# A German Odyssey

# A German Odyssey

## The Journal of a German Prisoner of War

Helmut Hörner

Translated and Edited by
**Allan Kent Powell**

Fulcrum Publishing
Golden, Colorado

Book Design by Jody Chapel, Cover to Cover Design

Library of Congress Cataloging-in-Publication Data

Hörner, Helmut, 1916–1990.
    A German odyssey : the journal of a German prisoner of war /
Helmut Hörner ; translated and edited by Allan Kent Powell.
        p.       cm.
    Includes bibliographical references.
    ISBN 1-55591-077-7
    1. Hörner, Helmut. 2. World War, 1939–1945—Prisoners and prisons.
3. World War, 1939–1945—Personal narratives, German. 4. Prisoners of
war—Germany—Biography. I. Powell, Allan Kent. II. Title.
D805.A2H67    1991
940.54'72—dc20                         90–85221
                                                         CIP

Printed in the United States of America

0   9   8   7   6   5   4   3   2   1

Fulcrum Publishing
350 Indiana Street
Golden, Colorado 80401 USA

# CONTENTS

# PREFACE

*A GERMAN ODYSSEY* chronicles the World War II experiences of Helmut Hörner, a common German soldier who, at war's end, found himself a prisoner of war in the United States. Drafted in 1938, Hörner became a good and brave soldier. He stood guard along the French-German border when Germany invaded Poland on September 1, 1939. The next year he marched into the Netherlands, Belgium, and France as part of the German invasion force in May 1940. In 1941 he landed in East Prussia, where he was one of the first German soldiers to cross the Russian border as part of Hitler's surprise invasion of June 22. Hörner and his unit pushed to Volokolamsk, sixty miles northwest of Moscow, where he was wounded for the third time during the Russian invasion. Sent back to Germany to recover, he was later assigned to train recruits in and near Karlsruhe before he returned to France in 1944.

A loyal German, Hörner fought for his homeland and was wounded again in France. On August 29, 1944, Hörner and his comrades were overtaken by American troops near Soissons, France. It was not until after his capture that he came to the realization that his homeland and the Nazi regime were not the same. This transformation is vividly portrayed in the following pages along with Hörner's struggle to cope with defeat, disillusionment, and the prospects of a dismal future.

Following his capture, Hörner endured miserable conditions in French prisoner of war camps until he departed for the United States on board the *Thomas Marshall* on April 3, 1945. The Atlantic crossing was an ordeal for prisoner and captor alike. While two friends were immune to seasickness, Helmut and another friend were not, and the agony he suffered is vividly portrayed. The prisoner of war experience in America was generally positive because the captives were usually given good food and comfortable quarters and interacted with a number of American civilians.

During his fourteen-month stay in America from April 1945 to June 1946, Helmut Hörner spent time in seven camps in five states: Camp Gruber, Oklahoma; Camp Greeley, Colorado; Fort Du Pont, Delaware; Fort Dix, New Jersey; West Point, New York; Camp Upton, New York; and Camp Shanks, New York. He was one of nearly one-half million German and Italian prisoners of war sent to the United States between 1943 and 1945. The prisoners were scattered throughout forty-five of the then forty-eight states in hundreds of camps holding between a hundred and several thousand prisoners each.

Of the approximately 2.5 million German soldiers taken prisoner by the United States during World War II, 371,000 were sent to the United States for internment. The United States in 1929 had signed the Geneva Convention, which outlined the specific measures to be followed in the treatment of enemy prisoners of war. Basically, prisoners were to be treated humanely and were entitled to the same housing, food, clothing, pay, and work hours as provided to the soldiers of the capturing nation. Only enlisted men could be put to work— as long as they were healthy—and they were not to be required to do any work that required the handling of weapons or munitions. Noncommissioned officers could only be required to supervise the enlisted men, while officers were not to be required to work. American authorities were committed to honoring the Geneva Convention for a variety of reasons: a genuine belief that the prisoners were entitled to humanitarian treatment; a sense of responsibility in living up to a treaty signed by the United States; as insurance that there would be no justification for the German government not to live up to the Geneva requirements in its treatment of the 95,000 American prisoners of war it held; a conviction that well-treated prisoners would be more productive workers; and as encouragement for German soldiers to surrender, knowing they would be well treated by the Americans if they did.

The official explanation for the decision to transport German prisoners to the United States was twofold: to help relieve American fighting forces of the responsibility and problems of guarding, feeding, and housing prisoners of war in the active theater of operations; and to help alleviate the critical manpower shortages at home. There was little extra cost in transporting the prisoners to the United States because most of the returning ships would otherwise be empty.

Some argued that American ships loaded with German prisoners of war would be less likely targets for German submarines, and in fact, during the course of the war no transport ships with prisoners of war on board were sunk. Others felt that if German prisoners could see the United States and experience at least some of the benefits of a democracy, they would jettison whatever Nazi or communist sympathies they had and return home committed to make democracy work in postwar Germany.

In August 1942, Great Britain persuaded the United States that it could no longer handle additional prioners, and American officials agreed to accept 50,000 enemy prisoners on an emergency basis. Ultimately the United States would care for approximately 175,000 German prisoners of war captured by the British, and that number was turned over to the British to help with postwar reconstruction in England. Among these prisoners was Helmut Hörner.

German prisoners of war were sent to the United States in three general groups. The first were those captured during the fighting in North Africa in late 1942 and 1943. By the end of 1943 there were 123,440 German prisoners of war in the United States. The second group numbered about 50,000 men, most of whom were captured during the fighting in Italy. The third group, which numbered 182,000 and included Helmut Hörner, was captured after the June 6, 1944, landing at Normandy and up to the German capitulation on May 8, 1945.

The initial plan for the German prisoners in the United States was to guard them in large compounds of approximately 3,000 prisoners in camps a considerable distance from the coasts, the borders, and strategic installations. As American officials realized that the prisoners could be used as laborers, the philosophy shifted more and more from security to the effective utilization of the prisoners. This led to the establishment of many branch camps, usually in agricultural areas, of approximately 300 prisoners. The prisoners became such an important part of the agricultural work force that farmers from all over the country demanded that additional prisoners be sent to the United States to help raise and harvest badly needed crops. Helmut Hörner's sojourn in America reflects the stages of this development: he started out in a large "holding" camp in Oklahoma, Camp Gruber; was then sent to a large centrally located work camp at Camp Greeley, Colorado; and then went to small branch camps in Glassboro, New Jersey, and West Point, New York. However, unlike most prisoners of war who either stayed in one camp or one area of the country, Helmut Hörner saw several camps in both the West and the East.

With few exceptions, the United States lived up to the provisions of the Geneva Convention admirably. Just like American soldiers, German prisoners were transported in Pullman coaches, much to their astonishment since in Europe prisoners and soldiers alike were transported in boxcars. Prisoners were issued regular army clothing, but were obligated to mark the exterior with large "PW" initials. The former German soldiers were housed in barracks and tents like those used by American soldiers—and often recently vacated by them. They were permitted to attend movies and religious services; participate in sports; set up classes for instruction (English and American history seemed to be the most popular); take correspondence classes from American universities; operate libraries; subscribe to American magazines and newspapers; engage in painting, woodwork, and other crafts; and produce concerts, theatrical productions, and variety shows. Medical facilities were available in the camps or, if the camp was small, under contract from local civilian physicians. Food was very good, and except for the period just after the war ended during the summer of 1945, there were no complaints. Prisoners often gained significant amounts of weight (twenty to forty pounds); civilians complained that they were hard pressed to find hamburger and hot dogs while enemy prisoners of war were enjoying steaks. Canteens were provided where the prisoners could purchase soft drinks, sometimes beer, cigarettes, and other articles. Enlisted men earned eighty cents a day, equivalent to the pay for an American army private. After the war noncommissioned officers could "volunteer" to work in order to earn the eighty cents a day. Otherwise, officers and noncommissioned officers were given a few dollars each month to purchase essentials like razor blades and toothpaste. Careful records were kept of each prisoner's earnings and a government check in U.S. dollars was issued to the prisoner for the balance in his account. These checks typically amounted to thirty to fifty dollars, but sometimes exceeded a hundred dollars.

Prisoners were allowed to write and send and to receive letters and packages. However, the letters often caused more anxiety than relief. Letters from Germany often reported on the devastation and lack of everything there, or were long delayed because of the disrupted mail service in Germany or the frequent transfers which many prisoners faced in the United States. German prisoners in the United States had no control over when and where they were sent or what work they would do. The forced separation from dear comrades, as Helmut describes, was one of the most difficult aspects of prisoner of war life in America. Equally disquieting was the indefinite information about when the prisoners would be sent home.

Official policy discouraged and prohibited contact with Americans; however, the reality of workplace situations provided some social interaction among civilians and prisoners. Following the defeat of Germany there seemed to be less need to follow a strict nonfraternization policy, and many prisoners of war developed friendships with Americans during the summer and fall of 1945 before they were sent away from the United States. Prisoners like Helmut seemed impressed with the American people—their generosity and goodwill, devotion to freedom, perception of equality, and common sense. They were also impressed with the size and richness of America and the value of a democratic form of government. In this sense, the prisoner of war program in the United States was a great success as nearly all of the 371,000 prisoners left the United States with strong feelings for America and a desire to see their homeland enjoy the same freedom and prosperity they had seen in America.

After leaving the United States, Hörner spent another eighteen months in England and did not return to his home in Karlsruhe until January 1948. Shortly afterward, he began writing a fascinating and detailed account of his sojourn as a soldier and prisoner of war, using the diary notes that he had kept between July 1944 and June 1946. Composed immediately following the war experience, this work is the first to chronicle the life of a common German soldier who survived the frantic days after the Normandy invasion in June 1944, capture by American forces, and internment in the prisoner of war camps in France and the United States.

In 1983 I began research on a book about German prisoners of war which was published in 1989 by the University of Utah Press under the title *Splinters of a Nation: German Prisoners of War in Utah*. In late fall 1988, newspaper correspondent Ingrid Sulich wrote an article about the German prisoners of war in Utah and my research on the subject. The article was published in over a dozen German newspapers, including the *Badischer Neuste Nachrichtung* on November 11, 1988. Helmut Hörner read the article and immediately wrote asking if I would be interested in reading a book-length manuscript he had written, part of which covered his time as a prisoner of war in America. I wrote Hörner that I would like very much to read his story. I realized that a well-written account would give a unique view of life as a prisoner of war through the eyes of one who experienced months of captivity. Still, I tried not to let my enthusiasm carry me away and reminded myself that many times in the past I had been disappointed when something of promise turned out to be less than usable.

There are few greater pleasures for a historian than to come upon a document or manuscript that magnifies his or her understanding of an event or epoch that has long been an area of interest. Such was the joy I experienced when Helmut Hörner's manuscript arrived in my office at the Utah State Historical Society on January 11, 1989. When I pulled the single-spaced manuscript from its box and began reading the 351 pages that had been untouched for nearly four decades, I knew this was no ordinary reminiscence of a World War II veteran, but a work of history and literature that revealed the thoughts, fears, and emotions of a common soldier and offered meaningful insights into the World War II experience in a way that no other medium could do.

A quick reading of the Hörner manuscript revealed that it was an extraordinary account by a former German prisoner of war in America. I was pleased that the manuscript revealed so much about the common but important aspects of prisoner of war life—the friendships, separation from friends and families, concerns about what was happening in Germany, the realization that they had been misused by the Nazi leaders, the struggle to look to the future with hope and faith, relations with Americans, and the constant longing to return home.

Helmut Hörner's account is important because of the insights he offers into the life and thought of a prisoner of war and a soldier of a defeated army. Like the majority of German soldiers during World War II, Hörner was not a member of the Nazi party. Still, as a witness to the chaos of the Weimar Republic and the disastrous depression that raged throughout Germany, Hörner appreciated the jobs that the Hitler regime provided and the restored national dignity.

Hörner's manuscript divulged insights not only into the life of war prisoners but also into human relations. The manuscript exceeded all my expectations and I anxiously pursued the possibility of publishing it in English. I tried my hand at translating several pages and found that, although it was a laborious task, it was possible. I wrote to Hörner and proposed that I continue with the translating and try to find a U.S. publisher interested in the project. In the meantime, I continued translating the rest of what appears as chapter 6 in the book.

A few weeks after receiving Helmut's enthusiastic letter to proceed, I traveled to St. Louis to attend the annual meeting of the Organization of American Historians. While browsing through the book exhibits, I noticed a new press—Fulcrum—located in Golden, Colorado. Since Helmut had spent some time at the Greeley prisoner of war camp in Colorado, I thought there might be some interest in the project by a Colorado-based publisher. I approached Jay Staten about the idea. She was most enthusiastic, urged me to draft a formal proposal, and championed the idea with Fulcrum publisher Robert Baron.

The acceptance of the proposal and continuing encouragement provided a helpful stimulus in keeping the project moving forward. Since the original manuscript did not cover Helmut's life before July 1944 or after he left the United States in June 1946, I asked Helmut to write an account of those periods.

The two accounts were finished in the fall 1989 and were used to produce chapters 1 and 7 of *A German Odyssey*. To provide explanatory material not covered in the original text, I have included notes and comments which are set off from Hörner's text at the appropriate locations.

As the project continued, I contacted Frederick Weber, who came to the United States from North Africa in 1943 as a German prisoner of war. He spent most of his time in the United States in Ogden, Utah, and emigrated from his home in Düsseldorf with his wife and daughter to Salt Lake City in 1954. Weber assisted with the translating of chapters 2, 3, 4, and 5. His experiences as a German soldier and prisoner of war were very helpful in explaining terms and situations to an American of another generation and language than himself and Hörner. Although there were times when Fred expressed some question and even disagreement about certain statements and descriptions, he was faithful to Helmut in helping translate the words and ideas with broad-minded respect for another man's story and opinions.

With the assistance of a travel to collections grant from the National Endowment for the Humanities, I was able to travel to Germany in April 1990 to review the manuscript with Helmut, clear up certain questions, and identify photographs and other documents that could be used to illustrate the book. Relying on the English he had learned in school and as a prisoner of war, Hörner read the manuscript and expressed complete satisfaction with the translating and editing. He did suggest that I use the real names of his comrades, which he had slightly altered in the manuscript, as a gesture toward preserving their memories: his old friend Willi Hocker, for example, was originally "Willi Hofer." Similarly, Robert Briller was "Robert Brehm"; Siegfried Neumeier was "Siegbert Mark"; and Schulz was "Scholz," although Helmut did not remember ever learning his first name.

During my stay Mrs. Hörner, Elly, was a very gracious hostess. Her willingness to do everything possible to further work on the book has been essential, especially because Helmut was in poor health during the last two years. She continued with correspondence when Helmut was no longer able, sent photographs when requested, and continued to cheer and encourage Helmut even when his doctors' diagnosis left no hope. (On August 10,1990, Helmut Hörner died of pancreatic cancer while this book was in production.)

My parents, Leland and Luella Powell, have encouraged and supported this book as they have all of my undertakings. My wife, Brenda, and our three children, Lee, Liesel, and Adrianna, have also enthusiastically sustained me in the effort. I am thankful that fate allowed Helmut and Elly to become part of our lives.

# Chapter One

# FRANCE AND RUSSIA

HELMUT HÖRNER WAS born in Karlsruhe on September 18, 1916, as the fourth son of August Hörner and Elise Kirchner Hörner. After his return from World War I as a sergeant in the German army, August Hörner continued his trade as a bricklayer and was employed as a foreman by a Karlsruhe firm. He also worked a small plot of land to provide produce for his family and care for his beloved horses. When Helmut was five, his mother became sick and lay in bed for nearly two years until her death on May 5, 1924, of pleurisy.

Karlsruhe, Helmut's birthplace, was a city of approximately 200,000 inhabitants before World War II. Located in Baden-Württemberg in south-western Germany on the east side of the Rhine River not far from the border with France, Karlsruhe lies just to the north of the Black Forest.

\* \* \*

When I was born in Karlsruhe on September 18, 1916, my father was fighting as a German soldier in France. After Hitler came to power in 1933, the employment situation eased considerably and I was able to secure a position as an apprentice dental technician. I intended to become a dentist. I completed my apprenticeship and was ready to continue my training when I was drafted into the German Work Service. Unlike most other young German men, who were sent far from home, I was assigned to work strengthening the West wall fortifications along the Rhine River. Our camp was located about ten miles from my home, between Karlsruhe and Rastatt.

1

I was drafted into the German Army directly from the German Work Service with orders to report to the Baron von Forstner Barracks in Karlsruhe on November 15, 1938.

The evening of August 26, 1939, I sat with my father over a glass of beer in the local tavern. The men spoke of work in their gardens and fields. I listened attentively until two military police entered and came immediately to my table. According to military procedure, I stood up. "Your papers, please," one said with a dead serious face. "Do you have a bicycle with you?" "Yes, certainly," I said and wondered if it still worked. "You are ordered to report back to the barracks immediately!"

The barracks were in confusion. Comrades were busy packing. A friend was already working on my things. "What is going on here?" I asked. "Mobilization, either they are playing around with us, or there will be war," they said.

By midnight the barracks were emptied and we were camped in the woods. Our heavy machine guns were set up ready to shoot down enemy airplanes. The following night we retreated to the West wall. On September 1, we learned that war had broken out as German troops had been fighting in Poland since five o'clock that morning.

But where we were, the Rhine flowed peacefully. Nothing stirred. No shots could be heard. We carried on as though on training maneuvers.

The calm held. Fourteen days later we heard the report of victory in Poland. Then we were taken out of our bunkers and marched to Mühlacker. There we were loaded on trains and transported to the area around Cologne and Düsseldorf. We were quartered in private houses and survived the bitter cold in warm beds. We threw away the food from the field kitchen and ate with the civilians who housed us.

About noon on May 9, 1940, we were ordered to pack our belongings, since we would not return to our quarters.

In the early dawn of May 10, we crossed into Holland. We fired a few shots at a harmless fortress. Then the infantry began to run. Our assignment was to clean out a few pockets of resistance and to take prisoner entire battalions of soldiers. Near Lille, we met a heavy barrage—our baptism of fire. In Antoing on the Schelde we encountered an English line regiment fortified on the other side of the river in a cement work that lay higher than our side and had a better line of fire. There we experienced war as our fathers had described it. The English surrendered after two days. They simply disappeared during the night.

We continued our march to the Marne. We found completely exhausted groups of French soldiers along the road. We did not see the Marne because we were ordered to stop. It was a cease fire and we fell like dead flies into the grass, completely spent. While other German units prepared for the festivities in Paris, we tripped off on good roads north toward Dunkirk after a few days' rest. Then we finally had fourteen days of complete rest. The first vacationers got ready. I went along with them. The industrious French opened their black market. We had plenty of money. We could not use it at home, but here you could buy everything. A pipe for my father and a nightgown for my mother was enough for me. We really did not need anything and I was too lazy to carry much around with me in my pack.

Around Dunkirk we swam in the warm ocean, lay in the sand, played cards, and drank French wine. The French refugees returned to their dwellings. We were amazed at their unusual way of life. They lived wonderfully, with plentiful food and drink. As an occupation force we were under strict orders not to disturb them. Signs hung on all buildings in French and German that whoever was found guilty of plundering or rape would be shot.

\* \* \*

Dunkirk was the site of the evacuation of English and French forces from the Continent after German armies launched their offensive against France on May 10, 1940, and overran neutral Holland and Belgium, outflanking the Maginot Line. On May 26, English ships began evacuating troops that had been pushed back to the French coast. A total of 338,226 men, of whom 112,000 were French, were taken across the channel to England between May 26 and June 5 before German forces reached the northern French port of Dunkirk near the Belgian border and captured the remaining French force of 40,000 men.[1]

\* \* \*

On September 18, my birthday, the planned invasion of England was abandoned. From then on German aircraft of all types thundered day and night across the channel toward England. The air battle had begun. The German army was without work. We were withdrawn back inland thirty miles from the coast. We enjoyed a wonderful winter in the beautiful city of Brugge.

On Good Friday 1941, the alarm was sounded in the night. Everything was loaded onto trains. My division headed eastward. As we crossed the Holland border back into Germany we stopped for a moment of silence, then rolled on toward Berlin. From there we continued on day and night toward East Prussia. Our trip ended in Johannisburg. That evening we unloaded and marched on to the Masurian Lakes in the vicinity of Suwalki. It was an uncivilized region. We were quartered in private straw-roofed houses without any electricity that were bitter cold and filthy. The roads were unpaved. We Germans from the south had no idea what Germany's breadbasket was really like.

It was the beginning of a hard time, training in the muddy land where the ground was still partly frozen. During the day all movement was westward, but at night we pushed eastward. Rumors flew wildly. We had signed a nonaggression pact with Russia. We would travel with covered windows through Russia toward Egypt to the Africa Corps, where we would attack the English in Alexandria from behind. Everything possible surfaced, but no mention of an attack on Russia.

The evening of June 21, 1941, we vacated our quarters. The companies separated and marched eastward, then rejoined in the dark woods along the Russian border. Mobilization was underway and all barrels of our weapons pointed toward the east. The masquerade ended by itself without any orders. We knew what was up. At 1:00 A.M. our leaders were instructed to appear for a battalion meeting. We received mail and could write a few quick lines home. Then the battalion commander rose to his feet calmly. He pulled out a note and his adjutant held a covered table lamp over it. He read softly: "The war against Russia is ordered by the Führer and will be carried out. Zero hour will be announced in the field. We will see each other early in the afternoon on the other side of the Neman, which we are ordered to clear for the tanks. That is all."

At 3:00 A.M. countless airplanes with the Iron Cross on their fuselages began thundering eastward. The war against Russia had begun. We crossed the border silently without any preliminary artillery fire. It took only ten minutes until the first Russian shots were fired at us. Shortly thereafter the first dead fell. Then the German artillery opened fire on the earth bunkers in the distance. In less than an hour we had battled down with hand weapons the surrounding resistance. Then we were attacked from behind. Everyone thought that we must turn around in order to clean up our rear. Instead we had orders to push eastward to take the Seenenge. We reached our goal. The tanks rolled mercilessly over the Russian infantry, or so it seemed! In reality the Russians made room for the tanks and then attacked us from behind. This was not France, it was a new eastern tactic.

We reached the bombed city of Lida. The inhabitants came out of their poor huts. Clothed in rags, they greeted us as friends. They even brought in beer. Our assignment was completed. For the moment, we had no new orders. We lay around and observed silently the unkempt residents. Then our field kitchen arrived. We had pea soup with pork. Chaos developed. The people were hungry.

We now learned that the Russians had attacked the field kitchens behind us and killed the cooks. This was a new war. Now we had a real enemy. So began the first day of the tragedy: Russia.

The land was strewn with dead, wounded, and morally defeated Russians. We could not stop and help the prisoners or wounded in any way. Our orders were to press eastward, mercilessly eastward. When night came we went to sleep in a woods twenty miles beyond Lida. Completely exhausted, we fell into the cool grass. We were all plagued by a terrible thirst. But the water carriers returned from the next village with empty pails. The fleeing Russians had poisoned the wells.

A sergeant and eight others mounted horses. About four o'clock in the morning, as it started to get light, two of the riders returned. God was with us, they had found a clean water source. And so it continued, day and night—eastward. There were a few small encounters, but we reached the city of Orsha which had been laid low by bombs and tanks. We were met by battalions of Russian prisoners marching westward. No German soldier accompanied them.

We pressed further eastward. Our goal was Smolensk, the gate to Moscow. But the Russians did not open the gate. As we reached within ten miles of the city, finally we were forced to halt. The sounds of battle reached us clearly. Fighter bombers and tanks were at work. We learned that a Russian general named Timoschenko, who was surrounded by German tanks and under air attack night and day, would not surrender.

While we dug into our foxholes to sleep and rest, the transportation of ammunition and provisions continued uninterrupted. Medics examined and bandaged the lightly wounded. We had lost seven men and three horses on the march to Smolensk. I received a grenade fragment in my right thumb. The stupid white bandage forced me to hide my hand in my pants pocket. Three low-flying bombers came at us from the east. No one worried about it since we all considered them to be German planes. With the exception of a couple of fighter planes, we had not seen any Russian planes. Suddenly we noticed that the bombs they were dropping were intended for us. It was too late for us to do anything. Half a minute later we saw the terrible picture. Our company commander, soldiers, and horses were killed by bomb fragments and several were wounded. Medics cared for the wounded and others carried our dead comrades away. The dead horses and useless vehicles were pulled off the roads by teams of horses and the company prepared to move out. We paid our last respects to the dead with birch crosses on which were placed their steel helmets.

After a few days and nights Smolensk was completely encircled by our divisions. On August 6, 1941, the surrender took place. We captured 310,000 prisoners, 3,000 tanks, and the same number of artillery pieces. To this point, our divisions had fought on foot over 750 miles in six weeks.

We continued eastward, disturbed by minor skirmishes here and there. We knew from aerial reports that the Russians were massing their strength around the cities of Gorodishche and Vyaz'ma and were waiting for us. The push toward Moscow stalled before Vyaz'ma and the entire middle sector of the east front came to a halt. Battle lines were drawn and we were ordered to dig in.

On August 27, 1941, we were shocked out of our midday sleep in a cornfield. Hand weapons cracked suddenly from the woods behind us. Our lines were not tight. The soldiers were either asleep or playing cards. A Russian cavalry troop slipped past us unnoticed and opened fire with machine guns. They were cut down in a dance of fire from our machine guns. The dead numbered three hundred. They were sent to their deaths for no reason by some crazy commissar.

On October 2, 1941, the middle sector of the eastern front went on the offensive against Vyaz'ma/Moscow. An artillery barrage of all heavy weapons, the worst that we had ever experienced, was launched against the surprised Russians. It was like the end of the world. The sun was blood red. In the cemetery-like stillness the German infantry, feared since the First World War, stormed the Russian positions. It was gruesome. Between the many dead, men still moved who no longer had human faces. They shot with their weapons and threw grenades that exploded immediately, setting our clothing on fire. Later these were called Molotov Cocktails. For seven days and nights we stood almost continually in close combat with the steadfast Russians. Early on the morning of the seventh day we finally reached the edge of the woods.

In the area of Wolokolamps on October 14, two spent Russian machine gun bullets hit my lower left leg. They bandaged me carefully and set me upon a saddled horse. I rode as quickly as I could to the main first aid station. There I was given papers sending me home. But it took time. At the main first aid station in Vyaz'ma the first wave of wounded had been transported, but there were still a large number who could not be moved that kept the medical personnel busy. Those with light wounds, like me, had to be satisfied with a fresh bandage. Finally, on the third day after my arrival, they carried me to the operating table.

The operating room looked like a butcher shop. Doctors and medics worked near collapse—rolled up sleeves, bloody hands, and blood-smeared clothing—while a few miles away destruction was in full force. A doctor and medic looked at my leg almost with humor. It was swollen from the ankle to the knee and red brown in color, but not yet black. The doctor probed in the two bullet holes, but could not get through to the bones. "The sergeant must be sent to Smolensk, we have no X-ray equipment here," he said.

Two Russian prisoners carried me out into a cold tent and I was very satisfied. Two days later we left for Smolensk, riding in a truck through a light snowfall. We drove up a hill and stopped in front of a large, green-painted stone house. It was the hospital. As far as Russian conditions go, it was quite comfortable, but naturally overfilled. A doctor was in attendance when my bandage was changed. The wound had built up pus. He also probed around. Since there were no exit holes, they gave me a small narcotic and when I came to they showed me the two bullets. The points were damaged, but they had come from a far distance and had lost most of their power. The doctor said, "These things only hit your bones so that there are a lot of little splinters in your flesh. They have to work themselves out. It will take time. You are lucky. We are sending you home in the morning."

\* \* \*

When Helmut was wounded on October 14, 1941, he was approximately sixty miles northwest of Moscow and among the advance units in the drive for Moscow. Volokolamsk was not taken by the German forces until October 28, two weeks after Helmut was wounded. (Helmut uses the German spelling, Wolokolamps. The English spelling is Volokolamsk.)[2]

\* \* \*

I traveled by train to Warsaw and then to Coberg. I was finally in Germany!

We were then transported in buses, deloused, our uniforms taken to be washed, and our bandages changed. By early afternoon on November 1 we lay in wonderful fragrant beds, provided with coffee and delicious cake by young ladies.

Within a few hours my fiancée knew about my situation. I obtained a telegram form, but only for Elly. My parents received only a card. Parents were afraid of telegrams from or about their sons on the front.

Twenty-four hours after I sent off my telegram, my dear one shook me awake. She stood at my bed looking at me, fighting with her feelings. We hugged each other affectionately and she cried and laughed at the same time. We looked at each other for a long moment of silence. There she stood, my Elly! Eighteen years old, young, blond, and beautiful.

We left early the morning of November 11, 1941, traveling over Nuremberg to Karlsruhe, where I reported to the hospital in Moltkestrasse. The chief doctor looked at my papers immediately. Then he gave them back to me and turned to the window and looked out toward the dark, bare trees. After a while he turned around, and observed me attentively. "How are you? You were in the middle sector? That is where my son is assigned to a main aid station. It's shitty, isn't it?" "At a main aid station he doesn't have much time to think about you, Doctor." "I know, he just sends a card once in a while. As a young doctor he always got sick when he had to treat stomach wounds. Were you satisfied with your treatment?" "Of course, doctor!"

He forced a laugh and said, "Especially since they sent you home. You came here with an escort? Walk around the room here, there are little slivers in your leg that will work their way out in time unless they move into your arteries. But don't worry, we will keep an eye on them with X-rays."

When Elly and I stepped outside, night had fallen. The city was completely dark under considerable cloud cover. But we knew our way very well. We walked hand in hand, even though it was forbidden for soldiers to do so, the hundred yards to the streetcar. To my surprise, the car was full. But there were plenty of seats for wounded soldiers.

The streetcar stopped. We had reached the street where Elly's parents lived in the south part of the city. We embraced and kissed in the dark entryway and then Elly rang the doorbell. Her father opened the door and beamed when he saw us. He gave me a big hug. Like my father, he too was a veteran of World War I. The fiancées of Elly's four sisters and her only brother were all in the army and at posts outside Germany. The girls quietly shook my hand. With wet eyes, Elly's mother said, "Finally one has come back."

We began preparations for our wedding. On New Year's Eve I invited my parents-in-law and Elly to dinner at a nearby restaurant to celebrate our engagement. Everything was rationed, so dinner consisted mostly of wine and a piece of sausage. No rings could be purchased in the shops, so my parents-in-law took the rings off their fingers and put them on ours. It was an unusually generous gesture. They were married shortly before World War I began. It was certainly a good luck piece. I was the second to wear the ring through the battlefields of Europe and return home.

We planned to marry in mid-May. In the meantime I did my assigned duty with the 109th Replacement Company, where experienced wounded or sick soldiers from the front were used to train new recruits. It was duty like in peace time. I had duty hours like any normally employed civilian.

With our plans to marry in mid-May, I was certain that nothing would happen before then. However, early in the morning of April 28, 1942, the duty sergeant woke me with orders to report to the clerk's office as soon as possible. There I was met by the sergeant major: "You are to go immediately to the quartermaster to be issued clothing and equipment to go into the field. Afterward arrange with your bride to meet you at the city office at noon. You do not need to attend roll call. After the wedding you are to return to the barracks to march with the others to the railroad station. The train leaves for an unknown destination at 2:00 P.M. Understand?"

Shortly before ten o'clock I rang Elly's doorbell. She was irritated that I visited her during duty hours. I could only say: "Is your blue dress ready? We are getting married today at noon!"

People adjusted to the war. Elly looked at me, confused, and only said: "And you must leave!" She did not cry, but she was so pale that I feared she would collapse. Her mother left us alone in the kitchen. We embraced. Our kisses could not be saved for a later time. Then I had to go, and said, "Be at the city hall in plenty of time, don't forget the papers. Where is father?" "In the vineyards, he has the day off. When does your train leave?" "Two o'clock from track eight. Please come alone."

At the barracks everyone was busy packing. I reported to the sergeant major that my bride had been told about our wedding; I was going to get something to eat and then travel to the city hall. He said, "That's fine, Hörner, be here promptly at 1:10 P.M. for the march to the station."

Only Elly, her mother, and her sister Erna were at the city hall. The others were still at work, not knowing about the ceremony. I could not reach my parents. They did not have a telephone. Inside I felt a miserable anger. Outwardly I could not let anyone notice.

The city official called us to the altar and suddenly everything was festive. Instead of receiving a bible as in earlier days, the city official gave us a copy of Hitler's *Mein Kampf.* Now Elly and I were a couple.

Only the hard clang of my boot heels still echoed in the stone stairway as we hugged each other with masklike faces on the street. I only wanted to see Elly at the train station.

On track eight stood girls, wives, and even a few children. But they did not have smiles on their faces. *Good-bye* is such a horrible word.

My wife also stood there. In all the confusion she seemed so lonesome and alone standing by the train with its opened doors. But her face beamed as she told me she was with child. I was happy that she had a large and good family at home and that she would be well cared for. She would be a good mother for our offspring. We embraced without words. Everything had been said that was humanly possible. Quietly, but distinctly, I felt in my beating heart that I would see her again.

Exactly at 2:00 P.M. the train rolled from the station. Early the next morning we reached Berlin, where the train stopped at the Friedrichstrasse station. We had to get out. A small committee was waiting for us. We were loaded on army buses and taken to an army hotel. We were fed breakfast and then a captain spoke to us: "Men from Baden, Hessen, and the Eifel, I welcome you to the capital of Germany—Berlin. You will be our guests in the city for three days. You will stay here and be cared for. We will show you the sights in the city."

For three days we visited museums, churches, castles, and monuments. Then they took us to the train station and we continued eastward through Frankfurt/Oder to Radom. There we underwent leadership training. We were treated like recruits the first week. The second week we worked hard, learning more about the use and care of hand weapons. The third week we began early in the morning with a three-mile run through the woods, then breakfast, and training with gas masks in a gas chamber. In the afternoons we had to write essays. A favorite assigned theme was "Those who will give orders must first learn to obey!" Other topics included "What is Comradeship?" "What does it mean to be a German?" and "How does one treat German women and children in view of the future of our people?" The subjects were assigned at the beginning of the hour and each essay had to be at least four handwritten pages long.

The last week was devoted to tests. After we were released from Radom we went by train toward Warsaw. We were amazed at the freshly washed wagons. A wise guy cracked, "Children, don't take any beer to Munich, no owls to Athens, and no lice to Russia. We are going home!"

No one laughed. He was lucky that he was not thrown from the train. But strangely the train went south of Warsaw to Lodz, and then westward. We became restless. The poison stove of rumors cooked on high. Westward! You could see tears in the eyes of men who seemed so hard. Somewhere we stopped. We smoked anxiously and became silent until someone suddenly opened the door from outside and screamed as though he were crazy, "I have just spoken with a railroad worker. He says our train is going to Breslau!" The joy that broke out cannot be described. Home, to Germany.

In Breslau we learned that the train was going to Dresden; beyond that the railroad workers did not know. We stopped in Karlsruhe and got out. No one knew we were home. We were given three weeks' leave. Our packs were loaded onto trucks at the train station and we could go home immediately. We drank a beer together in the inn at the station and then separated to hurry home.

I went by foot. As I turned the corner and stepped into the side street, I saw Elly standing on the sidewalk. She was talking with a young woman who was swinging a small child in her arms. The sun lay on their faces. A beautiful sight. Elly heard my boots clapping and turned toward me, then covered her mouth with her hand. I took it away and kissed her passionately. Immediately I felt how large with child she had become.

Our apartment was small, but beautifully decorated. Elly's parents had bought part of the kitchen items for us. The living room furniture was used but well built and assembled from relatives. We embraced and were happy.

We went to bed early at night. My right hand rested on Elly's growing stomach and from time to time I could feel the odd blows of a being pushing toward the world. Often my sleep was disturbed by dreams that terrorized me awake, and made Elly restless. I smoked many cigarettes in the kitchen, to brake myself, to try to restore order to things that one cannot control. I went with my wife into locales, drank beer, interrupted the young recruits, sat at the head table with the old World War I fighters and discussed strategy, answered questions for which there really were no answers and which bored my wife terribly. Then we would go into a movie, and gaze at depictions of the old heroic times that contradicted history. We watched the newsreels showing artillery fire from some sector of the front, taken well behind the battle lines since enemy grenades could destroy a camera.

After my leave was over I was assigned to training duty for the 109th Replacement Company located in the Kaiseralle, just about in the middle of the city. I could go home for lunch. It was a wonderful time, but it came to an end quickly. After a difficult farewell at the train station, we headed east. The 109th Field Regiment needed replacements quickly.

After a train ride through damnable Russia that seemed to never end, we stopped in Gzhatsk. We were instructed that we must get out quickly and lie under the cars. The Russian fighter bombers greeted us with bombs and machine guns. But our anti-aircraft was well placed. We did not have a single wounded man. The front lay about fifteen miles northeastward. The march did us good. About four o'clock in the afternoon we were at regiment headquarters. There were hardly any familiar faces.

\* \* \*

The Eastern front had stabilized east of Gzhatsk, a city approximately 110 miles west of Moscow, in early 1942 after the Soviet forces launched their Moscow counteroffensive in early December 1941, pushing the German armies back from Moscow to Volokolamsk, where Helmut was wounded on October 14, 1941, and then another thirty miles westward.[3]

\* \* \*

I was assigned to the 4th Machine Gun Company. My company leader was Paul Nagel, whom I had known since 1938. After a short private talk he sent me with a runner to my position. There I found only four grenade launchers; two of them were Russian. There were none of the old crowd among the young men. They were all glad that I had experience on the front.

The men's weapons were well cared for. The manner in which they carried out their assignments with the launchers was excellent. Each one knew what to do. An exercise with the launchers indicated that the men were in order. I was very satisfied and left them in peace.

It was the beginning of September 1942, a restless but sunny day. I had to continually pay attention to the Russians in the woods through my binoculars. There were none to be seen. But they hammered away at us harder than usual with the unpredictable weapons. You could hear when they were fired and when they randomly hit in our woods.

At 7:00 P.M. I was relieved. My legs hurt from standing in the hole and I lay down on my bed. There was hard sausage on my table for dinner. But I was not hungry and not even thirsty. I slumbered somewhat restlessly. As I awoke it came to me that I had not tested the grenade launchers.

I spoke with the sentries and looked around the area. Then I started to go from the firing position toward the bunker. At that moment a grenade landed about ten steps away. I heard the splinters strike a tree, then I felt the blow above my belt, in the left side of my stomach. It was not especially bad, but fear drove me into the bunker on shaky legs. I sat down carefully on the bench, took off my belt, and noticed that it had a frayed rip on the top side as though it had been cut by a poor saw. When I opened my field blouse the guard looked in from the door. He saw the bloody shirt and immediately called for help. I held my bandage on the wound. The medic said, "Let the blood run freely, that will clean the wound. Would you like to lie in bed, or is it more bearable to sit?"

I remained sitting. Every movement hurt. The splinter was stuck somewhere inside. When the doctor came, he asked immediately when I had last eaten or drunk anything. Nothing since noon. My supper still lay there. He was obviously happy and said, "You were lucky." Then he took some alcohol from a bottle, cleaned the hole free of blood, and tried to find the splinter with a probe. Then he gave instructions for me to be transported. A gut shot, the most feared wound among all front soldiers. I hardly felt anything, I was in a trance many miles westward where perhaps my wife was giving birth to our child.

At some point I must have fallen asleep. The wagon stopped somewhere. I heard voices. The foreign body in my stomach made itself painfully known with every movement. In the meantime a man got in and took my temperature. I asked no questions and he said nothing.

I arrived in Smolensk on September 14. The splinter was in my intestine, just as the field doctor had supposed. I became very mixed up with everything, the medication, narcotics, operation, the concern about the birth of our child, the rumors about partisan activities behind the front, the question about the security of the railroad line. I was sent to the reserve hospital Zichenau in Germany on October 10, 1942.

At the end of October I was assigned to a recovery company in Karlsruhe and received leave. I saw my son Günter, who was born on September 15, for the first time. It is impossible to describe my feelings. In a word: we were happy.

After my recovery I was assigned to the 4th Replacement Company, 109th Regiment, in Strasbourg. Once again I trained recruits. I had a nice single room and there was an excellent cook in the canteen. Later I found a room for my wife and child in the city. It was a wonderful time. Our Günter grew in strength; he was healthy and active. Every evening we went for a walk. As a soldier I was not allowed to push the baby carriage, but Elly was a proud mother. At home Elly thought about Christmas and worked to knit a new pullover while I played with our little fellow on the floor until bedtime.

Christmas came and then the New Year. You could not help but notice that everyone was sad. The men were away, no friends. The Sixth German Army was caught in a doubtful fight in Stalingrad. The whole German people was severely shaken. A glance at the map and anyone could see the dangerous situation along the entire southeast front where our troops, in their push to capture the source of Russia's oil in Baku, faced being cut off by the enemy. But the leaders in the Führer's headquarters always maintained that now the Russians had nothing more, that they were at the end of their strength. ...

Then we were hit, like so many other German families before us. My honored and admired brother August Hörner died in combat aboard his submarine.

Stalingrad sank in ruins. The Russians won—300,000 Germans devoured by the giant Russia.

\* \* \*

One of the objectives of the Russian campaign was the capture of the rich oil fields in the Caucasus region. Known as operation Blau, the offensive was stalled by heavy spring rains until June 28, 1942. Convinced that the Russian forces were nearly finished, a few weeks later Hitler ordered a major attack on Stalingrad, an industrial city on the Volga about 560 miles southeast of Moscow. Originally known as Volgograd, the city was renamed Stalingrad in 1925 for Joseph Stalin because of his association with the city during the Russian Revolution. With Stalin directing the Russian fight against Hitler's troops, Stalingrad was important not only as an industrial center and gateway to the Volga and Caucasus areas, but also as a symbolic objective for the German forces. Against the advice of his generals that it was impossible to conquer the Caucasus oil fields and Stalingrad at the same time, Hitler insisted that the battle go forward. German troops began attacking the city on August 20, 1941, after a period of heavy air raids. By September 13 the Germans were in the outskirts of Stalingrad, where each yard they advanced was taken with great difficulty. On November 19 the Soviets began a successful counteroffensive designed to cut off approximately 300,000 German troops of the Sixth Army by a pincers movement in the German flank. Completely encircled, the Sixth Army commander General Friedrich Paulus requested permission to break through the Russian lines to the southwest, but Hitler ordered Paulus to hold his position at all costs and promised that a relief effort would be undertaken. The relief effort failed. Without adequate food, clothing, ammunition, and gasoline, and with intense pressure from the reinforced Russian troops, Paulus surrendered the German Sixth Army on February 2, 1943. Of the 280,000 Germans initially in Stalingrad, 147,000 were killed, 90,000 taken prisoner, and 40,000 evacuated—most seriously wounded. Only a few thousand of those captured at Stalingrad returned to Germany after the war. Among those was General Paulus, who as a prisoner of war publicly condemned Hitler and Nazism. Most of the prisoners died by starvation, partly as a consequence of the inhumane treatment of German prisoners of war by the Russians. The defeat at Stalingrad marked the end of the German offensive against Russia. Soviet forces began an effort to push the Germans out of Russia and pursued them all the way to Berlin, which they reached in spring 1945. The siege of Stalingrad occurred as German efforts in North Africa suffered a severe setback when British troops under General Bernard Montgomery defeated German forces at El Alamein in late October to early November 1942. British and American forces also landed along the coast of Morocco and Algeria and within a few days controlled all of French North Africa to the Tunisian border. The defeats at Stalingrad and in North Africa marked the end of the German advance which had begun with the invasion of Poland in September 1939.[4]

* * *

I trained recruits. Often I felt sorry for them, but we had to be hard on them. Iron discipline had to be learned. I remained their comrade; finally, I knew what they would face. I spent evenings in their room, I concerned myself with their personal worries and troubles. Often those trainers who had not been at the front only had their work plan and training schedule in mind.

On December 5, 1943, nearly everyone was given leave. I had been determined fit for combat. Still I enjoyed the leave. My brother Willi was also home from the Crimea, where he was commander of the submarine hunter *Siegfried* on the Black Sea. We celebrated Christmas knowing that soon things would change.

I learned from my old comrade, Robert Luettin, that we were going to France. Every German soldier was satisfied with that news. I was especially pleased that all of the sixty-five recruits assigned to the grenade launcher detachment were men that I had trained.

We marched to the railroad station in Strasbourg and were taken by train to the training center at Münsingen, a miserable place. It lay on a high plain in the Schwäbische Alb. It was bitter cold; the snow was three feet deep. It was a gigantic army camp of only barracks buildings. Italian prisoners of war lounged around the camp begging for food. The poor devils could not help that they had ended up in this situation. We were fed primarily stews and soup and we could not put any of that in our pockets to help them. There was plenty of bread and so they had to be satisfied with that.

On January 6, 1944, we began our training. Our young recruits had been soldiers for only nine weeks. They had been in the Work Service, in the Hitler Youth, and were completely adjusted to the war. It was very easy to work with them. Even when we loaded them down with the heaviest weapons, they still laughed and sang with full voice as we marched: "It is so wonderful to be a soldier. ..."

I learned from Luettin that we would be in Münsingen for only a short time. Those who could had their wives or parents come for a visit. Naturally Elly was soon with me.

We had a couple of wonderful days together and then the train for France stood ready for us in Urach. Elly and I were not the only ones who had to say good-bye once again. But we did not have to go to Russia. By contrast, France was a highly cultured, European land with everything one could want.

The train left on January 15, 1944, crossing the Rhine through Metz and on to Verdun where the trenches from 1914–18 earned our attention. The train stopped and was unloaded in Bayeux in northern France.

Our assigned quarters were in some miserable barns, horse stalls, and sheds. But we were under the leadership of Luettin, an unbelievable scrounger. In a nearby village we found a small castle with a large yard, stalls, rooms, a hall—everything we could have wanted. Without asking the area commander, Luettin gave the order to move into the castle. He waved my warning off with his hand and everything turned out fine.

As always in life, the good times did not last long. We were transferred to Caen/Orne. But we had Luettin. He found quarters for us in an empty cloister school. In Caen we built fortifications, dug foxholes, and set out so-called Rommel asparagus against air landings by the English.

After Luettin left for his honeymoon, our division was transferred to Saint-Malo/Dinard. I was the commander. It was an unbelievably beautiful area. I wrote to my wife that I would like nothing better than for her and Günter to come to be with me. There was a wonderful castle on the edge of the sea, and the ocean water was delightful. When the sun shone, it looked like paradise. The sky was high and blue, the water green. It was clear to the dumbest private that the Allies would not attack here. There was no possibility for landing boats. Bare, broken rocks lay in the water. It did not look like any landing boats with invading soldiers could get a foothold. The defensive positions around Saint-Malo/Dinard were ideal.

Like on nearly every evening, I stood on the terrace of a bunker with a captain, the observer for the heavy artillery. The date was June 5, 1944. Our watches indicated it was 11:10 P.M. as our binoculars dropped to our chests. "Certainly not today," the captain said. "Look, Hörner, the waves are so high, the night is too bright. If any warships appeared on the horizon I could knock them out of the water with my artillery. Let's go until morning."

We separated and I went to those on watch. The beach was secured with barbed wire and mines, but because of the ebb and flow of the tide, they were constantly in need of repair. The men on duty were all at their weapons and wide awake.

The telephone rang exactly at 1:10 A.M. The report was that Allied airplanes were dropping dolls in the north that exploded when they were touched. I passed the report on immediately to our men. A little later the company leader was on the telephone. He said quite excitedly, "Hörner, sound battle alert immediately, complete battle alert immediately, report when it has been carried out! I do not yet know if it will be serious. Is there anything unusual happening there?"

We soon learned that the Allies had landed in Normandy, with heavy fighting around Cherbourg.

In Saint-Malo/Dinard nothing stirred. On June 9, 1944, we were pulled back. To the north, the Americans had secured a strong foothold and because of their total air superiority we could only march at night. Our division was hard pressed. Differences of opinion among our leaders tore regiments, even battalions apart. Casualties mounted because of the strength of the American air power.

By June 15, 1944, the Americans had reached Saint-Sauveur-le-Vicomte. We were pulled out of the advance and attached to the heavily embattled 91st Division. Now, for us, the fight began.

\* \* \*

The allied invasion of France occurred on June 6, 1944, at Utah, Omaha, Gold, Juno, and Sword beaches. These beaches are located just to the east of the northwest tip of Normandy known as the Cotentin Peninsula. Because of the large concentration of German troops in the Cotentin Peninsula and the importance of controlling the peninsula's key port city of Cherbourg in order to secure their right flank, American forces pushed west and northwest into the peninsula. After Cherbourg was captured on June 27, Allied forces regrouped, and on July 3, three divisions of General Omar Bradley's Eighth Corps (the 79th, 82d Airborne, and 90th divisions) began the offensive to push out of the Cotentin Peninsula with an attack toward La Haye-du-Puits, the key city for controlling the western side of the peninsula. According to military historians: "In the fighting that ensued, slow progress was made through the marshlands and borage country, where every field was a fortress and every hedgerow a German strong point. The Eighth Corps converged on La Haye-du-Puits, capturing the town on the 7th."[5]

# Chapter Two

# FRANCE 1944

*2 July 1944*

THE HEAVY AMERICAN grenades explode, bringing death and destruction to our positions. The air is saturated with iron and the stench of burned gunpowder.

Rifle squad leader Sergeant Hagerle and I spot an American machine gun position about four hundred meters away and destroy it with mortar fire from my unit. The enemy recognizes our observation post and responds with well-aimed fire. We both barely reach a tank ditch before the ruin of revenge plows down on us. I try to establish contact with the fire command using a field telephone. But the box is stubbornly silent; undoubtedly the cable has been severed by a grenade. Before I can lay down the receiver, I am blinded by a dazzling flash followed by a terrible detonation. My comrade collapses next to me, his eyes still wide open. A grenade splinter pierced his steel helmet and tore a fist-sized hole in the back of his head. I carry him on my shoulders to his company battle station. During the past few days, death has had a rich harvest. I return to my fire position, located about two hundred meters to the right and nestled in a cow pasture thickly planted with trees.

I sit in our well-built bunker covered with thick tree trunks and still do not comprehend why I am still alive. The fire has decreased. Only a few seemingly misdirected grenades unsuccessfully seek a target. Instead of answering the disturbing questions of my comrades, I lift my canteen filled with Calvados to my mouth and stare through the opening of our shelter at the meadow which has been plowed by American grenades. Gradually the good alcohol brings me to

18

my senses and brings a smile to my face. I turn and look into the young but hard faces of the men. "It's OK you guys, two of you see that the telephone line is restored immediately. I'll go ahead to B observation post; keep the telephone receiver occupied and prepare for action." Quickly I rise and walk out of the bunker, not noticing the relieved looks of my comrades.

Somewhat confused and slightly foggy from the schnapps, I reach the observation post located in the middle of the battalion defense line. Mechanically I shovel the fallen dirt out of the foxhole; suddenly the telephone rings. "The cable is in order," croaks a voice out of the earpiece. "Good," I say, "get ammunition to the position as soon as you can and report when you are ready to fire. Have Sergeant Hermann get two cars moving in order to fill up the reserves."

A little later Moeller, my messenger, kneels over the foxhole. "Did anything happen to you?" he asks. "I was concerned about you." "Don't worry about me," I calm him.

While Moeller digs the hole deeper, I search the enemy lines with my glasses. The machine gun position, which we destroyed earlier, is occupied again. The Americans apparently believe that a grenade will not land twice in the same location. While I watch an unconcerned soldier drag ammunition into the position, an enemy observation plane comes over us. Moeller has camouflaged the freshly dug earth with a tent canvas. We don't move, because we know from bitter experience that these fellows have damned good eyes. He flies over us headed south. The moment is right. The telephone rings. "Prepare to fire" is announced. I take over the receiver: "Hermann, how many grenades are there in the position?" "Ninety," he replies. "Good, prepare twenty and report when ready to fire," I order over the wire. My head is empty. In spite of the heat I feel my cold hands as they put my pistol on the rim of the foxhole. One thought dominates me: An eye for an eye, a tooth for a tooth, that is the law of war.

"Everything in order, Hermann?" I whisper into the receiver. "Keep that artillery observation airplane in sight. As soon as twenty rounds have been fired, everybody into the bunker. Don't forget the camouflages for the launchers; the Americans will certainly send their iron thanks by return post. Work carefully and fire when ready!"

I observe the enemy position with the field glasses, and hear the detonation of the launcher which drives the grenade out of the barrel toward the target. Before the explosions can be heard, the first fountains of earth shoot up to the sky. Seconds later the grenades explode with a murderous sound. Almost at the same time a machine gun from Hagerle's platoon concentrates fire on the enemy position. A gruesome picture of raging destruction stands before my eyes. Deadly silence follows the hellish uproar. The enemy position is totally demolished. Nothing moves. The work has been accomplished.

At 8:00 P.M. Sergeant Hermann comes to relieve me. We smoke a cigarette in silence. The Americans are keeping quiet. Fire is directed toward the roads and crossings. Twilight lies over the bruised earth as now friends and enemies collect their fallen comrades. Deep in thought, I stumble around the shell holes, back into the bunker. It has been damned hot today, but my evening report to the company does not contain any losses.

I don't want anything to do with food. My friend the good French Calvados tastes much better and I still have two canisters in the bunker waiting for their destruction. When the mail arrives I am no longer in any condition to read the letters from far-away Germany.

### 3 July 1944

I am awakened by the roar of an unfettered war machine and hurry to the bunker exit. The Americans send their usual morning greetings. Toward the main line of battle, raging machine gun fire is heard. My platoon is ready for battle. The American shells explode with murderous sound in the neighboring cow pasture, where a fake position was built to deceive the spotting planes. Only two unfortunate cows and a calf stand with hanging heads eating the shrubs which frame the meadow and serve as a fence. With a few jumps I reach our mortar position and I am greeted by the smiling crew. "Finished sleeping, sergeant?" asks the crew chief. "You nightingales, who can sleep with all this uproar?" I retort.

It is now nine o'clock and I am informed that the Americans have been shelling us since 7:20 A.M. "Why didn't you wake me up?" "Hermann wouldn't allow it. You had a hard day yesterday and need your rest." The crew chief grins. "I am honored with your love, pals, what happened in the meantime?" I ask. "About five o'clock an American scouting patrol was captured and because it did not return punctually, a whole company was sent to inquire about it, but the soldiers in front wouldn't allow the bad enemy to enter our territory. Now they are insulted and are throwing cracked peas into our garden," I am informed.

About ten o'clock I meet Hermann at the battalion command post. The weather is beautiful and the front completely quiet. "Too bad about the nice weather in the middle of the shitty rotten war," I greet Hermann. "You can't do anything about it, it's our turn." He forces a smile. "I am sorry, but you are right," I answer disgustedly and unfasten my canteen.

"I remember the Frenchmen we saw who were going swimming with their girlfriends while we Germans were hurrying with forced marches to the landing beaches to defend France from the invading troops." "That's the way it goes." He grins like an old drunkard as I hand him the canteen filled with Calvados. I believe we all will become drunkards who will have to be treated in hospitals after the war. "We are really lucky that the stuff is lying in nearly every cellar. It is something that we missed in Russia, but then Ivan fired at us day and night and all of that on a sober stomach, that forced many to change their pants fast if they did not want to dirty themselves." I smile and also take a healthy swig. "Stop talking about Russia," Hermann raves, "otherwise my entire body starts to tingle." "Calm down. I would rather be in France despite the American superiority in matériel; the only thing I don't like is the slack manner in which the war is conducted," I confide to him.

"Oh well, the main thing is that our division is in order and nothing can shake it. We have to hold out until the leadership is able to survey the situation and can bring battle-hardened units into action." He tries to cheer me up. "That may be true," I agree with him, "but I favor a strongly led attack instead of squatting in our holes waiting for the Americans to land their troops. Besides, it still puzzles me how Cherbourg could fall."

"A lot has happened in the last little while that we cannot explain, and it is better not to think about it but simply worry about saving our own skin," Hermann offers and squints at the enemy line with the field glasses. "Look thirty points to the right of that large poplar tree in the low shrubs; something is moving." "You are right, a group has nestled an antitank gun in the shrubs and that fool over there is just beginning to camouflage it." I lower my voice. "Measure the distance exactly, Hermann," I whisper to him, while my hand turns the handle of the telephone. "Throw one, second loading, in the basic direction, thirty additional degrees. Distance 380, report when ready!" I pass on to our launch position after Hermann has found the distance.

"Hopefully that thing won't fire before our mortars reach it," I whisper again. "I never liked those things; they are too fast for me. They reach their target before you can hear the shot. I am much more sympathetic to artillery; their howling noise gives you a chance before they kill."

Shortly afterward a loud shot roars. Without the binoculars I look at the target. An earth fountain rises and falls to the ground about 150 yards short of the target. Immediately I contact mortar launcher number 2 and change the distance to 100 yards farther while the well-trained fingers on launcher number 1 extend the distance to 530 yards. Seconds later six grenades leave the barrel of launcher 1. Six gray-black fountains cover the target and the distinct cry of at least one seriously wounded man can be heard.

The smoke is gone. I clearly recognize the badly camouflaged antitank gun. Two places next to the target are only burned earth. Everything is calm. Satisfied, we light a cigarette and grasp the canteen. Who shoots first and hits the target can live to be quite old at the front.

The sounds of motor engines approach us quickly. The fighter planes are coming. With bullets spitting out of all their holes, they chase like wild hunters over the main line of battle. They swing off and now come from the east along the defense line. The detonation of the light bombs and the fire from the weapons on board fill the air as if judgment day has arrived. After considerable time, the scare is over. Only a single enemy observation plane glides overhead. The medics go to work.

At 3:00 P.M. the battalion orders us to prepare everything for a concentrated fire strike against the enemy positions. The specific time is not given. We are to report when our preparation is finished.

At exactly 4:10 P.M. all Hell breaks loose as a huge fire dances over the enemy's line and back. Hot steel roars in merciless destruction out of all weapons of the battalion and into the American bridgehead on the peninsula of Cotentin.

The infantry, accompanied by light tanks, begin the attack. I have orders to follow with two launchers to help watch over the attackers and put down any obstacles that appear. Suddenly the whole front is thrown into motion. As during my first attack at the Schelde in Holland and later with all the attacks in Russia, an ice cold feeling rises in me. Then the shock and fear of gloom withdraw from me. Using every bit of cover, I move toward the enemy position in the immediate proximity of our battalion leaders. My eyes witness the usual picture of devastation as we breach the enemy without much resistance—a machine gun nest with its dead, there a soldier lies who took a splinter while already in retreat. In the foxholes lie broken cartons of crackers, packs of cigarettes, and chocolate wrapped in gray cardboard. Touched with sympathy, I look at an American whom a grenade splinter penetrated behind the ear, transferring him from life to death. He is at the most thirty years old. A reddish, scrubby beard covers his chin. The shirt is unbuttoned and a thin chain with a small silver cross lies on his hairy chest.

The attack rolls on. American prisoners come toward me. Their hair is cut short and their faces are distorted like masks. One has a naked woman painted on the back of his jacket, another a map of Europe on which Berlin, underlined in white, can clearly be read.

Two hundred yards in front of me, the hand weapons speak a distinct language. Even more prisoners come toward me, but the resistance is stiffening, and the attack is coming to a halt. On inquiry the battalion commander tells me that we do not have a specific goal, but are ordered only to advance in the general direction until we meet stiff resistance and then halt. Our task is to disturb the enemy and to capture men and matériel. At night we will withdraw and return to the positions from which we started.

Orders come through to dig in. We are situated immediately in front of a U.S. artillery fire position, which could make life difficult for us. Even though we are delighted with the grown-over hedges of our location, it is damned hard work to dig foxholes in the roots. Even before we are finished, the Americans begin their counterattack, supported by five tanks. It is exactly 7:25 P.M. With concentrated fire from our weapons we stop the counterattack, the break-through point is sealed, and the enemy is forced back. Two U.S. tanks are now smoking ruins on the landscape. A dead American bends out of the turret tower. This day has cost the enemy considerably in the high losses of men and matériel. As so often, today has shown once again what a well-trained and properly led troop can do against an enemy with superior matériel. I am proud to belong to this troop.

### 4 July 1944

After a careful shave and bath in an old wood barrel, I eat breakfast about nine o'clock. Today I feel especially well. A brief examination of our weapons and a few cheerful words to my comrades and I am on my way to the observation post to relieve Hermann. I take the shorter course across the cow pasture. The area to the left of the battalion is under enemy mortar fire. I should hurry to the observation post, but it is such a beautiful day that I find great joy in my walk across the meadow. Around the meadow, the engineer platoon is preparing some small jokes for the Americans in the form of stumble wire connected with explosive mines, and hand grenades skillfully placed without their pins. I remember ten days ago when they mounted a light pressure mine under the toilet seat of a latrine near a French farmhouse that we could no longer defend. I imagine with satanic pleasure how an American sat down comfortably on the seat only to have the mine blow both him and the stinking outhouse to heaven. But this treachery is a weapon against both enemy and friend.

Suddenly, not five steps away from me a gray-black mushroom erupts in which a fiery satan bellows and spits glowing beams from all sides. Even before the sound and pressure waves reach my ears, I lie down in an old shell crater, holding the steel helmet on my head as clods and rocks fall on and around me. Then I feel a hot burning in my left foot. With horror I observe a long tear in my left boot that reaches from the ankle to the toes. The pain increases. With difficulty I try to remove the boot from my foot, but it causes terrible pain. Determined, I take my knife and cut the upper boot from the top to where the tear begins. Finally I succeed in freeing the wounded foot from the boot and pull off the sock. I look at the damage, which at first glance does not look too serious. One toe is split open from the root to the toenail like by a hatchet. The blood gushes blue-red from the wound, soaking my entire foot. Calmly I stick a cigarette between my lips; let the red sap of life continue to flow, cleaning the wound; and prepare the bandage.

"Where are you hit?" an artillery man asks abruptly, standing at the rim of the crater and staring at my wounded foot. "You see for yourself, my friend, come down and help me bandage my foot if you don't have anything more important to do," I wave to him. "I am supposed to be scouting the destruction, but I think you need help," he utters as he kneels next to me with the bandage. In the meantime the whole foot has swollen. Lightly shaking, I am forced to lie on my back. "So," says the man, "the campaign is over for you. Whom can I inform?" "Just go straight north two hundred meters and there you will find Sergeant Hermann in his observation post; he can send me to Moeller," I inform him and nod my thanks in addition.

I take the splinter, which is about the size of a nickel, out of my boot sole, and play with it in my hands . . .

"What have you done?" Moeller asks, interrupting my thoughts. "Why didn't you take the passageway? Now we are sitting in hot grease and you are going to lie down in a white bed." "Shut your mouth, what is this nonsense about a stretcher," I scold him and the medic standing behind him. "Try it first before I go." Angrily I stand on my legs, but the toes hurt so much that I come to my senses. "So there," grins the medic, "now be nice and tame and lie on the stretcher." Carefully they carry their angry load out of the crater and a short time later reach the fire station, where the battalion doctor has already arrived. "It finally got you?" he says and loosens the bandage. "Only partly," I respond, although every time he touches me it causes strong pain. "Yes, my dear, the toe, including the nail has been split and damaged the bone. It will take several weeks before you are in order again. You will have to be transported to the main aid station."

While the medic bandages my wound again, I frantically consider how I can get away from these quacks, as the doctor fills out a red-rimmed form and hangs it on my infantry insignia. "It looks quite nice next to the insignia." He grins. "What does this mean?" I ask furiously. "You don't think I will just leave my men sitting here?" "Yes, you can't even walk, or do you want them to have to carry you around? One of your men can take a bicycle and you sit on the front and report to the regiment first aid station. That is an order. I will call your company leader so that he can send a replacement for you," he instructs, businesslike.

My eyes wander around, looking into the solemn faces of my comrades. I feel like vomiting. "Hermann will take over the platoon for the time being!" I arouse myself finally. "Here is my pistol, the maps, the binoculars and the compass," I say, turning to the battery sergeant. "Moeller, bring my shaving kit, fill my canteen full of Calvados, and get your bicycle. Don't you guys worry about me, do for Hermann what you did for me, and in the meantime I will see if I can't stay close by."

Perplexed, some of them wipe their noses and others rub their moist eyes. "Did you eat onions?" I ask, forcing a laugh to save the situation. With all my energy I suppress my own feelings that now bring to my consciousness just what these men mean to me.

Moeller goes down the hill quickly but carefully. The road is torn up by grenades and it requires his whole skill and attention. Thirty minutes later I am in the hands of a competent physician. "It is just enough to send you home," he says and gives orders to bandage me again. "Couldn't I let it heal while I stay here?" I ask. "Nonsense, the bone is gone, you have to go to the main aid station, and a truck is just about ready to leave." He remains hard-hearted. "I would still rather stay with the troops," I demand. "You don't hear very well, sergeant, or do you believe I will let you stay so that in a couple of days I will have to saw off your leg at the knee? Do what I tell you, the war is not yet over, you will still have your share of it in case you have not had enough already. Tetanus," he says to a medic and is already busy with somebody else.

Submitting to my fate, I turn my bare behind toward the medic and the syringe. The needle penetrates my flesh and brings into my body the protection against tetanus. Shortly afterward I stand on one leg in front of the ambulance and hold Moeller's hand tightly in mine. "So Moeller, thanks for everything. Say hello to the comrades and now go to Lieutenant Luettin. Tell him of my misfortune and that I will write him from the hospital as soon as possible. See that you all keep well so that I can rejoin you." "Come back to us again." He struggles, still pressing my hand until the medic is forced to separate us. Shaken, I understand once again the deepest meaning of the word *comrade*.

The medic drives quickly to the main aid station. The well-known ritual begins: bandage off, bandage on, fit for transport. "Couldn't I stay here for a few days until the wound reacts?" I ask the doctor after I have been taken care of. "Listen." He considers my request, somewhat amazed. "I don't hear that question very often. But do you believe we would transfer you if it were not necessary? We have to look at the wounds very carefully; some don't have any. Just yesterday someone arrived here with a fine bandage. His arm was completely wrapped in bandages and you could see the blood that had seeped through a hundred yards away. I thought to myself, he must have a hole as big as a grenade, but he didn't go through my station. By chance I saw him get on the bus. The bandage had not been changed and that caused me to pull him out of the bus. He protested strenuously. We called the military police, unwrapped the bandage, and found no wound. I tell you this so that you know it is not so easy to get away from here, but you cannot run or walk in difficult circumstances and then we will need the vehicles for the serious cases. We know that in the next few days the Americans will mount an offensive from their bridgehead and we have orders to send away all the helpless. Sleep now, your bus leaves early in the morning."

### 5 July 1944

At seven o'clock the bus, with its war-scarred load, rolls southward from the main dressing station. A medic, with a snow-white jacket and strongly oiled hair, sits next to the driver and is our only escort. The mood is very good because most are very glad to be out of the mess.

In front of me an SS corporal tells about the combat of his division. His right arm is in a bandage with wiring which we front soldiers call simply "stuka," because it looks very similar to the wing of the Junkers 87 airplane. He boasts of how his unit made pigs of the American tanks and I wait for him to announce that he has personally eaten a Sherman tank. In time we learn that he belongs to the SS Division "Goetz von Berlichingen," which is generally known as the "kiss my ass division," and of whose bravery no one has any doubt. But I let him speak without giving him any more attention, attributing it all to his youth and first experience in battle.

Silent and withdrawn, I sit on the green upholstered seat of the bus which is fleeing this Hell. My thoughts are with the fifty-five men who I was forced to leave. What will happen when the Americans actually start their long-anticipated attempt to break through? Will the thin German lines hold? What kind of a way to conduct the war is it when no complete division can be sent into battle and only single, isolated battalions are sent out in front of the enemy artillery? It is impossible that the German high command was so surprised by the enemy that they simply threw units against the enemy to be squashed in a few hours through the meat grinder of a determined opponent. Something is rotten about this affair and gives the current rumors about the high-ranking deserters and traitors a sense of legitimacy.

But why brood over such things which one cannot change and over which he has absolutely no influence? I force the troubling thoughts out of my head and look into the summer landscape while the bus, marked by Red Cross flags, pushes toward Avranches under swarms of enemy aircraft.

About one o'clock we leave Avranches and three hours later we arrive without incident in front of the cathedral in Alençon, where we are provided with food and drink and find overnight accommodations in a chapel.

### 6 July 1944

Three Paris buses stand in the courtyard of the good nuns who, without any consideration of persons, follow their self-chosen life work of service. They have made our night's stay as comfortable as possible. Like me, the wounded of this new theater of war wait impatiently before the opened doors of the buses. The doctors and medics strictly control the papers, identification tags, and transport slips which only an hour ago they filled out themselves. Within a few minutes it is obvious why such strict control is considered necessary. There are indeed German soldiers who seek to put as much distance as they can between themselves and the front. Fools, I think, now they will be court martialed, given a warning, and their chances to survive with their lives are lessened while the hardships are at least tripled.

Finally the doors to the fully occupied buses close. "Be good," the medics wave to us and the column rattles out of the courtyard. The way out of Alençon follows over the Sarthe toward Mamers, Bellême, and Nogent-le-Rotrou, where we make a brief stop to refresh ourselves. But the wheels of the mighty organization of the German Red Cross drive us onward and bring us into Chartres just before dark. As night breaks, I lie freshly bandaged, washed, and cared for in a bed intended for wounded who are in transit.

### 7 July 1944

About ten o'clock we arrive in Paris unharmed. "Reserve Hospital," stands over the entrance to a building near the north train station. We enter and are received by German medical personnel. Quickly we are sorted and distributed to the individual stations. Before an hour has passed, I lie washed and freshly bandaged in new pajamas in a white-covered bed in a nice private room.

My wristwatch indicates it is 1:00 P.M. as a young girl opens the door and brings me back to consciousness. "Mr. Sergeant, your dinner," she says, observing me curiously. It is unbelievable how fast life for a soldier in war can change, I reflect, while the young lady brings my food. The French girl serves me meat soup, noodles, salad, and goulash. I eat quickly and then end the wonderful meal with a swig of Calvados from my canteen, which Moeller filled for my departure.

Once again my thoughts return to the front. Why has fate been so openly generous to me, I ask myself, and a dull fear comes over me that one day I will have to pay for it. It is hard to comprehend that I came out of that fury with only a scratch. But finally I am not the only one whom the gods of war may have saved for later.

At 3:00 P.M. the doctor makes his rounds and tells me that on July 6 the Americans attacked and broke through our lines at several points. Even here the war still has me in its clutches. Alone once again, I see in spirit my brave comrades, how they hop from one hole to another and contend for their lives. Although the doctor spoke about only a few breakthroughs, I am still convinced that the 101st American Paratrooper Division landed in the middle of our position and that the thinly held line by La Haye-du-Puits came under heavy attack. At the moment I do not know what is stronger in me: the joy that I am here in safety, or the oppressive fear for my comrades and the eventual success of the Americans.

### 8 July 1944

Without asking if I am willing to leave, two French girls stand at the foot of my bed and hold fast to their demands. Everyday life in the hospital begins. Reluctantly I relinquish my territory to the two souls bent on cleaning and hop to the door. Directly across the hall the door is open. A man without a shirt, on whose left shoulder a bandage is taped, stands at the wash basin soaping himself.

"Good morning," he says, friendly. "Staff Sergeant Boger is my name. Where did you get hit?" he asks after I have introduced myself. "Up by Saint-Sauveur." He answers and blows a mighty cloud of smoke toward the ceiling: "I came out of that area too. I was with the 91st Air Landing Division," he lets me know while he waits excitedly for my reaction. "I know that bunch, a brave division, about the 12th or 14th of June we partly relieved you up there." "Then you are from the 77th Grenadier Division," he interjects quickly. "That's exactly right." I laugh excitedly over this accidental encounter. "Come, we have to drink to that. The women are finally finished with my room." He takes me by the arm and pulls me into his room. "Man alive, the Americans jumped directly from the sky into our positions; I can only say that was quite a racket." He continues with the theme after we take seats on the bed and he gets a bottle of cognac and two wine glasses from the nightstand and fills them. "Isn't that a little bit too much so early in the morning?" I toast him. "It tastes better than the so-called coffee," he indicates, smacking his tongue. "When did they get you?" he asks after another healthy gulp that empties half the glass. "On the fourth of July near La Haye-du-Puits," I say, becoming more serious. "That is only three days ago; what has been going on since the 19th of June?" he asks urgently. "It was not too wild. When we arrived the Americans were quite impertinent, but we quickly tamed them. The worst were the damn fighter planes and the heavy artillery. Naturally they pushed us nearly every morning at the close positions so that about eleven o'clock a counterattack from us was necessary. Contrary to the Russians, the Americans avoided any night fighting, which made our action considerably easier." I explain in a few words what was happening at the front.

"That's about the way they were with us after they established a foothold. But the first days were wild and they had to fight bitterly for every foot of ground. The devil knows how it was possible that they could take Cherbourg." He throws out the question which for all of us remains a riddle. "There was certainly something rotten about it," is my opinion. "It could not be anything else, because I know the fortress well enough to understand what it would have cost the enemy if the preparations for defense had been serious. Instead the bastion fell silently, to our horror, on June 27. No, it was actually the 26th." He corrects himself and I concur. "Drink your glass empty, the coffee will soon be here and we can talk later," he says as we hear the clatter outside in the hall, and I hop out of the room and crawl into the freshly made bed.

After drinking the coffee, the cognac that I enjoyed presses me into the pillows for an hour. But at ten o'clock the doctor stands at my bed with his secretary and an old nurse who takes my pulse. "Everything OK?" he asks as I open my eyes. "Thank you Doctor, I feel quite well," is my friendly answer. "Leave the alcohol alone, it will lead to nothing. If you are still too nervous to sleep I will be happy to give you a sleeping pill," he counsels in a fatherly tone. "I met a comrade this morning who was in the same sector as me and we had to drink to that," I excuse myself, as it is immediately clear to me that the doctor has a sharp nose. "So, it is Boger across the hall?" he asks with an understanding smile. "Yes Doctor," I confirm. "He likes to drink even without a reason; it may be a habit from Normandy." He nods to me and raises his index finger in warning. "Presumably we can heal you here." He changes the subject. "Tomorrow I will look at the toes." "I appreciate that, Doctor," I say thankfully. "First rest completely, and then we will see what to do." He gives me his hand and leaves the room with the others.

I reach for the remaining American cigarettes and watch the blue circles after the first little clouds hang in the room. "Oh, what bad air you have." A French girl named Janette disturbs my beginning thoughts. Quickly she closes the door and tears open the window. "Always smoking and drinking. All soldiers drink too much." She begins her completely unnecessary lament and plants herself in front of my bed. "I brought cognac for you, if it is OK," she breathes secretly. "How much does such fun cost?" I wink with my left eye. "Twenty marks, that is not very much for you. In the city your comrades pay more," she clumsily entices me. "Why don't you sell the stuff in the city?" I wonder. She does not answer, but only looks at me. She furrows her eyebrows, her nostrils seem to inflate, her breast swells then sinks. Slowly I take my wallet from the night table and lay the money in her small hand. "It is very hot in the room, Janette, please open the door." I turn away from the situation that has become so unpleasant. She understands quickly. Insulted, she rolls the bills together, sets the bottle on the night table, and rushes from the room. "Certainly you are still very tired." She turns back once more. "Perhaps I will look in on you tomorrow."

Amused and satisfied, I grin inside myself and take the oft-read letter from my wife from my bag. I think you have had bad luck, Janette, you are not the right one for me, and my thoughts wander back across the Rhine.

After twenty minutes the devil alcohol torments me until I am convinced that I must have a sip from the bottle. But I don't have a corkscrew. "It serves you right," I mumble to myself. "It is unfair to your comrade Boger to drink the bottle alone. Besides it tastes much better when you drink with someone." With these thoughts, I slip the bottle under my coat and make my way to Boger. I nearly drop the bottle of cognac in surprise. Janette is lying in bed and is being comforted by Boger. Assuming that no one has yet noticed me, I seek my salvation in flight. But before I can reach the door, Boger calls to me, "Slowly, you disturber of the peace; where are you going with the bottle?" "I thought I would disturb you, Boger, pardon me," I stammer in my embarrassment. "Nonsense, sit down," he chatters, obviously in a good mood. "So, Janette, disappear; tomorrow is another day." He turns to the girl and swings out of the bed.

In no way embarrassed, she dresses without forgetting to put on her makeup. As our glances accidently meet, I observe that now her eyes seem satisfied. Smiling, she shakes hands with both of us and leaves the room humming the hit song, "Please Come Back." While I light a cigarette, I observe how Boger pulls the cork out of the bottle. He is the proper representative of our warrior generation. About twenty-nine years old, long brown hair, lusty black eyes, straight nose, broad, sensuous mouth, and a strong, energetic chin. On his field blouse, which hangs over the stool, there is next to the other orders and medals the Iron Cross First Class. In the meantime he has filled the glasses and hands one to me: "Toast, my friend, we have to do something for our health."

### 9 July 1944

About 10:00 A.M. a medic enters my room, puts me in a wheelchair, and takes me to the operating room where the good doctor works with his skillful hands on me. After I return to my room, I lie flat in bed until noon because the wound has become very uncomfortable. Still the doctor expresses satisfaction with my condition and tells me that there are people here who put pepper and other material into their wounds in order to stay in the hospital longer.

I too have noticed that it is much more pleasant here than at the front, but to use such means to try and prolong one's life seems to me to be vile and cowardly. Nevertheless, no one can escape his destiny and what seems to be right at the time can prove to be wrong later, especially if one tries to deceive providence through crooked means. With a mighty gulp from the cognac bottle I rinse down the dull taste and then I light a cigarette. The next few hours are taken up with writing letters home and to the front.

### 10 July 1944

At 1:00 P.M., I hear a discreet knock on my door and in response to my invitation two sturdy, pretty, and well-made-up girls enter my room. They are helpers with the air force and they look wonderful in their uniforms. Smiling, they trip to my bed and extend their hands amicably: "Inge from Görlitz," and "Renata from Düsseldorf." They lay down a pretty bouquet of wildflowers on my night table and in response to my invitation take a seat. In contrast to the girls, who act natural and uninhibited, I become nervous and reach for my cigarettes and offer them one. Without any restraint they accept and soon rings of blue smoke drift comfortingly to the ceiling. They ask about the nature of my wound and I must tell them about the front, which I do quickly with a few humorous words. As we continue our cheerful chatter, they begin to unpack their presents: a small but very tasty cake with chocolate frosting and white powdered sugar, a notebook, and a silver picture frame. Soon everything is carefully organized on my night table and my wife looks out from the new picture frame, amused at the scene. Before I always had something against girls in uniform, but now I am asking in silence for these two to forgive me. Their conduct and manner is so nice and uncomplicated; the pretty faces beam with the joy of giving. I reproach myself earnestly for my stupid prejudices.

"How can I thank you?" I laugh, happy with this nice change. "If it has brought you joy, that is thanks enough for us," Inge says modestly in a most pleasing voice. "But I beg you, joy is not expression enough for what I feel," is my honest compliment as we hear a knock on the door and Boger, pushing two girls ahead of him, enters my room; they are warmly greeted by my visitors. Gallantly he extends his hand to the women, then turns to me and competently takes my pulse. "Quite high blood pressure, my boy." He shakes his head seriously and that brings everyone to laughter. I could tear my hair out because the crazy character has embarrassed me and no way comes to mind to extricate myself from the affair.

In the meantime his two lady visitors have found a place to sit at the foot of my bed with Boger, his arms crossed, between the two of them. "And such people sacrifice their free afternoon, and here in Paris." I pick up the thread again. "What is that in comparison to you men?" Inge explains, almost sad. "We girls will never be in the position to compensate you any more than in the most modest manner, for your hardship and suffering."

"It is actually not as bad as you may imagine. One grows quickly into it and even the constant danger helps one to value life more. Everyone, whether man or woman, does his duty regardless of where fate has placed him."

While the conversation slowly drifts into political and military matters, Boger disappears and comes back a moment later with a bottle and glasses. "So children," he says, filling the glasses, "that is enough of this fruitless theme; let's drink to victory and not the least your graciousness; we cannot do any more for the situation at the moment." "That is the most reasonable idea that I have ever heard from you." I raise my glass.

After the second glass of cognac, I have the utmost pleasure listening to the long-missed chatter of the girls, who discuss the shameless, cunning French women and in particular the simplemindedness of the German soldiers. The blond Ingeborg, who Boger brought into the room, observes, "It is very hard for a respectable girl to secure the man her heart desires. If she does what he wants then he stays away because he believes she would do it for everyone else. If she doesn't do it, then he thinks he is wasting his time."

### 11 July 1944

I get up after lunch in an unpleasant mood and soap myself at the wash basin. I am at odds with myself and wipe the foam from my face. Why should I shave if I can't leave the building? The shaving brush falls back into the basin filled with water. I have got to stop drinking. The women must stay out of my room. The radio should not blast so loudly. The wounds must finally heal. No, I should have visitors more often. There is a shortage of conversation and entertainment in this place. I should be able to go out. The noisemakers on the floor should offer better music.

"How are you doing today?" the doctor asks to the accompaniment of all the commotion outside. "When I lie down, it's all right, Doctor," I answer the good man. He steps closer and looks at me: "Haven't you received any mail?" "No, not here," I answer in a disturbed tone. "Were you satisfied with yesterday's visitors?" he wants to know. "Thank you, I can't complain." I keep it short. "Make a note to get him a cane." He turns to the secretary: "I will look at the foot tomorrow." In a friendly manner he takes my hand: "Don't make any trouble for yourself; even this will pass."

Finally I have a reason to be angry with myself. How can I act in such an impertinent way toward such a good doctor and man? Especially a man who has always approached me like a fatherly friend. Why is it that sometimes against my own will I hurt people who are dear and precious to me? He won't worry that much about me in the future for I do not deserve any better.

Dinner arrives. Janette seems to have a chip on her shoulder. "Angry," I tease her sarcastically as she serves the apple sauce. "Yesterday the girls were here and today I can't do anything right," she fumes. "You must not try to comfort so many, Janette," I try to kid her. She slams the door shut. Bon appetit, I grin maliciously to myself and in spite of it all, I eat well.

The joyless day comes to an end without having seen Boger.

### 12 July 1944

After breakfast I sit, clean shaven, in the wheel chair in which the medic will transport me to the examination room. After a nurse loosens the bandage, the doctor, just as friendly as ever, inspects the wound. "It is coming along all right," he says, looking up, "but continue to take care of your foot so that the toe will stay intact later. You will get a cane so that you can find something to do outside of your room." He then gives instructions to rebandage my foot, paying attention to where the splint is placed.

Half an hour later I am in my room. I have come this far, I can walk with a cane. Distrustful, I squint toward the club that the medic has so matter of factly hung on my bed. As I do so, I recall the story of a man at home who, because of a wound he suffered during the First World War, received a pension and was always seen with his cane until a new law took away the pension. He then threw the cane away, declaring to the amusement of his friends that if he did not receive a pension any longer then he had no more use for the cane. From that hour on he was never seen again with that companion of so many years.

Shortly before 2:00 P.M. I wander over to Boger. I have not seen him for a while and find him polishing his boots by the window. He grins unashamedly. "Today I am going into the city," he says proudly and spits on his boots to bring out the high shine. "My, my," I laugh, "the bordellos will be happy to see a stallion like you." "Rubbish," he contradicts, "I am not one for those stinking booths. Do I look like someone who would have to pay for it?" "Calm yourself, where are you going?" I probe deeper. "That's the problem," he screams indignantly. "I don't know my way around this damn nest! If I had known it yesterday, then one of the air force girls could be my tour guide." "The best thing for you to do is to go to where the girls live and have them darn your socks. That is something that awakens their wifely feelings and if you already have your boots off ... " "Keep your mouth shut," he interrupts me, "the devil doesn't even know where they live." "How long have you been a soldier, Boger?" I wink at him. "What has that got to do with it?" he roars. "Because you don't even know that in a military establishment all visitors must leave their names and addresses with the guards," I instruct him. A radiant smile appears on his face as if by magic. Suddenly he is in a hurry.

The rest of the evening I spend in the company of two bottles of beer bringing my diary up to date. At 10:00 P.M. at lights out, Boger still has not returned.

### 13 July 1944

First thing in the morning I look in on Boger. The stench of sour alcohol in his room nearly takes my breath away. Quickly I open the window and observe the unconscious sleeper lying with his mouth open on the bed. A nurse carrying a thermometer in a glass softly enters the room.

"You are visiting so early?" She is startled and glances in amazement around the room where Boger's boots, pants, shirt, jacket, cap, and belt are scattered all over. Irritated, she puts her hands on her hips: "Just look at this, that's the way men are without women. He deserves someone who would at least pull down the blanket and put his naked behind in the bed." Angrily she picks up the things and puts them on the chair according to regulations. No longer interested in Boger's temperature, she turns to the door and hisses to me, "Please leave the window open, it stinks worse in here than a bar in the Rhineland the day after Mardi Gras."

I discover in the wash basin a beautifully labeled bottle of Calvados, still corked. Quickly I step to the window to give the bottle a thorough examination.

"Yes, yes, take a good look at it," says Boger unexpectedly from his bed. "It belongs to you, Helmut. I finally talked an old bartender into letting me have it. Then I had to defend the bottle from the Paris hookers with more difficulty than my machine gun position at Stalingrad."

"I will take a bath to wash away last night's sins, and I will excuse myself to the sergeant major for being late. Really they cannot be angry with me when I could not find my way back in this foreign and blacked-out Paris."

About noon Boger returns from the administration office somewhat depressed. "My pass is now with the chief doctor," he says. "That could be bad, Boger. Can't the chief just let the whole matter fall through the cracks?" I ask with an unpleasant feeling in my stomach. "It is too late for that, I should have gone in sooner," he says, apathetic. "Try to talk to the head doctor, perhaps he will take care of the matter," I counsel him. "Oh, shit, they can do what they want, they will anyway," he answers, brushing it off.

From late afternoon on we play cards and do not end the stupid game until the lights are turned out.

### 15 July 1944

Two days have passed without anything meaningful happening. Today at 11:20 A.M. Boger comes back from the doctor in charge, to whom he had to report for questioning. I have been anxious all morning about how the situation regarding his furlough will turn out. As Boger crosses the threshold and comes toward me, no words are necessary. The expression on his face indicates that he will be punished. "You must open the Calvados, Helmut, I need it very much to get the bad taste out of my mouth. After that I will pack my things, I must report to the personnel office today for assignment to the front," he says, rather depressed, and sits on the edge of my bed. "What happened, Boger?" I ask, although I am in no way surprised with the outcome since I went through the same kind of thing in my earlier days. "Not much," he answers with a subdued voice, "everything followed its normal course. Instead of returning at 10:00 P.M. we did not trundle in until 1:50 A.M. The guard, according to his orders, noted the time, and the rest you can imagine. You know how these chamber pot swingers are and how they use their diagnoses or whatever they call the pile of shit. So, with regard to me, I am considered healthy. At 3:00 P.M. I can sign out!" He ends his report and tips a double shot of Calvados down his throat. "A toast to you, Karl," I give him in response. "You know I had always thought that we would inhale these drops on an especially nice occasion and I did not know that this Calvados would be the reason for our separation. That is why it must pay the debt with death. Knowing the two of us, we will have carried out the sentence by three o'clock."

We enjoy ourselves immensely and the troubled times seem much easier to endure after the alcohol has mixed with our blood.

"First I will go to the personnel office and get a twenty-four-hour pass." Boger seems to read my thoughts. "Each soldier who is in Paris for the first time can get it," he indicates with confidence.

"How long will this damned war go on?" I ask after a pause. "If it ends this year, then we are the losers. I don't want that. We have stood in the shit too long to have peace at any price," is his opinion. "That's my view as well, but how can it continue?" I would really like to know. "You will have to ask Adolf that personally. As we hear, the great blow is coming soon. But I don't believe everything anymore." He fills the glasses again. "These stupid rumors have been stuck in my throat for a long time. Ever since Stalingrad they have been feeding it to us and all the time we have been going downhill." I defend myself against the eternal propaganda rumors. "That is not really so," he encourages me, "some things do have their justice. There are really weapons that are nearly finished that will give another face to the war, but when that will be we do not know." "Let's hope for the best, Boger." I raise my glass. "Let's have lunch now." "That's the way it shall be." He rises, slightly swaying, and goes into his room to pack.

After the meal I take the bottle and glasses and go with deep sorrow in my heart to Boger. It is always the same in the military, I think as I cross the hall. One gets to know comrades that he likes and then loses them.

"You come as though I called for you," Boger receives me. "I have just finished." "I don't feel very good in my skin when I see you in your war paint." "Me neither, but let's not talk about it; there is nothing that can be done about it," he says with resignation. "Do you at least know where your group is?" I ask while he fills the glasses. "No, I think I can find that out in the personnel office." He hands me the glass filled with liquor from Normandy.

At 2:35 P.M. Boger gets up and takes a cigarette out. "The time is up, my friend, I must go," he says and extends his hand. "Be good, Helmut, I am happy I got to know you; perhaps our paths will cross again in the future." "Take care, Karl, be cheerful and greet Inge for me. I wish you all the luck in the world, perhaps we will see each other at the front." I press his hand firmly and accompany him to the door. A friend has gone from me. Dully his steps fade away on the linoleum-tiled floor.

*20 July 1944*

Since Boger's departure I have not left my room. I am reading the book, *The Command of Conscience*, and I have forgotten the world around me. In the middle of the night a medic awakes me. "The Führer will speak," he says and with these four words he tears me out of my sleep and my lethargy. "Now, in the middle of the night?" I want to ask the man, but he has already left.

Quickly I get out of bed and make my way out to the floor. Subdued march music sounds out of the loudspeaker. The wounded stand in groups around the speakers. Bits of conversation reach my ears. "In the homeland the swine are rising up trying to stab us in the back," I hear an upset man say who wears a thick bandage around his head. "The main thing is that the Führer is still alive," another interjects. "What happened?" I ask as I approach a group. "A plot against the Führer," nearly everyone answers at the same time. A feeling of distress lies on my heart and the picture flashes before my eyes of Hagen as he stabbed Siegfried in the back with his spear.

From the loudspeaker we hear the familiar voice of the Führer: "I am speaking to you so that you can hear my voice ... a handful of ambitious officers ... as a sign of providence. ..."

It has come this far: now the Germans are eating each other. That is what all those strange decisions add up to since the invasion. Sold and betrayed, all the brave German soldiers stand on the fronts and fight in hopeless combat.

"What do you say, comrade, to this situation in the homeland?" a man standing next to me asks as I turn to go. "I don't understand it anymore," I answer, subdued. "Hopefully they will push through and finally bring the men out into the open," the man fumes and balls his hands into fists. "There may be people in the general staff on whose feet Hitler has trodden, but the fact that in this hour of their country's greatest need they try to play politics which will lead only to chaos, I will never understand." The anger hits me. "They are saboteurs who have shifted the war into reverse and now they have revealed their cards," I hear the man continue before the door to the room closes from inside.

What do these officers want, who certainly have a vision of the highest war strategy? Why do they resort to undertake a plot in order to overthrow Hitler? Reason tells me there are only two possibilities. Either they intend through sabotage to bring about the inevitable defeat in order to turn the people and the army against Hitler and then seize power for themselves, or we are indeed at the end of our strength and they are trying now to save what can be saved. But where do these rumors about secret weapons come from? The fact that they have already put the rockets into action is proof that there is some truth to what is said.

How will things go from here on? He will fulfill his destiny in that the new weapons will be implemented and the war will come to an end sooner or later, I answer my own question, since this simple solution comes closest to fulfilling my own wish to go home. But still I lie in bed for hours, smoking continuously, until sleep finally carries me from this miserable world.

* * *

On July 20, 1944, at 12:42 P.M., a bomb exploded in the conference room at Hitler's headquarters at Rastenburg in East Prussia. The bomb had been brought into a conference room in a briefcase by Klaus Philip Schenk, Count von Stauffenberg, a career officer in the German army and member of an old and distinguished South German family. Hitler survived the explosion because another officer had moved the briefcase behind the heavy leg of the map table. Still, Hitler was considerably shaken. One pants leg was blown off, one leg was burned, his hair was scorched, his back was bruised by a falling beam, his right arm hung stiff and useless, and both eardrums were damaged. Convinced that this was an important turn of events for Germany, Hitler would preserve his tattered uniform as a future museum piece as evidence that Providence had indeed saved his life.

This was not the first assassination attempt on Hitler's life, but it came closest to success. Count von Stauffenberg's action was part of an elaborate attempt by a group of military officers and politicians to take control of the German government and negotiate peace treaties with Germany's enemies. Upon returning to Berlin from Rastenburg, von Stauffenberg pushed ahead with the planned overthrow. However, later in the day, when it became obvious that Adolf Hitler had not been killed, other officers loyal to Hitler suppressed the attempted overthrow and shot von Stauffenberg and several other leading participants. At 12:30 that night, twelve hours after the explosion, Adolf Hitler spoke in a broadcast carried over all German radio stations. This was the speech that Helmut Hörner and the other patients heard:

> If I speak to you today it is first in order that you should hear my voice and should know that I am unhurt and well, and secondly that you should know of a crime unparalleled in German history. A very small clique of ambitious, irresponsible, and at the same time senseless and stupid officers had formed a plot to eliminate me and the High Command of the Armed Forces.
>
> The bomb placed by Colonel Graf von Stauffenberg exploded two meters to my right. One of those with me has died; other colleagues very dear to me were severely injured. I myself sustained only some very minor scratches, bruises, and burns. I

regard this as a confirmation of the task imposed upon me by Providence. ...

The circle of these conspirators is very small and has nothing in common with the spirit of the German Wehrmacht and, above all, none with the German people. I therefore give orders now that no military authority, no commander and no private soldier is to obey any orders emanating from this group of usurpers. I also order that it is everyone's duty to arrest, or, if they resist, to shoot at sight, anyone issuing or handling such orders.

I am convinced that with the uncovering of this tiny clique of traitors and saboteurs there has at long last been created in the rear that atmosphere which the fighting front needs. ...[1]

The response by Hörner and his comrades to Hitler's speech was apparently typical of that throughout Germany. John Toland, in his biography *Adolf Hitler*, records:

The early rumor of Hitler's death brought hysteria and tears to scores of girl telephonists. The story spread and caused consternation until the reassuring newscast brought new tears, these of joy ... . These expressions of relief were not completely self-serving. The great majority of Germans felt that the nation's future depended on the Führer.[2]

In subsequent days, other participants were rounded up, and it is estimated that about five thousand people were executed because of actual or alleged participation in the conspiracy. Among those actively involved in the plot were General Ludwig Beck; Carl Gordeler, former mayor of Leipzig; Field Marshal Erwin von Witzleben; and General Franz Halder. Others who knew of the plot but had done nothing to help or hinder it also lost their lives. Admiral Wilhelm Canaris was executed by a firing squad. Edwin Rommel, the popular and well-respected "Desert Fox" of the North Africa campaign and later the general in charge of German fortifications in France prior to the invasion, was forced to commit suicide, although his death was made to appear as occurring in an automobile accident. The effect of the assassination attempt on Hitler was to increase his intense distrust of the army generals while at the same time rendering his own leadership more ineffective. The shock of the explosion further weakened his ability to concentrate while the dubious medication he took seemed to cause further physical deterioration.

\* \* \*

*22 July 1944*

While the events of the last days are anxiously discussed in the hospital, a large number of newly wounded arrive. They put a second bed in my room for a badly shot-up staff sergeant. He comes from the area around Caen and is still very numb, so that any conversation is out of the question even though the happenings in that area are of great interest to me since my unit was stationed in Caen until May 1944.

For days the doctor has carried around a very serious face, and after his visit today a transport slip now hangs on my chart. He told me good-bye with the words, "We must make room, sergeant, keep your ears stiff. You are going to Strasbourg."

"I wish I were able to be transported," my neighbor finally opens his mouth. "I would feel much better in Strasbourg." "Here everything humanly possible is being done for you. You will not find a better doctor in Strasbourg and the food could not be better than here." "It doesn't have anything to do with that," he indicates with an earnest face. "I want to get out of France. One of these days there will be no more room for us here."

"You must keep still and not upset yourself, Comrade. One sees only black in the first few days and believes it will not be better. But things change quickly; in a week you will be dreaming of your first furlough. By the way, so that I don't forget, a couple of air force girls will come to this room in a few days and wonder why I am not here. Be so good and extend greetings from me; they will thank you with a very fine cake." I encourage him and organize my things in preparation for my transfer.

After dinner I stand in my freshly washed uniform at the bed of the staff sergeant and hold his hand in my right hand: "Don't lose courage," I say in parting. "They will put you back together and life will continue even if we on the front fail." "Good-bye, thank you for your indulgence, perhaps later we can get drunk on my pension." He smiles bravely and lifts his healthy hand in salute.

Thirty minutes later I sit in a bus that slowly takes us to the north train station. The sun burns hot on the Paris asphalt while the girls in fragrant dresses promenade along the pavement, their eyes, hidden by sunglasses, glancing at the gentlemen who sit in front of the restaurants enjoying cool drinks. But we stand once again on the edge of life and without a word of protest allow ourselves to be taken out of this beautiful city into another one where they will make our shot-up bones healthy once again so that we can be thrown back into the war.

"Get out," a medic orders us after the bus arrives at the train station. Twisting and moaning, the suffering people leave the upholstered seats and make their way through the nearly empty station to the platform where a Red Cross train waits to leave. Faster than one would expect from soldiers outfitted with canes and crutches, we have disappeared into the coaches. People are always driven by their desires. This time it is the pull to get a window seat. "Where are they taking us now?" A Saxon turns from the window and looks around. "To the moon where they will shoot you if you don't soon sit on your ass." A Swab cuts him short. "Hold your. ..."

"Gifts, cigarettes, chocolate, and candies," someone screams from the window and thereby interrupts the beginning skirmish. "Come here with the stuff; twelve men are in this compartment." The Saxon turns to better things, sticking his head out the window in order not to be passed over. His efforts are rewarded. Just as proud as Santa Claus, he distributes the items he has obtained, without forgetting himself. But not long after complaints arise. "When do you think they will leave?" the eternally dissatisfied bleat. "At the moment when the man with the red hat raises his green sign." A wisecracker knows the right answer and brings out the laughter.

Exactly at 9:00 P.M. the train rolls out of the station and into the beginning night.

### 23 July 1944

As dawn comes, we stop at the Fontainebleau train station. Damn it, this is not the direct route to Strasbourg, I think, but comfort myself with the immediate thought that apparently a bridge across the Marne has been destroyed and the train must take a detour. Under normal circumstances, we should at least be in Épernay if not Châlons on the Marne. But all the unrest is useless. The train stands, like it had grown here in Fontainebleau, on a rusty side track and shows no sign of moving on to where the thoughts of its passengers have been for hours: Strasbourg!

How much I look forward to this city to which I am tied by so many dear memories. I will immediately send a telegram to my wife so that she can join me.

While I allow myself the anticipated joy of our reunion, the train reaches the Yonne, a tributary of the Seine, and every minute brings us closer to our goal.

Suddenly my thoughts are interrupted. The train stands at Auxerre and does not follow the direction toward Dijon, Mülhausen, Strasbourg as I had imagined. Along the row of cars medics of the Waffen SS appear. "Get out," the command roars. Dreadful curses fly through the compartments. But they do no good, we are soldiers and must obey. "Such a damn dirty situation," bellows a joker. "So close to the latrine to shit in one's pants." And once again the long-suffering men are laughing. The soldier's humor helps to overcome almost everything.

A little later we sit in buses and ride into a summer-calm little city. "SS Hospital Auxerre" stands over the entrance to a park in whose rear a long, stretching building can be seen. "Here we are then." I nod to a comrade who sat next to me during the train ride and who looks very serious. "Endure it with humor, then it will be easier for you," I advise him as he appears now to be indifferent. "What are we to do among the SS?" he asks spitefully. "A hospital is a hospital, regardless of what kind of insignia the people wear on their uniforms." I shrug my shoulders and go into the building.

A considerable time later, I lie in blue-and-white striped pajamas in the corner of a large room in a double-decker bed and I don't know whether I should be full of anger or wonder. The hospital is filled to the ceiling. Despite the overcrowding, the noon meal consists of mutton and macaroni, and as a special gesture of hospitality, an apple for dessert. The food, to the comfort of all of us, is abundant and well prepared. With a full stomach, but with mixed feelings, I fall asleep in the strange surroundings with their constant disturbance.

Bathed in sweat, I rise up when the whistle sounds for dinner and go to wash myself. The meal is set out on a long table. The dominating heat brings forth all kinds of undefinable odors and as a consequence restricts the appetite considerably.

After dinner I find a book in the library, *From the Tsar's Eagle to the Red Flag*, which I put under my arm and find a quiet place outside in order to read until bedtime.

*24 July 1944*

The newly arrived wounded are given a thorough examination today. A medic stands with a list at the entrance to the hall and calls out the names of the wounded who are to present themselves to the doctor. As the first return they report that a rough tone prevails here.

At 10:30 A.M., I sit in front of the doctor with my bandages removed while he reads my papers with interest. "You are a sergeant, Hörner, and were wounded in the area around La Haye-du-Puits?" he asks me as he passes the papers to a nurse. "Release him for assignment in about three weeks." He turns to a clerk and gives instructions to bandage me again. Condescendingly he extends to me his hand and his glance forces me to look at him. "Nearly half the people in this transport are nearly healed. Do you have an explanation for that?" "The people were probably in good hands," I answer with a double meaning.

"There are other reasons for it if you consider it carefully." He overrides my ironical answer. "For sure," I confirm the truth of his accusation, "in the last days many wounded arrived in Paris so that the authorities were forced to transfer those who could be transported." "So, it's good, you can go. The next please."

"What funny people are here," I think, while a medic accompanies me to my bed. In the room there is a feeling of oppression.

I have hardly made myself comfortable when I hear a soldier speaking to one of the SS medics, "Yes sir," he says. "Stop all that nonsense!" Suddenly I lose my senses and hop to the sergeant as though driven by an inner force: "I am Sergeant Hörner," I hiss to take the man aback, "and I want to ask you what you mean with this tone of voice. This comrade has stood as a man and if you want to risk everything like him, then I suggest that you go smell where fourteen days ago he spit. The front is waiting for big mouths like you."

Slowly my inner equilibrium returns. Ice cold, I observe the man across from me. He has turned red with rage, but he controls himself, turns around, and leaves. At the moment you could hear a pin drop in the hall. Satisfied, I hop back to my place, surprised at the fuss the others make about my action.

"You certainly shut his trap," a soldier in the neighboring bed says. "Hopefully it will do some good, I can't stand to see how they try to jump all over us," I say, relieved, and climb into my bed. "He will report you for sure," the man fears. "He can go right ahead, I can handle myself," I answer indifferently. "If we win the war, can't you just imagine how they will act?" He wrinkles his forehead with these dark forebodings. "We aren't that far yet, so that I have to worry about it. If it comes to that, we are all still here," I indicate as lunch is carried in. "In any case, enjoy the food." I guide him back from the future to the present and consider with light resistance the rubber-like macaroni in the gray broth. "Don't they have anything else to eat here than these disgusting ring worms?" The confidence of the men in the room awakens slowly. "They can smear this filthy mutton in their hair." The courageous soldiers take up their well-practiced complaining, although the most outspoken, as always, are already after seconds. The meal time is flavored with an ongoing humorous banter until the entire crowd has eaten themselves full and rack out in the beds to fall asleep.

"You must report at 4:00 P.M.," a medic wakes me with a malicious grin. "Didn't I tell you so?" my neighbor flusters to me. "Yes, you are really a prophet," I reassure him and look at my watch. "For Hell's sake, they don't give one much time." I get out of bed and button my field blouse. "You are right, comrade, show him your ornaments so that he immediately knows who he has in front of him." He glances at my medals.

Exactly at 4:00 P.M. I stand before the head doctor on one leg, supported by my cane. He is the same one who examined me. In response to my greeting he indolently lifts his hand and asks me to sit down. "You had a dispute this morning with Vogel?" He opens the inquiry. "Yes sir, Doctor," I answer, to which I immediately observe that he is sour at me for not addressing him by his SS rank, but his exact title I am not familiar with. "What were the circumstances?" he wants to know and in response I rehearse the entire affair. "Why did you get mixed up with it?" is his next question. "Because I saw red when a medic a hundred miles behind the front abuses the wounded." I give him my honest and truthful answer. "Everyone has to do his duty wherever he is assigned," he responds sharply. "I am of the same opinion, but the tone makes the music and I want to make clear that all of us have absolutely nothing against the SS. On the contrary, we know how bravely this division has fought." I clear an eventual misunderstanding out of the way. "Will you apologize to Vogel?" he asks, the words clinging in the room like metal. The blood thuds dully against my temples while my heart gathers to give a difficult response. But a way out does appear. "If Vogel will apologize to the wounded man, then I am more than ready," I am astonished to hear myself reply. "That's fine." The doctor sits down on the edge of the desk, satisfied. "You can go, I will speak with him."

"Did you give him a proper response?" A curious group gathers around my bed as I return. "It was a conversation among men and nothing more." I damp their rebellious souls and they disperse, disappointed. For dinner we have once again rubber macaroni, goulash, and salad.

### 28 July 1944

We have settled into our new environment. The relationship with the hospital personnel improves. Nearly every day some of the men are released and once again sent to the front. Corporal Vogel and I have apologized to one another in the presence of the doctor and everything seems to follow its normal course. This afternoon a troop of artists brings something of a diversion into the stale hospital activities. The inmates of the hospital, including the German and French personnel, assemble in the park where long rows of stools and benches have been placed. The artists have arrived and the magic begins. A good announcer immediately establishes contact with the audience with his jokes. Before the enthusiastic applause has ended, he introduces an old singer who tries with all means at hand to make herself appear young. But she is an excellent singer and through her songs she is able to break the remaining ice that surrounded a certain stuffy element among us. She is followed by two tap dancers, then two young ladies who bring magic tones out of their saxophones and earn the enthusiasm of the entire audience.

After the usual smoking break, a juggler shows his talents. Then four pretty girls and two gentlemen with musical instruments let loose with "The Black Panther," so that even the wounded with crutches stand up and begin to sway with the rhythm. Just as the last echoes of applause end, the artists launch into "Barcelona," to the accompaniment of immense applause. Again and again the six must go onto the makeshift stage and again and again the applause roars until even the most stubborn understand that this kind of effort leaves the performers exhausted. The program concludes with the wonderful song about the brave little soldier's wife. We return to bed with totally softened hearts. A day worth living comes to an end.

### 5 August 1944

Today I have my first pass to leave the hospital. Although my foot hurts terribly when I walk, I don't care. I must finally see something different than double bunk beds and men in blue-and-white striped pajamas. Before everything, I think about going into the city to have something respectable to eat; then the rubber macaroni nearly gags me. I report in at the guardhouse where a staff sergeant offers me his help to go into town.

We dawdle along a path toward the town in the scorching heat. "How do you like the hospital, Comrade?" my companion begins the conversation. "I had really expected more comfort from the SS," I express my opinion. "It is indeed a bad store," he agrees with me. "It seems that you are from southern Germany, as I hear by your dialect," he observes. "I am from Austria, Briller is my name, Robert Briller, from Vorarlberg." "It's a pleasure." I am happy with his open manner. "Hörner, Helmut," I introduce myself. "Pleased to meet you," he extends his glove-covered hand. "Were you fighting against the Tommys, or on the Cotentin Peninsula?" he asks as we continue to walk. "I come from the area around Portbail, Saint-Sauveur, La Haye-du-Puits." I explain to him where I saw action. "My God, I come from that area as well! Now tell me that you belong to the 77th Division." I am prepared for any surprise. "The devil can take me, if that's not true," he responds, overjoyed. "Here, you can look in my *Soldbuch*." He will prove it to me. "Here, Regiment 1049," he points to a page in his well-used *Soldbuch*. "I believe you," I comfort him. "I belong to the 1050 Regiment." "Such a coincidence," we rejoice together. "We must drink to that!" He begins to speed up the pace. "Slow down, otherwise you will already be full before I arrive." I hold onto his sleeve.

* * *

The *Soldbuch* (soldier's book) was the German soldier's personal identification and a compact personnel file that he was expected to have with him at all times. The *Soldbuch* contained such information as the dates of promotions; awards and medals; clothing and equipment issued; military assignments; leave when longer than five days; the name of hospitals along with the length and reason for stay; religious affiliation; occupation; blood type; and physical characteristics including height, stature, hair and eye color, foot length and width, and special marks. (Helmut Hörner's *Soldbuch* indicates he has a scar on his right index finger.) There was also space for the name and address of the spouse, parents, or relatives and fiancée. The *Soldbuch* was the soldier's identity since it contained every essential piece of information about him and his service career.

* * *

Twenty minutes later we reach the city and two German railroaders show us where we can eat. A pleasant coolness and soft dimness pull us into the guest room. It is exactly 3:00 P.M. as the innkeeper, an older woman, comes to our table. "Bonjour messieurs," she greets us, friendly, and looks in anticipation from one to the other. "Avez-vous une bouteille de vin rouge?" Briller orders a bottle of red wine just like a native Frenchman. "Don't we want to drink a beer first?" I offer as a suggestion, and he orders two beers from the madame. "S'il vous plaît, messieurs," the madame whispers as she brings the drinks to the table. "Merci, madame," Briller thanks her politely and extends his glass to mine. "To the 77th." "And to our meeting each other." He laughs happily and pours the entire glass down his throat. "Order something to eat; that is why I came into the city and you appear to speak perfect French," I ask of Briller. "Nonsense, I only know the few words that one needs for food and drink," he confesses, but waves immediately to the madame and after she arrives he orders two beefsteaks, french fries, and salad.

While the rattle of pots and pans can be heard in the kitchen, Briller tells me a story about a French bordello, which at the moment is of little interest to me as I lust after the beefsteaks whose smell penetrates the air. After the unbelievably long time of twenty minutes, everything we ordered stands before us on the table. "Finally, once again something respectable between the teeth," snaps Briller. "Keep quiet and keep your fork busy." I reject all conversation in order to completely enjoy the wonderfully prepared dinner.

But too quickly the contents of the plate melt together without any observable resistance in the stomach. As my eyes take in more porcelain than food on the plate, I become afraid and wave to the madame to come to the table. "Avez-vous omelettes flamée?" I ask her. "Oui," she beams at me joyfully at the business I have brought and hustles into the kitchen to prepare scrambled eggs sprinkled with schnapps. "What do you think this fun will cost us?" I bring up the dark side of our pleasure. "Today it doesn't matter at all." He shrugs his shoulders.

The schnapps burns bluish on the scrambled eggs. Ceremoniously the madame holds the snow-white napkin ready. Quickly she covers it up and smothers the flame. "Hopefully the old one did not pour alcohol all over it," Briller seems to mumble to himself. "No alcohol," the madame protests indignantly. "Bon schnapps." "Merci, madame." I calm her and reach once again for my utensils.

Briller shovels his omelettes à la flamée behind his powerful set of teeth, while the matron stares at him from behind the counter, apparently offended. "You made her angry," I whisper to him and he waves for the old dame to come to the table. "Une bouteille vin de rouge, s'il vous plaît, madame," he says with the most charming laugh and hands the empty bottle to her across the table. "Grand filou," she laughs back and waddles to the counter. "So." I am happy she seems satisfied again. "Shit," says Briller and wipes his mouth with his handkerchief, "that is why she cheated us, or do you really believe the steaks are from a beef?" "Cut it out," I respond, "the old one has really gone to a lot of trouble for us." "For sure," he says, emptying his glass, "but perhaps you are a little naive. The beefsteaks are from an old gelding." "What are you saying?" I ask him indignantly. But with the most content manner in the world, Briller picks his teeth with a broken match, while leaning back fully satisfied. "You are wearing riding pants, you must know what a gelding is?" he asks in return. "Naturally I know, but you can't be serious that they would put horse flesh in front of us?" I respond, slightly irritated.

"My God, don't get yourself upset." He passes me his pack of cigarettes. "This is not your first time in France. They eat horse meat, and there is nothing you can do about it, and while we happen to be here we eat it with them. What is wrong with that?" "And you knew that?" I wonder. "Of course," he responds, "why, didn't it taste good to you?"

About 7:00 P.M. we ask for the bill. The madame has everything ready and names an astronomically high number. Carefully she picks up the bills and goes to the bar, where she pours three double glasses of cognac without being asked. She comes with them to the table, sets the silver tray down, takes a glass in hand, and nods encouragingly to us. "Toast, madame!"

The empty glasses clatter softly on the tray. The friendly madame accompanies us to the door. Happy and well satisfied, we both stand on the street and bask in the golden rays of the setting sun. "The old one does know how to live, you have to give her that," I say, reconciled, and limp with effort out of the alley.

In the vicinity of the hospital we enter a little establishment from which the music can be heard on the street. The inn is completely filled with soldiers from the hospital. The atmosphere matches. I am greeted heartily by a number of soldiers in the room and the word is spread, "He is the soldier that told off the SS man and. ..."

Briller looks at me in astonishment. "Did you cause any trouble in the store?" he asks as a small place is made available to us in a corner. "I heard about it," he adds, "and I can only agree with you; then those brothers have been a stench to me for a long time." "A bottle of white bordeaux," I order from the well-endowed waitress when she reaches our table.

But we have eaten and drunk too much to have any taste for the lukewarm wine. Furthermore, we realize that we have stumbled into a camouflaged brothel. When we try to pay, the young lady explains in good German that the bill has been taken care of. "If you want to come on a more peaceful day," she says with a tempting wink as we stumble out of the place.

### 10 August 1944

Today I leave the Hospital Auxerre with Briller. With orders in our pockets to go to Paris for assignment to the front we report to the local commander to collect our pay and pick up some better clothes. Briller arranged to leave earlier than necessary so we could stay together.

It is 6:20 P.M. when we catch a German transport which is going to Troyes. The driver is happy to have someone with him since the area through which he must drive is supposed to be infested with partisans. He carries a rifle and several hand grenades under the seat. We travel along the road to Sens, which we reach without any trouble. Because our nice driver is still fearful of the partisans, he turns down our friendly invitation to drink a round of schnapps with us and keeps going toward Troyes after we get out and wish him a good trip.

Happy that we now have Auxerre behind us, we look for the area commander, who directs us to a hotel for the night in which French refugees from Normandy are being cared for. Briller and I share a spacious, well-furnished room with a bath. There is much going on in the hotel. In spite of their uprooted life, the soldiers and the refugees enjoy every available pleasure even when all morals and good health go to the devil. I turn down my companion's request to go down with him and instead wash myself thoroughly before I search for my bed. Just as I am falling asleep, Briller appears with a girl and asks me to go downstairs for a while. "Are you to be saved?" I scream, enraged at him. "Do you believe I am going to let my sleep be disturbed because of this feather duster?" Offended, he shuts the door and disappears. Undisturbed, I sleep until the bright morning.

Shortly after eight o'clock, Briller trots into the room like a beaten dog. "Pardon me," he says, "I did not know that you were so sensitive." "I am not sensitive at all, but you cannot expect to be able to amuse yourself at my expense. By the way, did you go to the medic station already?" I ask sharply and sense at once that I have used the wrong tone. He gives me a defiant no for an answer and slams the door shut with a bang. Not entirely satisfied with everything that I have dumped on Briller's head, I shave and take a bath.

An hour later I report to the commander and receive our travel provisions and ask about clothing and transportation. But they have neither the one nor the other. Disappointed, I return to the hotel, where I find Briller asleep in his bed. A receipt from the medic's office lies on the table. Crazy dog, I mumble to myself and shake him. Disturbed, he glances around. "Get up you old boar and eat, I brought your provisions," I say without looking at him. Obediently he gets up and goes to the wash basin. While he dries his hands our glances meet. We both laugh. Everything is forgotten.

We enjoy part of the excellent hard sausage, bread, butter, and Swiss cheese. Just as we finish, a corporal from the commander informs us that we can ride with a transport convoy to Melun.

Within half an hour we sit in the cab of a heavily loaded truck and roll out of Sens. Although the road indicates plenty of evidence of enemy aircraft activity, we have to seek cover from the enemy planes only once. The terrorists initiate no action at all. This strengthens my belief that all the talk about French snipers is a pure fairy tale, since I have been in France more than seven months and have not seen a single member of this legendary ghost army. Nevertheless the driver does not tire of telling us about the mean and cunning ways of the French partisans. We pass the first houses of Melun without any trouble and hope from here on to be spared from the ghosts.

"It will be better if we go to the commander first for help to continue on," I suggest to Briller after we thank the driver and convoy leader and stand on the street in this strange city. "Let's get something to eat first, I have a tortuous thirst." Briller looks at me, almost begging. "You should not have drunk so much last night, then you would feel better." I can't seem to avoid the stupid accusation. "Please, I only drank a bottle of wine with the little one, then we went to bed." He defends himself. "It's OK, let's go to the bar on the corner." I point to an inn that holds promise.

"Avez-vous une bouteille de vin blanc?" Briller asks the good-looking waitress after we find a seat in the restaurant. "Don't trouble yourself, we speak German here." She laughs loudly and hurries to the bar, swaying her nice-looking hips. "Here you are, gentlemen." She places the wine on the table after a few minutes. "Thanks a lot; we could not have found a better place than here with you." I offer her a compliment. "Don't say that; I can be pretty nasty if I don't like someone," she explains and pours the wine from the bottle into the glasses. "According to that, you like us." Briller pulls the conversation in his direction and peers unembarrassed into her low-cut blouse. "My, but you notice everything." She sticks out her tongue at him. "But don't let it go to your head. You are the first guests today, that's why." She rolls her eyes and withdraws.

"Fine woman," Briller observes and toasts me. "You didn't get enough last night?" I ask him ironically. "If you must know, the doctor has prescribed these dark-haired ones for me." He laughs cunningly. "In that case, hurry up and get to your medicine, we have to leave soon." I remind him of his duty. "We could stay here and early in the morning stroll into Paris." He winks at me with his lusty eyes. "What do you want to do in this nest; we will go as soon as we have an opportunity," I maintain stubbornly. "Good, I agree; let's drink the bottle empty and then go to the commander. But I tell you, in Paris we will have so much fun that the walls will shake." He slams his fist on the table. "Good, agreed, but now I want to eat something. I am tired of this hard sausage," I concur and wave to the waitress.

After we eat, Briller talks me into a second bottle, which is not too difficult since the wine tastes so good. In the meantime soldiers from a tank outfit on their way to the front have stopped in the locale. In the course of our conversation, we learn that their route goes through Paris and there is a possibility for us to travel with them. We immediately go to the leader of the company, who happens to be a very careful major. He goes through our papers very thoroughly before he authorizes us to travel with them.

After dark Briller and I sit in the vehicle of a first lieutenant on the road to Paris. The column travels without lights through the blacked-out villages and small towns. A light rain has set in. Slowly the conversation in the car drifts away. A little later we are asleep.

"Porte de Bercy." The first lieutenant drags us from our dreams. "What's that?" I ask, drunk with sleep. "We are in Paris and have just passed Porte de

Bercy," he repeats himself. "So, you mean the gate to sin." I am already prepared for fun, but in reality I don't know what it means. "Yes, you could call it that." The officer grins cheerfully and holds a lighter to my cigarette. "You must soon get out, since we have got something to take care of in the Avenue Victor-Hugo," he adds while we rush past the street sign "Quai de Austerlitz." "Pardon me, First Lieutenant, we don't know our way around Paris, how can we find the commander of the personnel office?" I ask helplessly and look into the dark waters of the Seine. "Never mind, we will take you to the Arc de Triomphe and then show you where to go," he comforts me.

Slowly the column rolls along the Seine. "So this is Paris," Briller mumbles to himself as his eyes scan the streets and the high, gloomy houses. "Are you looking for something special since your eyes move like searchlights?" I ask jokingly. "I don't know, perhaps, with the name Paris, I always think of girls, but I can't discover any," he explains with the look of a hungry wolf. "Don't forget that it is about 2:00 A.M. At this hour the brave daughters of Eve are already in their beds." I dampen his adventuresome desires. "Are you crazy, in Paris one does not sleep, especially not alone," he exposes his desire. "For today we have missed our connections."

"Place de la Concorde." The First Lieutenant turns to us after we have crossed a bridge and come to a large square framed to the left and right with parks.

"So, here we are, this monument is the Arc de Triomphe, the grave of the Unknown Soldier," he adds after Briller and I have set foot on the Paris pavement and our eyes focus on the impressive and mighty monument. "You simply go along the Avenue de Friedland until you come to the Boulevard Haussmann, then along the Boulevard Haussmann to the Place de l'Opéra, where you will find the commander's door." He says good-bye. "Take with you our thanks and best wishes for the front, perhaps there we can be of help to you." We shake his hand and set out along the Avenue de Friedland.

"Your division has been wiped out, Comrades," says the gray-haired sergeant at the counter of the commander's office and gives back our *Soldbuchs*. "What do you mean?" I fall out of the clouds and stare at the man who so mechanically has made this terrible disclosure. "I am sorry, I will write you a twenty-four-hour pass. Before it expires you must report to the front personnel office, where you will be assigned to a unit," he explains, untroubled, and reaches for the forms.

"Put the slip in your *Soldbuch*, Helmut," Briller says. Sadly I lift my glance and look into his moist eyes. Slowly we turn to go. "Hey," the gray-haired sergeant calls to us, "You don't know where you are supposed to sleep." "Then tell us." Briller stops. "In the schoolhouse behind the Opéra." He shakes his head in disapproval.

"And now, Robert?" I ask my fellow traveler as we stand in the dark of night on a Paris street with no person to be seen. He shrugs his shoulders and lets his head hang. "Life goes on, Robert, let's look for a bar and get ourselves loaded." "You are right, that is the only way to bear it," he agrees.

Cast down, we amble along the street until the dance music from a bar rings in our ears. Listless, we enter and shove our way through the smoke and drunken women to a table. "It's too bad we had to land in a dive like this," I scream in Briller's ears since no conversation is possible with this spectacle. "Perhaps this is just what we need in order to forget our sorrows." He bends toward me and opens the wine list. "How would you like a Breton muscatel?" he asks immediately as the waiter finally comes to us.

Finally the wine arrives. But before we can toast each other, two women saunter to our table and, unashamed, sit on our laps. "Would you like to make love with me?" they giggle to us, but the smell of sour alcohol streams from their painted mouths and we spontaneously stand them on their well-formed legs. Fresh as this sort is, they take our filled glasses and down them in one breath. "Merci," they wave to us and flitter toward another table where they repeat their act for two sailors from the German navy. Disgusted, we quaff down the rest of the good wine and squeeze out of the dive. Only with great effort are we able to find the schoolhouse where, without delay, we lie down to sleep.

### 14 August 1944

"So, my dear Briller, let's look for the army quartermaster office at the east train station and see if we can get a new uniform," I suggest to my comrade after I return from the information office. "Mine is still good enough for me; anyway, let's get down to business; we cannot squander our time in this city of sin." He laughs, ready for action, and sets his cap on his left ear. "I find it simply shameful to offer us a stall like this for quarters," he comments angrily about the hard straw floor in the schoolroom. Since the Metro is not operating we are forced to travel the wide distance by foot. But luck is with us. On the Boulevard Haussmann we catch a truck which takes us where we want to go.

"I'm going to the soldiers' house and I will wait there for you." I depart from Briller and I enter the quartermaster's building with the truck driver. "Everything is ready to be inventoried and removed; I am sorry that I can't give you anything," the old lifer behind the desk responds to my question about weapons and clothing. "Dammit anyway," I say, my patience at an end. "I can't run around Paris without a weapon and a complete uniform." "You shouldn't; report promptly to the personnel office; they will assign you to a unit where you will get everything." The impertinent bully of a sergeant shows no sympathy. "Apparently you have been so long at this shirker's post that you don't have any comprehension that others also want to see something of the city," I fling at him and slam the door shut.

With an undescribable rage, I go to the soldiers' house where Briller waits for me. "You really outfitted yourself fine," Briller mocks me as I sit down at the table. "They are really idiots in this Babylon of sin." I allow my anger free reign. "Imagine, they have everything ready to take away and that is why they cannot give anything out." "Drink it down, Helmut, they can all go chase their own ass crossways," he suggests and hands me a glass of apple wine. "That is what you say, but I can't run around here like a deserter," I scream at him, uncontrolled. "They are just clerks afraid to leave the base and you can't change that." He tries to dampen my scorn. "Look at how thirsty our comrades are so early in the morning!" He diverts me.

They are almost all from the reinforcement units, a couple just out of the stockade, and some, like us, just out of the hospital. No one asks them about tomorrow or the day after tomorrow. There is no purpose in trying to swim against the stream of fate; that is why we must allow ourselves to be carried until destiny spits us out somewhere.

It is exactly 2:00 P.M. as we stand at the head of a long line of waiting soldiers and lay our papers in front of the clerks at the personnel office. "The 77th Grenadier Division no longer exists," is the expected response from the lips of the oldest sergeant. "What do you think you will do now?" He turns to Briller. "Go home," he answers him promptly. "I am sorry, that's not possible," the clerk laughs, "but if you don't want to go into another troop, then you can go out to Le Bourget where the rest of the division is being assembled to be sent to a new position in Holland." "Agreed." I nudge Briller. "Of course," he agrees with me, "we will certainly meet a few of the old comrades." "OK, then I will write your orders." The sergeant reaches for the forms. "Yes," Briller turns, "this is our first time in Paris, how about a pass?" "Yours expires tonight, isn't that right?" he asks, rubbing his chin. "That's the way it is," I join in quickly, "but we have been wearing out our feet the whole time we have been here running after clothing so that we have seen practically nothing of the city." "I understand." He chuckles pleasurably and stamps the extension on the pass. "It is now 2:20 P.M.; be here tomorrow at the same time so that I can give you your orders and transportation pass." "Heil Hitler," is our response as we leave.

Thirty minutes later we sit in the front yard of the personnel office and eat the march provisions that we have received. In and around the building swarm stragglers and those who pretend to be. Bread-begging Frenchmen surround us, together with those selling nude photographs and fellow travelers of the German headquarters, while an oppressive heat brings the sweat out of every pore. Without feeling any hunger, the two of us gulp down the dry Swiss cheese and watch the activity on the street. Suddenly Briller springs from his chair and hurries to the entrance of the personnel office, where he happily slaps a small infantry sergeant on the shoulder and he in turn enthusiastically shakes Briller's hand.

After some time the two appear before me. "Hocker, Willi," Briller introduces the man to me. "He is from my regiment and wears the Iron Cross First Class for good reason," he adds by way of explanation while I stoutly shake the hand of this seemingly very sympathetic blond fellow. "When were you wounded, Comrade?" is my first question to try and learn something of the fate of our unit. "I was not wounded, but cut off. After the great offensive on July 28, the division moved south while continuing to fight. At that time we still held a small strip along the coast because the Americans had pushed east and then turned south. Near Avranches most of the remaining troops were pushed aside at Saint-Michel in the direction of Saint-Malo while my five men and I joined a tank unit which was moving along the point of the front. Three days ago I escaped with this unit from the encirclement at Falaise-Argenta and yesterday I reached Paris."

\* \* \*

The Battle of the Falaise Gap took place during the first three weeks of August 1944. It has been described by one historian as "a Stalingrad in Normandy," and "one of the greatest killing grounds." More than 70,000 Germans were killed or captured. Nineteen German divisions—including Helmut's 77th Division—were wiped out during the fighting, and German resistance west of the Seine River was all but eliminated. Still, between 20,000 and 40,000 German soldiers—including Willi Hocker—escaped from the Falaise pocket which had Montgomery's English forces to the north and Omar Bradley's American troops to the south.[3]

\* \* \*

"Will we stay together, Willi?" Briller asks after a pause in the silence. "If it is all right with the two of you, I would like it very much." "That is understood. Do you have a pass?" I ask. "It is just about to expire," he answers, slightly depressed. "Then we will get you an extension," Briller says and takes him by the arm and I follow the two into the office.

"Don't let me hear any wish like this tomorrow, otherwise I will call the MPs." The sergeant grins and extends Hocker's pass after Briller makes it clear that he is from his battalion, which is reason enough to stay together.

As happy as children, we sit after an hour in the Cafe Strasbourg, with which Hocker seems quite familiar. It is a large place with an orchestra and now, at 4:15 P.M., is already full. After the second bottle of white bordeaux, Briller has already made the acquaintance of a lady and excuses himself for an hour.

"Where did you dredge up this Casanova," Hocker asks after Briller has departed. "In a hospital." I laugh heartily because I immediately feel the mutual sympathy that unconsciously binds us. "At the front, old Briller is the most dependable of all comrades, but as soon as women step into his view, something happens to him." Hocker knows from experience what he is talking about. "I had to find that out myself, and I can only tell you that it was no small undertaking to bring this stallion to Paris and especially to the front personnel office." I give vent to my continual worry about Briller. "I believe that something is not quite right with his wife. He never took a weekend pass as long as we were with the replacement unit." Hocker expresses to me similar suppositions that I had come to myself. "If that is the case with him, then it is best to let him do what he wants; otherwise we will only quarrel with him. However, both of us must keep an eye on him." I pull Hocker on my side.

### 16 August 1944

Briller, Hocker, and I receive our marching orders shortly after 2:00 P.M. and after a light snack we roll at precisely 5:43 P.M. along the Gare du Nord, in the direction of Le Bourget. At 7:00 P.M. we enter the building of the front headquarters in which the rest of the division is housed and report to Captain Nollte.

"So," says the officer after the greeting, "slowly we are getting qualified platoon leaders again. I am not from your division, but that is no reason that we cannot work closely together and I would like to ask you to do everything you can so that in the shortest time we can organize an effective strike unit. That is all for today. Have the sergeant major show you to your quarters. I'll see you in the morning again at eight o'clock."

"The man makes a very good impression, but what does he want with a strike force? I thought we were being assembled to be sent to a new position in Holland," Briller asks with an annoyed look at the chaos in the gigantic sleeping room. "We will know soon enough," is my dampened answer. "Let's look around and see what old acquaintances we can find," Hocker says, completely free of any ill humor, going ahead of us into the hall.

Slowly Briller and I follow him, while the eyes of all those present search us. The place offers quite an impressive view. French refugees of both sexes, whose fear of the future is written in their faces, talk with the German soldiers in the room or else lie asleep in the double bunks. Among all this confusion part-time prostitutes buzz around making sleeping arrangements for the night. Everything is together in one place, and God should have mercy on us all.

Disgusted, we enter the yard, where my eyes finally come to rest on two familiar faces. With warm handshakes, we rejoice at seeing each other again. Still the question of our mission here hangs like a gray cloud over the members of this once brave division.

"It is a pigsty without comparison; I can't say anything more," one of the men from my former mortar platoon indicates in response to my question. "Then we are in the wrong place and we will make it known in the morning to the captain," is my firm intention, which Briller and Hocker immediately support.

At dusk a sergeant in full battle dress enters our room and demands that we follow him to carry out an assignment. A few minutes later we stand in front of the captain and listen in amazement to his words: "I am very sorry that I had to pull you out of bed," he says somewhat nervously, "but you must take thirty men immediately to a bridge in the vicinity and either drive the French guerrillas away or destroy them. Briller, you are the oldest and will take charge of the group. There is a truck in the yard; the men are already loaded. Sergeant Wahl knows the way and will point it out. Do a good job and report to me immediately when the assignment has been completed."

Silently we mount the truck and hold tightly to the back of the cab. Someone hands us automatic pistols and steel helmets. The motor whines as the noisy truck rolls out of the yard and takes a westward course.

During the trip we talk over the assignment. Not one of us has participated in guerrilla warfare. Briller decides to take the truck within two hundred meters of the bridge and approach the objective from both sides of the street. "Wouldn't it be wise to set up the available machine gun on top of the truck's cab to provide cover when we leave the truck?" I ask, recognizing the weakest point of his plan. "Right, I was just going to mention that. In fact I will go further and order the machine gun to spray the bridge with a burst as soon as the truck stops, since we will not be able to leave the truck without a certain amount of noise and

I don't want to show the guerrillas any consideration. Besides, it may be an easy game for us if they realize immediately that we mean business," Briller verbalizes his thoughts. "That's a good plan, Briller," Hocker agrees, "the fire burst can still challenge any return fire and we will be able to assess their numbers, weapons, and position."

After we reach agreement on how the mission is to be carried out, we instruct Sergeant Wahl through the rear window of the cab. A little later the driver turns off the motor and lets the truck roll nearly in complete silence. We reach our goal. The alleged occupied bridge lies like a phantom in front of us. "Fire at will," Briller orders the machine gun unit. The tracer ammunition racks across the bridge like fiery lightning. At the same time we leave the truck in two equal groups, one to the left and the other to the right of the vehicle, which immediately retreats backwards. Pressed flat on the ground, we await the enemy fire. Minutes pass, but our opponent does not answer. On the right side of the street I give orders to leapfrog forward so that no one is exposed to the enemy without fire protection. As we come within forty yards of the bridge, Briller, according to our plan, shoots a flare over the bridge and shortly afterward the entire objective is bathed in a ghostlike light. But still there is no enemy to be seen. Cautiously I make my way across the street in order to speak with Briller about the confusing situation.

"What do you think of this shitty war?" he receives me, somewhat disappointed with the conduct of the invisible French. "There is nothing we can do, old man, we have to get the bridge behind us," I answer with a parched throat. "I would like to know where those damned scoundrels are hiding!" He seems to be asking himself more than me. "There are only two possibilities, Briller: either the boys left long ago, or they want to have at us on the bridge." "You are probably right," he indicates, "let's wait another ten minutes, then we will push ahead onto the bridge, unless nothing happens in between." "In the meantime perhaps we can bring the machine gun into position," I counsel him. "That's OK," he answers calmly. "I will send the right group forward so that you can give me fire cover; then I plan to be the first one on the bridge with my men. Let me know when they start firing at you." "Good, Briller, but where is Hocker?" I ask him. "I have him positioned at the rear so that they don't attack us from behind," he answers quietly. Quickly I cross the road back to my men and pass the word that the machine gun crew should report to me as soon as they come forward.

Perfect silence reigns on both sides of the lonesome bridge. It is 11:20 P.M. We are pained by a tormenting thirst. In our hurry, no one thought about bringing anything to drink.

Then on the other side of the bank two shadows move on the bridge. Dammit, they didn't even give us a pair of night field glasses. Quickly I send a man to Briller and inform him of my observations. "Wait and continue to observe," is his response.

I concentrate my gaze on the bridge, but the shadows do not move anymore. Do they want to blow the bridge into the air? Who would be served by that? The Americans are moving forward and badly need the crossing. We are in retreat and cannot do without it. And the French cannot have any interest to destroy bridges in their homeland for no reason. I continue to spin the thread further: if they are partisans assigned to protect the bridge, then only the Germans could blow it up behind them to hold back the Americans. Under these circumstances there is nothing more we can do than take the bridge immediately since the partisans could fire on a lonely motorcycle rider from ambush and endanger the retreat of other German units or at least interrupt the connections. After these considerations I make my way back to Briller to share my thoughts with him.

"Perhaps you are right, but still we should not act in haste and fall into their trap. I don't want to cause any unnecessary danger for anyone. That is why my intentions are to wait a little longer. It is possible they will lose their nerve and show themselves, and we can attack immediately," he explains to me in a voice indicating an awareness of his authority in the situation.

Returning to my men again, the machine gun crew reports to me. Together we bring the weapon into position. Suddenly a flare rises from across the way. Nothing moves after it lights. Finally, after about ten minutes, two figures appear on the bridge. Slowly and cautiously they come toward this bank of the river. Staring through the darkness I see Briller and his men creeping forward. At nearly the same time friend and enemy reach the edge of the bridge. Seconds later Briller's men seem to grow out of the ground and faster than panthers they move toward their opponents, knocking them from their legs and dragging them to the left embankment. "That went well," he giggles happily, "come and see the two prisoners." "Keep the bridge in sight and stomp on every ant that you discover on it," I order the man with the machine gun and follow Briller across the street.

Surrounded by our comrades, two Frenchmen between the ages of thirty and forty sit on the edge of the road and quietly consider their fate. In response to our question of how many they are and what assignment they had, they speak something that none of us can understand. "Where are their weapons?" I ask Briller, whose attention is now focused on the bridge. "They were probably lost during the fight; we could not find anything in their pockets except for cigarettes and a few cents," a private first class answers me. "Then we must look for them because only with the weapons can we prove they were up to something." I turn to Briller. "We will take a look as soon as it is light," he whispers to me and at the same time prevents one of the prisoners from lighting a cigarette. Was this fellow so poorly trained that he does not know how far someone can see a burning match or a cigarette in the night, we ask ourselves. Or is he a fanatic who is willing to direct the fire of his comrades on himself in order to destroy all of us? In lively discussion we consider these questions and come to the conclusion that neither of these two possibilities apply to him. The man is neither a hero nor dumb. "Either their accomplices took off or these two are completely alone," Briller determines. "Then he should stand on the road and light a cigarette so that we will know what we are dealing with," is my opinion, and the Frenchman is told that he can smoke on the street. Without any reluctance he follows our direction and in the middle of the street he lights a cigarette. With the cigarette he stands in the direction of the other side of the river, which we observe from our safe covering. Minutes pass, but nothing happens.

"Let's go," Briller orders. "Now let's go across the bridge and see if the devil is waiting for us on the other side." Quickly we select five men from the two groups. While Briller and his men immediately step onto the bridge, my men and I follow twenty yards behind on the right side, ready to offer fire cover. Undisturbed, we reach the other side of the river. On the right side of the street stands a little house, lonesome and dark, to which my men and I march immediately while Briller covers our action. Carefully we surround the house and stand in the yard in front of the back entrance. Attentive to all the sounds of the night and from within the house, I slowly push down the door handle. It resists and only gives way with a terrible noise from inside.

Silently we push ourselves into the hall, in which we are surrounded by complete darkness. I light a match to get a quick orientation. A staircase with five steps leads into a kind of lobby with three doors which apparently branch off into rooms. Quickly I slide to the middle door and shove it open, dropping to my knees as I do so with the automatic revolver ready to fire. Tension-loaded seconds pass, but there is nothing to see of the enemy. Still, from someplace else the sound of human voices can be heard. Anxiously I light another match and enter the room. In the flickering light I look around quickly. Except for the usual furniture of a cheap room, on whose table wine bottles and half-filled glasses stand, there is nothing worth noticing.

Hesitatingly I grope for the light switch and suddenly I stand in a brightly lit room. Disgusted but relieved, I breathe into my lungs the cold cigarette smoke that hangs in the room. Within minutes the other rooms are searched by my men. No human soul is to be found. "I believe I heard voices from the cellar," the soldier who remained posted at the entrance calls. "Search the cellar," I order and stick a cigarette in my mouth. Before I have inhaled twice I hear the cracking of splitting wood and immediately afterward a woman's scream. With a few steps I am in the cellar and stand in front of two men and a woman, who continue to kiss the cheeks of their liberators. In broken German they report their misfortune. They are refugees from Saint-Lô and wanted to go to relatives in Romilly. Their wagon was stopped by five Frenchmen near the bridge and they were forced to get out. They accused them of collaborating with the Germans and locked them up in the cellar. A short time later they heard their wagon leave and the steps of two men who returned to the house.

Some time later I instruct Briller in a few words what took place in the house. "With that we have fulfilled our assignment and we can go home in confidence. They are not guerrillas, but prowling thieves who seek to enrich themselves at the expense of others during the chaos of war," Briller concludes and assigns four men to secure the bridge, after which we withdraw. We climb on the truck and return to our lodging, where Briller reports to Captain Nollte and delivers the two prisoners. It is exactly 3:40 A.M. as we reach the street and search for our quarters. A new day spreads its gray, dusky light.

### 17 August 1944

In front of the troop quarters, they have set up a machine gun. Mounted on a table, its steel blue barrel points threateningly into the surroundings. The entire building is surrounded by lounging soldiers. I have never seen a picture like this of the German army, and I imagine it looks like the revolutionaries of 1918. We observe a strange officer who has buckled on his pistol like a butcher and is arguing with several sergeants on the open street, while numerous privates stand around grinning. Driven by disgust, a few minutes later we stand before Captain Nollte and ask to speak with him. "What do you wish?" he asks, friendly, as his eyes flash from one of us to the other. "We would like to know what the plans are and if you can't tell us, we want to ask you to let us go so that we can join up with a fighting unit," I insist.

Slowly raising his head, his eyes glide across our faces, and he prepares to speak. "I have the assignment to organize the rest of the 77th Grenadier Division and whoever else turns up in this area into an emergency battalion. This unit will be used in and around Paris in case of unrest. In a few days we will have between six and eight hundred men and the necessary equipment. Sergeant Briller will take over the machine gun platoon, you the heavy mortar platoon, and Sergeant Hocker the sharpshooter platoon." As we agree with him, he continues, "Our emergency battalion will be completely motorized. Platoon leaders will have either a motorbike or a personal car. I am sure that in a short time we will have everything and can then go to work. I hope that you will help me with this assignment and beginning tomorrow or the day after tomorrow bring some order to this wild herd. Does anyone have any questions?" he asks to end the briefing. "Yes," I say. "How much time do you think we have, Captain, to accomplish this?" "That question is well justified given the situation at the front. According to rumor, the Americans are moving against Versailles and I admit that we are in a race against time. But I assure you that I have good connections with those above and will be informed in plenty of time about any changes in our situation," he smiles, convinced. "What would you do if we requested that you let us go?" I ask in dead seriousness. "Reject it, gentlemen; since I need you badly," he says in closing and raises his hand in salute.

"How does it look as far as clothing goes for this special company?" I turn to the sergeant major after the meeting. "It arrived yesterday and is in the second story. Take what you need and leave me in peace."

On the road a bus fully occupied by German military women rolls toward the east. At the corner of a house, a soldier is in the process of selling a pair of brand new army boots to a Frenchman. Furiously I go toward the two. "You filthy bum, selling shoes which German women and girls have provided for us in a hail of bombs so that we don't have to run around barefoot. Don't you have enough money, especially when everything here is furnished free?" "You are right, sergeant," he excuses himself. "I did not think that far," he explains politely and overwhelmed with regret, something totally uncommon for this bunch. "Take the boots back immediately to where you got them and don't let me catch you doing anything like this again." I shove him from me.

The machine gun crew sits in front of the quarters and dozes out of boredom. A brutal heat weighs heavily upon the streets and houses. But still the heavy vehicles of the German army thunder toward the east. Are they returning home to the Reich or going home rich? I ask myself as I stare at the mountain of baggage which is perched on the cabin of each vehicle.

"Where do I get a pistol?" I ask at the clerk's office. "They are in the weapons room, in case you are used to getting them out of the toilet," the staff sergeant answers ironically. "Thank you for the information; I did not expect that in your pigsty," I shoot back and go in search of the weapons room. This opportunity takes me pretty well through the entire building. In the yard, in the rooms, and in the hall, everywhere the comrades are drinking or speaking with the refugees, whose identity no one bothers to investigate. Nowhere is any order visible. Discipline remains only out of old habit. Finally I reach the so-called weapons room. "How about a pistol for me?" I ask the corporal in charge of the weapons, who is not thrilled with my disturbing his noon nap. "You are in luck, there is still one here," he indicates and lays a Luger P08 pistol on the table. "Is there any ammunition, or should I just throw it at the enemy?" I ask in a bad mood. "No, you get sixty rounds, and an ammunition case; you just have to give me your *Soldbuch* so that I can register it." The corporal finds the once common tone among comrades.

"How do things look with weapons for the entire battalion?" I ask after I have completed all the formalities. "This machine gun and the one in front of the house, and a few hand weapons are all that we have received in the last eight days." He gestures sluggishly. "But is there the possibility that we will get the necessary weapons in the next few days?" I ask, somewhat upset at his stoic quietness. "I drive to Paris nearly every day and ask what we are supposed to receive, but I tell you freely, either they don't want to give us anything to shoot, or they really don't have anything more and they should end this shitty war," he answers angrily. "Here, have a smoke, comrade, and don't upset yourself," I say, departing.

### 18 August 1944

At eight o'clock, under orders from the captain, we begin to divide the lethargic men into platoons and units. The men follow our orders with resistance. There are only a few among them who wear any decorations. When a division goes under, the only survivors are the baggage handlers, ammunition carriers, and a few clerks. But we go ahead and divide them. Paper is so patient. It does not make any difference if the term *marksman* stands next to the name of someone who only knows the end of a rifle from hearsay.

About ten o'clock we know what is up. Of the ninety-one men, twenty-three are trained for the machine gun and eighteen for the mortar. Of the five sergeants, two appear to be good platoon leaders. We have forty-four rifles, twenty-eight pistols, four automatic pistols, and two machine guns. After we are finished, the captain orders the men dismissed. Officers and noncommissioned officers stand in a half circle around the company commander who has no company. I observe the two officers carefully. The captain makes a good and trustworthy impression, even though he does not have much front line experience. The lieutenant is not completely unknown to me and is as conceited as a peacock. Despite his Iron Cross First Class, I do not believe that he is the hero he loves to play. In the shadow of the two men stands the payroll clerk with a stomach like a beer keg. A spiteful expression lies on his obese face. I don't like the man, even though fat people are generally known as jolly fellows.

"As you have seen for yourself," the captain crushes his cigarette as he begins to speak, "the men are in need of retraining. We will immediately take on a small training exercise so that the men can have their confidence with the weapons restored and in order to keep them off the streets. Whoever comes for duty under the influence of alcohol is to report to me immediately regardless of who he is. That is all for the moment, thank you."

Promptly at 2:00 P.M. our duty begins. For a full hour I explain the 98K rifle to the mostly older soldiers. With horror I observe the inexcusable ignorance of the men who wear the rank of private first class and corporal on their field jackets, but who have only the slightest familiarity with the most simple weapon of the German army. Still they grin arrogantly and disturb my efforts. From 3:00 P.M. until 4:00 P.M. I learn the same thing about the mortar crew. Suddenly no one claims to have been trained with the weapon, or at least that it is many years since they have had in their fingers what the soldiers call the grenade gulper. The whole sad affair makes me sick, especially since I do not have the necessary tools to demonstrate the proper procedures. Finally, I am able to keep only a few of the men from falling asleep.

"You couldn't even attack a shithouse with these people," Briller expresses the opinion of all after our first training session with this mob. In order to dissipate our worries a little bit and to avoid a drinking bout, we friends decide to take a walk to the airport. We find time to observe the stream of refugees as well as the retreat of the German air force companies. Here and there personal vehicles appear in which high-ranking German officers sit with their painted ladies. Our attention is drawn particularly to the large suitcases as these elite leaders move eastward, intending to take their precious lives to safety. Never before in this awful war have I had the possibility to glimpse behind the wavering front. But at this moment, it is fully clear to me that the rats are abandoning a sinking ship.

After a slow walk we reach the airport. An antitank gun stands at the entrance. The conversation with the men there is more discouraging. They await orders any moment to blow up the place with all its remaining fuel. An inner, overpowering unrest seizes me as I take it all in. The collapse of the front is apparent. I only wonder quietly to myself why the Americans don't launch a quick breakthrough to Paris.

We return earlier than intended. I meet the captain and ask to speak to him to share our observations. "Don't worry, my friend, the Führer will soon end the retreat. By the way, if we are in actual danger I will give you plenty of notice." He pats me comfortingly on the shoulder. "Isn't it time that we join up with a battle-ready group?" I press him. Angrily he forbids any interference in his affairs.

Bristling with anger, the three of us sit on the terrace near the swimming pool. "Here, sergeant." An old front soldier puts a bottle of champagne next to us and pats me trustingly on the back. "Have a drink, your throat must be dry from the long instruction. Long live the 98K rifle." Despite my low mood, this honest expression of soldier humor brings me to laughter. He then affably whispers with a heavy tongue in my ear, "Watch out for the officers and above all for the well-fed pay-pig. They will leave us sitting in the shit when things get hot."

You could be right, I think, after the man has left and I drink the lukewarm champagne until the "kiss my ass" attitude comes over me. After dark we move to the flat roof of the building and watch the flickering artillery explosions to the west. Looking to the east, we follow enthusiastically the fire tail of a V-1 rocket traveling rapidly in a northwest direction. For a long time we discuss how much the new kind of rocket weapon can influence the outcome of the war. Finally we take the path homeward with mixed feelings.

### 19 August 1944

We stand for a long time on the sidewalk because a long line of autos, horse-drawn wagons, and buses makes any crossing dangerous. Everything appears to have been set in motion, but our schedule calls for training with the machine gun.

At 8:00 A.M., the captain takes roll. After a second count there is no agreement with the number we had yesterday. One sergeant and nine men are missing, whose names are quickly determined. The captain, with a red angry face and accompanied by the sergeant and pay clerk, goes to the clerk's office to initiate a report for court martial proceedings against the fugitives. We three sergeants divide the group and begin the technical instruction, which the lieutenant supervises without any interest. The entire theater makes me sick and seems so senseless, just as if when a ship is sinking someone wants to learn quickly how to swim in a bathtub. But even with purposeless activities the hours of the clock turn and once again it is lunchtime.

After lunch the three of us lie down for a nap. The captain has informed us our presence is not necessary for the afternoon training. He has changed the training schedule, and between 3:00 P.M. and 4:00 P.M. he will instruct the entire battalion about the meaning of the oath of loyalty in general and in specific the consequences of desertion.

In contrast to this morning there are no vehicles to be heard on the road. There is barely a stream of refugees now. In the middle of our friendly conversation, a private enters and gives us the order from the captain: "The battalion will move out tonight toward the east. All platoon leaders are to report to the office!" We look at each other. "The last ones are bitten by the dogs," I say in the silence after the man has left, and we get up to carry out the orders.

When we arrive at the office, the captain receives us in suppressed agitation. Without any digression, he tells us that the battalion must be ready to march at 8:00 P.M. What provisions and clothing we can take are to be loaded on the three horse-drawn wagons. The rest is to stay where it is. With the unnecessary warning not to lose any time, the orders that I have never heard before as a soldier come to an end.

Almost unnoticed by the French, we leave Le Bourget like thieves in the night without song or sound. We march along both sides of the road. We move eastward toward an unknown fate as though a fist is in our neck.

### 20 August 1944

After a seven-hour march without incident, we land in a village and find quarters prepared for us by the officers, who naturally cover the distance in an automobile. But we must give them some credit in that during the course of the night they drove back and forth caring for their lost group and seeing that at each crossroads the three platoons stayed on the right way. Dog tired, we all fall into the straw. Because of my long stay in the hospital, the soles of my feet are so tender after the long march they now burn like the fires of Hell. The same for Briller, and so our friend Hocker must play nurse to both of us. But still we three inseparable friends look for an establishment about three o'clock and drink a poorly cooled beer, although the thoughts of the continuing march overwhelm us with dread.

After sundown the malicious French watch us leave their village. As we march, I feel as though I am going barefoot over hot corrugated sheet metal. But now I must be hard on myself. They told me to take a place on the vehicle, but I see so many comrades who creep along the road like they are walking on eggs and I don't want to be the object of their cursing. Never in my entire life as a soldier have I ever demanded more from someone than I was willing to do myself. I adopted this principle from the beginning and to this day I have been well served by it.

In the meantime the night has quietly laid itself over the landscape and wraps with pity the thrown-together, hopeless heap of humanity in its dark veil. In May 1940 I first set foot on French soil with the best-equipped and best-trained army in the world. Then the German troops overran this land with a victory march without comparison, destroying within thirty-six days the entire army, including the English expeditionary force that was so hard hit that their only possible salvation was the wretched flight to the fleet of ships assembled at Dunkirk. Today, four years later, I slip out by the dark of night toward the starting point, back in the Reich with the bitter feeling of shame in my soul at the way the rest of my brave division has dissolved, while troops from a continent four thousand miles away follow close on our heels.

### 25 August 1944

The rising sun finds us four kilometers before Soissons, having left the road of retreat and quartered in a little village situated only two hundred meters from the great artery of traffic. It is no longer so important where we sleep, but when and for how long. A few months ago a couple of days' or nights' march like this was quite common. But many have just come from the hospitals and others were always drivers and are not used to marching. No wonder then that nearly everyone has to endure the march walking on injured feet and they are so close to exhaustion that they nearly fall asleep while walking. To make matters worse, nearly everyone is wearing new boots which in most cases were selected without thought for a long march such as this. So it is explainable why we do not arrive in a tight column and the first ones already lie in a deep sleep before the last arrive. But no one is choosy. Instead, everyone collapses, wrapped in a blanket, into the straw of any barn or shed and within seconds finds himself beyond good and evil. After the last man is brought under a roof, the three of us can also find some rest.

After six hours of refreshing sleep, Briller shakes me awake. He stands barefoot before me with coffee, bread, and butter in his hands. His field blouse is open and his dog tags hang like a cheap medal on his hairy chest. "Let's go," he says, "drink some coffee, we have got to go see the old man." "What does he want from us in the middle of the night?" I ask, irritated. "It is nearly eleven o'clock and the sun is burning hot in the sky, my friend."

The heat is brutal, with no breeze. The dust-covered leaves on the trees are nearly wilted in the park where we turn and stand across from the captain.

Affably he waves off our formal German salute. "Good morning," he says and extends his hand to each of us. He is only dressed in riding pants and a shirt; his field blouse hangs over the stool on which he sits. "Please, take a seat, and smoke if you like," he begins and gestures with an open hand toward the stools. "You have seen the men during the march and have observed them as closely as I. It is clear that we must rest for a while in order not to completely ruin the feet of the men. I have made an inquiry by radio to the higher command and know that we can afford to stop for a while. The Americans are busy around Paris with our rear guard forces. By the way, we left at exactly the right time. The mob rose up in the metropolitan area the same day we left. Today we will nurse the feet of the suffering men. At 2:00 P.M. lunch will be distributed and every man will receive a bottle of wine from our stock. Assign your sergeants to insure order and discipline in the quarters. Except for officers and you men, no soldier has the right to leave the village. If any of you want to go to Soissons, you are free to do so after 5:00 P.M. Are there any questions?" He ends his explanation. "I thank you," he says as we indicate there are none and raise our right hands in salute.

"As necessary as the rest is, there is still a voice of warning inside me," I say in the cool dusk of the barn in which we have stretched out, protected from the glaring sun. "I am not overjoyed at it either." Hocker joins my side. "But the rest is absolutely necessary, you can be assured of that." "The rest is no luxury and if the situation allows it, I will praise the captain for his wisdom," Briller adds, then falls asleep almost in the same moment.

With an uncomfortable feeling in my heart, I sit and look at my feet. There are no blisters. The scar on the toe is protected from harm and the soles of my feet are very red because of the sweat working together with the tannic acid of the new boots, causing a very uncomfortable burning which I am able to nearly eliminate by rubbing them with butter. Acting on former experience, I decide to treat my boots with urine in order to deal with the tannic acid. I get some oats from one of the drivers and fill my boots with it because the oats absorb the urine and in doing so will expand the narrow part of the boots. After I ease my conscience with this primitive method, I lie down to sleep.

Freshly bathed and clean shaven, we set out to Soissons, where at exactly 6:00 P.M. we tip the first glass of cognac. The dive in which we find ourselves is full of thirsty soldiers and women. Mixed in are Frenchmen, who cover their heads with berets while their ears are tuned in to the conversations of the tipsy soldiers so that the bits and pieces of information can be transmitted to their collaborators, who will put the mosaic together and for which the German soldiers will pay with their blood.

The smell of sweat and cheap perfume hangs in the room. As the bartender fills our glasses, I instinctively feel someone staring at me and turn around. I am attracted to two girls whose eyes seem to radiate a mysterious fire. Without resistance I move in response to the invitation to the girls' table and bend to them, questioning. "Please sit down by me," one whispers in good German. "I am so alone." In amazement I look at her and sit down in the chair next to her. "You are alone in the middle of all this activity?" I ask somewhat sarcastically and observe her without restraint. "Don't you like me?" she asks as she observes my critical look. "Let's not talk about that," I evade her question, "but you said that you were alone, what is that?" "It may be that you consider it a lie, but it is still true," she twitters pleasantly and smooths her dress flat over her thighs. "And what do you expect of me?" I ask bluntly because this time I am really in doubt. "I want to talk with someone who has understanding. I want to escape the constant fear of the impending disaster," she answers and looks deeply into my eyes. "And that is why you come to a place like this and pick me out of the crowd?" I ask, shaking my head. "We both may be related souls. Just as you came through the door you made a distinct impression on me and the wish to speak with you became stronger and stronger the more I observed you," she explains with a light vibration in her voice.

Fighting back my stimulated vanity, I inhale deeply from my cigarette and see Hocker coming toward the table. "We are moving on, Helmut" he grins at me, "the innkeeper does not have any more ice and all the drinks are warm." "Now or in a minute?" I ask, looking at him angrily. "Immediately, if it is all right with you," he replies stubbornly and stands like a bully, his gaze lost in the notch of the blouse of the girl I am speaking with. "Then there is nothing more for us." I turn to the girl and get up. "May I come with you?" she asks quickly, her eyes resting on mine.

Undecided, I glimpse at Hocker, who gives me a "no" sign. "There is really no purpose," I say helplessly, "my time is short." "Aren't you going to stay in the city?" she asks. "We don't know," I respond, disenchanted, looking at her sharply. "You just said that your time is short." She pushes unmercifully further. "Our leave time, mademoiselle," I explain with a prudent smile. "Oh, then I can visit you tomorrow, if …" "Yes, on the moon," Hocker interjects energetically and pulls me by the arm to the exit where Briller is waiting.

"She is not a typical bee." Briller immediately receives me on the street. "I observed her closely, Helmut, and I suggest that we inform the security service; that beast can do all kinds of damage." "The only thing we lack is the proof, my friend. Besides, I don't think we want to spend this evening by such gangsters when that is their assignment anyway, to protect us from such women." I talk him out of it. "Man, she surely must have fire in her behind," Hocker mixes in, grinning from ear to ear. "It would really be too bad to let the security service squash such a volcano." "Let's forget this nonsense," I end the fruitless discussion. "If she really is an agent, then she can only be a very small cog since there are not any great secrets among the men in this joint."

Still undecided where we can spend a cozy evening in this strange town, we discover a hotel in a side street that suits our taste. In the dining room we find a comfortable corner and sit down. Plates are set on white-covered tables and the attentive waitress asks immediately what we would like. Quickly we reach an agreement over the menu and order three beers, a bottle of red wine, three beefsteaks, french fries, a green salad, and oysters for dessert. The girl laughs as she takes our order, then hurries to the bar.

The establishment is sparsely occupied, while in the connecting room, into which we can see through the opened folding doors, soldiers and girls are listening to the blare of a juke box while civilians temperamentally discuss the situation over an aperitif. Just as we finish our cigarettes, the girl brings in the food, then disappears, but not without first a charming wish that we enjoy the meal.

Concentrating on the food, I do not notice that in the meantime the locale is filled with new guests, until a familiar girl's voice asks if she can sit with us. Glancing up I recognize the girl with whom I spoke previously in the inn. Slightly embarrassed, she stands at our table looking at me with her night-blue eyes. Unconsciously my hand makes a gesture of invitation, in response to which she sits down without saying a word. Somewhat nervously I reach for my glass and in doing so glimpse Briller's face, in which I detect a twitch of rejection. Silently we busy ourselves with our food, but everyone knows that each one's thoughts are on the mysterious girl sitting next to me who has once again forced herself between us with her ample charms working on me.

Tenderly her hand caresses my hair. "Come with me," she whispers alluringly. The golden beams of the sinking sun slant into the room. The enticing words of the mysterious girl sound in me. My blood rushes through the veins and pounds at my temples. In one swallow I empty my glass, reach for my cigarettes, and stand up. As if bitten by a tarantula, Briller jumps up. "Stop, Helmut! Don't do that," he cries angrily and clings to my arm. "What is the matter, Briller? Am I a baby who needs a nurse?" I ask, irritated. "Let me bring this affair to an end, if you please." "I will watch out for myself." "Good," he says harshly and turns to the girl. "Where do you want to go with my friend?" "What concern is it of yours? Didn't he just tell you he is old enough to take care of himself?" she hisses back and looks at him with a mean expression on her pretty face which leaves me with a cold feeling.

Briller stands broad shouldered in front of her, his arms resting on his hips. "You disappear now at once and don't let me ever see you here again, otherwise I will call the SS," he growls at her determinedly and touches his pistol with his left hand. As if hit by a whiplash, the girl quivers at these terrible words from this enemy stranger. Slowly she turns on the heel of her brown pumps. With veiled eyes she touches me with her little delicate hand. "Farewell, mon cheri," she whispers and turns toward the door.

A cloud of her alluring perfume lingers and I watch her until the door snaps closed. Disappointed, I fall into the chair and consider my comrades with discord in my heart. Hocker sits with a mask-like face, nervously sucking at his cigarette while Briller sits in the corner with a gloomy disposition and blinks at the last sun rays of this day. Clearing my throat, I grasp the bottle and pour the rest into the glasses. Briller's fist comes crashing to the table. "The damned women are throwing the best comradeship before the dogs," he cries with a raging red face. "Take it easy, you good old timer, we have not come to that yet. While I rarely interfere with your activities, I know that you did it out of concern for me and perhaps I should be thankful to you." I laugh, somewhat forced, while my eyes meet those of my friends. "Let's forget the witches and let the ghosts rest. Three cognacs and fast," I whisper into the ear of the passing waitress. Understandingly she nods to me and hurries away. Two seconds later she puts the glasses before us on the table. "Those were to be for other guests, but I believe you need them more urgently," she whispers into my ear. "Now, down with it, guys," I toast my friends and three skilled hands guide the glasses to the mouths.

Soldiers sit at all the tables with women, playing the eternal game of the sexes. A tall drunken blond is shown the door by the owner just as three SS sergeants enter the room, looking in amazement at the blond. She throws her arms around the neck of the first one, kissing him so that his entire face is covered by her cheap lipstick. When he finally frees himself, his grotesque appearance brings out the laughter in those present. All three appear to be in a good mood and when they approach our table and ask to sit down, we invite them without hesitation.

"Are you stationed here?" I ask to say something to the new arrivals. "No," one informs us, "we are on the march toward Holland." "And you?" he looks at me anxiously. "We are on a foot march to the asshole," Briller throws in ironically and brings the entire circle to laughter. "Are you really going by foot?" the three wonder at the same time, to which Hocker responds with a short history of our experiences and the SS men listen without interrupting. "Come with us," they say after Hocker finishes. "We can't let the poor devils outside sit in this lousy place," I protest to them indignantly. "It is way too late for that." They nod their heads in agreement. "No, that would be a shame and unworthy of a German soldier," the youngest of them finally joins in the conversation. "You three are courageous members of the army, but unfortunately your type is now dying slowly, but surely out," the oldest indicates knowingly. "It's a pity about you boys, you would be in the right place with us," he adds. "I don't give a shit," Briller indicates. "We had bad luck, perhaps the sun will shine for us again." "Therefore let's drink another bottle." "Bring us another six beers," Briller calls to the waiter standing at the bar.

"But we must go back to our quarters and it is already 1:00 A.M.," Hocker notes seriously. "Sleep here in the hotel, boys," one of the SS men mixes in. "It would be dangerous to stumble the three miles back all alone." "What do you think, Helmut?" Hocker turns to me. "Let's see about a room, I don't have any desire to walk back and it will be hard to find a ride going back in the direction of the front," I answer in resignation. "We will have one shortly," the older SS comrade responds and goes up to the counter.

The man returns from the counter with a new bottle of cognac. "Everything is in order." He grins, satisfied. "The innkeeper will keep three rooms for six of us, but the place closes at 3:00 A.M." "How is it with the bottle, comrade? Naturally we will share the bill," I suggest to him. "Just drink, it is already paid for." He waves it off and pulls the cork out of the bottle with skill. With a steady hand he fills the glasses. "My friends call me Herbert." He lifts his glass and looks me good-heartedly in the eye. "I am Erich," the second chimes in. "And you can call me Dieter as long as you continue with your friendly face." "Then a toast, friends," I indicate with a clang of the glasses. "You have already heard my name."

We set our glasses down as Hocker returns. "So what is the big bad wolf doing with the child?" the older Herbert asks curiously. "He will eat it for sure," Hocker responds promptly and is met with ringing laughter. Still standing, he gestures with his thumb toward the hall. "You should take a look at the way old Briller is bringing the little one in on the line. She is only hot lava in his fingers. I am sure that she will give him her purse full of money if he will only go to bed with her." "I would like to know who ends up marrying these women!" Herbert throws in, shaking his head. "What does it matter to us?" Dieter laughs and turns his head toward the folding doors behind which Briller sits with the girl while in Dieter's eye the fire of desire burns.

"Every generation produces the kind of women that they deserve. The French failed in 1940 and along with them their women," Herbert indicates in an objective tone. "And how will it be with us if we fail?" I ask, somewhat shocked. "Not one jot better," he answers, troubled, and takes a cigarette. "After the First World War when the Rhineland was occupied, mulatto children were born," he adds in a contemptuous tone.

In the barroom only two tables are now occupied. It is 2:10 a.m. The gloomy words still ring in us as we step behind the folding doors and are greeted enthusiastically with bottles and glasses by the girls. In anticipation the girls skillfully make room, leaving to us the decision as to which place, that is which partner, we choose.

"Take the good-looking blond, Helmut." Briller, fully in his own element, takes me by surprise and pushes me down on the only empty chair at the table. "She likes you very much," he whispers with good intentions into my ear as I attempt to protest. "Keep one thing in mind, my dear Briller, I am in the habit of choosing my own friends." I refuse to let him push me around and reach for the cigarettes to offer one to the blond on my right, noticing an insulted look in her face. "Are you angry?" I ask, feeling some pity for her. "Take it how you want." She forces a smile and reaches for my hand which holds the burning match in front of her cigarette. Inhaling the smoke deeply into her lungs, she looks at me affectionately out of her slanting eyes. "Do you always reject little girls like this?" she asks, leaning back in her chair so that I can admire her figure. "Only on the outside, on the inside I generally like them very much," I state honestly. "So that is your tactic." She laughs, satisfied. "You have seen through me, mademoiselle." I drink to her.

"I would like to treat everyone to a bottle of cognac," Briller interrupts the conversation at the table and calls for service. The owner comes to the table with a negative gesture. "We are closing, gentlemen," he says, pointing to the clock, which indicates it is 3:00 a.m. "Avez-vous une chambre séparée?" Herbert asks in fluent French.

Undecided, the innkeeper plays with the gaudy ring on his little finger while we all anxiously keep our eyes on him. With an agile tongue Herbert speaks into his ear. Finally they are in agreement. "We can go to the room and he doesn't care what we do there. We can purchase drinks at the bar with hard cash," Herbert proclaims with a sovereign voice and is rewarded with a hot kiss from his long-legged partner, who accompanies him to the bar.

Ten minutes later Herbert, Erich, and I sit in my hotel room drinking with the two remaining girls after Briller, Dieter, and Hocker have excused themselves and their ladies for half an hour. Quietly the blond Blanche sits next to me on the bed in front of which we have pulled the night table and on which we set our glasses. Herbert and Erich are squatting with the long-legged and good-looking Colette in the middle on chairs, two of which they have brought from their rooms. It is very hot in the room and we decide to turn out the light and leave the blinds up so that we can leave the window open. A little later only the rising cigarette smoke and the clatter of glasses on the marble plate of the night table testify to our presence. Snuggled affectionately on my shoulder rests Blanche's head as she alluringly whispers in my ear, "Voulez-vous faire l'amour?"

I have known for a long time that this question was coming but still I don't know what I should answer. Out of embarrassment and with an unusual mixture of pity and personal desire, I stroke her silky blond hair. The smell of a pleasant good shampoo is noticeable and I whisper my "Oui" in her ear. In the silence the creaking noise of the straining bed springs in Briller's adjacent room penetrates our room and brings us all to laughter, relieving the tension at the same time. With five girls and six men, not even a university can reach an agreement without some compromise. But only the crazy Briller has brought us into this situation.

Finally Briller crosses the threshold, pulling a dark-haired female behind him into the room. "What are you doing squatting around here like the disciples on the Mount of Olives?" he asks cheerfully, taking a glass from the night table and offering it politely to the girl. "You have to bring your own chair with you, old fellow," I instruct him after he searches the room. "I will get one," twitters his darling with a voice as clear as a bell and goes lightly from the room. "She is thankful, isn't she, you tired warriors?" Briller smirks proudly and tips a full glass of water into his throat. "Where are the others?" He turns to me while looking for a cigarette. "Still in action," I growl. "Then disappear with Blanche in my room. Just look at the poor girl, she is crazy with yearning," he proclaims without any tact, awakening in me the wish to box his ears. "Lie down yourself in your rotten crib if you want to make prescriptions for others." I jump at him, angry. "Take it easy, son," he says in amazement at my irritated tone and sits down on the chair that the black-haired girl has brought in for him. "I only intended good for you," he begins in a conciliatory tone, petting the naked leg of his bed partner, who has rolled herself up on his lap just like a cat. "I am going to get some sleep." Erich gets up, yawning. "When are we to be awakened?" He turns to Herbert. "We have to get up around 6:00 A.M.," he answers, frowning. "Then good night, gentlemen. Don't let me disturb you," he waves tiredly as Briller tries to hold him back.

After a while I become uncomfortable sitting on the bed. Standing on one foot, I pull off my boots and take off my field blouse while the others look at me in amazement. "Do you want to get rid of us?" Herbert asks, uneasy. "Certainly not," I comfort him. "I just can't see how I can sit on the bed when it is much more comfortable to lie down." "Come Blanche, lie down, it is really a strain to sit without a backrest," I encourage her. "I can't do that, my dress will be wrinkled," she indicates, blushing like a school girl. "Come on, Briller, turn the light out for a moment and then Blanche, take off your dress, I will cover you with a blanket up to your neck if you want it."

Without protest, she gets up and turns to the bed on which I am stretched out. As the light goes out, there is the rustle of clothing as Blanche undresses. Before Briller turns the light back on she has slipped under the cover and has me in her arms. I would willingly crawl under the cover to her, but the lurking eyes of the others forbid such action. In order to kill the rising desire, I reach for a glass and empty it in one swallow.

After ten minutes even Herbert's girl has recognized that it could be a long session; she slips under the blanket with Blanche and a little later both are sound asleep. We waste the time debating whether it was right or wrong for Hitler to use the Waffen SS against the German army until we are no longer capable of any clear thoughts since the cognac has finally brought us to our knees. In a blur, I see Briller totter out of the room with his ballerina just before I slide into the kingdom of dreams.

### 26 August 1944

Awakened by the noise of a passing truck, I look in shock at my wristwatch. I see that it is 6:47 A.M. and I look around the room. Blanche and Colette lie in peaceful sleep next to me in the bed. My head is humming as though a transformer has been turned on. Carefully I get up and go to the wash basin. I hear an angry grunt and bending forward I discover Herbert asleep on his back, his hands folded on his stomach as though he is in a coffin. Slowly I climb over him and go to the wash basin. While I am occupied with drying myself, I look at the bottles on the night table and I am in doubt as to which I should drink from so that I will feel better. Blanche, laughing sweetly, reaches her arms out to me. Bewitched, I breathe in the fragrance of the warm girl's body and still standing lay my head on her firm breasts. "It's too bad, Blanche," I whisper excitedly, "we have wasted the time; now I have to leave." Tenderly she strokes my hair with her hand. "That is why I will hold you in my heart longer and hope for a fulfillment. You have behaved very decently," she whispers.

I raise the curtains on the window and let the rays of the late summer's morning sun flood the room. "Get up," I call into the quiet floor and knock on Briller's door. "What is going on?" he asks, ill tempered. "It is nearly seven o'clock, you old fornicator," I call impatiently. "I am coming right away," he responds, wide awake. "Which room is Hocker in?" I ask through the keyhole and see Briller step to the wash basin completely naked. "Number four," he answers calmly and lets the water run into the basin.

Discreetly I knock on Hocker's door. Immediately the inner latch slides back and Hocker stands before me completely dressed. "Good morning," he grins, somewhat embarrassed, while his turtle dove shoves a big bill into her purse and explains that she is going downstairs to order coffee.

It is seven o'clock. In the clutches of exodus fever, we all assemble at the table in the guest room of the hotel to drink coffee. One last cognac unites the souls of this war-defiant night. Knowing that we probably will not see each other again in this life, we shake each other's hands in farewell.

With our hands in our pockets we stand under the gate to the hotel and consider the fastest way to get back to our unit. "Here in the yard are enough bicycles," Hocker suggests and glimpses playfully into the sun. "If we take the bikes, then other comrades will miss them," I object. "They are here in the city and can secure others," he answers back coldly and I notice a determined look in his face. Calmly he goes back through the entrance to the yard and rides back a few seconds later on a nearly new bike. With a pounding heart, I turn ninety degrees and rush to the bicycles. I nearly run into Briller as I struggle out of the entrance and make my way to Hocker, who greets me approvingly. Shortly afterward Briller comes up with the rattling sound of tin. A cooking pot hangs on his handlebars and sounds like the trumpets at judgment day as he comes across the stone pavement. Angrily he takes it off the bars and bangs it into the street curb, where it rolls clattering to a stop.

"Slower!" Briller wheezes behind us. "I have a flat front tire." We nearly fall off our bikes laughing at the misfortune that has befallen the old stallion. Again and again we turn around so that we do not lose sight of Briller. We roll along the street leading out of town to the west until he yells for us to stop at a small hospital. We halt and dismount from our bikes. Briller calmly pushes his bicycle through the front yard of the hospital and puts it in the back. He then stands next to an ambulance into which are being loaded wounded who shake hands goodbye with a doctor in a white jacket. The two back doors close. The driver climbs behind the steering wheel and starts the motor. Leisurely the wagon rolls out of the front yard with its load of war-marked victims toward the city. Deep in thought, the doctor goes with his assistants into the building. Like electricity, Briller grabs the bike that stands in front of his and in the next moment is in the seat. "Stop!" screams the doctor, who happens to return out of the house.

"Where are you going with my bicycle?" "Is this yours?" Briller asks in amazement and looks down at the steel horse. "Oh pardon me," he adds, "naturally it is just a mix up, there is mine." He points to his flat-footed vehicle and stands the doctor's bike up against the building. "What are you doing here?" the doctor asks him affably. "Visiting comrades," Briller lies, looking serious. "Then you can help the stretcher carriers; unfortunately we are short of personnel," the doctor indicates absentmindedly.

Willingly Briller grasps a stretcher and together with a medic carries it into the house while six others remain in the yard. Doubled over with laughter, we wait eagerly to see how the good Briller will save himself from this situation. The medics come out of the house followed by Briller. "I'll take the last one alone," he says as the doctor falls in behind those carrying the stretchers into the building. Seconds later he rushes out of the building, grabs the doctor's bicycle for the second time, and rushes like a whirlwind out of the yard onto the street and nearly tips over negotiating a sharp right turn. Just as though the living personage were right behind us, we rush over a bumpy railroad crossing out of the city toward a nearby village. At exactly 9:40 A.M. we slip into our barn, completely soaked with sweat, and fall asleep on the spot.

We get up about 1:00 P.M., awakened by the clatter of our comrades' cooking utensils. We barely finish our meal when we are called to report to the chief. "How was it last night in the city?" the captain asks curiously, without any attention to rank. "Very nice," Briller answers shortly. "Oh, well, the main thing is that you amused yourselves without doing any harm. It is possible that we will stay here one more night, that is if I don't receive any other orders. Still, I wish to keep that among us. A little sleep would not hurt you, gentlemen. As I hear, coffee had already been issued before you stumbled in here," and with a cunning laugh he raises his hand in salute.

Afterward we sunbathe and smoke cigarettes. Afternoon quiet rules in this small village. During our discussion with the owner of the barn in which our quarters are located, which is confined to the beautiful weather and the senseless war, we are invited into his living room, where they cook good coffee for us for which we provide the beans and they the water. After they offer to make some fried potatoes in addition. I must donate a can of liverwurst, which each one of us has taken out of Le Bourget in our packs. The lady makes a concerted effort to make the afternoon as pleasant as possible with the apparent quiet hope that one of us will make the night sweet for her, since in the meantime she has forced herself into a very tight dress from which more of her anatomy can be seen than left to the imagination.

A man knocks on the windows from outside and asks us to report to the chief immediately. Excusing ourselves for a moment, we leave the room and report to the captain in the park, who is leaning against his automobile with a serious face, buttoning up his field blouse and staring at the radio transmitter.

"We have to leave immediately." He receives us nervously. "Our rear guard has had enemy contact with U.S. tanks only eighteen miles behind us. Sound an alarm at once to the battalion and have the vehicles gather ready to move out along the village road. It is now 4:40 P.M., we leave at 5:30, so get going."

The whistle sounds shrilly over the quiet place. The sergeant on duty calls through the village, "Get ready to move out immediately," and the place becomes a beehive of activity.

The packing and formation of the vehicles goes forward in the usual manner and without any friction. Exactly at 5:30 P.M. Briller reports to the chief that we are ready to move out, when suddenly the thunder of the fighter planes sounds above us and they begin a hellish shooting along the road toward Soissons. With the bicycles in our hands, Briller, Hocker, and I stand at the end of the convoy and wait for the fighters to return.

Because of the action of the fighters, no one notices the dull growling and chain rattling behind us. But like upset hens, old French women run across the road, through the small streets in the village, and disappear into the houses.

"For Hell's sake! There are tanks on the road over there!" I hiss to my friends and see a small tank which I recognize as an American Sherman tank rolling in the direction of Soissons, followed closely by larger tanks. "They are ours," the captain laughs, joining us. Before I can answer, a shattering cannon shell tears all illusions to shreds as it slams into the front vehicle on the edge of the village.

"Take cover," the captain orders. We run right through the park, climb over a six-foot-high brick wall, and try to pull half of the unit behind us toward a nearby wooded hill where we can reassemble.

In the meantime I take a map out of my bag and find that to the right of the hill about two and a half miles distant is a secondary road that parallels the main road we were following in our retreat. A sergeant volunteers to see if the Americans are on that road as well. If it is already occupied by the Americans, the only possibility is to break through during the night.

All together we number forty-two men, one machine gun, one automatic pistol, and twelve rifles. We sit around smoking and listen to the wild noise of fighting in the town until the sergeant returns and reports that the road is occupied by the enemy. A glimmer of hope is extinguished. We are surrounded.

We push to the east edge of the woods, from which we have a clear view into several parts of the burning town. The fighting noise from Soissons diminishes. Dusk spreads over the woods and valley floor. A night fog arises over the meadows and fields that separate us from the city, in which German soldiers still battle against the enemy for the right of occupation.

The captain and the lieutenant come crouching to us. "Do you have a plan to get us out of this dead end?" the captain asks in complete calm. "I suggest this, captain. After dark we move toward the burning house to the far right. The meadows and fields in front of us can be crossed quite quickly; then we can pass around the city as much as the terrain will allow. It is senseless to try to cross the Aisne over a bridge since they have undoubtedly all been secured. We must cross the river by way of the open land and cannot use any roads. After that we can find our way without much trouble," I express my point of view. "I think we will be able to do it," the captain indicates. "Pass the word to get ready," the captain orders the sergeant sitting next to him. The three of us get up and pass among the men to make it clear only weapons and ammunition can be carried and under no circumstances are they to make any noise.

A short time later one of the sergeants takes the machine gun and the three of us wait for the signal from the captain to move out. Silently we slide down the slope and after half an hour reach the open meadow that stretches out before us, now covered with ground fog. Keeping in view only the burning city with the house to the right, we move through the sleeping valley floor. The rest of our comrades follow like shadows. We stumble upon a field road which heads in the general direction that we have set. Following it, we are only about a mile from the edge of the city. The slightest strange noise from the shortest distance seems to ring in our attentive ears. Without a word we lie on the right side of the way in a potato field. The few noises behind us indicate that the rest of the group has understood. Raising my head over the potato plants, I look backward and see only the dusty, lonely road through the field.

"We must stay to the right," I whisper to Hocker lying close to me, "and continue in a southerly direction and single file." He passes my suggestion on to Briller. Straining to hear, we wait for the message to be passed on. Nothing stirs, neither in front nor in back of us. In the process of getting up, I hear clearly the voice of an American. "Shall I spray him with the machine gun?" the sergeant asks Briller. "That won't do us any good" I hiss back, "but just alarm the whole mob. Tell the sergeant," I whisper to Hocker, "that under no circumstances is he to open fire without an order."

It is exactly 12:10 A.M. and I have a terrible thirst. Forcefully I suppress a sneeze. I breathe deeply through my mouth and press the air out of my lungs through my nose to get the dust from some flower out of my nostrils. For the moment I am successful. Intensively my thoughts focus on the possible situation for the enemy. Thereby I come to the conclusion that during the late evening hours the infantry with some tanks had cleaned the Germans out of the town and that the tanks had moved on ahead. With the coming of night the invaders will put up a circular defense around Soissons and move undercover. In that way all the roads and streets that lead to the city will be sealed off by the opponent and we are lying right next to an American machine gun nest. There is no other choice but to try and go around the city in a wide circle.

I whisper my deliberations to Hocker and he passes them on to Briller. Like a snake Briller crawls toward me. "Man, I have landed in an ant pile. The beasts have worked me over so much that my skin burns like I am frying in Hell," he laments slowly into my ear. "That won't hurt you any, old fellow. You won't get to heaven anyway. In the meantime the ant's venom will save you from rheumatism here on earth." I console him and raise my head above the potato plants. "Can you see anything?" He tugs at my arm. "Nothing of any importance," I respond and lay myself flat on the earth. "I have come to basically the same conclusion as you, but I do not like the direction. We know that the Americans have penetrated further south of Paris than to the north. Besides, the Tommies are holding back quite a distance in the north." "That is clear to me," I answer back, "but you forget that we did not have any other choice since our quarters were south of the main road. Consequently we must try it in this direction." "Good," he agrees, "we can't lie here forever; let's get going."

Carefully we get up and prowl parallel to the city edge across the fields. Glancing to the right, I recognize the individual dark shadows that rise from the potato field and follow in single file until a few yards to the right a scuffling noise is heard when two rifles collide. We throw ourselves to the earth at once. Not twenty yards ahead of us we hear the excited voices of Americans and see a white flame rise in the sky. At nearly the same time, a machine gun barks its fire along the field road. Devoid of any common sense, the comrades break out like a herd of sheep backwards out of the potato field and seek security in insane flight. Hugging the earth, we wait until the Americans have calmed themselves. With our pistols ready to fire, we listen with every nerve for the approach of our adversaries.

The hands of my illuminated wristwatch move steadily and within half an hour nothing has occurred. "Who is still here?" I nudge Hocker next to me, who passes the question on to Briller. A barely noticeable rustle, which is gone in a few seconds, gives me to understand that Briller is going backwards to check on the number of comrades still with us. "I believe they all took off," Hocker mumbles to himself. "Then we are no longer responsible for them and can try to get through alone," I whisper to him and look over the top of the potato plants.

After fifteen minutes, Briller snakes between us. "Not one pig still here," he breathes angrily. "So we were not wrong in our judgment of this miserable herd," Hocker hisses through his teeth.

After a short war council, we come to the conclusion that we will try it alone and that we will keep to our intended direction. We crawl behind one another and after twenty minutes reach the edge of the potato field, and keeping to the left make our way across a meadow until a swamp with reeds requires that we halt. Without any hurry, we look for a suitable place to overcome this obstacle, which we succeed in doing after a few minutes, but not without severely taxing the ability of my indestructible comrades to keep from laughing when a stupid accident causes my right boot to slide on a slippery spot and I end up in the water. Dripping wet, I reach the opposite bank and with the help of my comrades pull off my boots in order to be rid of the stinking water. Under the amused grins of these malicious fellows, I wring out my socks and slip my boots back on. "Just wait, you scoundrels." I take the wind out of their sails. "Someone has prepared a surprise for you someplace."

Without delaying any longer than necessary, we continue further and after an hour come to a secondary road on which there is considerable traffic by American supply trucks. Pressed tightly against the embankment, we wait for a break in the traffic and then with a quick jump reach the south side of the road. Continuing in a southerly direction, we steer toward a burning building far to the right. Lulled by the hope that we will be able to skirt the city without being noticed, I hear clearly the loading of a weapon. Once again we kiss France's hotly contested earth, holding to it tightly. Dark clouds have appeared in the heaven. Only a few individual stars can be seen in the firmament and keep alive in us the belief in a good outcome. Time presses. Before it is light we must find a safe shelter. It is 2:20 A.M. as we retreat toward the west to make another circle in our third attempt to get through.

At exactly 3:00 A.M., as we are attempting to cross the railroad track running north and south to Soissons, two machine guns open fire several yards from us to our complete surprise and force us to take cover under the howling buzz that is tearing up the meadow. Amazed and sure that we had not made any noise, we look backwards and notice a tree about one hundred yards in the distance, on which the Americans must have seen our silhouettes. A short "turn" from Briller's lips is enough for us to execute a 180-degree turn on our bellies and, like serpents being pursued, slither back in a westerly direction. A new burst of adrenalin gives us a renewed shot of energy to our waning strength. We assemble behind the tree which was the reason for the Americans' fire. Just now, when we have no possibility of finding any secure cover, it begins to rain.

After a short discussion, we get up and follow behind each other further to the west. Not until we are sure that we are out of range of the American machine guns do we take cover in the underbrush. "This time the devil has his dirty fingers in the game," I open our conversation. "That's the way it looks," Hocker agrees, pulling a comb out of his field blouse to fix his hair. "Now it is absolutely necessary that we find shelter for the day; it will be light in an hour," Briller growls, lying on his back. "Unfortunately there is not a solitary barn or shed in this damn area," Hocker answers sullenly. "In every situation the German soldier has come out all right," I throw out, "and we will find a place to camp." "The best thing would be to return back to that woman." Briller suppresses a laugh. "Now I would not say no to her if afterward she would let me sleep alone in her bed." "That is not such a bad idea." Hocker reaches for this thought spoken in jest. "Does that mean that we should go back that far?" I object. "Be calm and listen," Briller says in a low tone. "It is obvious that we will not get anywhere trying to go south. I can imagine that the road to the city, I mean the main road from the north, is the open left flank as the Americans have pushed into Soissons. If that is the case, then in the coming night we just need to find an opening to cross the road and head in the direction of Laon to connect up with the German troops."

"Not to detract from your idea, Briller, but what it means is to bet everything on one card and to renounce the time we have already wasted foolishly," I mix in with my warning. "Then tell us what you think we should do, Helmut," Briller says. "We cannot lose any more time. You have seen for yourselves what the Americans have rolling across the roads. It doesn't look to me like it is just a matter of the situation around Soissons. They are well informed about our troop movements; they would not shy away from pushing into an empty sector in order to secure it. We should consider whether or not we should get going and try our luck to the south, or just find shelter here in this vicinity and wait for the coming night."

"So," Briller seizes the initiative, "let's look at our alternatives. Since it is now light, a march to the south is out of the question. That only leaves this piece of woods for our shelter since with this weather we cannot camp in the open meadowlands. If there is still fighting in the city, then my viewpoint is correct and we should try to get through to Laon. If it is quiet, then we are just as close to the northern road as the southern. As I said before, I think the northern route is better. Does anyone have a better idea?" he asks, pulling in his legs in order to stand up. "No," Hocker and I answer at the same time and get to our feet.

As quickly as the terrain allows, we make our way to the heights of the wooded hills straight to the northwest and after an hour we reach the southern side of the road. A convoy of trucks moves through, forcing us to take cover. Snuggled close to each other we stretch out in the low grass and stare at the passing vehicles loaded with American infantry soldiers. It is apparently no fun for the Americans either to be driven so early in the morning in this weather toward the German weapons. Quietly they sit on the benches of the trucks as though they were animals being driven to the slaughterhouse. "They would probably rather be with their wives lying in a warm nest instead of picking chestnuts out of the fire for the old Roosevelt," Hocker says out loud with sad eyes as the last truck rolls past. "That is what is the most shitty in this world," I agree with him. "Otherwise you did not perceive anything special about this funeral parade," Briller notes in the early morning. "What was there that was so special to be seen?" I ask curiously. "It was infantry," he says calmly. "That's right, Briller," I admit and immediately it registers in my consciousness what he means. "Now I nearly believe that you were right about your wedge; then it appears that to this hour at least, they have not brought any artillery forward." I laugh with admiration at his sharp vision. "That's nice of you," he continues to mock me. "I did not expect that you would tune in so soon; I thought you only used your hot head to dry your hat." "Ah, the old Briller still lives, then nothing can go wrong for us today." Hocker closes the circuit of our comradeship. "Let's go, you old wash women." Briller laughs and gets ready to start.

Like the wind, we sweep across the road and roll down into the grass. Securing all sides, we move as quickly as possible in a northwesterly direction toward the hilly section of woods from which last night we made the first attempt to break through with the miserable remainder of the battalion. In the meantime it is now 5:15 A.M. Despite the time of day, thanks to the light rain and the thin early fog over the meadows and farmland, it is possible for us to continue our journey. But still we slowly become suspicious, because while there is the loud noise of motors to the right and left of us, to this hour not one shot has sounded in Soissons.

In an area of thin scrubs and old dried up fruit trees, about five hundred yards from the ascending forest, we lie down for a council. Finally daylight allows us to light a cigarette without danger. Given entirely to the anticipated pleasure, we open the packages with nervous fingers and shove the sticks filled with gold-yellow tobacco into our mouths. "Light?" Briller asks in forced calmness. "Light?" I ask Hocker and clap with both hands on my pockets without hearing the familiar rattle of matches. In shock we look at each other. Is it possible that we have hauled 240 cigarettes around with us and no one has a match?

"That is the worst that has happened to us yet," Briller expresses, completely brought down. We put the cigarettes back into our pockets. Suddenly, and completely unexpectedly, from behind the woods the crack of artillery fire of four American batteries is heard, and seconds later the heavy projectiles howl above us through the rain clouds. Like steel springs from which the pressure is suddenly released, we pop to our feet and follow the flight of the shells recognizable by the roar. Seconds later four mushrooms of smoke rise toward the sky in the southeastern part of the city. "That makes me sick." Briller shakes his head. "We could be there right now, if we had listened to you, Helmut. There are still some Germans at work and we could have helped them."

"Nonsense, Robert, when they send the next salvo into the northeast section, then you will be right again. We are not going to get any farther right now. I am in favor of getting a couple of sheaves of oats and finally going to sleep for a while." I comfort Briller, laying my hand on his shoulder. "Why should we bring those things over here?" Hocker mumbles to himself. "It would be better to get under them where they are; the ground is certainly dry." "He is right," Briller indicates. "They could see us carrying the bundles." "Of course," I agree, "but each one of us would have to nestle alone in one of the pyramids and we cannot exchange any thoughts." "Let's get some sleep first," Briller decides; "we can tell each other our dreams later on."

We make our way toward the field and disappear under the stacked oat sheaves, where I immediately fall asleep sitting up.

### 27 August 1944

It is 11:25 A.M. The rain has let up. Torn shreds of clouds hang in the sky, through which the timid rays of the sun dare to come out from time to time. On the stalks of my tiny straw hut, silver streaks of water drops run down and disappear into the earth. Little bugs are busy at my feet on the fertile field. A light vapor rises two feet above the earth. Life will go on, even when I am stiff and rigid under the earth. A father cannot keep his son back from war anymore even though he breaks his heart over why he has raised him so that when he becomes grown he must be destroyed. A young wife will cry for her mate and press tenderly to her the child who will never see its father again. No news will reach the homeland about the manner or place of my destruction. Like a dog I will be thrown into a hole and covered by hate-filled strangers who only want to save themselves from the stink and danger of infection from the corpse. It will not be otherwise.

But the will to live rises powerfully in me. Determined, I reach my hand into the holster and bring the cold, hard steel in front of my eyes. Whoever is seeking your life, I whisper inside myself, has forfeited his own! My hot blood rages in my veins and drives me to my feet. Like the shells of larvae awakened to life, the oat sheaves fall apart. Committed to act, I call to my friends to depart and go about securing all sides of the hollow.

"What is going on?" both call, coming out of the oatfield into the hollow. "We have finally got to do something, friends, if we don't want to be cornered by the dogs," I give in response and keep my eyes on them. "I have been observing the terrain around us," says Briller, loaded with new energy, "and I don't think we will stumble into a trap if we can cross the five hundred yards and get into the woods." "Then let's get going immediately." My impatience pushes to my lips. "What happened to you, Helmut?" asks Hocker, mistrustful. "I want to have a decision, Willi," I respond coldly.

"Don't lose your nerve, one should not do anything rashly," he warns, raising his index finger. "Nineteen hours have passed since the Americans caught up with us. You cannot talk about acting in haste, rather the opposite is more the case," I insist. "Don't prattle unnecessarily and stick close to my heels," Briller demands and walks calmly out of the hollow. Obviously nervous, Hocker chews on a grass stalk as he pulls his pistol out of the holster and follows Briller. Securing the rear, I follow last.

Exactly at 2:00 P.M. we are sitting on the same tree trunk that Hocker collapsed on to catch his breath yesterday at 6:00 P.M. Now unmerciful hunger and thirst register. We have not had anything to eat or drink for twenty-two hours. Dull, tired, hungry, thirsty, and with soaking clothes on our bodies, the three of us sit, forsaken by God and the world, in a French forest from whose trees the water drips down our necks with the slightest breeze. Rage slowly but surely rises in us. In addition, we are surrounded by the enemy but we still struggle to keep the vague hope that for well-trained soldiers it will not be too difficult to get out of this encirclement. We forget that now, 1944, after more than four years of war, we have become weaker while the others have grown stronger.

"If we had only left Soissons with the SS." Hocker opens the round. "If we had only gone to a respectable unit in Paris," Briller joins in. "If this shitty war had only stayed with the devil," I add my two cents' worth.

Restlessly I get up and wander in a circle around my two companions, whereby I stumble upon the remains of the equipment and supplies left by the men from our battalion. Out of sheer boredom, I turn over with my feet the helmets, belts, and cartridge pouches until I come to the bread sack, which I pick up and examine curiously. "Well, well," I groan and pull a piece of Swiss cheese out of the bag. Sauntering toward my friends, I see their expectant faces looking at me. Then I feel something crawling on my hand holding the cheese and I quickly look to see what is there. Angrily I shake my hand vigorously without letting go of the cheese and twenty ants that were hanging on it fall to the ground. The last one I brush off with a branch torn from a tree, then I hurry proudly to my companions.

"So," I hold the cheese in front of their hungry eyes, "isn't that something?" "It weighs at least three hundred grams with the holes." Hocker laughs and reaches for the cheese as a red-brown ant crawls out of one of the holes. "Do these beasts also eat cheese?" Briller asks, observing the animal. "No," Hocker jokes in response, "they don't eat it; we will." Finally a laugh comes back to our serious faces as Hocker cuts the cheese into three pieces. "It will give the stomach something to do," Briller indicates and, struggling with the entire mass, shoves it into his mouth all at once. With a mighty effort, he swallows the entire gluey clod as his eyes bulge out like those of a frog. "Dirt grub," he spits out as his tongue makes a half circle between his cheeks, lips, and teeth while we struggle to suppress our laughter. "Don't laugh, you dirty sacks," he growls angrily. "Come on old man," I nudge him, "what will the madame do when we appear? Perhaps she has something that you can wash your mouth with." "You don't want to go down to the village, do you?" He jumps up with a jolt. Hocker looks at me, upset. "That is exactly what I want to do, at least to the edge of the village so that we can finally see what is going on there," I answer, determined. "Or don't you want to go over the road toward Laon?" I follow up. "Of course I want to do that, but it is still daylight!" Briller counters. "Then let's at least go far enough so that we can see the village and the vehicles," I demand dauntlessly.

Without further dispute we go into the underbrush so we can slip down the slope. Just as we reach a point where we can see the church and some of the roofs of the village, the bells in the village begin to clang. Loud shouts in the village streets are sure proof that Soissons is free of Germans.

"Liberté pour Français," bellow a pair of children's voices as the bells become silent. "This time we are really in deep," Hocker mumbles angrily. "Tonight we will look up the madame," Briller says gruffly. "We will learn from her where the Americans are," he adds. "She will turn us in," I warn.

We lie in the thick underbrush and await nightfall. Calmly and attentive to everything, we glide quietly down the rest of the hill and a little later stand in complete darkness before a high park wall that we follow to the left until it makes a right turn into the village. Carefully we work our way to the first houses and discover double guards with long, fixed bayonets on the village streets. "They are French," I murmur to my comrades. "Shall we try it further to the west or east?" Briller asks. "Eastward," comes from our mouths at the same time. "Then about face," Briller whispers, and I am now in the lead. Quickly we make our way over the small meadow that is nestled between the village and the woods and after thirty minutes reach the eastern limits of the village. We recognize the frame of our burned-out ammunition truck. But even there further eastward, Frenchmen stand smoking together with weapons on their shoulders. The French are in front and in back of us.

Inch by inch we make our way slowly through the meadow, then past a guard standing on the road. I do not have the slightest fear of the French. But to be in the situation with the Russians would seize me with terror. Briller approaches me from behind. "Just keep going, Robert, I will watch out for the Frenchmen," I say softly in his ear.

It is 1:35 A.M. when we stand up north of the railroad tracks and joyfully stride out in a northeast direction toward Laon, which lies about twenty-five miles in the distance.

### 28 August 1944

For an hour and a half we march unmolested across the fields, keeping Soissons to our right so that we can cross the railroad line headed north.

We later observe human shadows on the horizon above the railroad grade. They move here and there in typical American carelessness. Robbed of all hope, we let ourselves fall exhausted into the grass and stare into the heavens, from which comes no advice or means of escape.

"Further northward?" I say without any power in my voice. "It is certainly hopeless," my companions answer. "Then we must try and get some civilian clothes and see if we can go on during the day," I answer. "Where will you get civilian clothes?" they ask. "What about the madame, Briller?" I nudge him. "She just wants a man in bed and not to help anyone who is trying to flee," he snaps, depressed. "Then I will try it," I say and sit upright. "If one goes, we all go," they both respond. "OK, then let's go back again to the village," I say, filled with new courage, and stand up quickly.

Silently we retrace our steps. Exhausted, we stop close to one of the houses standing along the street near the main road of traffic. We fall into a thin clump of bushes and are immediately asleep.

A bright day greets us as we awake. The sun burns hot in the sky. Looking toward the street we are amazed at the convoys of Americans that roll eastward uninterrupted. "How are we going to get across this road?" Hocker flusters in shock. "They won't be traveling forever," Briller responds confidently. "It is already nine o'clock," I indicate with a laugh. "Time does not matter any more," Hocker reacts laconically.

Brooding, we lie again on our backs and blink into the sun. About ten o'clock the traffic on the road suddenly stops. Not one human being is to be seen in the entire area. "Let's go, men." Briller forces a grin and stands up. "Get ready to die," Hocker indicates.

Boldly we step into the road, our pistols ready. We make our way through small unfenced gardens, across the village street unseen, and follow the park wall into the woods, where we stretch out next to a pond covered with magnificent water lilies. We are now aware of the improbability of our luck, but also the carelessness of our conduct during the entire war. Unusual situations demand unusual decisions. As we discuss whether or not to test our lucky streak by knocking on the madame's door during the day, since it appears that the entire village is in Soissons celebrating the victory, our doom approaches in the figure of a stone-faced old Frenchman. He bends around the shrubs in front of the pond and begins in all quietness to pick the water lilies without even a glance around the area. Unable to move because the old man would notice us, we wait, hoping that he will soon disappear as quietly as he arrived. But suddenly he slides on the slick bank, falls onto his back, grabs the grass with his hands, and stares directly at us.

"Oh, soldat Allemand," he screams like he is insane and with his last ounce of strength slides back away from the water's edge. He stares at us with open mouth and immediately screams in a shrill, crackling voice "la guerre fini! American-soldat ici! Liberté Française! soldat Allemand part!" "Shut your damn mouth," Briller screams, going straight toward him and seizing him in his arms.

Irresolutely we stand around the old timer who, shaking with fear, begins to scream again. "What shall we do with the old boy?" Briller asks, puzzled. "Stick his head under the water until he becomes peaceful," Hocker says, reaching into the man's pockets and pulling out matches in his hand.

Quickly we light our cigarettes. As fast as his legs will carry him, the grandpa uses this instant to gallop back toward the village, screaming all the way. We follow him quickly and grab him by his jacket. He stops running, and whimpering he moans, "C'est la guerre!" "Yes, this is war, old man," Hocker hisses at him.

Undecided as to what we should do with this shaggy Frenchman, fate takes the unpleasant task out of our hands. Five Frenchmen come toward us on a fast run, their attention having been drawn to us by the old man's screams. The five men hold their rifles to our breasts. "Give up," one of them calls to us in good German, "the Americans have been in Laon for some time!"

Slowly we lower our pistols. The spokesman comes to us walking calmly. With outstretched hand he demands our weapons. Instead we put the pistols back into our holsters. "We are not at war with France," I say, looking him in the eyes. Laughing, he pulls a pack of American cigarettes out of his pants pocket and hangs one between his lips in typical French style. "You are lucky," he says, still laughing and holding a burning match to his cigarette. "I was a prisoner in Germany," he begins in a calm voice, "and I cannot complain about the treatment. You could have easily fallen into the hands of some fanatics who would have shot you without mercy. You can keep your weapons if you will follow me into the village, where I will turn you over to the Americans. You are certainly part of the people who rested here a few days ago and did not cause any trouble. Give up. The war is over for you and you will see your homeland again."

We look at each other. "We will not surrender to the French," I whisper to my friends and notice that one of the riflemen has disappeared back toward the village. "Let's run into the underbrush on the left and shoot it out with these guys," Hocker murmurs through his teeth. An unrealistic situation rushes through my consciousness, and I am in doubt whether I am awake or dreaming. Unexpectedly, four Americans, the size of trees, appear from around the corner. Shaking with fear and excitement, they remain about five yards distant from us, standing with their automatic pistols pointed at us. "Hands up, boys," one of them calls, and as in a vision I see everything that is dear and precious to me disappearing in an unending distance.

The most disgraceful moment of my long life as a soldier has arrived. Here in this lousy French pen it has come to an unworthy conclusion. "Raise your paws in a double German salute, Helmut," Briller says loudly next to me. Just now I notice that my friends are holding their open hands in front of their chests. Without direction from my absent spirit, I slowly raise my hands toward the sky.

* * *

From the time Hörner was wounded on July 4, 1944, at La Haye-du-Puits until his release from the hospital in Auxerre on August 10, the American forces made significant advances. Hörner's Division, the 77th

Grenadiers, was part of the 450,000-man German Seventh Army, which during the first two months of fighting after the Normandy invasion lost 160,000 men killed, wounded, or taken prisoner. The 77th Division was wiped out at the Battle of the Falaise Gap in fighting during the month between Hörner's wounding and his release from the hospital with orders to report to Paris for assignment. Hörner opted to take an assignment with an emergency battalion under the command of Captain Nollte composed, in part, of remnants from the 77th Division. Under Nollte, Hörner and the others were to occupy Le Bourget, a few miles northeast of Paris, and would presumably engage the enemy when it launched its attack on Paris. Hörner, Hocker, and Briller arrived in Le Bourget on August 16, the same day Chartres, with its famous medieval cathedral, fell to American forces and the day before Orléans was taken. The retreating German army was in no position to take up the defense of Paris and when Hörner and his comrades left Le Bourget on August 19, American forces had reached Mantes-Gassicourt on the Seine, thirty miles west of Paris, and French resistance fighters had begun open operations against the Germans in Paris. Four days later, August 23, French resistance fighters had Paris under control, and on August 25 French and American troops rolled into Paris. Despite some pockets of resistance from the nearly 20,000 Germans still in the city, Paris was free. Compared with the fighting in other cities, the Allied casualties were light. Only 628 Americans were killed, while the Germans lost 3,000 killed with 10,000 taken prisoner.

While Americans and French celebrated the liberation of Paris on August 25, sixty miles to the east in Soissons, Hörner, Briller, Hocker, and the others were enjoying their last wild night with the French civilians of that city. The next day, August 26, they were overtaken by units of the U.S. Seventh Corps, under Major General J. L. Collins, pushing northeast twenty-five miles from Château-Thierry. The Seventh Corps took Soissons on August 29. While Hörner gives August 28 as the day of his capture, it is possible that he lost track of one day, since his prisoner of war tag indicates that he was captured at 11:00 A.M. on August 29, 1944, in the vicinity of Soissons. Hörner was correct in considering it hopeless to try and escape to the south—the direction the Seventh Corps had come—and as they made their way north around Soissons trying to cross the Aisne and reach Laon, they were cut off by the Seventh Corps, which continued its rapid advance through Soissons to take Laon on August 30.

While Hörner had no clear picture of what was happening as he and his unit sought to outrun the Americans, he knew that the Aisne River, just north of Soissons, might pose some barrier to the advancing Americans; if they could cross the river, their chances of escape were much greater. But the rapid mechanized American advance meant that once the foot soldiers were overtaken, there was little hope of pushing on ahead of the American troops. The Seventh Corps continued to push northeast after taking Laon and by September 3 had cleared most of the army's zone south of the Belgian border.

* * *

# Chapter Three

# PRISONER IN FRANCE

IT IS DIFFICULT TO document the situation for German prisoners of war in France. Indeed, this is one of the valuable aspects of Hörner's account. It seems that his experience was generally typical of the thousands of German soldiers who were captured as American forces rolled across France and into Belgium. Hörner's interrogation was perhaps an exception because the Americans misinterpreted documents in his possession to indicate he was a member of one of the feared rocket-launcher groups rather than the sergeant for a mortar launch group. Still, at this point, most interrogations of German prisoners were very cursory because Americans realized that, with the Germans in rapid retreat, circumstances were changing almost by the hour. Furthermore, soldiers in retreat, hurrying through unfamiliar territory and often cut off from their units, had little logistical or strategical information that would be of any use to the Allies. Finally, so many prisoners were being taken that it was impossible to spend more than a few minutes with the common soldiers to identify those who might have special information and who thus could be held for further questioning.

While Hörner describes conditions for the German prisoners as very poor as far as food and quarters were concerned, those familiar with the war situation in France realized that this was not necessarily intentional on the part of Americans, but rather the result of a combination of factors over which neither German prisoners nor American captors had much control. Provisions were in short supply for the American forces, and as more and more German prisoners were captured and areas of France liberated, the demand for provisions grew. A few days after Hörner was captured, American tanks spearheading the advance through eastern France were forced to stop because of a lack of gasoline. Given the scarcity of rations to begin with; the difficulties associated with transporting the rations from the United States to England and from England to France by ship, and then by truck to the various prisoner of war camps; and the belief that former soldiers, now prisoners, would be more easily controlled if the amount of nourishment provided only marginally sustained life, it is understandable why there was so little food for the prisoners and why it was a subject constantly on their minds.

It also seems that the allied forces were unprepared for the large numbers of prisoners that were taken during the first few months after the invasion. Enclosing the masses of prisoners with barbed wire in isolated fields was the easiest way to handle the captives quickly and divert the minimum number of soldiers for the required guard duty. As far as living conditions were concerned, many Americans felt that the Nazi soldiers did not deserve better, while others found little difference between the hardships of confinement and the living conditions for their own front line soldiers.

* * *

*28 August 1944*

The tires of the jeep squeal sharply and raise an ugly cloud of smoke as they negotiate a left turn on the street going out of the village headed toward the main road. My two comrades, sitting to my right and left, clamp like iron onto my arms.

No, I do not dream. I am sitting on the wide hood of an American army jeep between my two companions and traveling back along our road of retreat to where we came from. Turning myself around, I see the disapproving faces of the American soldiers and the threatening manner in which they point their pistols at us. Once again a feeling of inner emptiness and infinite abandonment creeps over me. I try to bring some order to my thoughts while I stare at my field blouse, robbed of all decorations and badges. Where my national insignia was sewn, there is now a hole through which the white of my undershirt can be seen. On my left wrist is a band of white flesh where a short time ago my wristwatch kept the skin from becoming tanned. Only my shaving kit remains.

"Pull yourself together, Helmut," I hear Briller saying from what seems like a far distance. "Shut up," barks an American behind us over the windshield. "Kiss my ass," growls Briller and spits contemptuously onto the right side of the road.

The motor of the jeep hums monotonously as it distances us further from our intended goal with each passing minute. The thought comes: Why didn't I put a bullet into my head? What purpose is there to living without freedom, especially now after the world in which I believed, for which I fought and bled, has collapsed? Who are these people, who, like highway bandits with no feeling of shame, plunder soldiers in their most bitter hour and enrich themselves in the most base manner on the misfortune of others? What will happen to us, what must the homeland face if these Americans are successful in pushing into the Reich?

Like a strong stimulant, these thoughts make the blood flow hot from my heart through the veins and create a new determination in every pore of my body. In full possession of my old spirit for life, I grab the hands of my friends and press them vigorously in the hope that they will also overcome this humiliation. A fine smile on their mask-like faces thanks me for the gesture. A warm stream of inner joy pulsates throughout me with the certainty that I do not have to carry the coming misery alone. A quiet oath seals in me my readiness to stand by them in their highest hour of need. It is true that today we have fallen into the hands of robbers, but the fair fight in Normandy brings the conclusion that not all Americans are such miserable highwaymen as these. The fact that they have a sense of humor was proven during an episode that occurred near Saint-Sauveur. At that time some Germans fell into their hands, including an eighteen-year-old who had the face of a child. After a quick decision they cut his pants off above the knee, filled his pack with chocolate, hung a sign around his neck that read, "We do not fight children," and sent him back across no-man's land to his unit.

It will be a hard loaf of bread that the future gives us, but the belief and hope that we will once again see our homeland shall shine for us like a star in the darkest night and together we will endure what fate has prepared for us.

The driver cuts the motor and turns left onto a field road where fifteen tanks are assembled along the length of the meadow. The jeep stops by the tanks. With grinning faces the troops pull us from the jeep. Helpless, the three of us stand in the middle of these foreign soldiers and let their mockery pass over us. The four rascals to whom we surrendered our weapons show the others our decorations, which they pull from their pockets. A tall American examines our medals and insignias with interest. On the sleeves of his wind jacket are three raised stripes and two lowered stripes, which indicate that he is a staff sergeant, the same rank as we. With unconcealed admiration he walks up to us and pats us on the shoulder. "Good soldiers," he says, acknowledging us, and calls in incomprehensible English to the four soldiers who are busy examining the contents of our map cases. They respond by shaking their heads. Energetically he turns from us and steps among the group of curious who are examining our equipment. A hail of words shoots from his mouth upon the soldiers, to which one replies in the same intensity and tone.

We listen, surprised, to the terrible gibberish, recognizing that a fight is looming over our medals. With the painful feeling in our breasts that we are witnesses to and the cause of a strange family strife, we follow the spectacle that these farmer sons from the United States are carrying out. A pudgy older Yankee comes out from a tent situated between the tanks and goes toward the arguing soldiers. On his cap and on the corners of his shirt collar are two metal bars which identify him as an officer. After a few sharp words directed toward the soldiers, the rabble becomes silent. With a stonefaced expression he now comes toward us and remains standing three paces away. His gray eyes wander from one to another. Taking an enormous cigar from his pouch, he shoves nearly half of it into his mouth. From the pockets of his jacket, he pulls a match in complete calmness and then with a quick strike against the low-hanging pistol holster lights the match. Leisurely he guides the burning match to the cigar and seconds later an impressive smoke cloud rings toward the sky. Staring at us with an unchanging face, he calls several men to him with a snap of the fingers. Without taking the monstrous cigar out of his mouth, he talks to the soldiers in a deep voice. Their grim faces promise nothing good for us. In the next moment we are encircled by the Americans and feel their searching hands on all parts of our bodies. The entire contents of our pockets, including our wallets, fly before our feet. Before our eyes strange, dirty fingers sort through our possessions and take all money and photographs with military objects from our wallets. Bitterly I see the picture of my wife disappear into the pocket of a dirty thief.

Unmoved, the officer follows the shameless activity of his subordinates. Finally they are finished and indicate we can pick up the lamentable remains of our possessions. A small truck, built like a jeep, pulls out of the group of parked trucks with a howling engine and stops next to us. Five heavily armed Americans help us into the vehicle. They climb into the wagon after us and with their bodies block the open back end of the truck. Driving quickly we travel back along the field way to the main road and after fifteen minutes turn left onto a small paved street and stop suddenly in front of a large farm complex. Our guards spring elegantly from the truck and indicate with spiteful gestures that we are to do the same.

In stoic calmness we leave the vehicle, unimpressed by the conduct of the Americans, and march toward six Frenchmen standing in front of the gate to the farmyard with German rifles and pistols in their hands. They break out in a war cry when they see us. Under the idiotic roar of these failures from 1940, we are driven through the entrance to the yard, and stand next to each other with our faces toward the house wall. Ja, do it quickly you murderers, I think, expecting to get a bullet in the back of the neck. In seconds my previous life passes through my consciousness. But the seemingly endless minutes pass without anything happening until an unseen man calls Briller's name in German.

"Present," I hear Briller answer indifferently. "Come inside," the other one registers again. I glance to the left in the direction from which the voice comes. Unruffled, Briller leaves the wall and saunters through the open door of a shed toward a standing American. Almost politely the man leads him in through the door.

"They are going to interrogate us," I whisper softly to Hocker, and as a consequence I receive a hard, painful blow to my right kidney which takes my breath away and immediately silences me. Calmly and ready to meet with dignity whatever comes, I glue my hands to the wall and stare with hanging head at my boots until Briller, after nearly an eternity, is returned to us and my name is clearly called. "Don't give them anything," I hear Briller hiss, as I march like an unfeeling robot to the soldier at the door.

The guard leads me through the door into some kind of a carpenter shop which is set up as a temporary office. At a long table, sitting with his back to the door, is a massive being whose insignia indicates that he is a high-ranking officer. The guard shoves me in front of him. In military form I salute him with my hand on the corner of my cap and notice how the man across from me studies me critically. Bored, he thanks me for the salute and leans back comfortably in his chair while one of the four men in the room serves him a cup of heavenly smelling coffee and a plate with bread and corned beef.

Exerting all of the control at my disposal, I force my eyes from the splendors before me, which I assume are there to tempt me. I observe immediately his suddenly wide-awake look and wonder what his purpose is. Disappointed, he reaches for his cigarettes, throws one leg across another, and turns to me in exaggerated friendliness: "Since July 20th, the Nazi salute has been required in the German army; why is it that you salute me with the old military salute?" "My tactfulness forbids me from using this salute of honor on an enemy officer," I answer with a firm voice. "So?" He acts surprised. "Then you possess more tact than your Minister of Foreign Affairs, von Ribbentrop. Do you know that during one of his visits to the English king, he greeted him with 'Heil Hitler?'" "I am not aware of that," I give indifferently in response. "It is the truth." He underscores his words and reaches for the coffee cup. "How long have you gone without anything to eat?" He turns to me and continues the conversation. "For two days," I explain shortly. "Oh, then you must be terribly hungry. We will hurry so that we can get you something good to eat," he says to me in a concerned manner.

I am not going to fall for that, I say to myself, although a terrible feeling of hunger rages in my insides. But the voice of the officer interrupts my thoughts: "Your unit, please?" he asks and reaches for paper and a pen. "Here is my *Soldbuch*, mister." I answer calmly and finger my *Soldbuch* out of my wallet. Curiously he leafs through the pages and gives it back to me. "How is it that you have just now been captured; your division was destroyed long ago?" he asks. "I was in a hospital," I explain to him. "So, that's why," he indicates, satisfied, "but after that you were in a rocket-launcher company; where is it now?" "I was not in a rocket-launching company," I return his assertion. "But this is a record of your troop strength and ammunition stock," he declares sharply, and holds an old roster in front of my eyes that was in my pack. "Naturally that is from La Haye-du-Puits." I laugh at him. "Don't lie," he bellows angrily in response. "We have the means to make you talk; you can count on that." "Here is my *Soldbuch*; everything that I know and that would be of interest to you is in it, mister. Otherwise I do not have anything else to give you," I say to him with deliberate calmness. "I will give you the opportunity to consider it once again in quiet," he says, somewhat cooled, giving one of the men present the sign to take me away.

Prepared for any meanness, I go in front of the guard out the door, where another receives me, leads me across the yard, and shoves me into an enclosed pigsty. The gate slams shut behind me. In the half dark, I look at my new quarters and confirm to my satisfaction that the boars that were housed here before me were removed days ago and because of the excessive heat the straw is at least dry. Since it is impossible for me to stand up in the small stall, I shovel some straw into a corner and sink down upon it. It's too bad that I don't have any matches with me in order to smoke one of the few cigarettes that I still possess.

What did the American officer mean with his crazy talk about rocket launchers? I only saw those weapons in action once in Russia. That was on October 2, 1941, near Vyaz'ma. Damn it, those were the days. ...

Squeaking, the door to the pigsty opens and bright sunshine floods my dungeon. From the perspective of a frog I see the brown leggings covering the shoes and olive green pants of an American. "Come out, you Nazi pig," he calls in bended position into my quiet little chamber and grins from ear to ear. Dumb dog, I think and slip outside.

Blinded by the glaring light, I hold my hand for protection in front of my eyes, as the guard takes me by the arm and guides me to the officer. "Have you considered the situation?" he asks and looks at me cynically. "In connection with the matter, there is nothing to reconsider," I answer him honestly. "Shall I put match sticks under your fingernails like the Gestapo does to the Jews?" he snaps threateningly. "That will not make a rocket launcher out of me. I did not have anything to do with it," I answer him obstinately. "What is this written by your own hand?" He holds the list under my nose once again and points with a pencil to the signature on the backside of my old ammunition report. "Mortar ammunition," I say dryly. "And here," he points to the end of the list. "996 mortar grenades," I read to him. "So," he laughs triumphantly and folds the list together, "they are rocket launchers, isn't that true?" "No, just mortar grenades, 8-centimeter mortar grenades, mister." I laugh in his face at the error. "Why didn't you say that at first?" He becomes angry and throws the pencil to the table. "You didn't ask me about it," I answer calmly. "Get this fellow out of my sight," he speaks German in a rage, puffing on a cigarette.

Apparently happy about the failure of his superior, an older American, gray at the temples, turns to me and behind the back of the officer gives me a sign which seems to mean, "let's leave the fool." I salute, turn on my heels, and follow him. With the feeling that I have won a battle of wits against the officer and that I have avoided a medieval torture, I step to the side of the somehow sympathetic older soldier, out into the open, and across the yard, where he puts me into a shed. To my great surprise, there are about thirty German soldiers there, including Hocker and Briller. A quick glimpse into the individual faces of the prisoners is enough to know that, unfortunately, I am not acquainted with any of the others.

The shed does not have a door and is completely open in front, apparently having served the farmer as a coach house. As a consequence, two American soldiers stand several paces distant, observing us sharply and chewing with empty mouths in a manner that reminds me of cows ruminating in a meadow.

"They are chewing gum," a noncommissioned officer explains to me in response to my question about why they are continually chewing. "What did they want from you, Helmut?" Hocker asks, concerned. "They thought I was the leader of a rocket-launcher unit." "And that's why they locked you up in the pigsty?" Briller asks in amazement. "It wasn't that bad; if it doesn't get any worse, we can be satisfied," I answer him tranquilly. "Hopefully we will soon get something to eat; otherwise I'll die," Hocker mumbles to himself. "What time is it?" I ask, looking at the other Germans. "A while ago it was 3:00 P.M. according to the American's watch," the noncommissioned officer informs me. "Where are you from, comrade?" I ask. "From Neustadt," he sighs, depressed. "That is not too far distant from my home," I say lightly. "But unfortunately no longer can it be reached from here; the train has already departed," he indicates without humor, then continues. "We should have gone to the railroad station earlier, comrade. This morning they pulled me out of the arms of my girlfriend. The French must have betrayed me." "Where did they catch you?" I ask, interested. "Naturally in Soissons. I could have held out for a long time with this voluptuous prostitute. She had food in abundance, let me tell you." "Then it was about time that the Americans saved you; otherwise you would have had to serve at her court of love for a long time," I tease him. "Not so long, we will be home by Christmas," he indicates, convinced. "Do you believe that Hitler will finally put into service his legendary secret weapon?" I ask hopefully. "Hitler and secret weapons, don't make me laugh," he responds contemptuously. "No, the Americans will win the war and make us their forty-ninth state; then see how well we live." "So that's it." I whistle through my teeth and turn away from him.

My friends look at me with sad eyes. "Don't let such idiots bother you," they whisper to me. "It is unbelievable what kind of fools we have among us," I fluster back, shaking my head in disappointment. "How about smoking?" I ask my companions. Both shrug their shoulders. "Why don't we try it?" I say, taking out my cigarettes to offer them to my friends. Embarrassed, we ransack our pockets for matches while the guards watch. Regretfully we display our empty hands to each other. Without interfering, one of the guards steps toward us and in a friendly gesture holds a burning lighter to our cigarettes. With a deep drag we pull the long-missed smoke into our lungs and nod our thanks to the foreign soldier, who acknowledges it as he returns to his position. There are both good and bad among them, I conclude.

"Those two seem to be in order." Hocker seems to read my thoughts. "If they would just give us something to eat." "Be a little patient, Willi, we will surely be fed soon; the interrogation officer knows that I have not had anything to eat for two days." I comfort Hocker while my own terrible hunger torments me. "That is what I told him as well," he now laughs, causing me to lose faith. "Did you tell that fellow that you belong to an Alarm Battalion?" Briller asks, interested. "No, I was ashamed to utter the name of this heap and he did not ask at all," I answer softly. "We simply lay down our *Soldbuchs* in front of him and there was nothing entered in them. He already knew about our old division and so he did not ask any questions about it," Briller explains to me. "That's clear," I say, "the outcome has been decided and they are no longer interested." I add my commentary.

In the meantime rain clouds gather and the first drops drizzle onto the hot stone pavement in the yard, causing steam to rise. The poplar trees standing nearby begin to sway in the increasing wind. Our guards are relieved. Two others, covered in raincoats with small, rapid-fire weapons and ammunition belts, take the same places and stare at us, apparently in a bad mood. The soft hum of motors in the sky draws our attention. As the noise grows louder, our trained ears distinguish the familiar sound of the ME 109, which has been spread over all the battlefields of this war. Like a bolt of lightning out of the bright sky, it screams almost vertically out of a cloud bank, firing tracer ammunition into an American fighter plane below it. The American pilot guides the badly wounded metal bird upward as a black, ever-increasing stream of smoke pours out of the plane's engine. The ME 109 rushes over the farm at a low altitude and disappears in an elegant turn before the enemy anti-aircraft guns can fire at it. At the same time, as the American machine climbs toward the sky, a dark bundle falls toward earth until a white parachute unfolds and gently brings the pilot back to earth. The plane, now free of its pilot, wavers drunkenly in the sky for a few seconds and then, as though smashed by a gigantic fist, explodes in a mighty ball of flame and is scattered by the winds. We look with happy eyes at each other. Once again we are permitted to see war as we have known it.

Only slowly does the awkwardness of our own situation return to our consciousness. Instinctively I feel the eyes of the American guard resting on me and turn around, looking up at him. A faint smile can be seen in his face and the wink of his eye indicates his recognition of the German pilot.

"These guys are fair," Hocker whispers to Briller and me. "I would like to know that for sure," I say and dig out my cigarettes. Once again we squeeze the cigarettes between our lips and look inquiringly toward the Americans. A sergeant pushes his way to us on the outer edge of the shed, from whose roof the rain water trickles out in silvery drops from the leaky rain gutters. He tries to give us a light with his wet matches. The guards follow his vain attempts with interest. Finally, when they make themselves understood, one of them steps toward us and holds his burning lighter to our cigarettes. "No good, German matches," the sergeant babbles trustingly, but the American merely shrugs his shoulders and returns to his place. "You old fool," I hiss angrily at him. "For your entire life you have lit fires with German matches and suddenly now, in the eyes of the Americans, they are no good. Do you believe you can improve your own circumstances with this stupid prattle? I am convinced that every clear-thinking opponent has nothing but contempt for one who soils his own nest. What would you have thought of a Russian prisoner in a similar situation who chattered about his matches, which functioned fine in dry conditions and which he used just a short time before to light a cigarette while standing behind his machine gun to defend his land?"

Once again I turn in disgust away from this characterless scamp, who, without a word of response to my accusations, slips back into the dark shed and mixes with the other Germans.

"We will have a lot of trouble in the future with our dear comrades, if they continue to act this way." I bow my face in shame. "I would have liked to bust him in the nose, but we cannot show the Americans such conduct if they are to have any respect for us," Hocker cracks, just as angry. "We must hold out and watch out for ourselves; otherwise we will sink in our grief." Briller calms us with a warning just as the noise of a truck's engine in the back of the yard drowns out his last words. "Now, for sure, there will be something for us to eat," Hocker suggests, and all the men behind us become unruly like cows in a stall that can smell their feed. "Only two men at a time," a tall American calls, standing on the tailgate of the truck holding up two fingers. The truck is completely empty and the bed is freshly washed.

"Go ahead," the tall American indicates as we hesitate in front of the empty vehicle and look to Briller. Quickly we grab onto the sides and climb up, and Briller as the next follows. Happy to be together, we forget our disappointment and are already curious about where they will take us. Certainly there we will get something to eat since it is at least 6:00 P.M.

In no time the truck is completely occupied by German soldiers. The last to get on are three SS men with badly torn uniforms and swollen faces. The Americans chase them angrily back into the shed and slam the tailgate of the truck closed with one hand. Three powerful Americans armed with pistols make their way through the crowd and climb onto the truck. Slowly the vehicle begins to move with its sorrowful freight, reaches the main road in a few minutes, and starts to roll westward with accelerating speed. After about thirty minutes' travel time we see five American tanks encircled on the other side of the road close to the edge of a nearby wood. In the middle of the circle we recognize about three hundred Germans crouching on the ground. Slowly our vehicle turns onto a field road and rumbles toward the tanks. Our captured comrades look at us curiously as the truck stops and we are told to get out.

"Line up in two rows," we are ordered by an excited and unbelievably fat American whose shape brings us to laughter. "Macht schnell," he screams angrily, as he notices that we have very little respect for him. "That fellow has eaten way too much for us to take him seriously," I chuckle in high spirits to those around me and they in turn break out in laughter. We quickly form in two rows, in the firm hope that we will finally get something to eat. Once again the three of us stand in the front row and look for provisions, but none are to be seen.

Instead two Americans without weapons stand three steps away from us, and upon a signal from the fat one begin going through our pockets. Afterward we are driven through a line of cynically grinning Americans where a couple of U.S. soldiers, armed with red-lacquered clubs, urge us to sit down.

"Don't they give you anything to eat here?" is my first question to the unknown fellow sufferers next to me. "No, only the club, if you don't make yourself small and ugly," an older corporal answers. "That can be bad for us," Hocker indicates, sad and downbeaten. "Do you know when we will be sent on?" I ask the corporal. "Not today for sure," he answers, resigned to his fate and lying on his back in the wet grass.

Luckily the rain has stopped. We smoke without speaking. How long will we still have some? "I will make an inventory," I interrupt my friends, lost in their gloomy thoughts, and lay out the rest of my possessions between my widespread legs: a letter case with diary; four small photographs of my wife and me in Strasbourg; a list of my belongings in our apartment at home; the marching orders from Paris to Le Bourget; a telegram from my wife in which she reports the bomb damage our apartment had suffered; my *Soldbuch*; a handkerchief; a full pen and a pencil stump; thirty-one German cigarettes; the wedding ring on my finger; my shaving kit with a razor and twenty blades, a half-used bar of soap, shaving brush, a can of shaving cream, and a little bottle of after shave lotion. "You came away very good," the corporal indicates as I shove my riches back into my bag. "It's not the end yet," Briller throws in. "How many cigarettes do we have together?" I ask my friends, reporting my thirty-one cigarettes. "I have twenty-three," Briller announces. "And I have forty-four," Hocker laughs proudly. "Then together we have ninety-eight cigarettes," I conclude. "The corporal shall receive eight of them so that he can also smoke," I note, handing him five, to which Hocker also adds another five. "So that he has ten," the good Hocker laughs generously. "Many thanks," the man says, suppressing a little emotion.

Gradually the night descends upon us. Only the glowing points on the tanks indicate the location of the Americans. "Before I starve to death here, I am going to take off," Hocker whispers with a determined expression. "We would not get past the tanks alive, Willi." I try to talk him out of his insane intention. "Impossible," Briller agrees with me and as proof a tank machine gun peppers its tracer ammunition into the woods. "At least let us sleep in peace, you gangster," a man bellows out of the middle of our group, upset about the noise of the machine guns. "We are hungry," someone suddenly yells courageously. "Whoever mutinies will be shot," an American responds in a powerful voice from where the tanks are located, causing a brooding silence to lie over the captive soldiers. Overcome with fatigue and weak from hunger, we fall into a restless sleep on the cold, wet earth.

### 30 August 1944

After I awake from a terrible sleep, the first thing my eyes behold is the leaden gray sky. Tormented by absurd dreams, I need considerable time to find my way back to reality. I look at my surroundings, my entire body shaking from the wet and cold. Mist and thin fog clouds lie over the prisoners pressed tightly together. Here and there someone tries to warm himself through deep knee bends or running in place. The American guards stand on the ground and sit on the tanks wrapped in their warm brown coats with glimmering, yellow-gold brass buttons, their automatic weapons ready. A gnawing hunger rages in my empty stomach. Sleep still holds my two companions in its compassionate hands while my thoughts wander homewards.

Now the field mail service, which previously invisibly connected the front to the homeland, has been torn in two. Weeks will pass before my family will be informed by way of Geneva of my fate. Many days and nights of uncertainty will wear on them as they wonder about me. An immense longing seizes me and brings me to my feet. With numbed legs, I wander along the edge of the assembly area to restore some feeling to my limbs, to organize my thoughts, and to set myself in order. Since 1940 I have seen countless soldiers of the opposing nations fall into German captivity. Their fate was certainly no less difficult than mine. I estimate that since the war began over a million German soldiers have come under foreign custody in such places as Africa and Stalingrad. I cannot consider myself so important, especially not now, although a terrible hunger depresses me and all of the meanness and humiliation that I have recently experienced threatens to drive me to the edge of doubt. A number of situations that I have fallen into during the course of the war seemed hopeless and brought me to a confrontation with death. But still, to this day, fate has been kind to me and has provided a way out in every situation. The time in prison will also pass, perhaps earlier than I think. It depends completely on me if and how I come through it. I recall the saying I learned at my confirmation, which has accompanied me throughout my entire life: "My son, give Me your heart and let your eyes be pleased with My way." Good, we will see why I had to become a prisoner at this time. They will not allow us to starve, otherwise they would have executed us on the spot and saved the trouble of transporting and guarding us. A prisoner is ballast for the enemy, if not an immediate danger. We require guards and provisions. The first are missing at the front and provisions are dependent upon the supply convoys. Therefore we are not really as useless as I had previously thought. And then there are my two friends that, luckily, I became acquainted with while we were still free. Perhaps providence has arranged it this way.

During my wandering I come unexpectedly upon a group of German staff officers sitting on the edge of the camp area. Even a general staff officer with a red stripe on his trousers is among them. Amazed, I remain standing, looking at the gentlemen who still wear their medals. It is a mystery to me how these high-ranking officers, who must have known about the situation at the front, could have been captured. Or did they come to the Americans out of free choice? In the hospital I heard rumors about such officers.

"I think he is crazy," I hear an older major say to the others. Slowly I turn around and look at one of the tanks while my ears intensely take in the officer's conversation. "He did not listen to Rommel or Rundsted. Instead he just ordered a vigorous defense without allowing himself to get a correct picture of the situation," one of the men among them says with a sullen voice. "You could not expect anything better from a corporal," another throws in. "And I don't understand Keitel, who must be informed about everything and still accepts Hitler's orders." "He must be one of the first who realized that his Führer is crazy and still after the twentieth of July he announced in all openness his loyalty to him," another indicates in an objective tone. "What would you do in his position, when everyone watches every step and spies follow you?" the major asks angrily. "We don't know enough about the situation, gentlemen, so we'd better just drop the subject," a clear voice ends the conversation.

Deep in thought, I look for my friends, who sit smoking on the ground watching for me. "Back from your early morning exercise," they greet me, laughing. "I come directly from a section of the division staff and report to you obediently that the Führer is crazy," I answer and sit down among them. Obviously doubting my understanding, they look at me sharply and chuckle to themselves. "Have a smoke, Helmut." Hocker tries to distract me by offering me a cigarette while he continues to study my face. "I am not crazy, you sleepy heads, I only wanted to move around a bit and came upon a couple of high-ranking German prisoners whose conversation I indiscreetly heard." I remove from them all doubts about me. "Is there really a general here?" Briller asks, becoming curious. "No general, but a general staff officer with the rank of colonel," I explain to him and report what I have heard. "They always babble about such stupid things and then they lick the soles of Hitler's boots when they receive the Knights' Cross in their hands." Briller pushes away the talk about officers. "Hitler is crazy for them now that he can no longer use them," Hocker spits out contemptuously.

Still filled with bitterness, I look toward the wood's edge, from which a group of Americans are coming toward us. When they reach the German staff officer, they stop. After a short exchange of words, the German general staff officer salutes and goes into the center of the assembly area. "Listen up, all of you," he calls with a clear voice. "The Americans have just informed me that in half an hour we will be transported from here. They ask, therefore, that as soon as the trucks arrive we assemble in five rows so that we can be loaded as quickly and easily as possible. We are going to a collection camp in which we will immediately be given something to eat. Nothing will be taken from anyone. By this occasion, I want to ask you personally to keep order and discipline so that in our present situation we can impress the Americans."

Under the more or less loud curses and maledictions of the prisoners he turns and goes back to his place, where, his ego now built up by the Americans, he continues his conversation with the other officers.

"We want to make sure our cigarettes are secure," Briller indicates, taking his three packs of cigarettes out of his pants pocket. We follow, likewise taking all the cigarettes out of the packages and hiding them under the hem of our field blouses. In future searches, I will keep my wedding ring hidden under my tongue. Only my shaving kit, which I must carry in my open hands, remains in possible danger.

Two Americans armed with pistols mount the truck, which is completely loaded with Germans, and hold tight to the wooden stakes used for the canvas covers. Finally the black drivers slam the doors to the cab shut. With a jeep occupied by four Americans in the lead, slowly the convoy gets underway and reaches the highway. At a speed of about thirty-five miles an hour we roll westward through the area recently conquered by the Americans. After half an hour, we make a sharp turn to the south. We speed toward a village lying like a picture of pure peace, snuggled against the edge of the road.

In the village are beds and food, restaurants with cool drinks, and lusty girls—everything that a soldier longs for but which is now unattainable for us. Everything inside me strives to believe that this will be possible again. As the lead truck reaches the first houses in the village, it is greeted by the inhabitants standing along the street. But all too suddenly we see the raw reality in the form of rotten tomatoes, rocks, and fists raised in threat. In a frenzied rage and with wild, distorted faces, the French show their true faces for the first time in this war and what they really think about us. A hail of dirt and a cannonade of insults crack against us as we pass through this indignant mass of people. How is something like this possible, I grumble to myself as the whole affair is over and we roll through the poorly cultivated fields. You stupid German rube, I admit to myself, you always imagined that they liked you because you were so nice and friendly toward them. Greatly disappointed, I look at my countrymen who, like me, can only shake their heads about the French.

I feel that I have been forsaken by God and the world. My stomach cramps together and every nerve is in rebellion. An undescribable feeling of homesickness fills my breast which far exceeds all the bodily pain I have ever known. It is as though I have lost a loved one. But before I can control my feelings we travel through a small city and experience the same thing. We are lucky that the Americans sitting alongside us point their pistols at the threatening Frenchmen; otherwise they would tear us from the trucks and trample us to death. An old ugly hag, with a swelling on her forehead as big as a tennis ball, pours her chamberpot out of a window upon the defenseless German prisoners in the vehicle stopped in front of us. A hail of stones, which our comrades had caught from the French, cracks into the window of the old woman and she immediately clears out, disappearing into the interior of the house.

Finally the convoy continues on. Completely filthy, we escape from this awful town with its miserable people who act in raving madness to shower their hatred on defenseless prisoners. "That's the way it is with the 'Grande Nation'." I turn to Briller. "And we must handle them with kid gloves so that we don't hurt their pride," Hocker replies angrily. "Just once in my life, I would like to pass through this nest with my machine gun platoon," Briller thunders, slamming his fist on top of the cab, causing the driver to hit the brakes and then give the truck gas so that the passengers tumble on top of one another like sacks of potatoes. "Keep yourself under control, old man, otherwise you will have to get out and go by foot," I joke with my furious friend, who clamps a cigarette between his lips and waits impatiently for a light while another prisoner pulls, with considerable difficulty, a match from his deep coat pocket.

Gradually the ride becomes uncomfortable. Like animals for the slaughter, we remain squeezed together in a stupor. Finally the convoy nears Paris and we begin to prepare for the stormy reception we expect there, when the lead truck takes the road to Saint-Denis, which we reach after half an hour of slow travel. Prepared for everything, we stare at the few passersby on the streets, who hardly notice us at all. The quiet with which the citizens take our arrival seems unreal to us. To my complete surprise, I discover behind the closed window of a house an older man and two girls who wave furtively to us with their handkerchiefs. Not until we exit the city do a couple of young punks and pious hookers, with their repulsive gestures, blur the good impression that Saint-Denis has made upon us.

Already the sun is bowing in the west toward the sea when, in the vicinity of Chartres, we leave the main road and follow a secondary road to a meadowland surrounded by barbed wire in which about one thousand German soldiers are enclosed. I notice a water ditch which meanders through the meadows and awakes in me an insane feeling of thirst. Others in the convoy see the water too, causing a dangerous commotion. But the Americans have mastered the situation and have a large number of soldiers armed with clubs to maintain order as the trucks are unloaded. And it is only with brute force that they succeed after a few minutes in lining us up in marching order. Again and again they swing their clubs down on the dried-out bodies of the prisoners, bringing the half-mad men to reason.

I am pushed forward by the herd of prisoners, while Briller's tight grip prevents me from falling to the ground. "If we don't get something to eat here, then we will take off tonight," he cracks, full of doubt. Unable to utter another word, Hocker nods with sad eyes his agreement.

Finally the guards open the gate built of tree trunks. Once again our pockets are searched before we are allowed inside the enclosure. Only the thought of escape gives us the strength to stand upright and patiently allow ourselves to be searched. By now I no longer care what they take from me. My eyes see only the canvas bags in the enclosure where the first of our transport are gathered and drinking from the familiar spouts. Even before the searcher's dirty fingers are off me, I push my way forward and under one of the taps of the water container. Greedily I suck the precious water out of the bag like a piglet at the nipples of its mother and do not move away until Briller squeezes in next to me. Although my thirst is not satisfied in the least, I look around for Hocker and find him lying on the ground, his strength completely gone. I drag him next to Briller, who steps aside so that he can get some water. Only now I find the time and the interest to look around the area. The men from my transport lie in a wide circle like they have been mowed down, while a part of our predecessors mount the trucks in order to be transported on further. Still I feel the urge for water, but it is no longer possible to get to the bags, which are now encircled by a massive ring of thirsty men.

A considerable time later, Hocker reappears with a soaked field blouse and falls down in the grass beside us. "They will make perfect pigs out of us if this continues," Briller mumbles sarcastically to himself. "Perhaps that is what they want in order to drive the belief in a master race out of us," I mock. "They will only accomplish the opposite and will show us just how primitive they are," he answers in ridicule. "For the time being, I don't give a damn about that if they just finally give us something to eat. They are at least responsible for that after they have taken away our freedom," Hocker jabbers with tear-wet eyes which seize me with so much sympathy that I could commit murder to get him a piece of bread.

"Don't talk about eating, Willi, otherwise you will just get hungrier," Briller continues in an irrational tone. "It looks like the good air here is enough for you, and you are just happy to have saved your dirty hide." Hocker flies into a rage at Briller. "Put an end to trying to kill each other; then that will be the beginning of the end," I interject in order to prevent a useless conflict. Defiantly each one turns his back to the other and stares at the ground.

It has come this far. We begin to attack one another because of our hunger. This realization moves my heart to a previously unknown hatred for the Americans. We must undertake escape at any cost; the desperate decision to get out of this misery, or die trying, rips at me.

"Let's get some water to drink, friends." I try to bring about a conciliation. Without a word, they follow me to the water tank, where we lie under the spouts and fill ourselves. At least inwardly united, we return again to our old place and fall into the grass, where I keep a lookout for the Americans.

"What do you say about that?" I nudge my two companions and point with my finger to a group of Americans who come into the enclosure with boxes on their backs and then stack them up. "If there is no food for us, then I will eat grass the rest of my life," Hocker registers after a long pause. "You don't have to do that," I answer happily, then I notice that the Americans are tearing the bands from the boxes and taking the lids off. Already there is a steady movement toward the boxes. We too, shuffle in the immediate proximity of the feeding place, watching, with eyes like shy deer made tame by hunger, how the Americans carry in and open more and more boxes. Finally one of them asks me, "Speak English?" "A little," I answer him coldly. "Please put the men in five lines, right now!" he indicates to me, taking a small can out of the box which he throws into the air and catches like a ball. Fighting back my excitement, I mount a nearby stack of boxes and turn to my comrades. "Listen up," I call with a voice unknown even to me. "The Americans order that we line up in five rows so that they can distribute the provisions. Keep three steps' distance from each row and hurry up so that we can finally get something between our teeth."

If before I had imagined that I had learned somewhat how to handle soldiers, I am now bitterly disappointed. The men respond to my words like a scared herd of sheep chased by a fierce dog. Instead of lining up, they fight to get to the front while the weaker ones are run over without any consideration.

"Get in five rows, then we will get our provisions in the shortest time." I try once again to bring some reason to the herd. "Shut your mouth, you pretender," a private standing a considerable distance away bellows. "We don't need a sergeant any more. Get down off your throne and see that you get in line yourself."

Ashamed, I jump from the box and step toward Hocker and Briller, who are raging red with anger. "Come over here," a red-haired American waves to us, taking three small cans out of the box which he gives to us. "It's OK boys, we can wait until they get in the lines," he says to his comrades in a gloomy manner, whereupon we withdraw in anger about the lack of discipline shown by our fellow German prisoners.

"Such idiots." Hocker begins to cuss, staring at the small can in his hand. "No one would have thought it possible how they fall apart, especially in front of the Americans." "That's the way it is with the famous German discipline," I say dejectedly, "but let them do what they want; I am not going to worry about them. If they don't need a sergeant anymore, then we don't need any privates either." We watch the shameless action by the Americans as they beat the German prisoners mercilessly with their red-lacquered sticks after they try to use force to get to the boxes. "It had to come to this," I say bitterly and sit back down. "They do not deserve any better," Briller indicates, unmoved, staring at the can in his hand. "Damn it, I have such a hunger that I could eat a bloated cow. How am I supposed to get into this can of shit?" Briller laments.

I shuffle through my shaving kit for something to open the cans with while Hocker walks along the ditch looking for a sharp-cornered stone. Briller slams his can against the iron on his heel until a white broth gushes out of the hole. He quickly puts the can to his mouth and begins sucking out its contents. "What is inside?" I ask, shaking with greed and listening to the noises Briller makes trying to eat from the can. "It tastes like carrots and meat," he answers. Filled with impatience, we beat the cans against our iron heels. Finally, what looks like a hole appears in mine, but I can't get any juice out even though I suck on it like a crazy man. It smells like ham or eggs," I think out loud. "Then the junk in my can is decayed, and I have swilled the broth," Briller wails in despair, throwing the can into the grass.

Hocker returns with several stones in his hands. Busy like woodpeckers, we work with the sharp rocks on the cursed cans until a long crack opens in the side which, with the help of my razor, I spread apart. Now I squeeze the index finger of my right hand through the crack, and with it I drill into the soft contents of the can. Twisting it slightly, I pull it back out of the can and with a sudden motion pinch part of the pudding-like mass into my mouth. Not certain what it is that

I am eating, I continue this process until it is clear that the can is empty though hunger rages more strongly in my bowels. Terribly disappointed, I look to my two comrades who, still in doubt, search in their cans for any remaining bit of food. Angrily I throw the empty can into the ditch and stare at my index finger, which in contrast to the others is clean on the upper half. Not once did we wash our hands before we ate, although water was right under our noses.

Hungry and full of disappointment and despair, we fall on our backs into the grass and stare at the nearly cloudless sky where the first stars can already be recognized.

Along the barbed wire, the guards light small campfires. "We should find a place for the night," Hocker says, gloomily breaking our silence. "Here along the ditch it is very damp." We get up without a word and look over the fenced-in meadowland. "It doesn't matter," Briller indicates and begins to pull out the grass, preparing a place to lie down. "Don't bother with that, Briller," Hocker interrupts him with a weak voice. "Down there where I found the stones there is dry reed grass and bulrushes that will give us a good mattress."

Weak-kneed, we walk along the ditch to the place Hocker has discovered. Listlessly we collect the sparse grass and carry it to a dry place and pile it up. Exhausted, we lie down upon it. How long will it be until we will be able to sleep in a real bed? That is the thought that rattles in my tired brain. How good it would be if we could be changed into birds and could fly home. What are they doing and thinking at home right now? Do they sense that something has happened to me? I wrote my last letter in Le Bourget on August 17. Their letters to me will be returned and when they arrive the senders will be shocked terribly.

We must risk escape in order to save our loved ones the awful distress. We could simply head eastward during the night across the fields and feed on fruit and other plants from the fields. Within a month we would reach the Rhine or else a bullet would catch us and put an end to the whole misery. We don't know if the Americans will turn us over to a farmer as is the usual practice in Germany. Then we would at least have food and a bed. Perhaps the German divisions will return and bring us freedom. Certainly Hitler will counter the advance of the Allies on the Marne and in the Ardennes with his own offensive. Then the French will spit on the Americans like they are now doing with us. I certainly would not want to be a Frenchman in that situation because there are now too many bills to be paid after they have shown us their true face. Is it weakness or simply natural sleep that lulls us into such quietness and allows such thoughts to swirl through our minds?

It could be about three o'clock in the morning as I am awake. Still lying on my back, my eyes search the distant heavens as the gray of a new day begins to lift my spirits from point zero. My two friends lie next to me in a death-like slumber. Quietly I get up and attempt the first steps with my stiff limbs on this, the third day since we were captured.

Like a piece of iron drawn by a magnet, my steps guide me to the barbed wire that encircles us. With both hands in my pockets I stand staring at the awful barbs of wire. Only man, in his complete baseness, is capable of coming up with such a terrible means with which to spoil God's free earth. Do I see these rows of barbed wire for the first time today? Certainly not. During the long war years I too have set up the huge rolls to protect our positions. Even in my childhood I saw the cow pastures encircled with it in order to control the movement of the animals that were kept there. Why does this same wire look different in my eyes today? This time its barbs are directed toward my flesh and force me to finally respect it.

"Why are you standing at the fence and not sleeping?" A strange voice from the other side unexpectedly tears me from my brooding thoughts. Gnomelike, a figure stands in the dark gray of the early fog on the other side of the wire and points a rifle at me. "Shoot me if I am bothering you." My sleepy blood boils over while my eyes search for a good rock to throw in the American's face.

"Your dangerous words indicate that you are very bitter," he continues calmly in a quiet tone. "Why do you ask about a prisoner of war? Your comrades haven't shown such interest." I enter a dispute with him. "You must not believe that all Americans are scoundrels who want to rob you. In a few days you will be in a real camp in which you will be registered, clothed, and shipped to the United States. Then you will think differently about us," he indicates, hanging his rifle on his shoulder. "I am anxious to see if you speak the truth. Each time we are transported we are promised provisions, but for days we have received nothing except for the little cans last night," I answer him in a skeptical tone. "Go back a couple of steps from the wire and sit down, I will be right back. Here, smoke a cigarette so that I can find you again," he stammers, quickly throwing me a cigarette over the fence before heading toward the direction of the American tents.

Although I wonder what his conduct means, I sit a few yards from the fence and wait without expecting much when he returns. Then it comes to me that the fellow speaks very good German. I wonder if he is a German American or a trained spy. Observing the cold American cigarette in my fingers, after a few minutes I hear steps quickly approaching. With difficulty my eyes strain to penetrate the dark twilight and the thin fog. Like a shimmering figure, he appears at the fence and makes a soft sound which can only be for me. Cautiously I get up and respond with a subdued hello. "Come here, German," he whispers enticingly over the fence and I clearly observe a paper bundle that the man pulls out from under his coat. "Do you want to coax me to the fence so that you can do away with me?" I let slip unintentionally from my lips. "Here, take this and be at this place tonight at midnight. My name is Eric and my parents are from Stuttgart," he bubbles, ignoring my terrible suspicions and extending the bundle toward me through the fence.

Impulsively I spring to the fence, grab the bundle with outstretched hands, and dash back to my place. Without waiting for any thanks, the man disappears as though into the earth. Only the movement of the disturbed wire still vibrates in the early morning dark. With beating pulse I rip open one corner of the warm package and kneel in the grass, overwhelmed at the view. Spread out before me is a cooked chicken from which the steam rises, sending my senses into confusion.

As quickly as I can, I rewrap this fantastic splendor and speed back to my comrades as though I were being chased. "Hey, you sleepy heads." I shake them awake. "Look at this!" Still drowsy with sleep, they stare at the bundle, whose secret the paper covers. Suddenly Briller jumps up, seizes the package, and brutally tears the wrapping paper to shreds. Completely confused and unable to utter a word, he gapes in unbelief at the chicken, bread, cigarettes, and chocolate lying in the grass. "Divide it into three parts, Willi." I turn to Hocker with a trembling voice. With fingers like the claws of a bird of prey, he seizes the chicken and tears it apart exactly in the middle. Before I can describe the process, he separates the drumsticks with a twist. Without losing a single word, he shoves the two drumsticks toward me, takes half of the rest in his hands, and sinks his teeth into the yellow skin. Shreds of skin hang from his mouth like a bedspread. Satisfied, Briller and I grab our portions and then nothing but biting, chewing, and swallowing can be heard from three completely starved and half-crazy human beings. Minutes later the pale bones, completely cleaned of every piece of meat, lie at our feet. "Now divide the bread, Willi," Briller breaks out impatiently. With a few pulls, the bread is torn into three parts. It is just a small loaf of white bread, about three hundred grams, and is gobbled up in a second. Have we really had something to eat or is it a hallucination? Have our stomachs become barrels without bottoms?

"We will never be full, friends," Hocker forms my thoughts into words. "Let's eat the chocolate now and then drink the canal dry," Briller suggests, seized by his desire for food. "Listen to what I suggest, fellows," I attempt to persuade my companions. "As you can imagine, these things were given to me by an American. The man is a German American and understands our situation. He maintains that we will be sent by ship to America in a short time. Be that as it may, I don't want to starve to death either in the USA or here in France. Tonight at midnight I am supposed to go back to the same place where he spoke to me. Certainly he will not come with empty hands. If we save the chocolate now and that which we will receive tonight, then we will have a small stock and can eventually slip through the wide strand of wire after midnight. I believe, after my conversation with this philanthropist, that here will be our last opportunity to escape and later we don't want to regret that we have let it pass by. What do you think?" I ask my friends and look at them intently. "It is a good idea, Helmut, but have you found a hole where there are no guards?" Briller says thoughtfully. "No, but when night falls, we will keep the guards in sight. Certainly they are convinced that we are all too weak and no one is thinking about escape. For that reason they will not be very alert. Up to now nobody has counted us and they won't be aware of our escape once we have passed through the fence unobserved." I explain my thoughts completely. "Agreed," everyone declares at almost the same time. "Then let's get some water to drink, then go back to sleep so that tonight we can cover as much ground as possible," I encourage my friends as I stand to my feet and move in the direction of the water sacks.

With a proud feeling in the breast that we have a worthy goal in sight, I return with Hocker and Briller from the water tank back to our places. My companions close their eyes from the rising sun and fall into a deep sleep while I restlessly ponder the best way to get back home. If we can slip through the wire at about 1:00 A.M., we can cover about twelve miles toward the east before it becomes day. That will take us nearly to Melun. Once we cross the Seine, the next big natural obstacle will be the Marne. In any case, it would be the devil's fault if we can't accomplish what many before us have done.

### 1 September 1944

"It depends on what the Americans give us to eat tonight. I consider it nonsense to take off into the unknown without anything," Briller says to Hocker. "What do you mean here in the unknown?" Hocker prods him. "Is there perhaps something here besides the constant hunger?" "He said that the American told him about our upcoming transfer and I don't believe that they want to take us to America to let us starve to death," Briller utters his sentiment. "Apparently you have not yet been burned enough, my dear. Don't you remember the flyer we found by Saint-Sauveur in which they urged us to desert and they would give us the same provisions that they give the American soldiers? At that time, we did not believe it anyway and were not at all interested, but today we know that it is all lies and falsehoods. Just take a look at yourself, at what they have made of you. It's too bad that I don't have a mirror so that you could see your face," Hocker ends his speech.

"Thank you for the explanation. Your face is enough so that I can imagine what I look like. But don't misunderstand me, I am in favor of escape, it's just that there must be certain conditions," Briller explains. "Then once again we are united, old fellow," I conclude. "We will create the necessary conditions today. I suggest that we snoop around among the comrades and see if someone has a compass. Trust me, for chocolate or cigarettes you could buy a house in Germany." "First let's smoke one ourselves; I'll go get some matches; perhaps it will be the occasion to find a man with a compass." Hocker jerks himself up and goes away.

"Don't you have your heart in the planned operation, Robert?" I ask Briller after Hocker has left the two of us alone. "To be honest, Helmut, your plan is fantastic. But to cross the rivers and roads, we can't live from apples alone, and on the isolated farmsteads there are dogs that will prevent our approach. It is for certain that my heart is in it, but my reason wants security," he answers me truthfully. "I understand your inner struggle, Robert, but we really have nothing to lose and we can only win or fail," I pressure him. "Listen, Helmut," he falls into his local dialect and lies on his back. "You know that we have known each other for a long time and that we have fought many fights together, but don't take me wrong if I now tell you my opinion. You have changed during the last days. When I got acquainted with you, everything about you was based on reason. Only seldom did your feelings show through. At that time I secretly admired you because I was so careless and that is why I stayed close to you. I know that you did not like me very much in the beginning, but later I noticed a certain sympathy growing in you and I was very happy about it. Understand me correctly, I am still the same way today. But now as far as you are concerned, everything is based on your feelings. You nearly broke down over the mean actions of the French. I assure you, that did not bother me at all because I did not expect anything different from them. In Auxerre you were very angry because the madame tried to pass horse meat off on us as beefsteaks. That was a very small demonstration of feeling by you. But you washed it down with a cognac and that impressed me very much. To come to the point, old friend, listen to what I say. Use your understanding once again, throw your feelings overboard, otherwise I see only bad for you. One thing more, Helmut, I like you very much and I will stand by you regardless of what fate has determined for us."

I ponder Briller's words without being in a position to contradict him. I know only too well that he is right. But is it possible to step outside one's own skin? I want to go home, or at least to a German unit where I can be a man instead of rotting behind this barbed wire fence. How easily these words are said, even when they are meant to be taken seriously. Naturally they do not intend to let us starve, but a full belly is not the entire purpose of life. At least not for me. My grandfather had declared: "Man does not live to eat, but eats to live." Behind barbed wire there is no life, at the most that of a vegetable. But escape can bring life back to us!

"Hey, you sun worshipers, take me with you," Hocker calls to us, following from a distance. "Man, you have to haggle with those guys like an old Jew," he laments after he catches up with us. "You can't believe how expensive every pants button has become." "Do you have a compass?" Briller asks, abruptly stopping Hocker's surging speech. "No, but we can get a pocketwatch. But the fellow wants thirty cigarettes for it and it is an old clock that the Americans didn't even want," he observes further. "We can do business with him. If he is a smoker, then he will give us the watch for twenty cigarettes. In any case we must get the watch as a substitute for a compass," I say in conclusion and bend over toward the ditch.

Half an hour later we lie in the grass with clean-shaven faces and enjoy a cigarette in the warm sun. It may be ten o'clock and there is nothing going on in the camp. Only here and there a few German prisoners slip to the watering place. Bored, we doze along the fence in front of the American guards. Tonight we will flee from this unworthy life and, like animals in the free wilderness chased by humans, take up the fight for our existence. A joyful prickling feeling surges through my entire being with these thoughts. Happily I wink at my two comrades, who are deep in thought. Suddenly Briller jumps up and looks with complete interest toward the camp entrance. "What's going on, Robert?" I ask indifferently. "A whole bunch of Americans are coming into the pen," he answers, disturbed, and I raise up and look toward the gate. It is true, they are carrying tables and typewriters into the camp which they set up near the entrance. "Look out, they want to bind us with their papers." "Let them," Hocker pipes up cheerfully, "tomorrow morning they can cross us off their list."

A terrible, penetrating whistle shrills over the peaceful, sun-drenched meadow. "Everyone line up immediately in five rows!" a small, black-haired American bellows in perfect German. "Now we are in for it," I mumble, surprised. "If he is no German, then I will eat the broom and the cleaning lady." "Let's go men, let's see what's up." Briller springs to his feet.

Distrustful, but full of curiosity, we shuffle at a snail's pace toward the small American who has positioned himself, like a grown-up drill sergeant with a puffed-up breast, about twenty yards in front of the other Yankees, looking with apparent disfavor at the slovenly group coming toward him. Fully conscious of his own importance, he points condescendingly to the ground a few steps in front of himself as we approach, and proclaims in an authentic Heidelberg dialect: "Begin here, gentlemen, and please hurry up."

So, I think after I observe the man carefully, here is one of the victims of Nazi Germany. Triumphantly his black eyes beam at us while his hand strokes the brand new holster with the handle of an equally new pistol hanging out. Slowly the five rows are formed. A few U.S. soldiers, armed only with clubs, push their way deep into the camp and drive the laggards to the gathering place. Finally, it appears that all prisoners are assembled since the Americans begin to organize the mixed-up herd into fifty groups. Very much accustomed to our mentality, the outlaw German Jew throws out a few encouraging words of humor into the crowd, which accomplishes more than all the club swinging by his American comrades. The Germans respond voluntarily to the call for proper distance and intervals.

"The first group to the table furthest to the right, march!" the wiry man commands, exactly like a German master sergeant sending his company out on a detail. Automatically we march just like we were on an army post to the table, on which three typewriters stand, behind which three American clerks slump in their chairs in the most awful manner. Glumly they see in us only work to be done. Within our group, three American soldiers position themselves to keep order. The organization is good. We could envy them. After some minutes I stand before a typewriter and wonder at the agile fingers of the typist who looked so tired a few moments ago. After I give my name there follows my birthdate, birthplace, weapon type, the number of my division, and the place where I was captured, all of which is typed on a form A-4. Before I can retreat another American hangs a postcard-sized label on my upper left pocket button with the printed letters, "Prisoner of War." "That is your new proof of identity," he indicates affably and turns me over to one of the guards, who lets me back into the camp. I stop at the water bags and in complete peace I drink in preparation for the coming dry days. Directly afterward, something registers in me which I had not noticed since our stay in the valley on August 26.

Acting against all unwritten rules for prisoners, I run as fast as my legs will carry me to the slope of the ditch and drop my pants. It is not much that my body gives out as excrement, but one must be thankful for the smallest indication that everything is still functioning. Then I cover the signs of the saving deed, like a cat, with earth. "Man, why did you take off like you were crazy across the meadow?" Hocker asks, worried, and standing on the rim of the bank. "If you can guess what I have hidden, then you will get exactly half of it." I grin unashamedly. "Thanks a lot, I understand," he laughs. "Were you really successful?" "Just a little bit, but hopefully in the future it will be regular," I answer, satisfied, and step toward Hocker as Briller comes up behind him.

Together we return to our usual place, where we study the prisoner of war cards: "Prisoner of war surrendered at Soissons on August 29, 1944." "Very good," I say, "we will need this receipt when we get to our troops. It proves clearly that we were captured." "On the other hand, you should have had it dated before today, Helmut; then without a pass the Germans will certainly not take us in." Briller pulls my leg and spits in a high arc upon a flower which pushes up out of the earth. It is high time to think about our winter camp. At home the dahlias and the asters are in bloom. The wind blows over the wheat stubble. Fall and winter bring the worst time. We are going into the fifth year of this terrible war. Soon snow will lie on the graves of its countless victims.

"Let's look up the man with the watch." I turn to my comrades, who are busy removing the dirt from under their fingernails. "They are far from being finished with all their paperwork," Hocker answers, stretching his neck toward the gate. "Isn't it necessary for people to have three meals a day?" Briller throws out the long-feared question. "It is at least noon," Hocker adds, "and they do not make any indication that they are going to distribute any food." "Let's divide a package of chocolate, Willi; it would be wrong to rob our stomachs of the last piece of internal fat." Like a mean villain grinning at the tricks pulled on his companion, Briller takes in my words, wrinkles his face, and takes out of a side pocket of his field blouse the familiar American chocolate and throws it into Hocker's lap, still smirking at him. "Don't push the whole piece down your throat at once," Hocker teases him while handing him his share. "I hope a piece sticks in your throat so that in the future you will keep your mouth shut," Briller counters, letting a chunk of chocolate disappear behind his teeth.

"Shouldn't we go tank up on water?" Hocker asks. "The stuff is easier to swallow with a drink." "Do you want to bring this whole mob into an uproar?" I hiss at him. "What will they think when they see us munching on chocolate?"

"What they think is of no concern to me since yesterday, but you are right, we can't make life more difficult for the poor devils," Briller mixes in. After we get rid of the traces of our secret meal, we make our way to the water bags with thirsty throats just as the bags are being filled by a water wagon.

At least they provide water for us, I express my thanks. We can't complain about the treatment either. Even the Jew was not mean, but conducted himself correctly. With great care some Americans look after the water bags around which the spilled water has formed puddles. A gray-haired American takes a shovel from the truck and begins to dig a drainage ditch for the water. It does not occur to him to give the assignment to one of the many Germans standing around, which would have been expected. How different the Americans are. In general, their army is composed of older soldiers than the Germans. Is that why their treatment seems better? Their breakthrough at the Cherbourg bridge-head and the accompanying push toward Paris was anything but stormy, in contrast to our quick advances which resulted in lightning-like encirclements. But they have at their disposal an almost unlimited supply of weapons and matériel while after four years of war we are at the point of burning out.

The gate to the camp is opened by two guards. A truck rolls into the cage and stops in front of the gathering place. With great carelessness a very tall American twists himself out of the doorless cab and stands in front of the truck with both hands in his back pockets in a very unsoldierlike manner. The Yankees who arrive with him begin to unload boxes of provisions from the truck, the sight of which causes our hearts to beat faster.

This time everything suggests that the distribution of the provisions will be orderly. Without being asked, German soldiers, resigned to their fate, form up in rows. A few do try to dance out of turn and get to the front of the rows, but the majority have come to grips with the situation and work to educate the resisters.

After an hour of standing, the three of us sit on our mats made from reeds and hammer with stones at the cans we have received. Today there are two cans for each man and they are about two inches longer than our well-known "iron rations." From the outside, both cans look the same; there is only a difference in the weight. It is clear that we try to open the heaviest first, and after yesterday's practice, we are successful. The label on my can reads "Meat and Beans." Without speaking, we scratch for the beans and meat with our index finger through the crack we have made in the cans, all the time our hunger driving us to a frenzy. "Dear God, if we could only once more eat to our satisfaction," Hocker curses, then throws the empty cans into the ditch where they sink without a sound into the water. Forcing myself to rest, I sit next to my friends, staring into space and accusing God and the world. The cans shine in my hands like they are polished while inside my body a crazed dragon appears to be demanding food. When I received the cans I had the thought to save one of them for the escape, but now I can no longer resist the inner urge and reach for the second can. Again working with the tools of the first humans we attack the latest example of the progress that the white race has made in the field of food storage, the tin can.

Driven by the fully operating instinct for self-preservation, we pound without pause on the tin shells until they bend to human will and let their contents go free. For the price of our sweat we receive four cookies, three candies, and three cigarettes. "The damn Americans have nothing but dumb stuff in their shit cans," Briller bellows, foaming at the mouth. "They must take us for fools," Hocker joins in. "We must disappear, we've got to get out of here; otherwise, they are just making a circus out of us," I continue further. "Let's go get some water to drink and look for the man with the watch," Briller commands as though he wants to say good-bye to the Americans on the spot.

We stop at the water bags, to which are now tied several empty cans as water cups. A comrade, who seems to be shaking in his boots, offers us three cigarettes for three cookies. "We ate them all a long time ago," Briller says, undisturbed, to his face. "The cookies are only crumbs by the time you pound the cans open," I join in the conversation with this frail little chap. "We made knives from the steel bands with which the food cartons were wrapped," he tells me with lightly suppressed contempt. "Do you have anything against me?" I ask him, somewhat amazed. "Not particularly, but all of those of your rank are guilty of the shitty situation we find ourselves in," he accuses me through his small lips. "Man, you don't look that dumb, to make a sergeant responsible for the entire course of the war. Who put the bug in your ear?" I ask him, becoming curious. "Most of the men here cuss you three because you keep to yourselves instead of asserting our right to provisions with the Americans," he answers. "So that's it," I say slowly, "and what was your opinion last night when, at the request of the Americans, I asked you to line up? 'We don't need a sergeant anymore,' is what you screamed. That's why you ended up getting beaten into line by the Americans until you were finally eating out of their hands. Tell that to your dear comrades. By the way, in accordance with the Geneva Convention, which is now in effect for us, you can at any time elect a spokesman to represent your point of view to the Americans."

Still, I feel sorry for the poor victims of war even though I am one of them. But from now on away with such useless feelings. I suppress my rising sympathy and turn my thoughts to escape.

"Do you think you can find him again, Willi?" I ask Hocker after Briller and I catch up with him. "He is sitting over there with his buddies," he indicates with his chin toward a group of men lounging on the ground. "Hey, fatso," Hocker calls to the man and waves him to come to us when he looks up. "Do you still have your clock?" he asks affably while we drop to the ground. "Yes," he answers. "Let me see it," I inject myself into the conversation.

With dirty fingers he takes the watch out of the upper pocket of his field blouse and lies it in my hand. It is a very ordinary nickel-plated watch which could be purchased in France for three marks. "How much?" I ask the man. "Forty cigarettes," he answers without blushing. "This morning you asked thirty cigarettes," Hocker laughs at him. "Then the Americans had not given out any cigarettes," the man answers indifferently. "In the next camp a less modest American could find favor with the primitive thing and then you would lose it." I make an attempt to lower the price. "Yes, and your cigarettes, too." He turns the tables on me. "You have a good business sense, how about thirty?" I ask. "Nothing doing, forty and not one less." He remains firm. "Then keep it; what time it is doesn't matter anymore." I pretend to be uninterested and get up. "Good, give me the thirty cigarettes and it is yours." He finally comes around.

Exactly at 4:00 P.M. we lie down at our camping place. "From now on two can sleep and one stays awake. Who wants the first watch?" I ask without waiting for an agreement from both of them. "Me," Hocker volunteers. "Good, Willi, at 6:00 P.M. wake me; from 8:00 P.M. on we must keep a careful watch on the east fence, including the guards. I will meet my friend at midnight at the old place. I am anxious to see what kind of provisions he has packed for our trip," I say, snuggling into the mat of reeds.

Just as I start to doze off, I hear a loud engine noise. "Is something going on out there, Willi?" Briller asks sleepily without stirring. "There certainly is," I hear Hocker say quietly. "A truck convoy is rolling; I believe we will have company." "I feel sorry for them." Briller yawns and turns onto his other side.

A few minutes later a whistle tears us to our feet. Like an antpile that has been stirred up, the brown forms of the Americans pour en masse into the camp. Stiffened like pillars of salt, the German prisoners stand in their places and peer at the gate.

"Everyone line up in five rows in front of the camp exit," the black-haired sergeant bellows into the pen.

We are loaded into trucks with American guards. They distribute cigarettes and chocolate to those standing next to them. Although we are standing in the back part of the truck, the three of us also receive our share. Generously, the good man also makes his lighter available. Sometimes prisoners can be very thankful for the smallest sign of sympathy. But still the good-intentioned

American must energetically and repeatedly ask for his lighter back, which some scoundrel among us tries to keep for himself. Finally, under pressure of the entire group, the rogue returns the lighter to the good American after he has continually denied that he has it.

Slowly we roll into Alençon. I was here in the city before and my thoughts wander back to the past. How much has happened and what changes have taken place in the meantime, and it is only three months ago since I was wounded and spent the night here.

Silently and without sympathy the inhabitants of the terribly destroyed city stand on the road. Neither in a positive nor a negative sense do these people allow themselves to show their true feelings toward us. Who can they accuse? The defenders of the city, the Germans, are not the cause of the destruction. Only the attackers, that is the liberators, have turned everything into soot and ashes with their bomb carpets.

We now pass a church, made unusually beautifully golden by the sinking sun. It stands like a flare spouting heavenward in the midst of a crater landscape, as one of the last witnesses of this city to the downfall of all of Europe. Laboriously the column works its way through the rubble-covered and bomb-cratered streets. After we pass the last houses of a suburb, suddenly and unexpectedly we turn from the main street. Shortly afterward we reach our destination.

An enormous fenced enclosure lies before us, in which at least a division of German soldiers are crammed together. Vehicle after vehicle rolls through the gate and pours out its shocked cargo. It is a massive undertaking for the guard personnel to direct the new arrivals to the various components of the gigantic camp. Officers, noncommissioned officers, and soldiers are separated. Before the three of us comprehend what is going on, we find ourselves in a cage near the middle of the immense camp in what appears to be a section only for noncommissioned officers.

"A hearty welcome to you, comrades," an impressive man's voice sounds from behind my back. "Staff Sergeant Schulz is my name, presently a prisoner of war in Alençon, France," he introduces himself. We tell him our names and grin like Cheshire cats at the friendly man who has a pencil and a scrap of paper from a cement sack. "I am the man for everything around here, and I don't want to miss adding you to my list, since it is possible that our captors will eventually give us provisions either today or tomorrow based on the number on my list. By the way, you are in Compound 12, in case you missed it with your quick arrival. I am sorry I can't offer you a roof or a bed, but the sky has been considerate toward us and offers a wide star canvas over us. In this hotel there are no blankets or anything like that; therefore, based on my own personal experience, if you start to freeze, I suggest that you lie on your stomachs and cover yourselves with your ass."

"Do you always speak so much nonsense? Are you really that proud of your pig pen?" Briller smiles, already pleased with this fellow. "It pleases me that you at least deal with the situation with some humor. We have enough failures here who long ago lost their nerve." He follows up with Briller's joke and extends his hand. "When did they bring you to this side of the front?" he asks, keeping a sharp eye on us.

We give a short account of our story as a new circle of curious forms around us. "The Americans are already in Soissons?" is their only reaction, and they slowly separate from us.

Finally I have the time to look around my new surroundings. There is not much to see except for captured German soldiers, barbed wire, and a completely trampled meadow. Yet something does catch my attention that nearly stops my heart from shock. There is a tree in the compound whose roots have been uncovered by the hands of many men and the thin ends ripped off. The trunk is robbed of its bark. Only a few strands flutter brown and dead in the light evening breeze.

"Does the tree tell you anything, my friend?" Schulz interrupts my stare as he follows my gaze. "How long has this camp existed?" I ask tensely instead of answering his question. "I don't know, but this tree lost its bark and roots in the last few days." "Just like before, there is nothing here to eat," Hocker mumbles disappointedly to himself. "Where can you get a drink of water?" Briller asks, looking around the compound. "We only get water once a day, but that is supposed to get better, at least that's what the Americans have promised," Staff Sergeant Schulz answers him, but even he looks like he does not believe it. "It is slowly getting dark, men," he indicates, concerned. "If you want, you can sit next to me; I have a piece of cardboard at my place." Slowly we follow him into the right corner of the enclosure where he sits down next to a stick with his hat upon it shoved into the ground. His rolled up coat and an open piece of cardboard lie on the ground.

"Don't be bashful and take a seat, otherwise your legs will soon stick up into your empty gut," he encourages us, wiping with his hand the free spot on the cardboard as though he fears we might get our pants dirty. "Aren't you afraid that someone will take your coat?" I ask him after we have sat down. "Where will the thief go with it?" he laughs with a question. "He could go to the fence and sell it to someone else," Hocker answers in my place. "It's easy to see that you haven't been prisoners very long," he laughs, "otherwise you would know that behind barbed wire one does not go unobserved for a moment. Here you cannot even scratch your behind without at least twenty pairs of eyes seeing it." "Can you at least smoke a cigarette without being hit?" Briller asks cautiously. "Yes, you can, then some have them and besides this morning we received two small boxes which contained three cigarettes," he responds to Briller's question, who then takes a cigarette out of his boot. "Thank you, I don't smoke anymore." Schulz turns down the cigarette Briller offers him. "What do you mean anymore, comrade, have you given it up?" I wonder. "Yes," he indicates matter of factly, "if you can't get them, then the cigarettes really become coffin nails. In the beginning it is naturally hard to do without them, but I gave away the rest that the searchers left me and now it is easy for me to go without them." There is a lot of self-control in this man, I think to myself as I draw a deep breath of smoke which somehow makes me full but also weak. Tired, I let myself fall backward into the trampled grass and stare upwards into the stars.

Alençon, a city in France, on whose periphery today, September 1, 1944, at least fifteen thousand German soldiers are camping under the open sky under the control of American machine guns. Fate? Who can believe it? Where is the German military genius of which the history books never tire of reporting? Or with the invasion did they simply write us off in order to deceive the enemy and start an offensive from deep within our territory that will strike a blow of destruction? Questions, nothing but questions, which force themselves up during the long night and which neither I nor anyone else can answer.

### 2 September 1944

The warm rays of the mild September sun push aside the night and begin to change the dew into steam. A thick bumble bee circles around Hocker's nose, then lands on the small bridge of his nose, tearing him from dream land. "Man, I thought I was in the airplane that took me out of the encirclement at Stalingrad and I could once again feel the wound in my back. Instead the hum of this damn beast around my skull and a club of grass caused my back pains," he greets me with a sour laugh, disappointed with reality.

Nearly all the prisoners stand at the exits to their compounds, their hands in their pants pockets, gaping expectantly toward the main gate where a command sergeant major, whose face is covered with a Genghis Khan-looking beard, stands with other noncommissioned officers. "That fellow was appointed camp spokesman by the Americans and is the biggest swine that I have ever laid eyes on," Schulz continues his explanation. "He is from the eastern region, but describes himself as an Austrian and maintains that we are here thanks to the Führer. He barters with the Americans using watches and rings from our comrades and only returns a small part of the provisions he receives to those starving comrades who gave up their valuables. Later you can go with me and, if the opportunity arises, get acquainted with the American master sergeant who runs the entire store here. We consider him a rough fellow, but behind his rough exterior there is hidden the soul of a child which frequently pushes to the surface. Look over there; the completely rotten Austrian is raising his hand. That is the sign for the first three compounds to come and get their provisions. We must wait until he gives the sign a second time; otherwise he will put off the distribution for an hour or we will not get anything at all." Schulz ends his lecture and, with no shortage of volunteers, appoints eleven men to receive the provisions.

Finally the men come out of the American tents with boxes on their shoulders and follow in a file down the main street of the camp along which all of the compounds are located. Ready to move out, the eleven of us wait at the compound exit for the sign from the bearded one at the gate. When it comes, we move out in line and are joined by groups from Compounds 12 and 13. "How many men are there in Compound 12?" Genghis Khan receives Schulz with a domineering voice. In turn Schulz holds his list written on the cement sack paper under his nose. "How is it that you have 247 men today and there are only 244 on mine?" he asks Schulz bitingly. "I added three men to my list last night from the new transport," Schulz calmly answers. "They are not on my list!" he hisses and looks searchingly for help toward the tents from which a tall, broad-shouldered American steps toward them. "What is the matter?" he asks the camp spokesman. In fluent English the Austrian explains the situation. "Where are the men now?" The American giant turns to the like-proportioned Schulz. Quickly my friends and I raise our hands. "It's OK; the men are shaved and can't have been here very long," the Yankee observes keenly and disappears inside the tent. "It's all right this time," Genghis Khan finally responds, hard bitten, and clears the way to the tent. "The next time the lists must agree or you will get nothing." "Is that your food, perhaps, that the Americans are so stingy with anyway, you damned dog!" Schulz replies with considered calm and leads us into the tent.

In the half darkness inside the tent, the American master sergeant stands and sovereignly directs the German workers who pile up boxes of provisions on a rough-hewn, long table. In doglike submission and nearly overcome with fatigue, they wipe the drops of sweat from their faces after placing the provisions on the boards. Unstirred, the American observes them and rolls up his shirtsleeves, disclosing a row of German wristwatches which stretch from his wrist to his elbow. Like a child richly endowed by Santa Claus, he looks proudly and happily at his store of watches. It is out of the question that these Americans are aware of this injustice which they have perpetrated and how they have violated the Geneva Convention in taking these wristwatches; otherwise, they would not display them so openly.

"Let's go," he pulls me out of my contemplation, pointing with his red-lacquered stick to the tent exit, and I follow my comrades with empty hands. As useless as a spotlight on a bright day, I follow at the tail end of the column along the street, allowing my eyes to focus on the individual enclosures which do not differ in any way from each other. Everywhere German prisoners in dirty uniforms and beard-covered faces stand or lie waiting impatiently for the arrival of their food carriers.

"Ask the comrades to line up in two rows," Schulz calls after we reach the middle of the compound. "Helmut, you did not carry anything; please oversee the distribution and see that the comrades leave once they get their cans so that they don't come back to the feedbag twice; otherwise at the end there will be nothing left for you." He instructs me in this thankless assignment the way a veteran would handle a new recruit. Since my meal depends upon making sure that no one gets two rations, like a watchdog I observe each individual as he receives the cans from Briller and Schulz until he sits down someplace in the compound to eat.

"Here, watchman, you did a good job." Schulz throws me the last two cans after all 246 men have been fed.

Finally we can sit down to eat. At least the Americans here have given us a can opener so that we can quickly get to the contents of the cans. This time we have potatoes, yellow beans, and meat in the heavy can while the lighter can contains four cookies, coffee, and candy. Instead of acting like wild animals over this little bit of cold food, we keep an eye on Schulz, who takes a spoon out of the pocket of his field blouse and begins to eat with perfect manners like a cultured gentleman. After I stick two fingers into the can and shamelessly shove the solid mass of potatoes into my mouth, Briller and Hocker go after their cans and in a few minutes everything is gone. "If you don't have a spoon, then of course you must eat with your fingers." Schulz laughs and wipes his silver spoon on a clump of grass.

"Aren't you tormented by hunger, Schulz? After this thimbleful of food you blink so cheerfully in the sun," I ask the huge man in amazement while inside my stomach, still racked with hunger pains, a crazy struggle for the few calories is underway. "Do you believe that I would become full if I constantly talk and think about food? Naturally I have hunger like a lumberjack, but it is better if you don't talk about it and instead lie down so that you don't use up your strength," he answers, reclining on his back. "Let's have a smoke and then lie down ourselves." Hocker wrinkles his nose and points with his chin toward Schulz, whom he seems to regard as an unsympathetic snob.

Although Schulz's blameless manner strikes me as somewhat exaggerated, I still have a considerable measure of respect for him. The man is perhaps fifteen years older than we, but in any case he is much further ahead in practical wisdom. "How old are you, Comrade Schulz?" I ask. "In December I will be forty-three, if nothing comes up," he answers with a yawn. "You are from the area around Hanover?" I explore further. "Yes, but how did you know that?" he asks, sitting up. "Lie back down, I can tell by your accent." "So." He seems calm. "But you don't seem to have an accent, what corner of the world are you from—Schwaben?" "I am from Baden, also Hocker, but Briller is from the east." "I was just born there," Briller joins in our relaxed conversation as we close our eyes and allow the sun to shine on our dirty faces. "Most of my time was spent in the Reich. Later I married in my homeland and I still have a residence there." "It seems that you aren't happy with your wife," Hocker babbles out indiscreetly. For a long time I have felt Briller's secret sorrow without once poking at the wound.

"It was a disappointment, but otherwise not so bad," Briller communicates bitterly after a painful moment. "Now you know why I have led all the women around by the nose. With every whore who looked like my wife, I used all of the charm at my disposal until she was eating out of my hand and willing to renounce any payment. Then I went to bed with her so that in the morning I could leave her cold blooded," he divulges as though a long-plugged well is just unstopped. He then turns over and remains silent. We too fall into brooding silence.

At 3:00 P.M. we are scared out of a dull sleep. Tired and worn out, we bring our exhausted bodies to our painful feet, which have not been out of our boots for over a week. We finally receive water. A truck loaded with gas cans filled with water stands on the street and within seconds is surrounded by the thirsty prisoners. Like a rooster watching out for his hens, Schulz stalks out of the compound where he receives two cans of water from Genghis Khan and personally carries them to the middle of the camp. Automatically the inmates form up in two lines, three steps apart, with cans in their hands. However, things do not proceed without friction. There are outsiders in this camp but they are quickly brought to reason with a kick. A longtime prisoner describes to me the provision under which Schulz accepted the position of camp spokesman:

whoever cannot accept the discipline and order here must go to another compound. Naturally we receive our small can of warm water last. Schulz, who is much more familiar with American provisions than we, laughs as we cuss about the temperature of the water and takes a packet of coffee out of his pocket; grinning at us he pours the coffee into his can and stirs it with his spoon. Then, as though anticipating the pleasure, he brings the can to his mouth and with small sips lets the contents run down his throat.

"That's the way to do it, you greenhorns," he triumphs over our amazed faces. "Ja, does the rat poison taste good without being boiled?" we ask nearly at the same time. "Just try it; the Americans are a step ahead of us, and besides something like this is not possible with our stuff," he answers our question in a good mood. Quickly we fish out our packs of coffee and follow his example. He is right; the stuff tastes like coffee at Aunt Agatha's on a Sunday afternoon.

Somewhat stimulated by the coffee, we saunter around the compound and spy into the neighboring enclosure, in which noncommissioned officers are also housed. But the view offers only a little diversion.

Shortly before 5:00 P.M. the whistle sounds for roll call, which surprises us three newcomers. "What does that mean?" I ask Schulz in amazement. "It is just part of the daily routine and doesn't mean much. The Americans just want to make sure how many are interned, but they find out only when the French bring some back to the camp so that they can collect their bounty." "Take it easy and keep in line." I listen to Schulz's advice. "Is it possible to escape from here?" I ask. "It is possible, but the chance of getting by outside the fence is pretty slim. Besides, from here it is a long way to the front and the French are after every German they see," he answers me. "And they get a bounty when they turn in escaped prisoners?" I ask further. "That's what they tell us when they are brought back," he explains shortly and pulls me along to the camp street, where the men are forming up in five rows for roll call. "The faster it goes, the faster we get our two cans," Schulz whispers after we have taken our positions. That is why, I think, the huge group hurries so quickly into formation.

After thirty minutes Genghis Khan appears with the American master sergeant and separates the entire assembly into groups of fifty while some of the wisecrackers have all kinds of fun with him. Since Genghis Kahn goes ahead of the American Hercules and takes responsibility for the division, it is great fun for the jokers to quickly change places after they have been separated so that when the count is checked instead of fifty men there are forty-nine or fifty-four. This brings a reprimand from the Americans to the most hated man in the camp and the whole crew enjoys it with satanic joy. Of course the count is delayed considerably and the starving men worry about their small cans, although after they eat them they are more hungry than before.

Three U.S. officers enter the camp. Genghis Khan steps into the row and the master sergeant calls "Attention!" and reports. The rosters are compared. Minutes later the officers stride along the front row and inspect the compounds. A quick glance is enough to find that they are in order. "Do you believe that the count is correct?" Schulz asks me out of the corner of his mouth. "I have no idea," I answer, amazed at his question. "Tomorrow we will stand in the fifth row and then you can see how the prisoners deceive the Americans," he grins maliciously. "Exactly 6:20 P.M.," Hocker reports the time as Genghis Khan announces the count is over and dismisses the gigantic group. After about an hour we sit next to one another and devour our hunger rations.

Seven days have passed since we ate our last warm meal by the madame in the village near Soissons. Seven days? Unbelievable; it seems like an eternity. Pondering, I look at Hocker's face while my tired hands let the empty can drop. How small the fellow has become in these seven days. Deep shadows lie under his eyes which look at the world so sadly. What would one of the doves from Soissons now say if they could see him? In all likelihood they would spit at him just like nearly all French are doing today. Man, what miserable creatures we are.

"Are you day dreaming again?" Briller tears me from my thoughts when I do not react to his joke about a thimbleful of beans. "The less they give us to eat, the harder we must become." He thinks he must strengthen my resolve. "This time you are certainly right, Robert," I agree with him. "We must become bone hard because our flesh will certainly disappear with these miserable provisions." "Then that has its good side, because when the trumpets of Jericho blow on judgment day to sound the resurrection of the flesh, we can lie still since we consist only of bones." Schulz humorously follows the logic of our doubtful situation. "We laugh about it," Hocker joins in the topic, "but one thing is crystal clear; with what the Americans have given us during the past days, we will not survive past October." "Then let's make out our wills," I mock him and pull out my fountain pen.

Thirty minutes later we are asleep. In an unconscious state we are free of thoughts about our situation and our sorrowful existence.

### 3 September 1944

Crashing thunder and quivering lightning open the new day. With fearful hearts we sit and look into the sky at the cloud banks that are piling up and are being driven eastward by a strong wind. God be merciful toward us and let this bitter cup pass by us, is the hope of thousands of prisoners in the Alençon camp.

Woe to us if the sky now opens its sluices and sends rain to soak these meadows and fields where, surrounded by barbed wire and unprotected, we are subject to the weather. No drop of rain has fallen. Still the force of nature hesitates and seems to be in conflict with itself.

"In any case we must dig a drain ditch around our camping place." Schulz brings our attention toward the sky back to earth as he begins to loosen the grass with his spoon like a little boy playing in a sandbox. Listlessly my gaze hangs on the little tool while my brain moves lazily in thinking about the amount of work that such an undertaking requires. And still the three of us follow his example and begin to scratch with cans a small ditch around our camping place. In the course of time we become enthused about our progress and work with more inspiration to dig deeper into the soil until we are satisfied with what we have accomplished. We lie our tools down and sink exhausted upon Schulz's coat which he has spread out for us.

In the meantime the wind has blown the clouds into shreds and driven the threatening weather eastward. Individual sunbeams shine out from the grotesque images in the eastern sky. Around us comrades hesitatingly follow our example and now stand in the middle of their work with one group trying to outdo another. The American guards stand at the fence with grinning faces and observe the digging Germans.

"It's twelve o'clock," Briller announces the time as we get in line and Schulz returns with ten carriers. "Soon we will have food, you fidgety heinie." I grin at Hocker, who nervously shifts from one leg to another. "If we could just get full only once, then I would sleep all day long and would not have to trouble my brain with finding a way out," he laughs tiredly to me. "Haven't your efforts been rewarded? I mean, whoever searches so carefully for a way out must sooner or later come to a resolution," I ask him jokingly and then I am ashamed of myself that I might have angered the fellow. But he does not indicate any concern; instead, he suddenly bends to me trustingly and whispers in my ear, "Yes, I have a way out. Tonight we will sneak into the provisions tent and steal a whole box. You don't need to do anything more than stand as a lookout and take the chest for me. Before it is light we will have eaten it all and buried the remains." "You are crazy, Willi," I respond. "The tent is guarded and Genghis Khan and his helpers sleep inside the tent. Get that thought out of your head." "Then I will do it alone." He remains firm. "That is all we need, that you throw yourself to the dogs by such a hopeless act of despair. Do I have to play nursemaid tonight so that my old companion doesn't do anything foolish?" I growl. Somewhat disappointed at my words, he avoids my gaze. But from this moment on, I know that he is in danger. Once he has planned something he will transform it into action. From now on I must pay attention to the fellow. I clearly remember the same look on his face by the entrance to the hotel in Soissons when we needed the bicycles to get out of the village. It is the same face which in broad daylight and with empty weapons made its way through front yards of blooming flowers in the enemy village and pushed on to the nearby grove of trees. This obstinate mouth is the same one that counseled Briller to hold the old man under the water until he became calm.

"Schulz, is it possible to secure a box from the provisions tent without being shot full of lead?" I ask, much to Hocker's surprise, in the quiet afternoon. "You are wasting your time thinking about that. Let me tell you of an episode that occurred here shortly before your arrival," he explains as though he had expected the question. "I will make it short," he begins. "The thought to get full at the source comes up quicker than anything. It is no wonder that the second night after the tent was set up a break-in followed. The fellows went to work carefully. Like snakes, they worked their way past the guards to the back of the tent and loosened two of the tent stakes. Calmly they made their way inside the tent and took three boxes of C rations and brought them back undisturbed to their compound. But one committed a serious mistake. Out of pure arrogance he took the guard's rifle that was leaning against the tent. At the same time a second group of prisoners was on its way to the tent and they had no idea that they were following behind the others. They arrived at the tent shortly before the relief guard detachment and they were discovered by the Americans who were searching for the rifle. You can imagine what an uproar that caused. Still, the second group escaped and reached the first compound, where the men worked their way through the barbed wire back into their own compound. The first group took advantage of the spectacle. They cut their way through the two rolls of concertina with stolen wire cutters and took off with the rifle." "And if they haven't died, then they are alive today," Hocker interrupts Schulz's story with an unbelieving smile. "I can almost believe that," Schulz continues undisturbed, "but the entire camp had to suffer through two hard days. Not only did the Americans dig up every mole hole in the compounds, but we didn't get any provisions. Since then the camp spokesman and his helpers sleep in the tent and the guards shoot at every mouse that moves in the area of the tent at night. If you want to commit suicide and burden the camp with additional suffering, go right ahead." "I have nearly forgotten my hunger." Hocker kids him further.

"Haven't you heard what is waiting for us up there?" I try to straighten him out. "I am going to see for myself how watchful the Americans are," he throws out, getting up to go to the latrine.

"He will try it for sure," Briller flusters, dispirited, and stomps an innocent can with the heel of his boot. "From now on we will have to keep an eye on him at night," I whisper to Briller. "The boy is not that dumb that he will run blindly into destruction," Schulz protests strongly. "You don't know him," Briller speaks to him. "He was the best reconnaissance patrol leader in the entire battalion and whatever the fellow gets in his head, he will carry out, you can be sure of that." "Tonight let's go as food carriers and take a close look at this future scene of action," I suggest. "Perhaps he will come to our point of view, or perhaps there is a possibility to get to the fodder trough." "It is all nonsense," Schulz interjects. "Don't think that you are the most cold-blooded among the fifteen thousand men here. I will sell the coat to fill you up and that is all. Others don't have a coat and they have not frozen." "I would just like to know how our dear comrades are doing in the Russian prison camps when the civilized Americans allow us to starve," Briller seems to be asking the Almighty.

My own thoughts wander to the eastern front. Briller's question is nearly as complicated as the question asked by all of mankind about what will happen in the afterlife. In both cases no one has returned to give an answer. But I know one thing for sure: just as the curious could transport themselves to the other side through suicide and will not do it, I do not want to change my place in an American prison camp with one in a Russian camp. Although I know a number of comrades who are in Russian captivity, I am thankful that fate has kept me out of the hands of the Russians and from perishing on the endless steppes or tundra.

Hocker joins us again and lies down silently next to me. Either he has given up his intentions or the decision still stands anchored in his unconsciousness. Whatever, a nearly cheerful glow radiates from his small, suntanned face. "We must look for other possibilities to get some more food," I whisper to him in order to find out his secret and not to disturb our slumbering friends. "Oh, let's forget about it and close your eyes; then your stomach will think it is night and leave you in peace," he explains softly as he closes his eyelids. "So that's it," I conclude and turn over onto my stomach to take a nap. The loud sound of engines in the sky disturbs my sleep. "Oh, now they are taking part in the war again," Schulz mumbles, half asleep, surrendering to fate. "Is there an airfield close by?" I ask, observing a transport in the sky. "Yes, from here the Americans send food and supplies to the front," he explains sleepily.

Around five o'clock, a gentle kick wakes me from my short midday nap. "Time for roll call," an ill-tempered passerby explains to me. "Let's go to roll call." I wake my friends and then stand up stretching and yawning toward the sun. Once again we shuffle along the camp street and foully hang back in the last row. This time I observe the play with Genghis Khan and enjoy it immensely. I only wonder where these guys have the desire to undertake such mischief since it does cost a great deal of energy to crawl on all fours as fast as possible through the rows and endure a painful kick or two given in anger by humorless prisoners. In response to my question about this, Schulz shrugs his shoulders, noting, "They are the ones who know how to live here among us. There is no shortage of provisions for them here. For the bashful prisoners who still have something, they act as intermediaries, or they rub dried shit into dust and sell it for cacao. The devil only knows what they already have behind them; in any case in the present situation they stand above us." "We must fit in, Schulz, and not wait until the fried doves fly into our mouths. It is the strong ones that survive such times." I offer reproach about our inactivity. "Don't confuse the issue, Helmut. The street dogs are those who nourish themselves from garbage and keep above water that way. I will bet you that these fellows grew up in the poorest of circumstances, if not in an orphanage, or a boarding school. If someone perishes here, it is the intelligent ones. It does not have to be hunger that kills them, but the spiritual depression that finishes off useful people behind barbed wire. That is foreign to these fellows. Either they never did have it, or it was stifled at a very early age," he corrects me with father-like sympathy.

After the distribution of the water, Schulz slowly stirs the powdered coffee in his clean can. Like an animal of prey, Hocker watches Schulz's hand which holds the much-desired spoon. Schulz is oblivious to his surroundings and lost in his anticipation of the drink. Just in time I notice Hocker's fluttering nostrils, which indicate an imminent explosion that threatens to disturb our good situation. Without speaking a word, I take the spoon out of Schulz's hand and pass it to Hocker. "Stir your own coffee first, Helmut; some people maintain that they think about others, but in practice it seems to be different." He cannot resist this biting observation. Amazed, Schulz looks at Hocker, but only shakes his head and drinks the first swallow of coffee.

After we hold the empty cans in our hands and are feeling sorry for ourselves, I conclude that the moment has come to offer a serious word to my companions in order to avoid future dissension. "How would it be," I tear them from their lethargy, "if in the future we undertake to treat each other with better manners and more consideration, as is common among most human beings, rather than allowing every trifle to cause trouble among us? Nearly every hour we look at others and see how minor the causes of their strife are and laugh about it. Naturally our own nerves have been severely tested with what we have experienced and are considerably weakened by the lack of nourishment under which we are now suffering. But for reasonable men who understand one another that cannot be justification for any more senseless confrontations which only make life more intolerable." "Yes, that's my opinion." Schulz supports me immediately. "It is just that I don't want to insert myself into your group since you've known one another much longer." "I regret it every time I spout off," I continue, "that is the reason that I would like to prevent it in the future." "I see by your last words that this topic is not directed toward me alone," Hocker takes up the thread I have spun, which is intended to give us a better grip on ourselves, "but everyone should have understanding for those who despite everything still bust their necks." "Agreed; in the future we will conduct ourselves how we all wish it to be," Briller joins in.

### 4 September 1944

"He has dared do it; Hocker is in the tent." I shake the unknowing sleepers awake with my ice-cold voice. "Are you crazy? Damn it all," Schulz hisses, ugly, while Briller, like in a dream, pulls his boots toward him. "We must go look for him," he mumbles as though we were once again at the front. "Have you all lost your good sense?" Schulz bleats, whom I can sense more than see while I put on my boots. "Stay here and wait until we come back, Schulz," I whisper to him and follow Briller out of the compound.

Without a word we leave the compound exit. Crouching, we make our way separately along both sides of the camp road to the main road, where we are reunited. Only the glow of a burning cigarette gives away the location of the guard. Every nerve is strained to the breaking point, but we remain in our place. Minutes pass like hours, but the tent and its surroundings protect its secret. It seems that nature herself is holding her breath, as the hellish darkness and graveyard stillness lie in a wide circle where more than fifteen thousand souls are cut off from the outer world and are dreaming of better times.

"I don't believe anymore that he went into the tent," Briller whispers into my ear. "I can feel it, Robert, he is inside," I whisper back. "Then I will take a look," he sounds quietly. "Stay here; if you meet him you will irritate him. He does not suspect that we are following him. We must wait here in case the guard notices him and then we can help him." I dissuade Briller from his proposal. "You are right, Helmut, the only threat is from the guard, so we must get closer to the fellow so that we can hinder him from shooting if it is necessary."

We work our way to within five steps of the guard, who yawns loudly and flips his cigarette butt into the grass. Then a barely perceptible shadow glides past us to the right and changes directions at the main road. "Follow him, I will cover you," Briller whispers, not allowing any contradiction.

Faster than the shadow, I follow the way back and wait at the main road leaning against a post. Minutes later Hocker appears like a black panther at the post across from me and, breathing deeply, comes to a stop. "Pssst, Willi," I chirp, barely detectable across the road, and the shadow immediately collapses into itself. After I call for a second time, he answers and cautiously approaches my hiding place.

"Did you really notice that I disappeared?" he whimpers. "Robert is lying right by the guard; we must bring him back," I indicate, half in anger. "I only have a pail of lard. The bread is still behind the tent. I must get it." The little robber exhales happily and departs silently like a butterfly in the night. It is still dark, but the relief guard could come or the guard could hit upon the idea to go behind the tent. I concentrate all my senses in watching the guard, considering what I would do in his position. Since a sergeant is always prone to criticism, I find the guard's behavior rather careless. Certainly he believes that his superiors have disturbed his night's rest out of pure meanness, because the damned Germans have lost all desire to visit the tent at night since the last attempt. That is the only explanation why the fellow, acting in obvious boredom, continues to yawn loudly and spit on the tent wall and other places. In an emergency it would be an easy task for Briller to pull the legs out from under the fellow with a sudden jerk, bring him down on his face, and cover his mouth with bare hands to cut off the air.

Forgetting his duty, the guard lights another cigarette. The flickering flame of the lighter lights his face for a second. He then snaps the lid shut. That would have been the right moment to make him pay for his carelessness. At such moments of weakness, soldiers die day and night on all fronts on all sides. Even I am infected by his carelessness and I feel an almost uncontrollable desire to leave a calling card for the fellow. But Hocker creeps up to us like a dark breath and saves us all from my arrogance.

The pitch black night is about to change into a blue-gray color as Hocker makes his way on knees and elbows with a box in his hand past the main road and with no trouble follows the barbed wire in the direction of the compound. Since I am not sure if Briller has noticed him, I am forced to let him know. Halfway to his position I see the old warrior coming toward me and turn around to go back toward Hocker's post along the main road where I suspect he left the pail of lard. My suspicions are confirmed. A little later we separate and make our way back to the compound along both sides of the camp road. At the entrance to the compound Hocker meets us with hands in his pants pockets and a smug smile on his face.

Schulz squats on the ground staring into the breaking gray of a new day, unenthused about the bounty we set before him. "Don't think that I will stay behind the next time," he moans in relief like a woman in childbirth who has just withstood the first labor pains. "Take it easy, Schulz, and eat up. One of us must survive, when we face death, so that the future world will know how its sons decayed," Hocker whispers to him as he loosens the lid of the pail and I reach into the box.

Here, on the edge of Alençon in the middle of fifteen thousand hungry captured German soldiers, four men, four soldiers sit in the dawn of September 4, 1944, crying like children while working away on the cracker bread and lard stolen under the most dangerous of circumstances. No one is ashamed of himself in front of the others. But everyone is there for the other.

At eleven o'clock the whistle sounds to get our provisions. Sleepy, and quite awkwardly, Schulz gets to his feet. "It is useless to ask you if you want to go up today," he says yawning. "I want to go with you today for sure," Hocker grins. "Let's all go," I suggest, looking forward to seeing Genghis Khan.

I step into the tent and observe the fellows from whom Hocker stole the bread and lard. Even to this hour they have observed nothing. The prisoners work diligently with sweat on their faces. The tall American provokes them, throwing the ugliest abusive words over their heads. "You goddamn son of a bitch," he lets fly at a lame German who drops a box from the table. The man does not react any more to the barrage of curses from the Yankee than to simply grin like a coolie and work faster. It is terrible how the fear of hunger alone can change a man and can make him into a willing tool of his oppressors. If they continue to be so stingy with provisions then in a few weeks they will have broken the backs of the strongest among us and degraded us to helpless good-for-nothings.

Even this time I remain mute since the entire allotment can be carried by three men. Hocker, Briller, and I follow the carriers as escort personnel and find enough time to consider in the light of day the theater of our last night's adventure. It easily could have gone bad. But as always in such situations there were a number of favorable circumstances which made the theft possible. Hocker will not try it a second time. As nice as it is to be full once again, to get a bullet in your hide for a pail of lard and some cracker bread is stupid because there is no return from the world beyond.

It is ten o'clock, and still sleep escapes us. For hours the last of our carefully saved cigarettes has gone up in blue smoke. Everyone is busy with himself. We lie on our backs and await with fear the first raindrops to hit our faces. What will happen to us when it begins to rain? It is an unimaginable thought that the Americans will let us sink into the morass. Perhaps it would have been better if

I had supported Hocker's suggestion to go to the Americans instead of lying in our foul skin and allowing ourselves to be pumped up with false hopes. Even if they had turned us away, it is always better to try something than to do nothing at all.

However, my self-accusations come too late. The heavens open their sluices without mercy. The first drops thump on the packed and dried-out ground and begin to unite in little rivulets and swell to streams in a few minutes. The cans that we have saved stand on the rim of the drainage ditch ready to catch the much-desired drinking water. We sit under Schulz's coat, our legs pulled up, and listen to the tinny clank as the precious drops of water hit the cans clanging like music in our ears. Our arms stretch out from the protective roof, reaching for the cans. The refreshing moisture almost sizzles on the tongue. Those who share our fate are hopping around the compound at this late hour like happy children at play, paying no attention at all to their wet clothes as they gulp down the wet rainwater. The ground of the compound is softened up and the sleeping places are changed into sticky mud. There is no dry place where the tired body can find rest.

In groups of three, five, and seven men, the prisoners stand pressed close to one another and hold their completely soaked field blouses, which hang like wet mop rags, over their heads. And still the rain gushes down to the earth. The air has cooled off. Chilled, we four friends snuggle tightly together, squatting on our boot heels in order to keep the water away from our camping place. Despite our hurriedly dug drainage channels, the water still quickly spreads over our grassy area. We eat cracker bread and lard. In disbelief we look into the box whose contents, now threatened by the water, is nearly gone. This evening, at the latest, the booty from our robbery will be gone. Unlimited grief penetrates our hearts, while the sky continues without mercy to shower its water down upon us. Schulz's coat, which has long been soaked, no longer offers any protection. It is senseless to remain in this position any longer. Standing upright, we wait patiently, like cattle in the meadow, for a change for the better.

### 12 September 1944

Eight terrible days have passed. Eight horrible nights lie behind us. The rain has stopped. Clothed in wet, now-steaming uniforms, we work in defiance of death to put up the tents that arrived early this morning. Prudently the Americans provide better nourishment to the work details who are busy in several enclosures erecting the heavy tents. There is enough to do to make the new accommodations weathertight. Drainage ditches must be dug around the tents. Stakes must be driven into the ground and the tents securely tied to them.

Above all the foot-deep mud which has built up in the last days must be taken out from inside the tents and dumped behind the latrine. But there is no complaining to be heard even though all the work must be done with tin cans.

Shortly before seven o'clock, twelve large tents stand in our compound that are still too small to provide 247 men with enough room to sleep. Fortunately Schulz had the wisdom to organize the tent communities before the work began, leaving it up to the various groups to decide who would occupy the tents so that no circles of friends would be separated to sow seeds of future strife. It remains up to the individual communities to organize themselves in the narrow space that is available. As the work detail informs us, one of these tents is used as quarters by twelve American soldiers. That means that we must find room inside the slanting walls for more than twice as many men. After five minutes, the testing of the space is over and everyone knows his place. Most important is that we finally have a roof over our heads.

While we were erecting the brand new and obviously expensive tents, through carelessness a three-foot-long rip was made in the tent roof. While we Germans stood stiff with shock staring at the gaping hole in the tent, the sergeant said "It's OK, go ahead," and sent an American G.I. to get some material to repair it. Every German soldier can imagine for himself what kind of thunder and lightning a comparable German sergeant would bring down. Somehow the American soldiers take such things easier, or if you will are much more generous about it than we, which probably is connected with the natural richness of their country.

"Is everyone taken care of?" Schulz asks after there is quiet in the tent. "Yes, yes, staff sergeant." We sound like a choir. "Then good night,... good night."

### 15 September 1944

A sheer intolerable heat weighs heavily on our tent even though it is only nine o'clock in the morning. Hardened by the long time out of doors, I now find the air in the tent suffocating. My comrades still lie with closed eyes between consciousness and their dreams. So as not to disturb anyone, I get up carefully and slip out of our quarters. There is a wonderful sun shining over the tent city. Here and there blue smoke rises between the dark gray-green tents of the camp, indicating the well-being of the people even though thick concertina wire restricts their movement. At all four corners of the gigantic camp there are small wooden houses built upon posts several feet high, occupied by American soldiers who watch the activities of their fellow men and halt the surge for freedom with short but well-aimed bursts from their machine guns.

Shame on you, I think as I sit on the top of the drainage ditch and cross my legs. Not exactly sure of the day's date, I reach for my fountain pen and in a few minutes forget everything around me as I become preoccupied writing my diary. It doesn't matter to us whether it is Tuesday or Sunday. There is no sound, no report of what is going on in the world, and that works on our sad existence. Only gossip and latrine rumors reach the ear as they slip uncontrolled from compound to compound through the narrow strands of the barbed wire.

"You are writing?" Schulz asks from the corner of the tent after I have spent two hours alone. "Be so good and write down everything that I am going to tell you," he interrupts me and hands me a sheet of white paper. "Where did you get this paper?" I ask in amazement. "From the Americans," he explains happily. "From the Americans, how and what for?" I ask, still amazed. "There was a meeting for the compound leaders with the sergeant," he begins. "We put some heat under his chair. Now we are supposed to write down our wishes and he will pass them on to the commander. By the way, Genghis Khan is no longer the leader; he is going to be taken with a hundred men to another camp today. At the moment he is standing next to Compound 1 with a full sea sack and chain smoking."

Like wildfire, the news about Genghis Khan spreads throughout the camp while I complete the wish list with Schulz. No one is promising anything will come from the wish lists. They will be filled out, turned in, and finally thrown into an American garbage can. Hunger will remain our true companion. Blankets and coats are requested. Underwear, handkerchiefs, and shaving equipment are included in the wish list. The amount of water and provisions should be increased. Oh, paper, how patient you are. ...

At eleven o'clock the food carriers bring sauerkraut and cracker bread. "Poor Hocker, you must count the strands before you divide it up," I tease him regardless of my own depression. "I am nearly finished," he indicates, opening the flat round cans. "I will simply hang four strands on the ears, give them a slice of cracker bread, and you will see how proudly they march away. You don't need to watch out, no one will come a second time because it takes more calories to come up and get it than you receive."

The double rows follow our dialogue with questioning glances. "Watch out that you don't confuse the sauerkraut with your beard and swallow it down." The third one in line cannot resist pulling my leg. "That won't happen to you with your billy goat's beard." I bring the laughter to my side, as this comparison hits the target exactly.

Once again Schulz stands with a strict face next to Hocker and Briller during the distribution of the provisions. And once again the distrustful prisoners eye the food. It is sauerkraut and cracker bread taken as booty from the German army supplies in the bunkers along the Atlantic wall. We have nothing against the origin and also nothing against the kind of food on today's special menu. We are easily satisfied. The one and only issue is the small amount of food, which is not enough to live on, only enough for a long and slow death. The first sick in our compound are already lying in the tents. They are supposed to be putting up a sick bay in the main camp up by the barracks. The German doctor is supposed to have spoken to the Americans. No one knows for sure. But we don't believe any of the prattle because usually within an hour the rumors burst like a soap bubble.

But now life is coming into the camp. American guards cross the grounds going toward the provisions tent. "Compounds 1 through 3, step out to the camp road," a fat American bellows in poor German. Quickly Hocker, Briller, and I hurry out of our compound across the camp road and work our way through the several enclosures to the compound opposite Compound 1. We believe the prisoners will be searched and Genghis Khan has a wonderfully filled sea sack whose contents we would like to see very much!

Slowly the street fills with the men from Compounds 1, 2, and 3. We are amazed at the baggage that some of the prisoners of war carry with them. There are people with completely filled backpacks. There are men with suitcases looking as though the Americans had taken them away from their vacation, and they all fear that the grinning Americans will take their possessions. At their head, clothed in the blue coat of the navy, proudly decorated with the Iron Cross First Class, and with a thick American sea sack between his legs, stands Genghis Khan, the man from Vienna.

"The first three men, let's go!" the leader of the Americans calls. The rows begin to move. The first three men step lazily toward the Americans. "Put it down, and open it!" the American orders Genghis Khan who, in contrast to the poor devils to his right and left, still has his sea sack on his shoulder and makes no attempt to put down his bag and open it to be searched. Before he has the string untied with which the bag is fastened, the searchers' nimble fingers are into his clothing and disappear into his pockets. What they pull out in a few handfuls would, in this the fifth year of war, fill any European jeweler with enthusiasm: watches and rings in every possible form and price range; lighters, cigarette cases, and fountain pens in large numbers, to the delight of onlookers from both nations, are spread out before his feet. The Americans make short work of the sea sack as Genghis Khan reluctantly takes out an olive green blanket packed on top. In a sudden movement an American grabs the sack, lifts it up, and dumps the entire contents out onto the ground. There are items we have never seen before—cans of corned beef, white bread, C rations, cans of meat and beans—which offer an amazing picture for the hungry prisoners.

The Americans look at the pile of provisions indifferently and give their full attention to the valuables, which their leader sorts through and holds up in his hand a wristwatch for the others to see, then shoves the watch into his pocket and pulls out a handkerchief with which he blows his nose. "That's not your property." The leader turns to Genghis Khan and sticks the handkerchief back in his pants pocket. "I ... bought it," Genghis Khan stammers, downtrodden as he sees how the Americans are loading his goods into a box and setting them to the side. "Shut up, and go forward." He dominates him and gives him a shove so that he nearly trips over his own feet. "Stop," a lance corporal suddenly calls from Compound 1. "It is my Iron Cross First Class that he is wearing." "What is the matter?" the leader asks in confusion at the turmoil. "The Iron Cross is the property of this man," I translate quickly and point with my finger into Compound 1. "OK, you get it again," the American reacts immediately with warmth in his voice and waves to the lance corporal to come while at the same time he demands the Iron Cross from Genghis Khan, which he takes off his jacket with a dirty grin. Nearly ceremoniously he hands the decoration over to the German prisoner, who receives it happily and disappears back into the crowd. "Good-bye, Genghis Khan," those remaining behind bellow. "I'll see you in Hell," he waves back sarcastically.

"We are rid of him, Robert," I express, satisfied, turning to Briller while we remain spared by the Americans for the moment and make our way back along the road toward our compound. There Schulz listens with only partial interest to our report. "It always depends on the individual what he makes out of the situation," he lectures us at the end while looking at a picture on his knee of his wife, who holds a charming, pretty young girl of about five years in her lap. "Is that your wife, Schulz?" I ask, to which he responds with a tired nod of the head. "Yes," he says while looking through me, "and my child. Hopefully she is doing better. She is somewhat sickly and quite fragile." "Can I see it?" I ask, now interested. "Yes, go ahead, you cannot make her vanish." He forces a laugh and hands me the picture. "Are you jealous, Schulz?" I ask him, amazed as I now observe a new side of this usually self-confident man without looking at the picture in my hand. "Take a look at her first, Helmut, and don't talk about jealousy; I really don't have any," he indicates, somehow becoming uncertain, which amazes me even more and stimulates my curiosity, as I now hold the picture in my hand before my eyes. "Man alive," I exclaim unintentionally as my

:yes view the color-painted photo. Although before I had not paid much attention to the picture on Schulz's knee, the blond locks of the child did intrigue me, but now I am really surprised at the full-formed woman whose expression-filled, nearly green eyes rest upon my own. In a charming oval face, framed by magnificent blond hair, there is a mouth which creates a longing in me. The slightly opened lips disclose a row of small, pearl-like teeth that sparkle with good health. The white neck, which is graced by a skin-thin gold necklace, carries in all majesty this exceptionally beautiful woman's head.

"While we were away were you thinking about home?" I ask him as I give the picture back. "That's right my boy, so often one has his private sorrows which push themselves into the foreground when one is alone," he explains. "It is not curiosity, Comrade Schulz, perhaps I am too young for you, but if you are being tormented by some sorrow, wouldn't it be better for you to talk about it? I don't believe that your sorrows can be so tragic and unusual that we cannot speak about them and perhaps offer some advice." I encourage him to empty his heart. "I told you that my wife is sick. Shortly before I was captured I received a letter in which she informed me that she would be operated on the seventeenth or eighteenth of August. That is everything. You can imagine how much that troubles a person," he maintains as one friend to another. "That certainly is a worry that must be carried. There is nothing more that we can do than to hope with you that everything went well and that your charming wife and the mother of your sweet child might be preserved," I tell him with deep feeling for the situation. "Thank you for your understanding and your concern, but don't let it spoil your joy over the departure of Genghis Khan," he indicates somewhat absentmindedly as each one of us shakes his hand and he puts the picture of his wife away.

"She is more than beautiful, your wife, Schulz, but there is always something foul about wives." Briller inconsiderately tramples, with his unusual hate/love complex, the tender feelings Schulz has for his sick wife. "You are carrying your damn hate too far, Robert. You can't simply deride feelings that are holy to someone else." I get after him before Schulz can answer. "In general he is right," Schulz, much to my surprise, comes to Briller's defense, "but men must bear part of the guilt themselves." "Now you have made me curious, friend. Speak up, what is it with your wife?" I ask him, relaxed. "Nothing unusual. I only loved her too much to give her up," the big man answers bitterly and he tries to lead a lady bug that has just landed on his hand away with a blade of grass. "How am I to understand that? One does not give up what he loves, especially when it is his wife who also shows him love." I attempt to tear the secret from him.

"Don't demand of me that I reveal bedroom secrets. Be satisfied when I tell you that my wife was very foolish before I got acquainted with her and even though I knew it, I still married her because my heart forced me to. Our love has continued unchanged. But we have had to pay for it; then I have a sick wife and she has a man who is not very happy. It requires a large measure of tact and goodness of heart not to bring out these shadows of the past at every appropriate and inappropriate opportunity and thereby cause the martyrdom from both sides of this relationship which is already built on a shaky foundation. The necessary operation came as a consequence of my wife's earlier indiscretions and my only fault is that I knew about it from the beginning and I still married her. So that I can be spared your pity in the future, you should know that I do not regret it, but today I would do exactly the same thing. Now leave me alone for ten minutes, and please don't laugh at me; otherwise our comradeship will come to an end." He smiles painfully in conclusion.

"Now I would smoke a cigarette if I had one," I say to Briller as he looks toward the rusty barbed wire as though the world were lost. "And I would drink a bottle of cognac empty in order to forget this shitty life," the brave farm boy sighs. His thoughts are at home as I speak to him and I conclude not to disturb him anymore.

18 September 1944

Today we are to be registered. We stand on the grounds of the U.S. tent camp and have the opportunity to wonder at the good-functioning organization of the Americans which is the equal to anything in the German army. When I report my birthdate, the American clerk who had been so deep in his work suddenly looks up at me with interested eyes and says, "Your birthday is today," and then continues to pound away at the keys of his typewriter. "OK, take it easy," he sends me off with a snap of the fingers and hands me my prisoner of war number, under which I will be registered with the Americans from now on throughout all eternity.

"Today is your birthday, Helmut?" My companions congratulate me once we return to the grounds. "Why did you keep it a secret?" "Unfortunately I did not know for sure that today is the eighteenth."

Four soldiers from a work detail accompanied by an American enter our compound. Equipped with shovels and picks they pass by me quickly and follow the way to the latrine. One of them has a roll of copper tubing hanging on his shoulder. Curiously I follow him and observe them from a respectable distance, as they stop at the latrine, lie down their tools, and take off their shirts. But it is not their work as such which interests me, since it is immediately clear to me that they are going to dig a new hole, but the copper tubing has worked on me and brought me to a fantastic idea. I approach the group as it begins to work. "Do you want to help us?" the guard asks in a sarcastic voice when he becomes aware of my presence. But I act dumb and laughingly shrug my shoulders. "Do you want to help us?" A chubby-faced soldier translates the American's well-understood question. "I have become too weak for such things," I wave tiredly to him. "Sergeants can only show off," a lance corporal bawls as his seven years of service can be distinguished at some distance. "Keep your mouth shut, you are just jealous because you have not amounted to anything." Another spares me an answer. "Go ahead," the American fortunately interrupts the unpleasant conversation. "Lick my ass," the lance corporal spouts to the guard and angrily swings his pick into the earth and begins to work like a wild man.

"Do you have a toilet, or do you also shit on your billy club?" the red-cheeked prisoner asks the American in a kidding tone after a long pause. "Yes" the guard says unknowingly, to which they all break out in frantic laughter and the Yankee irritatedly chews his gum. "Hey, what are you going to do with the copper tubing?" I decide that the time has come and throw out the question that has been burning on my tongue. "So that the latrines can be fenced in and the side toward the outside of the camp covered with a tent canvas in order to spoil the desire of the French for looking at the asses of German boys," the staff sergeant, who was so spiteful before, volunteers freely. "That is exactly right," another confirms his words as I furrow my brow in doubt.

"Tell me, do you think you could pass me a piece of the wire without the guard seeing it?" I finally lie my wish on one card. "Of course we can, it just depends on what you are going to lie next to it, my dear fellow. If it is necessary, I will take the American's gum out of his mouth and let him continue to chew on a condom without arousing his attention," the big mouthed lance corporal answers. "Lay something down." I respond, "Can you reach into the pants pockets of a naked man?" "Oh, well … you do have something." He remains hard headed. "How about three razor blades?" I ask jokingly. "All right, but they must be as new as the wire." He agrees to the offer. "You will be through in an hour; before then I will be back with the razor blades." I turn toward my tent.

"Your tubing is even with the earth under the pile of dirt," the old fellow whispers to me as I shake his hand and pass to him the razor blades. "It's in order, greet the homeland for me," I continue loudly and return happily to the tent where I persuade my three companions to make a round of the compound with me.

Finally to ourselves, I reveal my plan to them. "The Americans have created an especially lucky coincidence for us with their plan to enclose the new latrine with copper wire. I am planning to exchange the copper as gold with the guards along the fence for food items." "Do you really think that the Americans are that dumb that they will take a piece of copper tube for gold?" Schulz interrupts me immediately. "Of course not. Open your ears and close your mouths so that I can explain everything to you in peace. Afterward you can talk as much as you want. You know how interested the Americans are in watches and rings. They buy wedding rings without seeing them and which they cannot recognize as being genuine. That is the point upon which my plan rests. Nothing is easier for me than to make a wedding ring out of a half circle of tubing. Unfortunately I do not have the necessary tools. But now we have the necessary material. Underneath the dirt that has been dug out for the latrine there is hidden a piece of copper tubing which I exchanged for razor blades with prisoners from a work detail. This piece of tubing, whose length I am not sure of myself, can be divided into pieces about six inches in length. It is work that any fool can do with a pair of pliers. It is possible to break the tubing by bending it back and forth. But then the ends must be cut straight. Later they can be fused together so that the swindle will not be obvious immediately. It is clear that the whole operation can be carried out only once since right afterward, when the happy guards look closely at their purchased jewelry in good light, it will be obvious to the dumbest hick that he has been taken. That means for us we must work hard to produce as many rings as we have material for and then on one evening carry out the big coup. Now I want to hear your opinion," I end my explanation.

"You have really hatched something, but I like it much better than your previous doubtful escape plan," Briller opens the discussion. "The whole thing might work, if you have enough skill with your fingers to manufacture rings with rocks. But you must consider that there will be ridges and bumps on the rings which will raise suspicions immediately," Schulz objects. "Let me worry about that. The deep ridges, which you are right about Schulz, must be rubbed down with a flat stone. The smaller ridges can be eliminated and the rings made shiny by rubbing them with sand and on our leather pants." I sidetrack Schulz's objection. "Your idea is the best and the last possibility to get something more to eat, Helmut," Hocker agrees finally without any conditions. "Just one more question for you. Are we going to do it alone, or involve everyone in our tent community?" I bring up the basic problem among prisoners who want to carry out such a project.

"Let's try it alone first," Briller indicates, becoming serious. "It will be hard to keep secret such work. The whole tent will become suspicious for sure when we crawl into a corner and hide ourselves in order to work on the tubing. I am in favor of involving the other comrades," is Schulz's opinion. "It would be better to try it alone first, then there are not that many guards if twenty-four men are producing rings for them," Hocker gives for thought. "It is also my opinion that it would be better to keep the matter among the four of us, Schulz. Then, as good as your intentions are toward the other comrades, there is certainly a man among the twenty-four of them who won't stay with us.

"The tubing at the latrine would be stolen in a few hours and then the entire coup would be botched. Besides, no one will have anything when the available material is divided into twenty-four parts," I register my thoughts against Schulz's good intentions. "I agree, you are right, but let me stay out of this game. To tell the truth I don't think I would be very good at this work and with my views I would just be in your way," Schulz expresses himself freely. "Naturally that is out of the question, Schulz. As much as I appreciate your points, they are not correct this time; then I don't see it to be any deception against our comrades or against the Americans. It will not hurt anyone since the Americans will just steal the provisions that they will exchange for the rings, or else they have extra food because they do not distribute it to us; then it is just when we exact a little well-deserved revenge. So Schulz, you are a part of the party and you do not have to do anything more than to cut the wire into pieces, which is just a matter of patience. You don't seriously believe that when we get our bellies full through our work that we will let you wither away in your vanity. Besides we need you in order to reach our goal quickly; then it would really be a wonder if no one else came up with the idea but me. Agreed?" I ask in closing. "Yes," he sighs as roll call is sounded.

After roll call and after we receive our sixty grams of corned beef and four biscuits, I stay in the vicinity of the latrine, where I keep my eye on the three ends of the wire. Should something change during the course of the night, then speed is all important in order to beat the competition in doing business with the Americans. While I keep an anxious eye on the latrine, Hocker and Briller saunter around the compound collecting stones that we can use. Because the earth has been dug up around the tents, the necessary tools of the stone age can be found which otherwise would be scarce on a meadow such as the one where we are located. In addition I need one of the finger-thick, round iron bars on which the lower strands of barbed wire are fastened. That is Hocker's assignment. Everything is prepared. We must only wait for night, since I do not dare pull the tubing from under the hill with so many prisoners watching.

Finally the moment arrives. Darkness has silently crept over the land. Only small groups of men stand chatting in front of their tents. The time for exchanging items with the guards has not yet arrived since the guards are not inclined to barter during daylight and it is impossible to carry with them larger exchange items without their superiors noticing. After the first guard change at night, then life begins along the fence. But that will slow down since hardly anyone in camp still has anything to exchange.

Indifferently I step toward the hill of earth. My boot tips scratch at the spongy earth until I feel an elastic resistance that sounds like metal. Thank God the man did not deceive me. Buried deep inside of me, the ugly doubt gnawed at me but I did not want to admit it. Yes, one must believe in something if he is to succeed. The good lance corporal! As I pull the wire out with my hands, I think, perhaps someday I can do better for your good deed than the three razor blades. Holding the wire tightly like a sword, I saunter toward the tent while part of the wire sticks above my head like an antenna. Unobserved, I slip into the tent and lie the wire on the ground. "Everything is in order," I whisper to my friends and fall asleep happily.

*19 September 1944*

Before the first gray is visible in the eastern sky, Hocker and I stand at the latrine and inspect the fence. Relieved, I tell Hocker that nothing has changed. But there are more latrines with copper wire in this large camp. There is no shortage of men with understanding and good ideas. Restlessly the fear of competition drives me around the compound, until finally the sun overcomes endless Russia and lights the western half of Europe.

Without delay we begin our work. The six-foot long tubing is cut into two equal parts in a few minutes. With a sharp-edged stone squeezed between our knees, each of us begins rasping away the ridges on the tubing. With strength and endurance that none of us would have expected anymore, we continue to work the material over the sharp stone under strong pressure. Before the first one heads to the latrine, I hold two six-inch-long pieces of tubing in my hand.

"Now we must separate ourselves, Willi. No one can notice the context of our work. Under no circumstances can anyone get the picture that we are working on rings. In case of an emergency, you can explain to the all too curious that the wire was forgotten by the work detail and you are going to make a hook for your cans. I will sit at my usual writing place behind the tent where no one is inclined to disturb me since I have already driven the gapers from that place. I will bend the rings. No one can surprise me because I only keep one tool in my hand and all the others in my pocket, something that I advise to all of you." I make my way to my usual writing place behind the tent where Hocker has placed the iron bar and a red sandstone which is very good for my work.

Industriously, but without haste, I begin to grind the surface of a piece of copper to give it the necessary half-round form. I only interrupt the work on one if it gets too hot because of rubbing too fast, and then continue with the second one. After considerable time the first success is apparent. The pieces have been shaped into their half-round form. Nearly crazy with joy, I rub the deepest scratches out with moist sand until they sparkle before me from the first rays of sunshine. Bathed in sweat, I suddenly become dizzy and nearly black out as I begin to smooth and polish the ends. My tired hands no longer obey my will. Exhausted, I drop the tubing to the ground. I feel like I am going to faint. Before my closed eyes dance thick slices of corned beef and a heaping box of biscuits. "Water ...," I stammer from my dried mouth before I completely pass out.

But it could only have been a few seconds that I was unconscious; then I see the same picture of sun and wind as I open my eyes again. Only a laming weakness makes me aware of my true physical condition. It is high time that we take our fate in our own hands, and an outflowing of hate against the rich Americans who trample around this island of misery like fat pigs, withholding the most necessary provisions from us, drives me to continue to work. Filled with sheer rage and the satanic anticipation that in a short time I will stick it to them with their own copper tubing, I bend the first ring around the iron bar and hammer the ends tightly together with a round stone. Becoming ice cold inside, I peel the nearly finished ring from the iron bar with considerable effort and contemplate my work with satisfaction. With ill-concealed wrath I proceed with the finishing work. All the dents and scratches are eliminated by careful rubbing with sandstone, which is not any rougher than a middle-range grinding stone that is used in any workshop. The final work involves the use of sand and wet dirt. I watch to see that the ring does not open and that it retains its brightness, brought out by polishing it on the buckskin seat of my pants.

So, I have earned the first meal in captivity. Now I will test it. Quickly I change my authentic ring with the false one and go to my friends, whom I find are not working diligently. "Man, this is a shitty job," Briller receives me. "Really shitty work, Helmut," Hocker joins in and I feel like boxing their ears. "How far did you get?" I ask in a harmless tone. "Each one has cut through one, but we wasted a lot of time trying to find a better method," Hocker answers me shamelessly. "You fools," I jump on them, "don't you believe that I did not do it before you? There is no other possibility here. I hope that you did not tramp around the compound with the wire and ask for a saw or pliers." "Not that, but we wanted to ask a soldier from the provisions tent for some pincers. Unfortunately there has been a guard on the main road since this morning where they are just finishing a guard house," Briller confesses in the most harmless manner this attempt of unbelievably stupid proportions. "Just continue to work so that your brain can finally get some nourishment, since it has suffered great need in the last while, as I can tell by the way you have gone about this." I satisfy them and me. "Look here." I hold the finished ring on my hand under their noses. "They must look like this one if we want to succeed." "Have you polished your own ring so that you know how the others must look?" Briller asks sarcastically, looking at the fake ring without any perception. "That is exactly what I wanted to know from you, you fool. Don't you see that it is made of copper?" I take the ring from my finger and hand it to the two of them. "Boy, oh boy, that is quite the thing." They become enthused about the project and stare at the ring from all sides. "Man, the most the American will think is that he has received a broken ring. In any case days will pass before they realize that this time they have lost at the party," Hocker revels happily. "Then let's get to work, men." I leave them reassured that things will go forward now.

### 27 September 1944

While several changes have occurred in the camp in the past seven days, my friends and I carry on with countless hours of work the plan we developed on my birthday. We tell no one of our work. As though under a hypnosis, we rasp, hammer, bend, and polish wedding rings for the Americans which they can put in their noses on their wedding days as a reminder of the German prisoners of war in Camp Alençon, who through starvation were forced to such desperate measures.

It is nearly ten o'clock. In a few minutes the guards will appear and we will approach them with our export items. Fifteen pieces of jewelry, created from desperation with the most primitive tools, wait in our pockets for their future owners. Everything has been reconnoitered and discussed. Nothing can go wrong. No competition can spoil the business. The price has been set with some flexibility. Only Schulz must be separated because of his striking stately appearance as a salesman. And now, at 10:10 P.M. we step toward the compound exit to smuggle ourselves into other compounds. The fox does not steal where he himself lives. Like this sly animal, I prowl, protected by the night, along the camp road to Compound 15 and enter. In the meantime Hocker and Briller have reached Compounds 2 and 31, which adjoin each other. Unhindered, I mix among the few men who stand at their latrine watching the individual Germans who are at the fence doing business with the Americans.

The last hesitancies have been fought back. Determined to get the highest price possible for my idea and work, I step up to the fence and point with my left index finger to the ring on my right hand. An American turns on his lamp quickly and looks at the false piece of jewelry for a second. "How many cigarettes?" the first interested American asks. "No cigarettes—food," I demand coldly. "OK, this tin." He reaches to hand me a two-pound can out of a clothes bag sitting on the ground. "What's in it?" I fake fastidiousness. "Pork," he answers importantly. Pork? What is pork, I break my head trying to remember. "It is very good!" He tries to encourage me to take it as I resist. "It is very fat pork sausage," my neighbor explains and licks his tongue. "OK," I say as though disappointed as I take the ring from my finger. The American shoves two roof rafters between the barbed wire to establish contact while the other guards keep their weapons pointed at me. Contemptuously I frown and lie the ring on the board. Carefully the Yankee sets the can on the second board. Drawn by our hands, the objects of exchange pass one another and change owners. With shaking hands I hold the cold, heavy can in my hands. Caressingly cool, the breeze strokes my hot cheeks as I sail out of the compound. It went all right, I think and breathe easily once I feel the camp road under my boot soles.

"Number nineteen" stands in faded paint on the small wooden board at the entrance to my second field of activity. The strange latrine lies lonesome and, lighted by the moon, ghostly, like an open grave before me. There is no guard visible along the corridor. The entire compound appears to have died. Becoming discouraged, I am about to sit down on one of the cross-beams of the latrine when I hear a metal clank on the barbed wire. It can only be the weapon of a guard that has struck the wire, I think, happily excited, and look in the direction from which the noise has come. Finally a huge shadow comes closer. Barely perceptible in the milky moonlight are the shiny coat buttons of the American. "Why don't you sleep?" the unexpected soldier asks. "I am hungry," I answer honestly. "Are you Nazi?" he asks with surprising sharpness. "Since I am here, maybe," I respond without thinking. A rash of cuss words streams through the barbed wire upon me, but I cannot understand one word. Suddenly he jerks his left hand out of his coat pocket and throws something, which I presume to be a hand grenade, over the six-foot-high fence, then continues on his way. Pressed flat on the mound of earth by the latrine, I hear the dull thump of the metal object as it lands just a few steps away. My mind registers that it is a dud after a few seconds pass and the expected detonation does not follow. Bad luck, you scoundrel, I mumble to myself and search the trampled grass looking for the projectile. Deeply ashamed, I stare at a small can on the bare ground. But still, responding to experience, I resist touching the thing but instead kneel down and take a close look. "Milk," I am able to make out as I strain my eyes. I have to force myself not to laugh. The devil can try to make sense of these damned Americans, shoots through my mind as I shove the can into my pocket and leave the compound.

I cross the camp road and enter Compound 21. "Is anyone there who has a watch to barter?" the exchange minister of this compound calls in ordinary black market jargon as I step among the group of prisoners assembled around the latrine. No one responds. With the upper parts of their bodies bent forward, their hands buried deeply in their pockets, bearded and ragged, stand the brave sons of Germany, shaken in despair behind American barbed wire, waiting for a crust of bread that may fall out of the pockets of the well-nourished guards.

Filled with rage, I push my way to the fence. Once again I raise the right hand and point with the left one to the ring on my finger. "Two breads." I entice the two Americans standing between the walls of wire. "No bread, only pork," the thick-necked garden dwarf crows to me from under his steel helmet. "OK, two cans," I demand boldly, taking the ring from my finger and holding it in my open hand as they shine their light upon it. "OK, catch it," cracks the voice of the small one and a can flies over the fence into my outstretched hands. Once again a board slides through the fence. With a light heart, I lie my ring on the altar of our guards. "It is broken," both of them cuss at the same time once their light rests again on the piece of jewelry. But their next words are lost on the wind. The person to whom they were directed has already fled to Compound 24 for rest and recovery.

Schulz's coat lies heavily on my shoulders as the heavy cans in the pockets await our destruction. A still heavier burden is the doubt weighing on my mind about carrying out the rest of my plan. There was nearly a problem and I would have left empty handed. We still have three rings to exchange for food. Two cans of pork and one can of milk are now in my possession. "Let's go." I drive myself and stride through the compound.

"No food, only cigarettes," is the laconic answer from my new bartering partner in answer to my approach. Silently I take the package of cigarettes bound with an elastic band from the rifle barrel and hang a ring on the edge of the barrel. The cold eyes of the American, with his finger on the trigger, rest determinedly on my hands and observe sharply their actions. But his concerns are unfounded. I do not intend to withhold my masterpiece from him. Lazily I lift my hand in farewell and disappear into the darkness. You will also think of me, I rejoice inwardly.

Leisurely I wander out of the enclosure and turn again toward Compound 19. The guards must have been changed in the meantime. I stand at the entrance listening and looking up to the few stars. Dead silence lies over the camp. The shadows of the row of tents stand gloomily, with their points raised like an index finger in the pale moonlight. There is no inner warning. Therefore, off to the enemy, I jerk myself and shove off from the post on which I am resting.

From far away I discover the guard by the glow of his cigarette. Not entirely sure that the change of guards has taken place, I sit on the latrine cross-beam like an ordinary user and turn my neck in order to make out the figure of the guard. Under no circumstances do I want to come into view of the unusual milk giver. Yes, the man along the corridor is smaller than the can thrower. Still I am reluctant to approach him. In order to draw his attention toward me, I step away from the latrine and in front of the guard stuff my shirt into my pants. Schulz's coat lies thrown carelessly over the parallel beam on which the cross-beam rests. Just then the American flips his cigarette butt in a high arch over the fence near my feet. "Don't you smoke?" he asks in amazement when I do not jump upon the butt. "I am hungry," I repeat my line. "Do you have a watch?" is the prompt response from the soul of a businessman. "Only this ring." I point to my right hand. "How much?" he asks, slightly interested. "Two bread," I respond and reach for Schulz's coat. "You get this can," he pulls out one of the familiar cans of pork. "Damn it all," I mutter angrily, "just sausage." "What?" the Yankee asks since he did not understand. "Bread." I repeat my demand. "No bread." The man slowly becomes sour. "It is good," I explain. I am in agreement and for the fourth time this evening pull a ring from my finger. The can rolls behind me while the guard sticks his weapon through the barbed wire. Unconcerned, the American draws the ring-decorated barrel back again. Quickly I turn away and pick up the can. Ashamed, the crescent moon hides behind the shreds of clouds after the fraud is finished and I slip out of the compound.

Compound 15 silently admits me. The last ring sits loosely on my finger. Wouldn't it be better to deliver the goods I have acquired to Schulz instead of chancing the last attempt so heavily loaded? No, I order myself and creep like an overcooked profiteer along the fence. A civilian whose story is known throughout the entire camp stands at the concertina wire and speaks every evening, like a wandering preacher, to the guards in perfect English. There is hardly an occupant of a tent in Alençon, be he German or American, who is not acquainted with his fate. But he takes himself much too importantly and considers his situation very unusual, even though he notices the mild laughter with which many hear his account for the second or third time. When war broke out with France in 1939 he was living as a rich German tradesman in Paris. At that time the French naturally put him on ice immediately, and he was set free by our troops in July 1940. He returned to his comfortable dwelling in Paris and continued his business activities. After August 1944, when the Americans turned Paris over to de Gaulle's troops, he was once again in the hands of the French and landed safely in Alençon. Naturally he was a civilian and should not have been brought to a prisoner of war camp, but it is a big joke that he continually identifies himself as the most innocent sacrifice of the war among fifteen thousand of his fellow countrymen. No one is bothered by his daily lamentations and so he continues to speak on and on. It is only that at the moment he irks me with all the babble out of his gold-filled mouth and I am afraid he will keep the guard's attention until he is relieved.

"Do you have anything to exchange?" he finally interrupts after I call attention to myself with a cough. "I only have my wedding ring, but I will trade it for some provisions," I answer him despondently. Apparently trying to get rid of me so that he can continue to speak, the German acts immediately as an intermediary. The transaction occurs unexpectedly quickly for me. Certainly he has talked the American's ear off, then without looking, he shoves the ring into his coat pocket while I shove another can of pork into my pocket, bid them good-bye, and leave the deceived American to his long-winded visitor.

My work is over. Heavily loaded, I shuffle along the camp road toward the tent that has become my home. The seducer rages in my breast and demands that I open the can of milk I received as a present. I deserve it since I have carried out my assignment to the full satisfaction of my friends. But you are a fool and still believe in the honesty of your world.

"God be thanked that you are here, Helmut," Schulz greets me at the entrance to the compound. "What is it, my boy, that you look at me so disturbed?" he asks, concerned, and attempts to read an answer in my face. "Nothing, Schulz, I am only happy, finally happy, that you are here and that you waited for me," I answer the good man and feel a relief as the devil in my breast disappears. "Hocker and Briller have been back for nearly an hour. Where have you kept yourself so long? I can tell you, the work paid off, even if you did not get anything. But come, let's go to the other two; they have been sitting for a long time in front of the opened cans waiting for you," he whispers hastily and takes me behind our tent to my writing place where Hocker and Briller greet me with a laugh.

Without losing many words, Hocker presents an opened can of pork that he holds between his feet. Without a sound Briller tears two loaves of bread apart and holds the not quite equal parts to us with closed eyes. Schulz's silver spoon makes the rounds as each one of us shovels his mouth full and then passes it on to the next. Like animals we gorge ourselves on the slippery sausage and cram the bread in afterward. After a while the thought enters my mind that later on I will only buy this kind of sausage.

"Full?" Hocker asks, looking around the group, answering himself as the empty can slips out of his hand. "Full?" We wonder ourselves about Hocker's question and shake our heads no. "Open another can, Willi!" Briller hisses greedily. "That's enough." Schulz counsels against it. "We are going to ruin our stomachs." "Open it!" I shove Schulz's warning to the side because of the insane urge raging in my intestines.

Hocker runs the can opener around the lid and smears each portion into our hands. Just like monkeys, we eat the sausage with dirty fingers. "We have sunk much lower than the pigs," Schulz mumbles, ashamed, folding his fat hands over his knees.

In contemplation, we stare at the five empty cans. "The rest, gentlemen," I turn our attention from the gluttony and pull my four cans of pork, the pack of cigarettes, and the can of milk from Schulz's coat pockets. "What took you so long?" Hocker asks with a concerned voice as my eyes rest on the can of milk. "Everything went all right, just once I had to make a quick exit when the boys discovered the crack in the ring. One of them gave me the can of condensed milk. I just needed more time than we had planned to get around to all of the compounds," I give the truthful answer. "But how is it that you returned so quickly?" I ask, surprised, looking at the booty they bring out from the hiding place, which far exceeds mine. "You fine dandies." I cannot restrain myself as my hands joyfully burrow into the box. In total the two have acquired twelve cans of pork, two loaves of bread, and a box of biscuits. "All of this from only three guards," Briller triumphs with a shameless grin on his face. "It was the easiest thing in the world," Hocker smirks proudly. "Against your suggestion, we stayed together, and in three quarters of an hour we sold all ten rings in Compound 2 without any incident. None of the boys noticed the swindle. The cans came like hail over the fence after we showed them the rings." "We only had to endure a little anxiety." Briller sums up the experience in military shortness. "Then our trick was a success and our work richly rewarded. Now, friends, we just have to secure our success." I end the conversation and get up.

Together Hocker and I lie the entire booty, except for the cigarettes and the small can of milk, in the box, which we then bury in the hole that we had prepared. A stone covers our food cellar from the view of the uninitiated. After the work is finished we rejoin Schulz and Briller, who were positioned as guards to divert others from our secret work. Restless from the entire event and satisfied that my plan has been carried out, we slip into the tent and lie down on the hard earth for a well-earned sleep, with our stomachs somewhat satisfied.

*3 October 1944*

For hours a cold rain has been pouring and has changed the entire camp into an unconnected pond. In the neighboring compound the latrine has overflowed and its stinking broth has penetrated our compound as the former meadowland drops sharply in the direction of the city. Shaking with agitation and weakness the famished comrades push toward the tent entrance and stare, with eyes which have receded into their sockets, at nature's fury. Our thirst has long been quenched and the faces washed clean of the preceding week's dirt. Others sit silently in their places. A strong wind rips at the tents and we fear the worst. We four friends are busy outside of the tent cleaning the drainage ditches, making sure that they work properly. Without concern for our soaked clothes, we monitor the tent stakes, which threaten to pull out of the softened earth. Now our extra provisions are of great use; then we are the only ones who have the strength to keep the tent anchored in place. Already single tents are blown over by the wind in various compounds and lie crumpled together a few yards distant from their original locations. The American guards stand wrapped in their gray-green raincoats between the barbed wire walls with annoyed faces. Threatened by nature, both guards and their captives are concerned about the posts and ropes which hold up their miserable quarters.

Yesterday new prisoners arrived in this blemish on mankind. Part of them are sailors assigned to the gun turrets around Paris who were supposed to defend the city on the Seine. They are a colorful, thrown-together heap, partly dressed in tropical uniforms with short pants, others in blue navy dress, and some in the gray coats of the marines. Among them are the countless clerks from the headquarters in and around Paris. Their uniforms are torn and soiled with blood. Their faces show the horror of the peril they have survived. Today, for the first time, they speak hesitatingly of the mental devastation of their experiences. They were assured by the honor of the French that when they capitulated they would be well treated according to the provisions of the Geneva Convention. Their understandable distrust was confirmed when the negotiators turned them over to the Americans who, in something of a demonstration of reassurance, provided them with protection in the form of several tanks.

As a marine reported, they paraded them through Paris after they had laid down their weapons. At the first meeting with civilians, they knew what was in store for them. They were cursed in the most evil manner and had everything possible thrown at them. The closer they came to the city center, the more audacious the French became. When they finally reached a certain point in the city, there were so many enraged people assembled that the Americans could no longer provide the necessary protection for the prisoners without using weapons against the civilians. But despite the burst of fire from the tank machine guns, the French broke into the ranks of the unarmed Germans and beat them to the ground, tearing insignias, medals, rings, and watches from them. It was especially bad for the higher-ranking soldiers who marched in front since the U.S. tanks followed in the rear. According to the report, in one case less than half of a 350-man company was able to escape the massacre. The rest were thrown into a Paris jail, where it was somewhat tolerable. Not until after numerous interrogations and much suspicion were they delivered to the Americans, who then brought them here. It is understandable that while these men are not pleased with the conditions here, still they are happy to be surrounded by barbed wire and American guards. These descriptions of the conduct of the French—"The Grand Nation"—cause a flaming hatred to spread throughout the camp. This is understandable because every German soldier remembers how the German leaders insisted that the vanquished French be treated carefully like they were raw eggs. All too often a German soldier who would have a small conflict with a Frenchman was threatened with arrest.

\* \* \*

Hörner is describing the accounts by Germans captured in the liberation of Paris during the last week of August 1944. The perspective is certainly that of soldiers, who hoped, if not expected, that they would be treated according to the provisions of the Geneva Convention. The scenes of captors promising soldiers who gave themselves up that they would be well treated, and American troops trying to protect German prisoners of war from an enraged citizenry, were not uncommon throughout the European theater of war; even Hörner had experienced the same as he traveled as a prisoner of war through France. Historians have recorded incidents of the mistreatment of German captives after the fall of Paris. David Pryce-Jones, in *Paris in the Third Reich: A History of the German Occupation, 1940-1944*, notes: "About twelve thousand Germans in all were captured, with some three thousand casualties, indicating that few of the garrisons had attempted to break out. Some surrendering Germans were gunned down, notably in an incident when a grenade was thrown close to a column of prisoners

marching around the Etoile, and a machine gun then opened up on them."[1]
Martin Blumenson records:

> When Paris was liberated, the German occupiers suddenly
> became prisoners, and the Parisians had a chance to take
> revenge on their enemies. They mutilated portraits of Nazi
> leaders, ripped down swastikas and threw clothes and papers
> out of buildings where Germans had lived. When the military
> commander of Paris, General Dietrich von Choltitz, was taken
> to police headquarters, people spat on him and clawed at his
> uniform. They did not know that Choltitz had saved their city by
> disobeying Hitler's orders to burn Paris to the ground.[2]

Larry Collins and Dominique Lapierre, in their history of the fall of
Paris, *Is Paris Burning?*, record:

> As, little by little, the sound of gunfire slackened in these streets
> spilling over with sunshine and joy, the occupiers of Paris began
> a last, sorry parade through the city they had ruled for four
> years. At the sight of their first sweaty and haggard files, the
> people of Paris exploded with all the hatred pent up during
> their long, bitter months of occupation. They beat and pum-
> meled, cursed and spat on them, and, on occasion, killed them.
> But of the thousands of Germans taken prisoner this sunny day,
> the sorriest lot of all were the officers of the Gross Paris general
> staff. For those men who symbolized the heart of the Nazi
> tyranny that had oppressed them for four years, the people of
> Paris reserved a particular violence. All along their path the
> crowd jeered, spat at them, struggled to leap past the screen of
> FFI guards to rip at their uniforms, club them, kick their shins.

One member of the general staff, Captain Otto Kayser, a literature
professor from Cologne, was shot and killed when a screaming Frenchman
wearing a blue beret broke into the ranks of the prisoners and, pointing his
pistol at the head of the German nearest him, pulled the trigger.[3]

* * *

A fifth man has joined the four of us: Siegfried Neumeler, a marine
corporal. He arrived here with the last transport and survived the march
through Paris. Snuggled close together we sit in our wet clothes inside the tent
on the bare earth and listen to his stories. We are very sympathetic toward him

since his views happen to agree with ours. But he has brought us a present which we would have gladly done without: lice! Since this morning we know. Naturally these little animals have settled in other tents for a long time already and it was only a question of time until they would favor us with their pinching. Now they sit in our hair and lay eggs so that their species will not die out. "In the French prisons there are swarms of these cursed beasts," Siegfried says as he pulls a prime example out of the red hair on his chest and squashes it with his thumbnail into the next world.

"But what I wanted to say," he continues his speech, "Guderian is really positioned on the Marne with his tanks and ready for a counterattack. The V rockets will be heavily used and make the Western allies ripe for negotiations. As I said, the war is not yet lost. In the Paris prison they speak with excitement about secret weapons which are soon to be implemented. Naturally no one knows anything for certain, but the people there are full of hope that they will be freed shortly thereafter. Imagine if the air force could drop a battalion of paratroopers and outfit us with weapons, what magic we could work on the backs of the Americans."

"Do you seriously believe the air force still has enough machines?" I ask him doubtfully. "Yes," he responds, "they have only kept them back to deceive the opponent. Now the Americans have all of their equipment on the continent. That is what Hitler wants so that he can completely destroy them. It is known that Rommel has two theories: first, to destroy the opponent on the water; and second, to allow him to land, pile up his equipment in France, and then surround and defeat him. The disadvantage of the first plan is that if the enemy is not successful in landing, he can try the invasion at another location. In that case, the many divisions and the available matériel would be a continual threat which would tie up in France an enormous amount of our strength. The second plan, which the Führer's headquarters selected, also has the disadvantage that some divisions must be sacrificed. It is our personal misfortune that we happen to belong to these companies. But our imprisonment will only last a short time since the Americans are not in a position to ship us away from here in time although we would be an important pawn in their hands during any cease fire negotiations."

Impressed by his enlightening explanation, we turn on our sides with new hope and doze until it is time to receive our provisions.

### 12 October 1944

"Comrades, we will sing the first verse of 'A Mighty Fortress is Our God'," the American Protestant chaplain says to those assembled on the camp road. No,

I am not imagining it. There stands a pastor in an army uniform and begins to sing. There are no decorations on his chest, only a large cross, the symbol of Christendom. And now the German prisoners of war join in song. Softly at first, then louder to the climax: "And He shall reign forever more."

"I have come to bring to you the word of God in your troubled existence," he begins his sermon. "Jesus Christ did not differentiate between people. You are here as prisoners of this terrible war, but believe me, we are all prisoners on this earth. Imprisoned until the Lord comes to make us free. Do not give up your hope in God. He has not forgotten you here; this beautiful October day is proof, even though it may be hard for some of you to still believe in God because of the hard fate that has come upon you. But who believes in Him will be free, even though he is surrounded by barbed wire. ... It is possible that mountains can be moved and hills made low. ... Amen. Hallelujah."

While the believers return to their tents moved and comforted, those who remain behind receive the churchgoers with mockery. "Are you now satisfied, you stupid sheep? Did he give you the sacrament to keep you from starving? Why didn't you bring anything back for us to eat ...?"

The opinions rebound harder and harder until Schulz puts an end to the strife. "Stop the theater, now," he calls the fighting roosters to reason. "Each can believe what he wants to. Whoever wants to discuss it must do so with the usual respect for the opinion of the other person. By the way, there is enough room outside for the screamers."

"Did the pastor say anything about the war theater, or better, about the care and provisions for us?" Schulz asks me after he has calmed the waves and we enter the tent in peace. "No, he only prayed for us," I answer him indifferently. "He could have done that in America; he did not have to make an extra trip here." He closes the topic with light derision and pulls the bill of his cap over his eyes to doze further.

### 18 October 1944

The five companies selected by the first sergeant stand in the center of the main camp at attention. The analysts have arrived. They want to examine our political views. A light cloud of irritation lies over the German prisoners standing weak-kneed in the rows.

What an affront they have allowed themselves against us. What does it matter to these strange people what we think? That is the last thing they have left us. Now they are reaching for it and want to degrade us from subjects to objects. I recall the radio station, Atlantic, on whose propaganda we were fed before the invasion as it screamed about the worth of the human being and how Hitler was in the process of eliminating humanity. What do they expect from the hearings? Do they seriously believe that each one will actually tell them what he thinks? Or do they believe that we will betray our own people now that we have got to know the Americans? Did they intentionally put us in our present situation so that we would respond with hate-filled words to their questions and they could say we still stand by the Hitler who suddenly attacked the whole world? Now you are to blame for your misery! But we have already prepared our answers, although not one of us knows what we will be asked.

The hearings get underway. Twenty paces from each company stand the interrogators and ask their questions of each one as they must step from their rows. Already the spirits are being divided. After a successful hearing the Americans send those who have been interrogated to the left or right corner of the yard where they are received by the guards. They are dividing us into Nazis and anti-Nazis.

"It doesn't matter at all what stamp they give us; we must not let ourselves be separated," is Schulz's whole concern. "Then you start Schulz; it is up to each one of us individually if we stay together," Hocker suggests. "I don't want to hear any criticism from you if after the hearing they give our camp a bad mark. I am inclined to say what I think," Schulz warns us. "We know that, but don't worry, it can't get any worse than it already is, so let's march." I comfort him.

As proud as a battalion commander, Schulz steps toward the Americans. He cracks his heels together as he salutes the officer three paces away. The American thanks him idly and Schulz stands comfortably.

Slowly the hands turn on our communal nickel watch. It indicates 2:23 P.M. as Schulz proceeds to the larger group in the right corner of the yard and I march forward, preparing myself for the interrogator.

"At ease," is the friendly instruction as his brown eyes take in my profile. "You are not one of Himmler's preferred northern types," he opens the conversation. "I am from the Germanic tribe of Alemannians," I answer boldly. "Do you believe that nonsense?" he asks, laughing. "It is no nonsense, but the history of my people." I try to enlighten him. "OK," he dismisses my answer with a lenient smile. "Have you ever participated in an election?" "No, before I was too young and later as a soldier I did not have the right to vote," I answer. "Do you believe in the final German victory?" is his next question. "I hope for it, because otherwise the future looks very dark," I respond frankly. "Now you are very bitter, but you will get to know a different America. Go to the left corner," he says pleasantly, but I go to the right corner once I am behind his back. Briller follows my steps after two minutes. Hocker then points with his outstretched index finger to the right corner and the officer gallantly grants him his free choice. After an anxious wait, we are delighted to receive Siegfried into our crowd. The fear of being separated is over. The hearing was a nice, if ticklish, change of pace.

After roll call the two groups mix back together and return united to the old compound. The cube of pork that was issued as an evening snack has long been digested and we can still hear from the big mouths how they supposedly told off their interrogators.

*26 October 1944*

Our situation is almost hopeless. Only a few members of our tent community are moving about in the open. Trade on the fence has stopped. Hardly anyone possesses anything of value. Like stupid, sick animals we squat or lie with sunken cheeks in our places. No reasonable word passes from our lips. Vexed and quarrelsome because of hunger and thirst, we are tormented spiritually because of the uncertainty and chaos that threaten to break out at any moment. However, few possess the strength to beat up another, though in the eyes of some the fire of madness glows.

"Dear God in heaven, have mercy on us!" a paratrooper in our tent, who has become despondent during these days, bellows suddenly. He then jumps to his feet and seconds later collapses like an empty sack. Of course he has enraged the entire crowd, who shower their anger upon him with wild curses because of the disturbance. Schulz and I try to calm the excited ones, although we are not free of the prison psychosis ourselves. In the light of day, everyone must confess that he is seldom capable of a normal thought.

Are you normal, am I normal? Are the Americans normal? What does normal mean? The boundaries have been erased. The world is upside down. Its masters have become insane.

"Wasn't that a shot?" I jump up, startled. "It was a shot!" a tough east Prussian confirms and rushes out of the tent. We lie down again after no further sounds penetrate the tent from outside. "A man has been shot!" The east Prussian stands at the tent entrance in shock. "Shut your mouth, you idiot," a Rhinelander barks at him, ready to throw his boots at him. "It is a fact, they are taking him to the doctor," the bringer of bad news insists, wringing his hands. "If you are lying, the devil take you, and if it is true, the Americans," Schulz responds and goes outside.

"The fellow is crazy, the Americans would not go that far," is the opinion of those in the tent who have not troubled themselves about the situation, and they continue to doze. "Shut up!" "Quiet!" is the only utterance they make about this turbulent situation.

"The man is dead! Shot! A blast directly into the breast! Right by the garbage pile! The guard is standing there looking at him!" Shaken, these words fall from Schulz's mouth in the room.

"I must see the face of the murderer," I hear myself say after a pause and go out of the tent.

The prisoners stand in groups close to another and stare at the guard, whose eyes circle the compound nervously. What could have caused him to fire this carefully aimed shot? To simply shoot down an unarmed prisoner of war during the bright of day? If he is insane, why does he not fire another deadly round into the crowd?

An officer with four soldiers comes and places him in the middle. Willingly he allows them to take the weapon from his shoulder. Unruffled, he takes the first steps toward prison—we hope!

A mighty animosity has seized the entire camp. Immediately the Americans strengthen the guards. Thoughtful men admonish peace. But the rumors act as poison among the inmates as they wind their way into every corner and find listeners everywhere. The camp is in an uproar. The weak nerves of the starved men are enraged. And the gunbarrels of the nervous Americans are pointed threateningly into the compounds.

Finally, after an hour a calming or at least diverting rumor circulates that a colonel, the commander of the prisoner of war camp at Le Mans, has arrived up in the main camp and will set things right.

The rumors stumble over themselves. Four o'clock: witnesses to the murder are to be taken up to the Americans. Four-thirty: the colonel is in the camp. Five o'clock: the commander of the Alençon camp has been taken into custody. Five-fifteen: the whistle sounds for distribution of food.

"Let's go," Schulz breathes to Briller and takes up his manifest to go with us to the provisions tent. "Now, what is going on here today?" We nudge each other as the carriers from Cage 10 pass by us, heavily loaded. "Today is the last meal," they tell us to our astonished faces as a truck rolls up to the tent and new provisions are unloaded.

This time no one returns empty-handed. Everyone has a box on his shoulder. "Tent chiefs come and get the provisions," Schulz calls. A can of pork for every four men, about 240 grams for each man! And for each man a small package of cracker bread.

Silently we receive the gigantic portions. Like animals, we gobble them down. The group then lies on the ground without moving. Death has reached into the camp today.

*Chapter Four*

# NEW CAMPS

*29 October 1944*

THE SUN HANGS blood red in the west over the ocean and with its last rays turns to gold the drops of rain hanging on the rusty barbed wire so that they glimmer like fiery rubies. The day comes to an end.

Still camped on this foreign meadow on the edge of Alençon are German soldiers, prisoners of the United States of North America. But we have reason to hope that things will begin to improve for us. Since yesterday we receive provisions three times a day. The individual portions have been doubled for each meal. Milk, butter, white bread, and sugar, all the things we have only known in freedom, are now a part of our daily fare. Who is in a position to measure what joy has been brought into the hearts of the once-confused prisoners of war? But one had to be a random sacrifice to set the stone in motion. Not one of us knows for sure what really transpired. The guard as well as the former commandant have been taken from here. It is further rumored that up to now the available provisions had been shifted to the French. In any case, even our first sergeant has not been seen by any camp inmate since October 26. The guards are correct and committed to making our hard situation easier. Today blankets were issued, but the rumors state that the entire camp is going to be disbanded and cleared out. Now, for us at the moment at least, next to a happy return home, there is no greater wish than to leave this Hell.

I still sit at my place behind the tent. When we arrived here, the barbed wire was new and sparkled like freshly poured lead. Now it sags and is covered with rust between the barbs. The raindrops have stopped. A hateful wetness lies on the wire. Each man should take a piece of it with him home so that he will be protected from now on from petty and narrow-minded views.

"Come in my tent, my boy, it is cold." Schulz tears me out of my contemplation. "Here, Schulz, shouldn't we secure a piece of the barbed wire as a souvenir from Alençon?" I ask him and pull at the wire. "We are still here, my friend. I will never forget this spot on the globe, even without a souvenir. Now come and let's drink our milk before it is completely dark."

### 31 October 1944

"All sergeants are to report on the camp road with their blankets and personal belongings!" a call sounds immediately over the graves of the still-living prisoners of war in Alençon.

Finally it is true! Shaken, we stare at one another. Some shake their heads in unbelief. To leave Alençon alive? That must be a mistake! How many years have we been here? Are we the last survivors from the great war?

"Hurry up, get ready, you fools; don't stand there like blockheads looking for additional holes in your rotten socks," Briller thunders and rolls his eyes like a wild boar. "And now?" Hocker asks, the dimples having left his cheeks. "Temporarily only a better camp, Willi," is my answer. "Whether it is a better grave, that must be confirmed." Schulz mixes in. "Poland is not yet lost. In a short time we will be free, so let's go." Siegfried drives us out of the tent.

Dirty, full of lice, torn, gaunt, a stinking pile, the refuge of the war, that is what assembles on the camp road. A few more than eight hundred noncommissioned officers of the great German army are counted. Is it really eleven, twelve, or fourteen weeks since all these men stood with weapons in their hands against the enemy, instilling fear and horror in them? Unbelievable! But it is really so. Here, Staff Sergeant Robert Briller, thirty-two years old, a member of my division. The picture of the ideal soldier, powerfully built, a brunette with a slightly receding forehead, black, jovial eyes, hawk nose, small, turned-up lips, and a vigorous chin, I got to know him in the hospital in Auxerre. At first he imposed himself on me, but later he proved to be a brave soldier and a good comrade. Well-acquainted with nearly all the battlefields and whorehouses of this war, he is an example of the modern farm boy.

Then Sergeant Willi Hocker, twenty-six years old, a small fellow, blond and blue-eyed, a slightly turned up nose and a girl-like mouth and chin. Always open to the joys of life, he was a soldier of undaunted bravery. A survivor of my division, I got to know him in Paris where our mutual affinity sealed the unbreakable bonds of friendship. From that moment on, in good as well as bad days, my trusted companion. I now beg to heaven that our future paths will never be separate.

The vehicles have arrived and the provisions distributed. The resurrected look at the searchers that have arrived. What do you want? Yes, we know, it is your duty. But put on your gloves, you men from God's own land, otherwise you will be infected with the pestilence in our lousy pockets!

The road looms before us. The searchers become helpers. Either with humor or in seriousness, according to their individual nature and temperament, they assist the weak into the trucks. The black drivers start up the motors. In the American camp the American flag is raised. It is eight o'clock in the morning. A bugle sounds. "Do we hear the trumpets from Jericho?" Schulz says with a broken voice and wipes his eyes.

Slowly the black soldiers drive their dishonored white freight out of the camp and turn into the road. Behind the barbed wire walls stand thousands waving a tired good-bye to us—men who in the next days will follow us. Before we reach the first houses, the name of the city stands on a bent sign—a city that will remain burned in the consciousness of more than twenty thousand German prisoners of war: Alençon!

The city is behind us. Quickly the convoy speeds to the south. Our beards flutter like flags in the wind. Although our eyes have a free and unhindered view over the land colored by fall, no one sees the beauty of nature. No sound comes from the lips of those raped by the war and barbed wire. A glance into the eyes of our comrades is enough to know: we have escaped. But have we really? Mistrust is still awake. No one has said where they are taking us. Only the motor of the truck sings a monotonous sound, as though it was happy itself to take us away from here.

At 2:00 P.M. we reach Le Mans, turn right from the main street, and our goal is in sight. An ocean of barracks and tents, snuggled between low pines and soft ground swells, appears before us. Joyfully agitated, we discover frail smoke clouds rising up from the oven pipes in the kitchen barracks. Where there is smoke there is fire! Where there is fire there are people! Where there are people there is cooking! And where there is cooking means that we will finally get something warm to eat!

Dear God, why can't we leave the truck? Why is the convoy turning onto the open meadow? What are the many American soldiers for? Do they really think we could still escape?

"Please leave the trucks and line up in five rows!" a German staff sergeant orders. With feet like clay, we drag ourselves to the assembly place. We are divided into companies. Company leaders are appointed. The American searchers touch us with disgust.

But now the blacks come, armed with spray cans and sacks from which they shake white powder as they go through the open ranks. "Unbutton your shirts and pants," the staff sergeant laughs, and soon the blacks are spreading their pulverized poison in the dirty, louse-infested clothes of the men from Alençon. Covered in white like flour mill workers, we stand and follow with all our senses the running and crawling across our skin as the lice poison begins to work. Relieved, we breathe easily as the tenants give up the ghost.

"Man, that worked," is the expression from all.

The march into the camp begins. The guards have opened the wide gates and allow us to pass by, simply shaking their heads. We make our way into Cage 3 by way of a wide asphalt street which is cleanly washed on both sides and lined with well-fed German soldiers who stand without speaking and as they look at us do not know whether to laugh or cry. Minutes later Schulz has divided his company into the barracks. Satisfied, we observe our new quarters. A sparkling clean room with straw strewn along the wall on the wood floor. Finally solid housing! Just as quickly as one heart beat follows the other, we lie down on our backs on the soft straw which smells of summer and thank the gods for our salvation. But before we are overcome with sleep, the door is thrown open and a man dressed in the white work clothes of a cook appears and calls us to receive our food. Whether we are awake or dreaming is not clear, but we do get up and step outside in an instant.

In the front of each barrack stand three tin containers out of which steam rises and whose smell threatens to completely confuse our tormented spirits. With the last bit of energy, Schulz is successful in getting the men into rows and distributes to them the cans with hot food.

And now it is my turn. With the feeling of a predatory animal that smells blood, I step up to the bucket and hold with shaking hands my two cans under the ladle, which has a capacity of about one liter. The can in my left hand is filled with spinach, meat, and gravy. Five potatoes about the size of tennis balls are placed in the other can. As quickly as possible I hurry to a sand hill and kneel to set down the cans that have become very hot. Carefully I begin to peel a potato with my fingernails until suddenly all reason leaves me and in an animal-like eating frenzy I shovel the potatoes with their skins into me, mixing the gravy and spinach into a fluid to help swallow down the potatoes. After I have also gulped down the meat, I drop to my side exhausted. Black curtains appear before my eyes. I feel sick as a dog. My stomach is turned inside out. My neck is stretched. My first warm meal trickles into the sand. Mechanically I once again shovel in the unchewed pieces of potato.

"That was a bad move, my dear," Hocker whispers to me, annoyed, as I open my eyes. "Damn it anyway, how can that happen to me?" I ask, looking at him in amazement as he calmly eats his food in small bites using Schulz's spoon. "Calm yourself, take a look around, all of them are throwing up," is his entire comfort.

We lie warm and cozy in the straw. The nausea has eased and my stomach is as empty as a drum. It is 6:00 P.M. From outside they call for us to get our tea.

"Are you feeling better?" Briller breathes in my ear. "Somewhat, I do feel a little better." I smile feebly. "What do you think of this hotel?" he asks, squinting roguishly with his left eye.

"It's OK until something better comes along," I answer, satisfied. "Earlier the mess sergeant was with Schulz. According to what he said, the Alençoners, as they call us here, are to receive extra provisions. He maintains that in less than four weeks he will have us back to our old selves," the good-hearted Briller reports, full of hope. "Then let them bring on the food; we have to eat by ourselves." I grin at him happily. "Keep it to yourself this time," he teases, "and don't spit it in the sand again." "It was just too hot and I ate it too fast, that will be a lesson for me." I nod to him.

"Here, you lazy stinkers." Hocker hands up a gigantic can of wonderfully smelling hot tea. "Man, where did you get that pail?" we stammer at the same time to the freshly washed Hocker. "Did you fall into a teapot; you shine like a monkey's ass?" Briller asks him and carefully takes the handle of the cup after I have carefully taken a few sips of the sweet tea. "No." He beams all over his face. "There is running water in the camp." "I am going crazy! Water lines, here in this cage?" I ask, unbelieving. "Are there also cleaning girls who will fluff up the straw?" Briller bursts out laughing, causing the tea to go down the wrong pipe. "Boy, that cup is the size of a marmalade bucket! Tell me, where do you get one of those things?" the old farm boy wants to know. "There is a whole mountain of them behind the kitchen barracks," Hocker informs him. "And how is it with the water lines?" I ask, in danger of being laughed at. "Come with me and see for yourself." He acts insulted. "Come on old man, we are going to go wash," I encourage Briller. "I can't do it right now. Look here, my legs are swollen," he says, pointing to his bloated calves and ankles. "You must go to the doctor, Robert, that is a bad sign," I say firmly so that he will not pass it off, then I follow Hocker out of the room. Surprised, I stop in my steps. In the meantime it has become night but in the camp it is still quite bright. "I am astonished!" I clear my throat and blink at the electric lights!

Like a mountain spring, the silver water dashes heavily over my hands. Childlike, men are playing in the cold wetness. "There is water, friends! Drink yourself dead and you will die happy," a half crazy shrieks.

"Now for a towel and soap, Willi; then we could really get clean," Hocker expresses across from us. "Even that hour will come, Helmut, you can count on it." He comforts me optimistically, while I take out my dirty handkerchief and wash it for the first time in weeks before I wipe off my face and hands with it.

"... and now listen up for a minute," Schulz speaks to his people as we enter the barracks again. "The Americans require that we keep order and discipline. We are responsible to keep the camp clean. Streets and walks must be kept clean all the time; the same goes for our quarters. In order to organize the cleaning details, I think that we should organize a work detail of volunteers who will be rewarded with extra provisions. I would appreciate it if the longest in rank would take on the responsibility as barrack leader and those who wish to work can report to them. As far as I can tell in the other barracks, there are enough men who are ready to work. I don't need to tell you that you don't have to work yourself to death. Whoever is willing to work for extra provisions, please raise your hands. Thank you, there are more than enough. Who is the oldest in rank? Your name, Comrade? Good, Staff Sergeant Meyer is assigned as barracks leader here. Who wants to work can report to him." Schulz ends his work for the day as company leader and lets himself fall exhausted into the straw.

For the first time I notice that his beard has been shaved and his hair cut. The upper part of his face is very pale, but free of dirt. He smells of soap. "And now friends," he lifts his head just once out of the straw, "sleep well, we will see our homeland again."

### 1 November 1944

Exactly at 8:00 A.M., we are called to get coffee. With large cups in our hands, the men from Camp Alençon stand in double rows behind the coffee containers and breathe in the aroma of the hot drink. At the same time the personnel in the kitchen are preparing our breakfast, which will be given out one barracks at a time to the barracks leader. Before half an hour has passed, the groups sit in their places drinking the wonderful bean coffee and eating white bread with marmalade.

Cautious because of yesterday's terrible experience, I sip my coffee slowly, although the desire rages bitterly inside me. Once again it is demonstrated what self-control our Comrade Schulz possesses. He takes in no more than what a mother would give her suckling baby. With the exception of Siegfried, whose stomach could apparently digest iron nails, we follow our friend Schulz's example. Admittedly the provisions that we secured by deceit kept us from nearly starving. We can tell which few, by trading with the Americans or through other means, were able to obtain some extra nourishment once in a while. Naturally they camouflage themselves by talking about their good constitution and so forth, but the others are not so dumb as to believe it and the traders and middle men are well known. Before, the poorest of the poor kept quiet because in their helplessness they always hoped that something might come their way, but now with the coming of the golden age, they are not bashful about expressing their opinions and showing contempt for the others.

Because we have friends involved in these quarrels and since we do not feel comfortable ourselves although we did not harm any comrades, we keep quiet about our coup. To our great surprise, one of the men who shared our tent tells how he, with three others from our tent, swindled the Americans. They made knives with the iron banding strips and cut the parchment-like paper in which the biscuit boxes were packed into notes the size of five-hundred-franc bills. Then they colored them with crayons to look like French banknotes and sold them in the dark of night to the American guards for food. After this mean trick is revealed, laughter rings throughout our barracks and we are freed from our own feelings of guilt.

In the meantime it is 10:00 A.M. and a new joyful event awaits us. The main camp leader stands in the doorway and wishes to speak to Schulz. "Present yourselves for a bath," he says to Schulz, so loud that we all can hear. In unbelief we all stare at the man. Bath? Where? How? "In the camp, in a transportable bath, and with water and soap, naturally," he willingly informs us and then leaves the room shaking his head.

It is exactly 11:30 A.M. as Hocker, four companions, and I strip the last rags from our lean and dirty bodies in the dressing room of the bath wagon. But we do not have time for any long observations because a gigantic black, who functions as the bathhouse master, drives us to hurry with his loud screams. The bath wagon is like a beehive. The coming and going is well organized, but instead of honey, it is the stinking filth that is stripped from the human bodies.

"Let's go." A black, standing on the right side of the entrance to the showers, waves to our group and passes each of us a piece of soap, after which we separate under the showers. A torrent of hot water floods over our bodies when they turn a handle on the wall. Just as I am beginning to enjoy my bath, the stream of water stops. "Soap up." The black grins, holding the handle, and shows a row of wonderful teeth as he watches with pride the results of the German words he has spoken while we go to work to soap our bodies. Although it is the best soap, it simply will not produce any foam on our bodies. Once again the black bath master turns the handle. A second shower pours over us. "Let's go," he orders us from the shower room while another throws an olive green towel on our heads and then a moment later collects them without us having had a chance to dry ourselves. We are then shoved into the dressing room where another black sprays disinfectant over our bodies just like he has done with the clothing lying on the floor. With a feeling of disgust, we pull on the shirts—which seem more like coal sacks—and jump into our pants and boots and with our field blouses in our hands escape from the wagon only to have the "lice killer" throw our forgotten hats after us.

We saunter along the asphalt road to Cage 1, where we reflect on a mosaic work done by the camp inmates. Spread out before us in the sand and made of white and black stones set down together is the American flag.

"Nicely done," I utter in passing. "It is only a little too wearisome for me." "How many small cans do you think the man got from the Americans for it?" Siegfried asks, hungry. "The talent and the endurance of the man would have been worthy of something better," Schulz says lightly, upset, without taking up Siegfried's question. "Let the man have his fun, perhaps he will be able to preserve his health with it. Some make rings and some gold. He just made a flag." I harmlessly defend the unknown artist. "A flag . . . , when I hear that. He made the American flag, that is what it is about." Schulz flies into a rage. "Don't get excited." I try to calm him again. "He really can't lay a swastika in front of the American's door if he wants to earn extra provisions." "In my view, the man has no character. The Americans would have recognized other kinds of work. Or do they believe that the American prisoners of war in Germany build the German war flag out of stones?" he asks, somewhat cooled down. "They are in the first place businessmen, and then Americans, at least as far as I have been able to learn. If they can increase their health with busts of Hitler or whatever, they will do it because their thoughts follow a different track than ours. That is not to say that they don't spit on the busts before they prepare them for shipment. We must become more familiar with the mentality of our guards if we want to pull off another swindle. We will not get far with them using a straightlaced Heil Hitler." I pick at Schulz's correct but inelastic thoughts. "Shut up with your wise ass ideas." Briller mixes in. "They should give us enough to eat; then the whole nonsense will stop by itself." "Right." Siegfried falls in. "They should ship in the feed so that we can begin to think clearly again." "That is exactly what they will not do. As long as we are hungry, our thoughts revolve around eating. That way we are not dangerous to them." Hocker also takes part in the conversation. "You are right, Willi, my stomach is growling again; let's go in the cage; perhaps in the meantime they have put something else there for us," Siegfried picks up the pace.

As we enter the barracks, Schulz is told to go to the camp leader. "What does he want at nine o'clock at night?" Schulz asks the man angrily. "He didn't say." The spokesman turns, unconcerned, back to his buddies. "In any case, the man turned around and hit the American with two hard slaps to the head so that he fell to the ground." The speaker continues his tale, which had apparently been interrupted by our arrival. "Yes, and then?" all of those assembled ask him with curiosity. "Then the sergeant disappeared into the crowd. The American stood up, asked the name of the sergeant, and when no one answered, he turned around and marched back into the headquarters. That is all I know," the man ends his latest news report from the camp at Le Mans. "This could be fun," Siegfried suggests after we sit down in the straw. "The American struck the German from behind without any reason," Hocker adds to the report since, in the meantime, he had made inquiries of an eyewitness.

The episode is being discussed all over the barracks; while the courage of the sergeant is praised, there is fear of consequences from the Americans. When Schulz returns we go outside. "The camp spokesman thinks that the sergeant should turn himself in if the commandant intends to carry out reprisals against the entire camp." Schulz opens our council. "Now I want to hear your opinion," he says, looking us in the eyes in anticipation. "I think that he should not report," Briller expresses firmly. "That's my opinion also. Besides it is not for certain that the American will do anything about it. He was clearly at fault. The American hit first. This time he met up with the right man. In fact I am in favor of hitting back immediately in the future. Who doesn't do it should be assigned to the Honey Wagon as punishment, since that is work for cowards." Hocker joins in. "That's right, Willi, you have said what I was feeling," I agree. "I also think that the man should be hidden," Siegfried reports. "I see that I am in the right company. I am proud to have such friends. The sergeant already reported to me. He is from the tank corps and is ready to turn himself in to the Americans, if that is what they want—that is, when the entire camp is to be punished for it. I talked him out of it. Now we will see if unity still exists among the old Germans. This is the appropriate situation to determine it; then the American hit him from behind without any reason and right is on our side without question. I am going to go explain it to all our comrades. I am anxious to know if anyone will step out against the sergeant or whether the old saying, 'One for all and all for one,' is still valid. Otherwise I will give up this job and just take it easy. See you later." Schulz departs.

### 2 November 1944

"We have some real despicable punks in our company; that shames me to be a German and a soldier," Schulz says to me after the meager breakfast. "You must give the men a little time, Schulz. The terrible experience of Alençon is still in the bones of the crowd. None of us are full yet. Everyone still thinks only of food. It will take weeks before we have enough strength for our thoughts to follow their normal course. Not until then can you ask me my opinion." I try to persuade him from his prejudgments. "It could be that you are right, but I consider myself too good to represent such characterless scoundrels," he answers as he observes his tin can. "What did the men actually tell you last night when you went through the barracks to get support for the sergeant?" I ask him in order to have a clearer picture of why he is so upset. "Answered?" he asks slowly. "Yes, that is what makes me so sick. Most of them said absolutely nothing, but some murmured because they fear that the Americans will hang the feed bag even higher. If the Americans identify the sergeant, that means someone from our ranks has betrayed him, and I will go in the desert." He postpones his decision as roll call sounds. "You are not Jesus Christ, but even He came back from there and began His work," I offer him for thought after we have left the barracks and make our way to the road, where we meet Hocker, Briller, and Siegfried.

"Comrades, last night there was a regrettable incident on the camp road that appears to threaten our good relationship with the Americans," the camp leader begins his speech after the end of roll call as the American officers in charge of the roll call look up in the sky. According to the Americans, the man who struck down the soldier last night is to report for a hearing. He has until eleven o'clock to do so. If he is too cowardly to turn himself in, then Cage 3 can expect their provisions to be withheld. Dismissed!"

Silently the crowd disperses. The men come back together in groups in front of the barracks. The troublemakers meet in the latrine. After about twenty minutes a pair of representatives of the majority opinion come to Schulz. "Nothing can happen to the sergeant since he acted in self-defense," they say. "In his position as company leader, Schulz should order the man to report. It would be nonsense for the entire cage to go hungry because someone is too cowardly to stand up for what he did." "The company is to assemble in front of the barracks," Schulz answers and points with his finger to the barracks exit and, like whipped dogs, they leave our quarters.

"Don't take a vote, Schulz," warns Siegfried. "Let the reins loose," counsels Briller. "Don't burn your fingers," Hocker adds. "Do what you think is right," are my last words on the matter.

"Who is in favor that the man, who last night on the camp road was hit by an American soldier and who defended himself from his tormentor with two blows, should go to headquarters and receive his punishment, please step to the left!" Schulz demands in one sentence that the assembled company of Cage 3 decide for themselves.

After a short pause movement begins in the ranks and more than half the group move to the left side.

"The sergeant please come forward," Schulz calls with a stone face. Tension-filled minutes pass, but the man does not come in front of the company. Slowly Schulz goes along the front rank looking in every face. Upset, he then returns to the center. "Where is the tank sergeant?" he asks more himself than the men in the company. A tall man from the tank grenadiers goes toward Schulz. Curiously the men, now divided into two ranks, fix their attention on the man, who speaks softly to Schulz until a handshake ends the conversation.

"The man has already gone to the Americans. Someone betrayed him last night. That is the work of a pair of miserable creatures, but the majority is in agreement. It is a scandal to be with these rogues as long as there are men dying on the front for whom the expression 'comrade' is not an empty word. For me personally, no one should expect that I will continue to play the jackass on whose back this characterless horde can ride. As of now, I willingly resign my position and will inform the camp leader of it immediately." Schulz ends his speech and calmly leaves the cage.

"The pretender can go to the devil; he only took the position in order to get better provisions," observes a skinny corporal with insane fire in his eyes. "We don't want a calcified rod as our company leader any more," another says. "We don't need any leader at all. Something to eat and peace is what we want," sounds throughout as the crowd disperses.

We have beans, carrots, and corned beef for lunch. The whole thing is cooked with potato powder and tastes wonderful. Feelings have calmed down. Bent over the plates, we shovel into our bodies the food that has so long been withheld from us. The sergeant is forgotten. Schulz has returned from the company leader. The Americans have already demanded his removal since they were informed already about his conduct. Downcast, we friends stretch out in the straw and fall into a restless afternoon sleep.

Around 4:00 P.M. a shrill whistle brings us back from dreamland. In front of the barracks someone bellows that before evening roll call, the company must choose a new leader. We remain lying in our places. "They can worry about that themselves," Briller indicates lazily and with such a great yawn that he cracks his jaw. Our friend Schulz, who in the beginning could find no sleep, turns completely over on his back and continues to snore peacefully.

Our new company leader is introduced at evening roll call. He is no man of importance. Gray, uneasy eyes look out from black-framed glasses almost spitefully at the company. He is of small build and the silver star of a lance corporal glittering in the sunlight gives the impression he is a slimy pusher. The American sergeant, to whom he reads the attendance report, does not thank him for his salute, but instead looks past him and moves on to count the soldiers himself.

Before the U.S. sergeant has left the camp, the entire crowd disperses without giving any attention to their new company leader. It is even worse when the food is distributed. Like wild sows, they all shove their way to the food containers brought by the kitchen personnel, and everyone tries to push the other from the bucket. Helpless, but full of rage, Schulz's replacement stands before the men and watches the resulting chaos as his first words about order and discipline flutter, unheard, in the wind. Already most are murmuring about the obvious inability of their new spokesman, but now it is too late. Among prisoners of war, it is not enough to have two stars on the shoulder in order to create respect, but simply and singly, one personality. When the kitchen personnel finally become tired of the whole scene, they hold their ladles under crossed arms and refuse to give out any more food until the wild herd becomes reasonable again. Naturally, the final result of this unbridled behavior is that we end up spending twice as long standing around.

Again Schulz proves his pure character in this critical situation. Immediately after the food is issued, he sets his two cans down by us and goes through the barracks. "I ask you comrades," he says in each building, "be reasonable and follow the instructions of my replacement. He certainly gives it with the same good intention that I did. I ask you to consider that the Americans keep a watchful eye on what we do. They will certainly not listen to a company leader who cannot establish and maintain discipline among his group. I have established a good impression among the American camp leaders. This camp is, I believe, in good hands. It is only up to us what we make of it. Order, cleanliness, discipline, actually the natural characteristics of our people, and firm control, are the things with which we can accomplish nearly everything in our camp. It is not always important who demands something, but the main thing is for whom it is ordered. Again, I ask you in your own interest and in the interest of everyone, to stay together; then we will be able to come through these hard times in prison."

### 10 November 1944

"It is too bad, really too bad, this hair could be worked into a nice wig," the man says over me while he is busy with the scissors and comb cutting my long mane back to the length of a match stick. "They are more suited for a street broom," Briller laughs next to me, unashamed about his own joke, hindering his barber.

The men from Alençon sit in a wide circle under the clippers. Last night we received Red Cross items. Each two men now possess a razor, two blades, a brush, and a piece of American shaving soap. In addition everyone received ten cigarettes. No wonder that today great joy rules in the cage. But now the barbers are at work. Schulz is one of the first who parades back into the cage completely clean. In amazement I stare at the well-known, stately figure with the nearly completely new face. Clean shaven, the hair cut and combed, freshly washed, with a cleaned suit and polished boots, he stands before me smiling while the machine is directed under my chin by the trained hands of the barber. What a man, I think. Certainly he would be the object of attention by many women if they would let him out to promenade on a boulevard or a street.

"I have something to announce to the company," our company leader says after evening roll call. "The Americans are pleased with the cleanliness of our cage, especially the barracks and the latrines. They were also very pleased with how we looked today after the barbers were here. Unfortunately there are still some among us who are unshaven and unwashed. The barbers have been instructed to report here tomorrow between ten and twelve o'clock. Bathing is at 2:00 P.M. By this time it would be very nice if the last ones would leave the bath wagon shaved and with their hair cut. I ask the barracks leaders to see that such will be the case. It is in our own interest not to tolerate anyone among us who does not keep his body clean. One thing additional to announce: There are school classes being offered in Camp 2. Every afternoon there are lectures on literature, art history, and philosophy. Whoever wants to do something for their education can show up there each day. Silence!" he interrupts himself as the statement about the lectures brings forth some muttering. "Now we come to the last and most important point for today," he continues. "There have been rumors that tonight we would be able to write. I have the following to say about that: After the food is distributed, the barracks leaders can obtain writing paper from me. Every man can have only one sheet. If you ruin it, you cannot get a second one since they will be counted out exactly. Only letters that are written on this special paper will be sent to Geneva. You cannot identify any places, no political or military commentary or things of that sort. Only those things of a familiar nature, for example: 'I have landed in prison and I am doing well …' "

"No way," the entire group bellows in response to these words and disperses.

"Such garbage, 'I am doing well … ' " you can hear the men curse as they hurry into the barracks to get their eating utensils since it is nearly time for supper.

After finishing the evening meal we friends are tightly squeezed together with the writing paper in our hands. There is a continuous roar of voices in the barracks so that it is impossible to think clearly. "I will report to the folks at home the pure truth about our conditions here with the Americans," someone screams and waves his white sheet of paper like an important document over his nearly clean-shaven skull. "You fool," another bellows laughing, "then your letter will end up in the wastebasket and the people at home will know nothing of you." "So lies, nothing but lies, is what we are to serve up to our relatives at home," observes a sword-thin sergeant, "then I will avoid writing anything." "That's right," a couple of others join in, "we refuse to write if we cannot report the truth."

"Such idiots," thunders Schulz and gets up from his straw mat. "Listen up." He turns toward everyone. "Be a little reasonable, men! It is nonsense what you are prattling. What good will it do your relatives to know the truth? Nothing but worry, once they are finally free of the uncertainty about your situation. They know anyway that imprisonment is no visit to a resort. Besides, such a letter will never get out of the camp. Look at the little sheet. Do you think you can write very much? Let your relatives know that you are still healthy, that you hope to see them and your homeland again, that life behind barbed wire can be endured, and call on them to have courage, even to hold out so that together we can go about healing the wounds of this war. Don't forget that we had a censor in the German army and there it was not possible to report back to the homeland about the negative aspects of the theater of war because they simply did not want to see relatives at home upset. Let's please have some quiet within these four walls so that we can finally get down to writing."

The largest part of the men agree with him as Schulz lies back down on the straw. "It really is true, damn it anyway. Sometimes this place seems like an insane asylum," he says to us and looks with a furrowed brow at the lined sheet of paper in his hands.

About nine o'clock the letters are collected and taken to the camp leader. There is almost a festive calm in the barracks. Everyone is alone with his thoughts. Germany, the homeland, how are our loved ones?

### 15 November 1944

The new day is cold and foggy. "The devil is loose in the camp," a broken voice announces behind me as I wash my upper body with cold water. "The Stars and Stripes made out of stone was destroyed during the night. The Americans are withholding this morning's coffee, and the threat of cutting off our provisions hangs over the entire camp," rocks throughout the washroom. "Fall out by companies along the street," a call sounds in our wet ears.

"Here we go again," says Siegfried in our concerned silence. "What idiots were at work? How can someone be so dumb as to bring the entire camp into difficulty with his impertinence?" I am overcome with anger. "The fellow must be punished by us." Schulz also boils over. "Let's go," Hocker says, depressed. We take our washing and shaving items back to the barracks.

A storm of indignation rages in our quarters. "Such imbeciles should be beaten," a choir of voices sounds in unison. "No, the one who put the flag together to enrage us should be whipped," can be heard from one corner. "It did not bother me at all; it does not matter what someone does to get something to eat," comes from another direction. "Yes, as far as I am concerned, they can put Caesar Nero either in charge or on top of our shithouse as long as my plate is filled up three times a day," another speaks out. "Come out, I will cover you with shit, you monkey." "Stop, this is not the way, men." Schulz steps in. "Fall out." Someone tears open the door and slams it against the wall so that the dust comes out. "They can lick our asses." Someone goes after the man. "Damn it anyway, come out." The black glasses of the company leader appear in the door frame.

All Hell has broken loose. The spirits are confused, the weak nerves are ready to snap, and the empty bellies call for the nourishment that we have become used to. Hunger, the most terrible ghost on earth, floats over the camp grinning and showing the poor half-insane men its ugly face.

Along the camp street stand the companies of the prisoner of war camp Le Mans. The entire leadership of the camp is on their feet. The brown figures of the American guards armed with red clubs scurry around the entire camp like chickens. Rain starts to fall softly. The whole theater makes me sick.

The counting begins. As every day, the rosters are compared. A second counting follows. The Americans are nervous. The count does not agree. Guards are sent through the empty barracks. They return without success. Eight men have disappeared. A third count brings the same result. Camp 3 is ordered to the barracks. The barracks leaders must stand in the door with their rosters and the men must sit at their places. Eight prisoners have disappeared during the night. They chose freedom.

Slowly the pressure on the hearts of the imprisoned is released and they glide slowly into a satisfied smirk. There are still real men among us who have not been broken by all the misery that has come upon us. Now they are gone from us; may their fate be a merciful one.

At eleven o'clock breakfast is issued. The mess sergeant is ordered to return eight portions to the camp leaders. A truck loaded with items for our noon meal is being unloaded by the kitchen. The Americans have decided against any reprisals.

"This time we were mistaken, Schulz," I admit freely as we sip the hot coffee. "It was still foolish for the escapees to destroy the flag and leave their visiting card behind. It would have been easy if the entire camp would have had to do penance for it and if they are captured then they will also be punished for the act," he answers, not completely without envy for these men whose courage is being spoken about throughout the entire camp. "What do you think, Schulz, shouldn't we make our way eastward?" Siegfried hazes him in good spirits. "Shut your mouth, it still eats at me because these boys did not have any trust in me even though I knew one of them very well. He is from my home town and is a well-known athlete there," Schulz responds. "He will say hello to your little wife, if his flight is successful." Siegfried continues to tease him. "Knock it off, I tell you, you damn asshole," Schulz roars, completely out of composure, and glances around the barracks with hate-filled eyes. Astonished, we look at each other. Slowly the connection comes to me. "Stay here, I will talk with him," I say and follow Schulz.

"Does the man know your wife?" I ask with little diplomacy, coming right to the point. "Yes," is the toneless answer from his lips, as he puts his right foot onto a sand hill, shoves his hands into his pockets, and gazes out over the barbed wire eastward. Perplexed, I pick a piece of straw from my field jacket and twist it playfully in my hands. "Very well?" I ask after a pause. "Yes, that's the hell of it, they were once friends," he discloses. "And you hope that the escape is not successful?" I bore further. "As a soldier, yes, … as Mr. Schulz, … , no," he answers coldly. "A twisted affair," I say slowly. "Don't you have any trust in your wife?" "Yes," he turns to me, "but no longer any in him since he disappeared without saying good-bye."

"Now I remember the man. Is he the tall, slender sergeant from the tank grenadiers that you spoke with from time to time?" I ask curiously. "That's him," he answers, taking a cigarette from his ration package of six cigarettes. My God, he smokes! No, he sticks it back in and puts the pack away. "Hey, give me a light, comrade," he calls to a passerby and pulls the cigarettes once again from his pocket.

"Here, Helmut, smoke one with me," he says, subdued, and lights a cigarette on the match that is offered to him. "Thank you." He dismisses the man as thick clouds of smoke begin to encircle him. "Damn it, it is still raining." He acts amazed as he hands me the match and the white cigarette paper shows gray spots. "Ah, that does not taste good anymore; why are we smoking anyway?" he asks in his confusion, throwing the cigarette into the wet sand and spitting contemptuously afterward.

"What do you think about trying to escape? I mean, do you think it could be successful?" he asks suddenly. "The chances are one to ninety-nine. Whoever just takes off without any preparation has no chance at all," I answer him coolly since the purpose of his idea is clear to me. "Do you believe the eight men will make it?" he asks further. "I hope so," I respond. "My acquaintance speaks fluent French and is not conspicuous in his appearance here in France. That is a powerful advantage for him." He nods his head several times in recognition of the ability of his adversary.

"Listen to me, Schulz." I pull my confused friend toward me. "The man who is causing you to worry knows your wife; they were once friends. Good! He also knows you and apparently your one weakness, your love for your wife. I have put myself in his place and considered why he did not tell an acquaintance whose character he knows well. You were not the best of friends; otherwise you would not have joined with us. A predecessor is always painful for a man, but we have little interest in the one who comes afterward."

"Stop," he tries to interrupt me. "Be quiet, I am talking now." I deflect him. "So, the man said to himself that you are jealous of him and in such a condition might not think clearly and could jeopardize his escape. I tell you openly, that if I were in his situation I would not have done any differently. Finally, he was also responsible to the seven others. But believe me, he did not undertake the escape because of your wife. That is behind him, either because he lost her to you or because she was just a passing affair for him. Who is in love does not believe that what is so important to him is of little interest to another. But it is really so. I will prove to you that the escape of this man does not have the slightest thing to do with your wife. He went through the wire into a dangerous freedom. Assuming that he is successful in getting back to Germany, which would take weeks, then he must calculate that your letter from here has already reached her. With the difficult military situation in Germany, he cannot assume that he will be allowed much time before he is once again sent to the front, where he is in real danger of becoming another victim of the war. It is absurd to think that someone would take on such a danger just to try and take another man's wife, even if it were possible, while on the other hand there is an almost certainty that her husband will return home healthy and well. No, my friend! There are other reasons that drove him out of this cage. Lack of freedom, humiliation, depression, and all that which we call barbed wire sickness is enough to explain his escape. Send your fears to the devil. With a man like you, such abnormal complexes are a basic contradiction to your personality. You must be told that. Don't be mad at me because I am the one that does it. But don't forget what I have told you and wish your acquaintance all the best luck for his flight; he will need it."

"It's time for lunch, let's get our plates," he says, overwhelmed at my words, and turns tiredly to go.

"What do you think, Helmut, are you going with us for the class?" Siegfried asks me after lunch. "Yes, of course," I answer him. "I still have to make up some classes." "Then get out of here so that we can sleep," Briller hisses at us. "I'm going with you." Hocker decides at the last moment and receives a disapproving smirk from Briller. "Sleep good," we wish the two lazy fellows and make our way to school.

"It may be that for most of the prisoners of war in this camp it is presumptuous or even quite crazy that in our situation we organize a school," one of the prisoners opens his lecture after a short welcome. Even the stiff soldier's coat cannot hide his civilian profession. "But the fact that the tent is completely filled confirms for me that this undertaking is right, that the desire for knowledge within the barbed wire, especially among the younger generation, is big enough to justify a series of planned lectures. It may be that this or that comrade who is present today will stop attending sooner or later, since he is only here out of curiosity, but there will be others who come who are not only tired of the boredom in the barracks, but simply because they seek intellectual nourishment. In order to take all the wind out of the sails of possible intrigues in advance, please allow me to say that the idea to undertake a kind of school instruction does not come from pure love for our neighbor. The teaching faculty who are present have no other reason in their hearts or minds than to prepare themselves for their civilian occupation. That may sound quite brazen, but if you are smart, you will take advantage of it and become smarter with our help. Knowledge is power, ignorance is weakness. It is up to each individual with what knowledge he will take up the struggle for existence in the homeland. With this explanation, I think I have painted a realistic picture for you and now turn the time over to Comrade Piotrowski, a future professor of literature," the sincere man finishes his speech and a frail little man in his fifties climbs onto the box which had served his predecessor as a podium.

"Ah, our boys are here." Schulz receives us sitting in the straw, well rested. "Where did you leave your school packs?" Briller kids us in a good mood. "Your brain is already dying, otherwise your hair would grow again." Siegfried strokes his bald spot. "Just the opposite, my dear, when the understanding comes, then the hair must retreat," Briller trumps. "Nonsense, hair does not grow on chalk," Siegfried says, already bored. "By the way, what do you hear about supper?" He swings around and sniffs in the air. "Cheese?" Hocker asks. "That is what it smells like." Siegfried circles with his nose until we all break out in ringing laughter, and finally he also discovers Briller's naked feet. "Get out of here and wash your tank treads," he orders the old farm boy, who sits grinning and massaging his toes. "I was just in the process of leaving, but your appearance kept me back," Briller discloses and then leaves.

Because of the misty rain, we are forced to remain in the barracks. Night comes earlier. In our barracks there is the depressed mood of a useless November day that has passed.

"I thought about your words from this morning, Helmut," Schulz says to me after supper. "Did your reflection do any good, Schulz?" I ask, at the moment little interested in his conversation. "Yes, but I notice that I came at a bad time for you," he answers, disappointed. "It is past; go ahead, shoot, I am all ears," I encourage him. "OK, the situation is just right since the others are still washing. To make it short," he begins, "I agree with your point. At the time this sport star left my wife in a bind when she could have used a good friend. I know that she was blinded by his passing fame and that is why she gave herself to him. He revealed himself to be a scoundrel, something that she will certainly never forgive."

"If she was only blinded by his fame and became friends with him, then she did not deserve anything better than to be misused," I say objectively. "Show me your better side, otherwise in the future I must keep everything inside." The large man pleads for understanding for his feelings. "Were you the man who saved her from her miserable situation after the other one refused?" I ask now, completely tuned in to the matter. "Yes, I had seen her earlier," he answers. "Did she notice you earlier?" I probe further. "She was not indifferent to me; there is plenty of proof of that," he answers laconically. "Did you try to get closer earlier?" I hold tight. "No, never, I was afraid of this woman. She was too beautiful and lightminded, something that one man seldom possesses alone."

"So why in the Hell did you marry her anyway?" I ask. "Because everything in me longed for her. I simply could not do otherwise. We both would perish because of it," he acknowledges in a curious happiness. "A man like you does not die because of feelings, Schulz; something like that can be overcome. It appears to me that you were dragged into the whole thing and could not get out of it honorably," I express my suspicion. "Now you are sitting in the wrong train." "Nothing had occurred before I asked her to be my wife." He smiles. "Yes, then did you buy the cat in a sack?" My patience slowly disappears. "Watch out, what do you think I am?" He becomes indignant. "Then damn it anyway, something did happen before," I insist. "Please, not so loud, this is only our business." He puts the brakes to me and continues softly. "Apparently you are too young to understand everything. A man becomes responsible only when he is the first one. Obviously that was not the case with us. The will to do it, and the pleasure that it brought, was equally large on both sides. Any obligation did not come from it. That is only for your enlightenment. No, it was just love which caused us to be married. You can sleep with anyone and go with everyone; all you need is a little sympathy."

"Man, Schulz, I don't understand you anymore. Your wife was once a little loose, as you said yourself. You knew her for a long time. She was never indifferent to you. You did not make a play for her earlier. You were afraid of her. She was too beautiful and lightminded for you. OK, that is an everyday story. Then somehow she ended up in a dilemma. You played the knight and then slept with her. To this point I understand you. That is a normal course, a logical point of conclusion. But, excuse me, you don't marry something like that! And where is your former fear of her beauty and her lightmindedness? Where did this sudden unconquerable love come from on both sides? And how do I explain it against your distrust today?" I press my interrogation.

"Are you afraid of a little rain? I do not want to have any listeners when I tell you the pure truth, but the others will be returning any minute," he says instead of answering me and gets up.

We leave the barracks together. It is still raining. Shivering lightly, we press ourselves against the back wall of the barracks and sink our hands into our pockets. An awful night, I think, as Schulz picks up the conversation in a dampened voice.

"After I got my degree, I entered into the banking business with my uncle and got acquainted with a beautiful girl. The First World War was just over without me having to become a soldier. The men were in shortage, just like the food, but the people were already looking to the gold bag. That did not bother us at all. After the bank closed, we gave each other a quick kiss in the stairwell and then met each other nearly every evening in a nearby park. We loved one another, but still it did not go further than kisses. A year later it was explained to me that it could go no further because my great love came from poor circumstances. Her father was killed during the war; her mother earned a living working in a factory. Outwardly I obeyed, but I promised my love that I would marry her later and went to work with great energy to earn enough to stand on my own two feet. Half a year later she was married to an old codger. Finished, over. From then on I looked at women with other eyes. Love was not enough; I learned about pleasure in its place. So I deceived everyone and let myself be deceived by everyone. The years passed. One day I saw her again ... , in the arms of another. Beautiful, reckless, and very young. It was in a night bar with red and green lights. I admit I was slightly drunk; we had visited most of the bars in the vicinity celebrating a birthday. But on Sunday afternoon I awoke with a clear head and remembered clearly the young, beautiful girl in the arms of a man who could have been her grandfather. That evening I looked for her in the bar, but she did not come. Four months later I met her in a clothing store. She did not overlook me, but did help a salesgirl persuade me to buy a shirt that I did not like at all.

"'I would like to get to know you better; how about a cup of coffee?' I asked her on the street. 'You can read my thoughts,' she said. 'I would really like to.' We conversed over coffee about the shirt I bought and parted as acquaintances. I used the following weeks to observe her. She was a little bitch. Again and again I arranged it so that we met by chance. One evening in April, she was apparently free and so she accepted an invitation to a dance. Afterward we drank coffee in my bachelor apartment until four o'clock in the morning. After Easter I saw her again at a sporting event at the side of our escapee. Then it happened. They ignored her, and treated her like filth. The man also showed her the cold shoulder. After she asked him to leave the event, he continued to converse with the respectable daughter of a town counselor. I saved her from this humiliation by asking her to dance with me and then taking her home. The next day she called me in my business and thanked me sincerely. A month later, in response to her request, I found her a job and a cheap apartment. She was healed.

"At the beginning of September 1938, I returned as a sergeant from my eight weeks of training to my home city and took up my work again. Some days later I held her savings book in my hands. At the beginning of each month she had paid in fifty marks. Immediately I got in touch with her and congratulated her, and she invited me to dinner in her apartment, the one I had arranged for her. For the first time I got to know her. She was not only very beautiful, but also an excellent homemaker and hostess. On September 16 we celebrated her birthday together. She paid for the first meal, and I for the second. She paid for the first bottle of wine, and I for the second. Later, in her apartment, she prepared coffee that would have brought the lame to walking. From Radio Station Luxembourg we heard slow dance music. We had found one another.

"At Christmas I asked her to become my wife. She nearly drowned in her tears and begged me to leave everything as it was so that we would not upset my family and friends. A week before Easter, we were married. I had trouble finding enough witnesses. After the wedding we ate in a hotel and then traveled to spend eight days in the Harz Mountains. It was a beautiful and happy time. War came in September. I was in Poland on her birthday and in Denmark when our daughter was born. Since then my wife has become sick. Her stomach is ruined. Now you know. Say what you want, I have nothing to regret."

"A strange love story, my good friend, and no longer something ordinary for me. Your happiness did cost you something, but I understand you, and we have to pay for everything," I respond, full of sympathy, looking into the dark night which does not allow any star a glimpse of this earth. "Yes, that is the way it is, Helmut, sooner or later one must pay for everything. In the end the bill is paid and we laugh at the completely unnecessary struggles of our youth," he agrees softly and leaves without paying any attention to the mud holes as the dirty water splashes to the sides under his quick steps.

### 19 November 1944

The pale sun spreads its sparse beams over the thick clumps of earth-colored, torn figures of the prisoner of war camp Le Mans. An interrogation is in process. We friends have it behind us and stand condemned as Nazis, with another three hundred prisoners on the other side of the majority of the prisoners. It is not easy to be recognized as a Nazi, since the American investigators apparently do not need many.

This time the American spent a long time with Schulz before he sent him into the right corner. Even Hocker's outstretched index finger pointing to the right corner is not enough. The American wants to know today exactly what we think. But we do not permit him this favor. He is given such foolish answers that he must consider all of us crazy. In the end each one has reached his goal. We are together again and the Americans have their Nazis.

A Navy petty officer forms up the mob and leads us, accompanied by the American guards, back into Cage 3. In front of the barracks we halt and face left. We stand in front of the barracks. "The Americans demand that we go into our quarters now, get our blankets and personal items, and return here immediately. We are being moved. Dismissed!" the sailor says with a frown. "Shit," bellows the mob and collects their things as fate has directed.

"Not bad," says Briller, looking around the tent and kicking with his foot the straw bale that will serve as our mattress. "At one time there would have been twenty-five men in these tents; now there are only nine; hopefully it will remain so," I express my satisfaction with the new quarters. "We did not think that we would be the ones to occupy the newly constructed cage when we stood at the fence feeling sorry for the prospective occupants of this compound." Schulz remembers our conversation on the third night after we arrived here.

Now we are separated from our former companions and stamped as the hated Nazis. What nonsense these kinds of interrogations produce. Do the Americans seriously believe that they can separate the wheat from the chaff? It seems so to me; then when I consider the men who experience the misery of imprisonment with me in this new barbed wire cage, I must be satisfied that they are the best, sincerest, and most upright from the old camp of Alençon. Three hundred and eighty men have been identified as politically dangerous and have been separated from the rest. No one complains about it. It was possible for each one to tell the interrogators what they wanted to hear. But we voted for comradeship and did not worry ourselves about the unknown purposes of the American interrogators probing our ideology. Not one man within this enclosure could have wanted war anymore than those who examined us today. God forgive them, then; they know not what they do.

At three o'clock we receive our noon meal. Our secret worries prove unfounded. We receive the same rations as before. It is a well-prepared meal of hash and pork. The extra provisions consist of a raspberry-red sweet soup. "Why are they feeding the Nazis so well?" Siegfried asks, resting after gulping down his food as usual. "Because hungry predators are more dangerous than full ones," Briller answers him. "Then they are really going to have to make a mighty effort if they want to fill me up." He takes up his dearest topic and tips the rest of his can into his apparently bottomless stomach. "Feedbag," Hocker laughs at him, collecting the plates and turning to the wash barracks.

The inmates of the Nazi cage stand ready for evening roll call. An officer, accompanied by two sergeants and four corporals, receives the count and returns the salute of our leader. "You have been sent to this cage today," he begins his talk in a German not entirely free of an accent after the count has been conducted. "I am the officer responsible for this cage and expect the greatest order and cleanliness from each one of you inside these walls. Whoever comes closer than five yards to the barbed wire either during the day or at night will be shot. I recommend to the company leaders that they place warning markers along the wire. I especially call to your attention that every attempt at escape will be punished severely." "Attention," the petty officer calls as the U.S. officer and his entourage leave.

"Remain standing for just a moment," the petty officer turns to the group with a wide grin on his face, "I would like to say something to you. I don't care whether or not I am the company leader. I would be thankful to anyone who would take it on. If there is none ready to do so, then I am willing to work for our common interests to the best of my ability. I ask you only to observe the conditions that I set down, which probably are not necessary. Is there anyone who will take over the work for me? No? That is what I thought. Then listen to me. I am pleased to be with men who still possess a little backbone. No one can know what the future will bring, but as long as we are here together we want to make life behind the barbed wire as easy as we can for one another. I would be pleased if all the comrades who are willing to work together in whatever manner for the group will remain here for a moment after you are dismissed. I am thinking in the first place of a regular cleaning service. In addition, it would be nice if we have a few teachers or attorneys or of a similar occupation among us who would establish a school so that we can get our minds working again. We all know boredom and the accompanying nitpicking tears at the nerves and in the end leads to hate-filled, even if unwanted, conflict. Whoever would like to help to make our stay here better through a little work, please remain. The rest are dismissed."

"That man is all right," Schulz says during our evening walk. "That is because he is from the navy," Siegfried asserts, not without pride. "If he eats as much as you, then it does not look good for the rest of the inmates." Hocker brings him up short. "It would be nice if we did have a few teachers among us so that during the afternoon we could learn something that might be of use later." I direct the conversation toward the topic that is most important to me.

### 26 November 1944

In the Nazi compound everything has turned out for the best. Here there are men with whom we really can do something. Within a few days, the entire cage has turned itself into a place worthy of human beings. All the sidewalks and other places could have been in a park. In front of each occupied tent are located sand beds which contain thoughtful little sentences or sayings written out with colored stones. "We are without weapons, but not without honor," stands in front of our tent. Within the quarters the best possible cleanliness rules. At ten o'clock in the morning, the straw pads are loosened up and the floor swept with homemade brooms. The occupants stand cleanly washed and shaved as best as possible, ready for an inspection by the company leader. Between 10:30 and 11:30 A.M. there is an hour of work for every prisoner, which serves to keep the entire area clean. Between noon and 1:00 P.M. we eat. Between 2:00 and 3:00 P.M. we rest. The rest of the day is free and we can use it to attend school, play games, throw dice, or walk around the area. The long, dark evenings are spent inside our quarters and the time is filled with whatever we want to do. Some tell jokes, some practice solving math problems in their heads. In our tent we have presentations that last twenty minutes for each man and he can pick whatever topic he likes. Even a singing group has developed and they raise the hopes of the comrades with their songs.

Time passes quickly. Even the weather, despite the lateness of the year, is comparably mild so that life inside the thin tent walls is nearly tolerable. But what is to become of us when snow falls or a cold spell hits? The fear of winter is close to everyone, and there are no reliable reports from the front. Still, two men choose to escape tonight. After long preparations, they go through the wire after midnight with all the necessary equipment. If the result is good, then they will see the homeland again.

"An American is standing in front of the tent with a weapon," I hear Hocker whisper to me between waking and dreaming. "You are dreaming," Briller mumbles sleepily with an angry tone. "Walrus, old one, look over there with your cow eyes," Hocker hisses, becoming nasty.

"Get out, get out," the American crows in a strange accent, waking the quiet sleepers. Disturbed by the sudden noise at this early hour, we lift our heads out of the straw and rub the sleep out of our eyes. "Let's go, hurry up." The fellow drives us to action because nobody has made a move to get up.

"What does that maniac want in the middle of the night?" the entire group howls, now awake and putting on their boots. "Fall out immediately in front of the tent with your blankets and personal articles," the voice of the company leader sounds through the cold veil of fog into the tent. "They found the hole in the fence," Schulz whispers to me as we step out into the open, where we are met by the Americans. The entire camp is in an uproar. An armed American stands in front of each tent entrance. Another spectacle has befallen the camp.

Every tent is thoroughly searched by the Americans. Even the sandy ground is shoveled up.

"Who cut the wires to help the two men escape tonight?" an American officer asks after roll call and all attempts have failed to find the wire cutters. But no one answers. Three hundred and seventy-eight German soldiers remain firmly silent. Hours pass and still the Americans know nothing. The fog-shrouded November day hangs gray on the prisoners, who are denied breakfast and who, as they sit on the ground, slowly become impatient.

Finally it is noon and the entire column marches out under orders from the Americans. The cage in which we felt so good remains behind. Within it, hidden under a sandpile, are the wire clippers which the German work detail quickly but carefully hid.

The group stops on the asphalt street. The main gate opens and a sandy path leads toward a comfortless looking enclosure. "Here German prisoners of Russian nationality were recently housed," the American sergeant begins his speech. "Bring this cage into an acceptable condition, and we will forget what happened."

The heavy beam which bolts the cage gate shut bangs into its iron holder. Two guards lean lazily against the woodwork. We are alone and left to ourselves.

"What a pigsty," our comrades comment about the condition of these quarters. Scattered throughout the entire enclosure lie rusty cans. In between them are rags, potato peels, and coffee sludge. The straw in the tents is wet and decaying. Nothing can be said about the condition of the latrines. Sadly and as though abandoned by nature, two crippled pines stand at the rim of the cage and bid us welcome.

"So men, that does not help any; we must create order, and immediately," the company leader calls to his downtrodden group after his inspection of the neglected place. "Every sixteen men, that is two tent groups, get together. First we will clean up the tents and establish a new latrine. For that I would like two men from each tent who will cover the Russian filth with chlorine powder and then bury it while the other groups dig out two new trenches. There is only one water tap in the entire camp. I ask you, comrades, to be especially conscientious of one another and avoid all conflict. By evening everyone can wash. I will try to get new straw from the Americans for the tents and find out about today's food. Please take up the work with your old energy so that our quarters can be put in good order before nightfall and with the hope that our two escapees can reach Germany healthy." He then leaves us to our work and goes with an interpreter to the gate.

The groups go to work and thoroughly clean up the quarters. The rotten straw is piled up behind the tents. The sidewalls of the tents are rolled up so that the odor can be drawn out and the water ditches cleaned out. Before dusk the quarters and surrounding area are cleaned of all garbage, but the new straw and our provisions have not arrived. The responsible officer informs us that there is no straw in storage and the provisions for our food have not been arranged. Therefore he reinforces the guards. The shadows of Alençon seem to lie anew over the cage and bring with them a tremendously depressed mood upon the inmates.

### 1 December 1944

"You have done that very well," Schulz says to Hocker and me as his moist eyes admire the advent wreath that we have made out of plants and which Briller and Siegfried have fastened to the tent pole. "We need candles; then tonight we could celebrate it right." Hocker laughs in good spirits like a little boy who is watching his mother bake Christmas goodies. "Perhaps the Americans will give us some on Christmas," Siegfried suggests and jumps down from Briller's shoulders, which served as a ladder while they were putting up the wreath. "Write to the Pope; perhaps he will send you a whole wagonful," Briller counsels him thoughtlessly. "Tell me, don't you have any feeling for anything?" Siegfried growls at him contemptuously. "Yes, for a tasty roast beef, a bottle of good wine, and afterward a beautiful woman in bed," Briller answers him. "You are a farm boy, and nothing more." Siegfried turns from him and lifts his view to the advent wreath while Schulz, Hocker, and I breathe easier. "This imaginary magic sticks in my throat," Briller notes to himself and stamps angrily out of the tent.

"Leave him in peace, Siegfried, he does not believe in anything but his own strength." I hold Siegfried back since he wants to follow after him. "I am really not bigoted, but today is the first Advent and, as long as I can remember, my father has been hanging a wreath under the lamp in our living room. Because I will do it later, I will not be mocked, even by Briller. I was really excited and happy as the two of you came in with that thing; then to tell the truth, I really did not know what the date is," he gives vent to his anger. "You must understand Briller, Siegfried. He was raised without parents and does not know the light in the eyes of brothers and sisters when the candles burn. It is magic that holds us to our childhood. Thank God for it. But we should not forget that this feeling does not exist with him since in his young years he was shoved from one place to another," I explain to Siegfried since he does not know very much about Briller. "Sometimes I think he is completely without feeling." Siegfried finally comprehends. "On the other hand again and again I find I like him very much. What is actually wrong with him? Something seems to be bothering him."

"That's right," Briller says from the tent entrance where he has suddenly appeared and stands with crossed arms. "That's exactly right. Something is bothering me. But it is not your childish actions about a wreath; rather the continual derogatory remarks about me in the last little while. I ... " "Stop, Briller," Schulz interrupts him. "No," Briller energetically rejects his intervention. "I will not be hindered from speaking. Every day you imagine more and more that you are better than other people."

"But Robert." I take advantage of the short pause. "Be quiet; even you have an excuse for everything and you search for all possible apologies instead of stating your opinion concisely and clearly." He goes after me. "I am not the vagabond highwayman that you think I am," he continues to speak, unhindered. "When I was six years old, my mother died of a stomach ailment. My father followed her two years later and left me alone in the world. The sister of my father, a stingy spinster, raised me and took from me the inheritance left by my parents. When I was fourteen years old, she sent me to a strange city as an apprentice and after three years I earned my license as a painter. From then on I took care of myself completely. I earned enough, but the glory only lasted two years and then I was unemployed like most men during that time. This blow fell on me in Munich. After I wore off the heels of my shoes looking for work, I volunteered for the national work service. In 1937 I was drafted into the army. In the meantime I had become a group leader, but this rank was no good to me. I began my military service as an infantry recruit—an ass in the third row. Still I was able to save five thousand marks. During a field exercise before the war broke out, I got acquainted with a very rich farmer's daughter. But it was not her money that attracted me; I was only interested in the girl. It goes without saying that she was beautiful. Men only get to know pretty women; the devil only knows who it is that marries the ugly ones. That is only incidental. In any case, she was slender, racy, and black-haired, with a face like an angel whose tender white skin was interrupted only by slightly pink cheeks. I came, I saw, and I conquered, as the silly saying goes. After the end of the invasion of France, it was very urgent for me that we marry, but this brought only resentment from my future parents-in-law and the entire family.

"Because of the circumstances, our wedding night passed with only the movement of the little one in her womb. Three weeks later, when little Heidi was just five days old, I had to catch the train back to the front, first to Maastricht and then by bus to my unit at Saint-Omer. In the middle of February 1941 I was given leave and during the entire train ride I was as excited as a snow king about the reunion with my wife.

"The disappointment knocked me to the ground. The old man was still upset with our premarital sin and hardly noticed me when I entered his farmyard. In my anger, I gave to a Polish prisoner of war the nice shirt that I bought for him in France. My dear mother-in-law greeted me in the living room with a hasty handshake without asking how I was or offering me anything to eat. Only a cousin of my wife, a sixteen-year-old teenager, swarmed over me and told me that she still liked me even if I was not a sergeant or did not have an Iron Cross. Since I sensed what this dumb band had expected of me, I pressured her and she told me that my father-in-law was ashamed of me because I had returned from the French campaign without a decoration for bravery in facing the enemy. After I recovered from this idiocy, I wanted to see my wife and child. I went looking for them and found them in the stable. It took everything to recognize her again. I almost passed her with a short greeting, thinking she was a maid because she had a red shawl covering her previously well-cared-for hair. My disappointment about her looks did not evade her, but she passed it off on the war, in case I had not noticed, and that all of them had to work. I asked her, with suppressed anger, if she had not received my letter with the day and time of my arrival. 'Yes, naturally, but my father did not want to know anything about it,' she answered. 'Where is our Heidi?' I asked with a pounding heart. 'Go in my room; I will come shortly; but be quiet, she is still asleep,' she informed me and then crawled under a cow with a bucket.

"What a wonderful reception, I thought to myself as I made my way into the house, and struggled to think what I would tell my comrades if I were to return early from my leave.

"Softly I entered my wife's room. Little Heidi lie there in her small pink bed, sleeping so beautifully with her fists formed into balls. Carefully I opened the locks on my suitcase so that I would not disturb her sleep, but then something moved in the pillows behind me. I thought, what if she is afraid of the strange man, so I kneeled to the floor and put back into the suitcase the little shirts, pants, and jacket that I brought for her and squinted frightfully toward the little bed. But she didn't stir anymore, except to wave her tender little hand in the air above her. Then I stepped to the bed and bent over her. Unconsciously I had taken a blue-white rattle from my suitcase and then noticed it in my hand. Joyfully I gave my daughter the colorful toy and she immediately made a great racket with it. About the same time, my wife stepped into the room. She was still in her work dress and smelled like cows, but the joy over the child shoved this invisible wall between the two of us away. The barrier was broken. We kissed passionately. Heidi pounded her enthusiastic applause on the edge of the bed with her rattle.

"Then I unpacked the other presents. I gave my wife a wonderful robe, stockings, and lingerie, all of which made her very happy. Enthusiastically she slipped into the suede robe and looked at herself in the mirror, until she noticed the ugly scarf and tore it from her head. You could hear how her soft hair fell in waves around her shoulders. 'Turn around,' she asked me like in the first days of our young love, and I immediately obeyed. Behind me I could hear the clattering around her dresser and then the wonderful smell of powder and perfume spread throughout the room. 'Do you like me now?' her dark voice rang. 'Very much,' I said. 'This is how I carried you in my heart through half of France.'

"The squeaking stairs put a brake on our rising desire. Without knocking, the door opened. 'Come and eat,' my mother-in-law said from the doorway, staring listlessly at her changed daughter. Quickly I bent down and pulled out of my suitcase a length of black silk material and handed it over to the woman, who took it hesitatingly but thanked me kindly. 'Come right away; otherwise the food will get cold,' she repeated. Quickly I took from my gas mask container a pound of coffee and a pipe that I had intended for myself. I followed my wife, who in the meantime had taken off the robe and picked up the little Heidi, downstairs to the dining room.

" 'You can hurry and wash in the kitchen,' the old man received me, somewhat friendly. 'Mother has drawn bath water.'

" 'I hope that you like it,' I explained and gave him my pipe. 'It looks like it's a good one,' he said after a while. 'Can you still buy everything in France without ration coupons?' 'For the time being, apparently, as long as they are in stock,' I answered 'Then it will not take much longer if everyone takes as much out as you,' he growled with a bitter undertone.

"In the following days I worked as hard as the dumbest horse, forbidding my wife to work. I sent her and Heidi into the city every day to prevent them from becoming peasants like me. I did not work on Saturday or Sunday; then I accompanied my ladies. For travel into the city we used a wagon pulled by a Hanover horse which we left at an inn at the edge of the city without charge. On Thursday before the end of my leave (I had to leave early Monday morning), I decided at the last minute to join the trip to the city and quickly put on my dress uniform while the old man personally harnessed the horse. Surprised at my sudden change of clothes and the crazy idea that I would accompany her, my wife talked with some embarrassment about a walk in the forest, which she had not taken for a long time. But I wanted to see a film and especially the newsreel. That is why I packed both of them into the wagon and drove out of the farmyard, although my wife continued to try and keep me out of the city.

"The month of March reigned over the weather and changed the snow in the fields into water which ran in small rivulets along the edge of the road, although the road itself was completely dry. I left the horse and wagon at the inn while my wife and Heidi disappeared into the dining room to warm up. As I came into the building, I heard my wife speaking on the telephone. 'My husband is with me today, so we can't meet, my dear,' she said excitedly. Determined, I stepped behind her and took the receiver out of her hand. '… it's too bad not now, but for sure on Monday afternoon?' a flattering man's voice sounded and then I slammed the telephone down. 'It is only a harmless acquaintance,' my wife lied, looking up with theatrical eyes. 'How long have you known the man?' Amazed, my own voice sounded strange even to me. 'Since you took over my work and sent me to the city,' were the accusing words from her now pale lips.

"That evening I sat in the train going to Maastricht. Everything inside was empty and broken. I longed for my comrades.

"At Easter my company was transferred to East Prussia; then on June 22, the fight with Russia began. Now I finally had something that I needed: the war! But it did not devour me, instead it spit me out on July 1942 with a shoulder wound by Rzhev. From the hospital in Vienna I wrote to my wife, but she did not visit me. She wrote only that I was expected home after my recovery.

"At the end of November I entered my parents-in-law's house with a heavy heart. In the meantime I had become a master sergeant and on my field blouse hung the Iron Cross, Russian Campaign Medal, and other decorations. Perhaps now they are satisfied with you, I said to myself, and took the few steps leading to the house in one jump. Once again the reception was cool. Only the wish to see my daughter kept me from leaving. In addition, I still loved my wife.

"That evening after the old ones had gone to bed, I looked in amazement at my wife as she started to prepare a bed on the couch even as her broad hips looked especially appealing to me. 'Who are you making the bed for?' I wanted to know. 'For you; I do not feel well; we will talk about it tomorrow.' She thought that she could keep me away. 'Are you pregnant?' I jumped up and grabbed her by the wrists. 'Yes, it is not enough for me to be married on paper,' she hissed at me like a prostitute.

"The rest is quickly told. Thick clouds of fog took in the lonesome wanderer as he went toward the city with his murdered soul now completely conscious that for him at that hour no goal existed. At the inn inside the train station, I tried to get some schnapps, but by the end of the third year of war there was none to be purchased openly. Finally in the canteen of my replacement company I was able to drown my sorrows. My unrestrained drinking and whoring stirred up quite a sensation, so that I was shoved around from one replacement company to another since I was still considered unfit for service and could not be sent back to the front. At the end of 1943, I finally landed in Münsingen training camp with a newly formed field unit which was transferred to France at the beginning of 1944. The rest you all know. Now I am going to get some water, because my throat is dried out from talking so much," he said, pushing off from the tent pole and leaving us alone in shock.

### 5 December 1944

"Why is the road there, for marching, for marching into the wide, wide world … "

"Left, two, three, four, left … , you love it don't you?" a tall blond American bellows in perfect German after we have left the camp and march along a poor secondary road under heavy guard toward the city of Le Mans. "They castrated that fellow in Africa and now he believes he can relieve himself by bellowing," I hear the man behind me say to his neighbor, and all those around him break out in laughter. "Cut out the laughing or I will beat you," the words of the blond eunuch sound in between the laughs. "Bravo," the entire column yells with one voice, and even the dumbest realizes that it will be hard to deal with us today. "Halt!" orders the officer and his unbridled hate brings his own men into an uproar.

"I have the assignment to bring this damn mob of Nazis to the train station," the short, half-insane Yankee screams at the crowd, who are still seized by humor even after they finally come to a stop. "Bravo," sounds again. "Whoever tries to hinder me in my assignment will be considered a mutineer and will be shot," he threatens further. "Hurray, we'd rather die than obey a lame jackass," the ranks threaten. "March!" the weakling commands with his last energy and takes the lead.

The horribly pale winter sun looks out from behind a cloud bank while we divide into groups of forty men and disappear into the gray American box cars. The doors roll shut. Forty pairs of eyes blink in the half dark. "Now it is perhaps ten o'clock on the nickel watch that a searcher took from me in the camp," Hocker says tiredly without finding a place to lie.

"There are our provisions and an empty bucket," someone calls from the corner of the overfilled car. "There is a note on top," another explains. "Go take a look at the things, Schulz." I nudge our best man in order to prevent any irregularities regarding the food. "OK, men," Schulz speaks a little later to the group. "The note indicates that these are provisions for three days. The empty bucket is to be our latrine. I suggest that we piss through the crack in the door and keep the shit in our intestines as long as we can. Whoever must, can use the bucket, and then can throw his own excrement out of the wagon. As soon as that is necessary we will knock out the window. It does not matter to us what the car looks like on the outside; the main thing is that we do not suffocate from our own stink. A few comrades and I will review the travel provisions and calculate the individual rations. If it is possible, and when all of you are in agreement, we will divide up all of the food among us so that everyone can be responsible for his daily ration."

"Give us the food." It sounds like a choir. "Good, I will count out what each one is to receive. Whoever appears before me twice will be sacrificed to the justice of the people. There are twenty-four crackers for each man, two light and two heavy cans, about 250 grams of corned beef, half a box of pineapple, and some sugar. Don't push, I will call for the next one thirty-nine times and once for the last one, and that is me. Whoever wants can count with me. The next ... "

"We just passed the city of Laval," a man reports from the window. "Then we are going to Bordeaux ... " another hollers. "Hello, we are from the men's brothel of Bordeaux," a couple of fellows begin to sing a dirty soldier's song and each one tries to outdo the other. "Bordeaux?" asks Briller. "What will we do there?"

The songs become silent. The singers are tired and sobered. The reaction sets in. The snoring starts. The unpleasant part of a trip begins. "It's a travesty that we have to sit in such a garbage can for a three-day trip," the complaints rise. "The warmongers belong here—to be locked up and chased around the earth." "Where shall I lie my tired head?" "Shut your mouth, you castrated cat, we are all standing so that you can lie down." "Kindly take your sweaty paws out of my nose, or I will kick you and ruin something." "Lick my ass, you idiotic sheep, I am entitled to some space."

And the wheels turn further on the axles carrying us into the new day.

### 7 December 1944

The gloomy light of this gray December day scarcely penetrates the wet cold air into the rolling dungeon. The cities of Flers and Coutances lie behind us and the train heads in a northerly direction toward the Cotentin Peninsula. The names of long-forgotten battlefields from the summer of this year, 1944, hang like a single accusation between the four wooden walls which hold captive now the living sacrifice of those battles and carry them on past the graves of their fallen comrades toward an unknown fate. England or America, that is now the question which fills all hearts after the train rolls into Cherbourg.

Encircled by a gigantic detachment of American and French soldiers, we climb downtrodden out of the stinking box cars. Before anyone can comprehend what is wrong with our conduct, we are shoved with hard rifle butts into the well-known five rows. The liberators and the liberated count their bounty and appear not to be satisfied since they do it again and again even though the results remain the same. Three hundred seventy-eight Germans were loaded and sealed up in Le Mans. Three hundred fifty-four arrive in Cherbourg. Twenty-four disappeared behind the locked doors. That is too many for the oppressors with their loaded weapons, who now stand with open mouths and appear to believe in ghosts. Too late do they discover that in one wagon the floor has been torn out and they did not count the men as they came out of the cars to insure that the numbers would be correct. Now the opportunity has been lost since the prisoners have all mixed together. No one knows anything about the escape and no one was in the box car from which the escape was made. At least for the time being!

But now the rage of the guards floods over the gloating group, we defenseless victims, in the form of blows with gun butts and clubs after the wretched group reaches the road leading uphill, which is surrounded by willows and shuts out the view to unparticipating witnesses. Softened by rain, the mucky field road has become bottomless and the limbs of the weak threaten to stop functioning. Woe to the poor ones who stop. But the merciless fellows drive their victims further up the hill and into the unnoticed oncoming night.

After an hour's march, the road becomes better. A short time later, lights appear which seem to frame a large camp. The men in front speed up involuntarily and suddenly come to a stop in front of a gigantic gate. Spotlights from countless guard towers slide over huge barbed wire walls which enclose what seems like more than several square miles. A stiff wind blows in from the sea and leaves the lips of the thirsty with a salty taste. Apparently we are in the extreme northwest corner of the Cotentin Peninsula, the Cap de la Hague.

"Absolute order and cleanliness is the rule in this camp." A haggard figure in an American coat and German field cap stands in the muck and greets the new arrivals. "Only those who indicate a willingness to follow my orders have the right to the relatively good provisions that are given out by the generous Americans. Because of the rainfall in the past days, the camp threatens to sink into a morass.

With the support of the American leaders of the camp, the rubble from Cherbourg will be transported here and we will construct a road that will allow us to go with dry feet from the tents to the kitchen, office, clothing room, etc. It is necessary that every available man participate." "Stop your nonsense and tell us instead where in this pigsty we can get some water to drink," a group on the left wing interrupts him. "So that's the way you want to start, it will come back to haunt you, count on it," the speaker answers, ready for a fight. "Keep your mouth completely shut, or you can observe your camp road from the bottom up. Send us to our quarters and disappear." The provocation continues to grow. "If you don't behave yourselves, I will let you stand in this muck until you grow roots," the chap mocks us brazenly, pushing us over the brink.

Before someone with sense can step in, he is encircled, shoved down into the morass, yanked up, and sent off with kicks. "Don't let us see you here again, you miserable dog," is the advice of the furious ones that accompanies him out of the cage.

"We have gotten involved here too," Schulz laughs, somewhat troubled, shaking his head in thought. "I would rather have it this way; then I prefer clear situations," I take the side of the resisters. "Everything is right and good. ... "

"Listen up," shouts the company leader from Le Mans, who now stands in front of the debating mob. "We are not going to get anywhere this way, men! There are at least sixty or seventy tents in this monkey pen. We must determine which are unoccupied and finally get under some shelter. The rest we will find in the morning."

"The tents with the numbers 41 and 67 are unoccupied; see that you disappear into them; we want to have our peace and sleep," a voice sounds from the row of tents behind us. "Thank you, friend," the sailor calls back and turns to his people. "Divide up into groups of thirty men in the large tents and rest peacefully; in the morning we take care of things and take the idiot in our teeth if he shows up again. Now good night."

### 8 December 1944

Under the shattering sound of a bugle, the Stars and Stripes is raised on the flagpole and stands stiff in the wind. It is eight o'clock in middle Europe and on its furthermost reaches behind mountains of barbed wire nearly thirty thousand of its sons, completely isolated from the outer world, are held prisoner. The white stars shine proudly from their blue background and proclaim the might of her forty-eight states which they symbolize and together with the red and white stripes constitute the flag of the victors.

Now their representative, armed with a thick cigar, stands in front of us and begins to speak: "You arrived here last night and introduced yourselves in the worst possible way. I have been informed about your unbelievable conduct on the march here, how you beat up the German spokesman who was assigned by us and who, in the final analysis, only had your best welfare in view. In case new attacks are reported against the discipline, I see no other alternative than to take whatever measures are necessary to dampen your impertinence."

"Now you have heard how affairs will be handled here." The man from last night follows the speech of the American after he leaves. "As I have just been informed, you are all sergeants from whom, in the first place, discipline can be expected." "Are you starting that again?" the sailor interrupts and goes toward him. "Who do you think you are other than a miserable traitor? Do you really imagine that we will be intimidated by you?" "Bravo, Herbert," the entire group supports him and the man puts his tail between his legs and trots in the direction of the cage exit.

In no time a delegation is formed which goes to the gate and asks to speak with the American while the rest of us, under Schulz's direction, take up shovels to bring our quarters into a liveable condition. Not until we begin to work is the mess sergeant justified in giving us something to eat. So we pick up the tools and wait to be surprised.

About eleven o'clock there is an undefinable thin soup which is gulped down in a hot hunger. But it only serves as a stimulus to our stomach nerves. The delegation is still standing at the gate waiting to be heard by the American. We continue to work on our quarters. All of the slime is shoveled out and the wet ground as well until we have dry ground to lie on. There is no straw here; even the long-time inmates lie on the bare earth. They are mostly troops which fell into the hands of the Americans around Rennes and Le Mans. Some of their comrades were shipped out to the States in the fall, and that was what awaited them until suddenly the transports were canceled. The men maintain that the shipping will resume any day and they firmly believe that one day they will land in the USA, unless the war situation changes to our advantage and throws all of the Americans' plans overboard.

The food is quite miserable, despite the impudent claims of the camp speaker. The camp leadership is living splendidly at the cost of the rest of the inmates. They fill their bellies full and then use food to buy up the valuables of the whole camp. The so-called German camp policemen act as intermediaries because they are the only ones who can move freely inside the outer barbed wire which encircles the entire camp. The consequence of this grievous situation is great bitterness in the camp. But the poor devils are simply not in the position to get rid of these parasites since the Americans have complete trust in them. That is why the good soldiers were especially happy when their hated spokesman was so thoroughly rejected by us and even after the speech by the American that we are not willing to crawl on the cross for this miserable creature.

After we finish the work we are sent to the clothing room and receive two blankets, a German army coat, and, when necessary, American shoes. We are now protected against bad weather and winter is already beginning to show its worst side.

At evening roll call the sergeants stand aside from the thousand or so men in the enclosure and follow furiously the bold arrogance of the speaker, who handles his comrades like they were galley slaves. When the Americans arrive to conduct roll call, this miserable worm of submissiveness falls all over them.

"You were told already once today that we place the greatest importance on discipline. Still the spokesman was attacked once again and hindered in carrying out his assignment in maintaining what was excellent order before your arrival. Whoever wants to register a complaint with the American leaders of the camp must do so through the spokesman. There is no purpose for unruly elements to believe that they can speak with the commandant. All commands and arrangements will be made by us and we expect that you will follow them, otherwise the issuance of provisions will be suspended."

"We do not oppose the American measures which serve to bring order," a dauntless man in our row suddenly answers the American. "It is simply the manner in which the speaker is attempting to institute them that we don't like." "He is a German and certainly cannot do otherwise," the American hisses contemptuously through his teeth and goes on.

### 10 December 1944

"We don't have any place to stay," says Schulz as we pick up our belongings and march, accompanied by guards, through the endless rows of barbed wire in Camp Cherbourg.

"… we must wander restlessly in Flanders, far from the homeland …" a couple of defiant ones sing from the ranks, bringing the Americans out of composure. "Shut up," the responsible sergeant bellows and waves his red-lacquered club threateningly. "Certainly he wants to hear another song," a high-pitched voice sounds above the crowd.

"… and we run up the pole our flag as red as blood, dirallalla …," it begins again as we go through the gate along a small cement entry into a cage while the guard detail forms up outside and marches away.

"I greet you on behalf of all the comrades here, and in my position as spokesman for this Nazi cage I welcome you heartily. I hope that we will get along well with each other although the personnel here consists only of simple soldiers. We have our own kitchen here and in case there is any doubt, I permit anyone appointed by you to be present at any time when we receive the produce, by its preparation and distribution. My name is Moehler. I welcome any suggestions that will improve things and I would be thankful if someone would take over my post; I certainly would not stand in his way. So that we can get you into your tents now, we want to put together a crew and I ask for the support of some experienced men."

"The corporals are still the backbone of the army." Schulz smiles proudly as he hangs his blankets over his shoulders and offers his help to the corporal.

A little later we move into the long, barrack-like tents in groups of sixty men. The ground is dry, but there is no trace of straw or anything else. Immediately we test the amount of space and our fears are confirmed. The quarters are too small for sixty men. "'There is room in the smallest hut for a happy loving couple,'" Siegfried quotes Schiller and observes the two tent poles. "Too bad that they are so far apart, otherwise I would make a hammock out of my blankets." "Didn't I always tell you that this fellow slept in the coal shed at home and in the navy like a monkey in a swinging nest?" Briller teases him. "You can still go out and wash your mouth; then you have talked shit the whole time," the seaman recommends to him, undisturbed.

"When you two are finished, I want to make an announcement." Schulz, who in the meantime has entered the tent, ends the dialogue. "Is the war over?" Hocker asks spryly. "Use your poisonous beak on someone else, little one," Schulz counters, "but listen all of you for a moment: lunch will be ready in half an hour." "Hurrah!" "Quiet! From every tent five men must carry the honey buckets from the latrine to the gate because the shit wagons are coming soon and the soldiers are still out working." "No way!" "Naturally there will be extra rations for those who volunteer. Who will do it for our tent? How about it Gerhard, will you take charge of it?" Schulz turns after a long pause to the latrine director from the camp in Le Mans. "I am not going to carry the shit of other people through the area," the man mutters. "Then hurry out and put some of your own in. How about it?" Schulz asks once again without receiving an answer. "Damn it, the trucks are coming soon and the pails are full. Where are we going to take care of our needs in the next days?" He becomes displeased.

"Carry the filth yourself," another makes the suggestion, and all eyes stare at Schulz, whose tall, wide figure stands in the tent entrance while his hand rubs his right cheek as though he has been slapped. "Good, then I need four more men," he says calmly after a while. "Let's go." Briller nudges us. Without a word, we four follow our friend Schulz out of the dim tent, leaving the others behind and ashamed.

"Do you know anything about the situation at the front?" Schulz asks the speaker Moehler after we five companions have eaten the well-earned extra rations and sit in front of the primitive kitchen barracks. "The Americans are at Aachen. They will enter Germany in the next few days." "Where did you get this damned rumor?" Schulz asks, excited. "Unfortunately it is no rumor, but a fact, friend, but there is still no reason to get upset; then they will certainly fly out of there in a short time." "You say it like you are really convinced, like you are in contact with Hitler's headquarters," I toss in the middle. "Not that, but once in a while I have the chance to read a newspaper," he answers idly. "A newspaper," we both stammer. "Yes, the American soldier newspaper *Stars and Stripes*, which the work details sometimes steal from the Americans." He clears things up for us. "Then you are well informed," Schulz rasps, still in unbelief. "Do you happen to have a copy in your possession?" he asks in doubt. "Unfortunately no, then as I said, I can only read it once in a while," he explains. "And who is the mysterious owner of the newspaper?" Schulz asks with a ridiculing laugh. "Perhaps you will get acquainted with him, it is entirely up to you." "You certainly make the situation difficult, or do you think that you have traitors among you?" Schulz inquires. "No, just the opposite, otherwise I would not converse with you. It is just that today one cannot be too trusting," he indicates as his blue eyes hold us in view.

"How long have you been a soldier?" I ask the man since the corporal stripes on his arm do not seem to belong there. "Hm, is that so important for you?" He grins at me. "Sometimes you can draw conclusions or find an explanation for something." I grin back. "You don't seem to me to be a corporal, either," Schulz chimes in. "Perhaps I am a general in disguise." He laughs ironically. "Unfortunately I must end our conversation since the food is ready and we don't want to keep the men waiting unnecessarily," he adds and extends his hand to us.

"If he is a corporal, I will swallow salt all the days of my life," Schulz whispers to me as we walk along the clean walk where our friends have already gone in advance of us back toward the tent. Twenty minutes later we hold the filled cans between our knees and, with the brand new army utensils which the food carriers brought along, we enjoy a very good lunch. The rations would have been sufficient for well-fed people. Nevertheless the split pea soup is quite a bit thicker than in the cage of the deserter. Without having to think continually about those pimps who divert part of our provisions for their own purposes, our anger disappears.

"I hope you are not upset with me, Comrade Schulz," the latrine director Gerhard says as he wipes his face with a napkin. "You know, I hate the laughter and teasing of the comrades although the fools know that the latrine is just as important as the kitchen. In Le Mans it did not bother me as much, but here it has to do with the filth of the infantrymen and I thought that it would look bad for a noncommissioned officer to transport their sewage." "It's alright Gerhard, you see yourself, we are all still alive, but take note: the shit of common soldiers does not stink any worse than that of noncommissioned officers." Schulz pats him on his bull neck. "I know, I have experience with that, forgive my rude conduct and know that in the future you can count on me for any work," he says ruefully and goes calmly to the latrine.

About 4:00 P.M. the work details return. They are almost without exception young air force men. Somewhat piqued, they look at the silver stripes and stars of their new neighbors. "What are the drones doing in our workers' cage?" they ask loud enough for us to hear. "We flung your honey for you today." Schulz laughs at a pair of the young pups. "How long were you unconscious afterward?" one wants to know. "The blow brought us back to life," I joke back and all laugh and go cheerfully into the washroom.

At evening roll call a taciturn sergeant appears with three corporals. He refrains from giving a speech. Instead spokesman Moehler turns to his people: "Today we have 350 noncommissioned officers sent to our cage and I hope that we will all get along well together. In the future the noncommissioned officers will see that the camp is kept clean since they cannot be assigned to work outside the camp. I am asking the tent leaders to arrange for men to take care of the chores, who will be given extra rations. For the older residents that does not mean they can pay any less attention to order in the camp. The latrine detail has the right to require anyone who is caught making a mess of things to immediately clean the dirty pails. Just one thing more: within the cage there are men who all hope for the final victory. At this time we cannot contribute much to it, but through our orderly conduct, keeping ourselves clean as well as the enclosure, we can show the Americans that the Germans are not gangsters as the propaganda in their newspapers maintains, but human beings who, because of different needs and experiences, possess a different world outlook. In order to accomplish all of this, we must all keep things to a minimum and recognize that they will grant us only when we are able to gain their respect by our attitude. On that account there should not exist behind barbed wire sergeants and soldiers, but only German prisoners of war who are bearing the same fate as men and who are trying to lighten each others' load. Perhaps the day is not far away when we will be freed of our bonds and can join the oncoming German divisions to bring about the final victory."

"What did you think of Moehler's talk?" I ask my companions after we have eaten dinner and make our rounds about the compound. "I can only repeat that he is no corporal and by all appearances he is either crazy or actually does have contact with the outside world," is Schulz's viewpoint, which I silently share. "The fellow risks his neck speaking out like that," Briller indicates. "I like him very much. What he has suggested is a mighty powerful idea." Siegfried beams in faith and hope. "Man, to have a rifle in the hand again and to be able to end this filthy war, that is worth every risk," Hocker mumbles between his teeth. "A dangerous game, which could bring us nothing." Briller dampens the weak glimmer of hope. "Then you would rather wait here until our comrades have pulled the chestnuts out of the fire and set you free?" Siegfried asks him sharply. "If the end is coming, I don't want to bite the dust because of a couple of crazies. I have a bill to take care of at home," Briller gives him a cool answer. "So, you want to take revenge on a weak woman instead of fighting and starting over?" Siegfried rubs him. "I don't know you any more, Robert." Hocker wonders about the brave soldier.

"The barbed wire has given me time to think. I don't want to hear any more about the whole swindle. After the war I am going to open a paint shop and marry a French woman from Normandy. My letter from Le Mans did not go to Germany, but instead to this girl." He pulls us out of the clouds with this new confession.

"Now I believe that your brain has suffered strongly since Alençon, old boy," I comment after the friends have calmed themselves. "Absolutely not; if you hadn't been so stiff-necked, I would have initiated you back in the Paris soldier's home and instead of going to the commander, we would have gone to Saint-Omer where her father has a paint store." "So, do you believe that I would have gone with you?" I ask, slightly irritated. "No, that is why I gave up my plan. I did not want to do it alone. Then we met Hocker and I knew he was straighter than you." He allows with complete calm a further view into his dark soul.

"Briller, for Hell's sake, that would have been desertion and would have meant the firing squad for you," I yell at him. "With our conversation in the soldier's home, I thought that the end of the war was here. Naturally I was lucky that I didn't get myself drunk, otherwise I might have succeeded in persuading you," he laughs. "Aren't you ashamed of yourself, to drag up such stories?" Schulz goes after him. "The Americans are in Aachen; lay the cards on the table; we have lost," he says softly, with conviction.

Pressed closely together we lie wrapped in our coats and blankets on the hard earth of the Cap de la Hague. The strong gusts of the cold winter wind blast against our fluttering dwelling. Like death in a mass grave rest the bodies of the captive soldiers. But the ghosts are awake and haunt the brains of those of us blown away by fate. Briller, who are you? A soldier of unquestionable ability, your blazing hate stands in uninterrupted combat with the bleeding heart of the man full of love for a woman. Where is your poor tormented soul being driven which cannot be freed from this fate-filled longing? Just when I thought I knew you and understood everything, then you open up a new side. Still the disappointments of life would have caused you to make a big mistake and carried you to a whole new life. The call, "Paris is threatened by the enemy," was enough for you to commit desertion within your own heart. Lay the cards on the table, we have all lost, you say, because the enemy stands on the border of Germany. Perhaps this time you are not completely wrong, but how many borders have we crossed without being able to end the war in victory? That which I do not give up, I have not lost.

### 14 December 1944

"Every man will receive a postcard which he can fill out in block letters. This card is to inform your families about your status, and therefore, as it states on the card, cannot be used for any further messages," spokesman Moehler calls into the tent and begins to pass out the cards. "We have already written a letter and we have not received any answer; why do we now send a note that we have ended up in prison?" a pessimist asks.

"In the meantime you have been sent here, which means a change in address, which the people at home do not know," the spokesman responds while I look at the funny card on which everything has been printed and we can only check the appropriate boxes. "I am fine," those at home will read next to my name, rank, birthdate, and my family's address, I conclude, and reach for my pen.

"You can accompany me, Helmut, that is if you are not too lazy," Schulz says after he has collected the postcards and is ready to go to the spokesman. "Don't you find it unusual, Schulz, that we still have not received any answer to our letters?" I ask on our way to Moehler. "As long as no one receives any mail, there are two explanations: either everything at home is falling apart so that the mail cannot be processed, or the enemy simply threw the letters to the dogs," he indicates thoroughly. "And you don't think of a third possibility, that our letters from Le Mans are still in France?" I ask. "Yes, but we do not speak about it; otherwise the next printed forms would go back to the Americans without any writing." He smiles shrewdly.

"Are you smokers?" Moehler asks after we meet him and take our places on empty food boxes. "No, not any more since I became a prisoner," Schulz answers. "According to what the sergeant told me today we are to receive tobacco," Moehler informs us. "I don't consider that to be good, because they will not deliver that devil's stuff consistently and when the stock is used up, then those that are addicted will face hard days and that will cause difficulty for those of us who must live with them," I offer for reflection. "You are right, comrade, but there is nothing we can do about it; if I burn the stuff up in the kitchen, then they will stone me," he suggests lightly.

"But what I want to know," he becomes more serious, "is there something that can be done with the noncommissioned officers, or has the barbed wire finished them?" "Yes and no," Schulz takes the answer out of my mouth. "We need some kind of hopeful news about the war situation to tear them from their lethargy." "We may not have to wait much longer for that," Moehler says seriously, but convinced. "Then if Germany is to save itself from the present situation, it is necessary to mount an offensive to break through and bring the Western powers to negotiations. In the east, the Russians are pressing heavily against Germany. That may be just as unpleasant for the Yankees as it is for the English. If Bolshevism conquers Germany, then they have made their sacrifice without purpose. Stalin is known as a bank robber and these people will not willingly give up any of their booty."

"Then Hitler must turn back the Russians in order to spare the women and children the horrors of occupation," is Schulz's opinion. "From a humanitarian standpoint that would be right, but the considerations of war require something else," Moehler declares. "If we spend our last strength in the east, the Americans will rest on the Rhine and wait patiently until we have been bled dry. The American desires would be fulfilled. Germany would lie smashed to the ground and Russia would be standing on weak legs in Poland, Hungary, and Rumania. The Allies would move in quickly to occupy Germany and then invite the Russians to the round table, that is if they did not get in each other's way." "Wouldn't that be better for our people? I mean if we are no longer in a position to continue the war to a successful conclusion wouldn't it be better to avoid the worst consequences, that is, the entry of the Russians, and simply ask the Western powers for peace?" I express.

"You forget that the Americans have demanded the unconditional surrender of Germany and to this moment have rejected any talk of a separate peace. Under these conditions we must allow the Bolsheviks to slowly stream into Germany and with all of our available strength undertake a blow against the West in order to bring England and America to reason. When they realize that they will leave the war weak and Russia strong, then they will save what can be saved and together with us move against the East," is Moehler's viewpoint.

"Your prognosis is very enlightening, but really a fantasy." I remain tied to the floor of facts. "Think about it; the Americans are no Italians who simply let their flag blow any direction in the wind. Besides, they are so rich in matériel that they must conduct the war so that they do not suffocate. The Russians may always have enough troops, but if the Americans stop the transports, then the air will go out of the Russians. In the middle of 1942 we had them on the floor, and only the Americans saved them with their matériel. Perhaps it would be good diplomacy on their part to meet Russia at the negotiating table, because Stalin waited in vain for the opening of a second front in the West, while Rommel was storming through Africa bringing the English into doubt and threatening Russia with an offensive from the south. Instead, we stumbled into the second Russian winter of war while the Americans landed in Africa and left us in the murderous battle over Stalingrad and the loss of the entire Sixth Army. It makes me sick that in the fifth winter of the war, while we are behind barbed wire, we now hear the names of German cities in connection with the front. Who in his right mind can still believe in victory?"

"I assume that you told the Americans different, since you landed in a Nazi cage." Moehler laughs. "What does that have to do with it? Didn't I say with reason?" I trump him. "Naturally, no one can be angry about that; the main thing is that your heart still beats true for our side. I will reveal new facts for your understanding which you have either overlooked or apparently did not know. After the defeat at Stalingrad, it was clear to the German war leaders that we were not going to win the war with our conventional weapons, at least not in the near future. The scientists have been at work for many years in the laboratories searching for new possibilities which would bring victory for Germany. Success has not avoided them. Just look at the V-1 and V-2 rockets and their frightful consequences. Unfortunately their implementation was carried out by idiots or saboteurs and at the beginning of the invasion they were not fully deployed against England; otherwise they would have destroyed the invasion forces. A whole list of modern weapons is being developed, such as the jet plane, which can fly faster than sound. There is also a lot of talk about a new kind of bomb in connection with a new type of airplane and its deployment will turn the war in our favor. It all takes time to test and implement it. Naturally it is not hidden from the enemy and that is why they are bombing the industrial cities day and night and have succeeded in retarding its implementation. But hopefully by spring we will be far enough along to launch an offensive that will bring Germany's foes to their knees. Concurrently with this continental offensive, the oceans of the world will be crossed by a new type of submarine which will send up in smoke the embarkation facilities of the Allies and cut the nerves of the troops that have already landed as well as the supply lines of the Americans to the Russians through the Arctic Sea. Then we will reach the point which our Führer prophesied at the beginning of the war: 'The last battalion will be a German one!' "

Silently Schulz reaches into his pocket and pulls out six cigarettes. "Who are you really, Moehler?" Schulz asks without looking at him. "A German corporal prisoner of war, that must be enough for you," he responds. "Good, let's assume that is so," Schulz says. "Where do you have your knowledge of things which we would label as rumors of secret weapons, but which have never been so precisely identified in connection with the last drum roll of this war?"

"I was captured near Metz and was able to bring my experiences with me. To be sure, I did not belong to a regular battle unit, which I hope you will forget after this conversation. But I have a question I would like to ask you, which must remain among us." "You know how to make one curious." I grope toward him. "Fire away, we are your good friends," Schulz presses.

"Good," Moehler flusters. "Can I count on you if situations arise which make possible escape in a grand style?" "Without question," I respond, giving it no thought, "but how is that to happen?" "At the moment that is not open to debate. I said, in case the situation arises, and the earliest would be in February or March when it all comes together. Then we will talk about it further. In the meantime, work carefully with the other comrades and avoid any unnecessary meetings with me. The American responsible for this cage is well meaning, but also very intelligent. Avoid everything which could bring him against us so that we will not be torn apart. If I do receive important news, I will inform you. And now leave me alone. Forget what could be fateful for you. Work carefully and keep yourself ready for the day."

"Hopefully we have not let ourselves in for something that we will regret," Schulz breaks the silence as we go to our quarters. The night lies cold over the tent city and wraps everything in dark secrecy. "Whether we are included or not, Schulz, if the dam breaks we will land in the torrent anyway. It is better to know what is going on rather than to be in the dark. Something is going on in this camp, and I do not believe that Moehler is the main figure. I no longer accept that he is just a corporal."

"That is why I now have my doubts. I know that certain officers are trained with the assignment to enter the prison camps in order to build a bastion in back of the foe, which, if the occasion arises, has the possibility to tie down a tremendous number of the enemy," he explains without enthusiasm.

"Now Schulz, have you messed your pants?" I ask like a heretic. "Don't joke around." He brings me aright. "I know that you are drawn to such an adventure, but I am too old for such plans." "I think you do want the final victory." I reach in. "Certainly, but we cannot do very much in the enemy's back with only our hands," he explains his rejection. "They will not expect that of us. Don't you remember that Siegfried spoke once about paratroopers? They will supply us from the air and then just imagine what kind of trouble we could cause to the enemy's supply system." I paint a bright picture of the adventure for him.

"When you look at it that way, the picture does have a frame and does not simply run off the edges. That would have to be a well-planned and prepared action whose success would play together with an effective breakthrough offensive in order to turn the war decidedly in our favor." He finally follows my train of thought. "It must come, Schulz. If they can hit the Americans in the winter, it will strike them just as hard as we were by the Russians before Moscow. Then in connection with the new weapons there would be no doubt of success," I chatter away. "You still have your doubts?" The Adam's apple in his throat rises and falls. "Certainly I have them, but I also have the hope which will take me through the saddest Christmas of my life," I confess shamelessly the self-delusion I have acquired behind the barbed wire.

*16 December 1944*

"Checkmate," Hocker says to Briller and puts his queen in a position so that his two bishops cannot offer any defense. "I did not count on your simple-minded shepherd move," Briller growls angrily. "The simplest way often leads to the goal more quickly than the most complicated subterfuges." Hocker laughs at him. "What do you know about it?" Briller bawls and shoves the primitive figures again into their starting positions.

"Give up, old boy," Hocker waves. "Today you do not have any luck with the game. Perhaps you should try it with romance." "You know even less about that," Briller responds. "You only mean that because you consider yourself irresistible." Hocker laughs cunningly. "I have already seen how the women treat you like a stepmother." Briller pushes him.

"The rotten whores only serve as a spittoon and do not count," Hocker hisses contemptuously. "And you cannot get anywhere with the others, and with that your repertoire is exhausted." Briller tries to silence him. "That is right where you make your great mistake, old timer," Hocker contradicts him and lets the wood figures fall into a rusted can as his long eyelashes sink like curtains over his eyes. "So, I would have liked to see one that would have fallen in love with you," Briller sneers further.

"Unfortunately that is no longer possible," Hocker whispers. "So, so," Briller becomes curious, "did she drown herself in the village pond out of love to you?" "Don't puff yourself up, you chimpanzee, she died as a sacrifice in the bombing," Hocker hisses at him. "Excuse me, I couldn't have known that, you never spoke about it," Briller says, ashamed, as three angry pairs of his friends' eyes stare at both of them.

"When was that, Willi?" I ask to bridge the painful pause. "The beginning of summer 1943," he answers, lost in thought. "I had met her about a year before in a hospital in East Prussia. Her name was Gerda and she was from the Ruhr region. At the hospital I had my first pass when I met her in the hall and she also wanted to go into the city. I was using a cane because of a bullet in the upper thigh. She offered to help me to the streetcar. We found out that we had the same goal: to go to the movies. From that day on she looked after me every day. After I could walk better, we took a Wednesday afternoon walk. The weather was beautiful and we enjoyed ourselves like children. We discovered a patch of deep yellow flowers on the edge of a stream. While we were picking them, her dress got under my boot and it left a terrible spot on the bright cloth. Together we tried to wash it in the stream. She slipped and I finally had the opportunity to take her in my arms without any resistance from her. After she could breathe once again, she invited me to start on the way back with her. But I was in love with her and I also noticed her confusion. After some hesitation she sat next to me in the young grass, but I had to promise her that I would be good. We did not say much; we each knew how things stood with the other. So we looked into the flowing water and listened to the beating of our hearts. An hour later we went back.

"The next day I had to look all over the building for her, since it was already 4:00 P.M. and she had not seen me. I learned from one of her friends that she had been reproached by one of her superiors because she had flirted with a patient. But I knew where I could find her and a little later I met her at the deck chairs.

" 'Are you crying out of anger because of the charges that they made or because of love for me?' I asked after I saw the tear traces on her face and the wet handkerchief in her hand. 'The charge would not matter to me, if our feelings in the middle of war had some purpose. Believe me, I am nearly twenty years old and never have I felt so miserable and yet so happy as in the past days,' she answered, breaking out in tears.

"I calmed her and said I would speak to her superior and we would become engaged. 'Now I must be the happiest human being under the sun, Willi, but I am not. Not yet; then I cannot become engaged without having first introduced you to my parents,' was her answer. 'Who are your parents?' I asked with a pounding heart. 'Respectable people, the rest is not important,' she answered defiantly. I asked her to also tell me what, in her opinion, was the rest that did not matter and I learned to my shock that she was the child of rich people.

"Immediately I made my plans to return to the front as quickly as possible. 'Does your leg hurt?' she asked, concerned. 'No, it is doing well; I will report tomorrow to the doctor in charge,' I explained. 'Aren't you satisfied with the treatment you are receiving?' she wanted to know. 'Yes, very much,' I said and felt an unusual hate rising in me against the beautiful rich girl.

"Why is she not poor? Why am I not rich? Angrily I sprang to my feet and went quickly into the house to escape her and my thoughts. But she held me back. 'What has happened to you? Is it a crime that my father has been luckier than yours? I do not know who you are or where you come from, but I do know that I love you and whoever I love my father will not reject. It is only the war that stands between us.'

"Two weeks later we left the hospital together. She had completed her year and I had my recovery leave pass. The trip for most of the travelers in the overcrowded leave train may not have been very comfortable, but the closer we were pressed together, the happier we felt. In Hanover we said good-bye. She wanted to prepare her parents and I had to visit my father.

"At the end of June after only seven days at home and after talking everything over with my father, I stood with her across from her parents. I immediately recognized that the gray-haired man, apart from his money, was still a butcher. Raw, but with a heartfelt greeting he received me and continued to shake his head. 'My Gerda had to go to East Prussia, can you imagine East Prussia, to find the most dainty butcher boy.' 'The boy must be hungry,' the old lady said and forced me to the table.

"The next morning Gerda showed me her father's business. It was not as large as I had imagined, but the man had really made something out of it. An hour later I had exchanged my uniform for the butcher's apron and began making a type of sausage from my home in Baden in this Rhineland shop. In the following days, my happiness lacked for nothing. It was perfect. Only one thing was too much, and unnecessary as a goiter: the war.

"In September it grabbed me again and guided me a few weeks later into the Hell of Stalingrad. Just as the Russians had enclosed us in the bitter cold kettle, I was hit in the shoulder by a grenade splinter. After a few anxious days, I lay on my belly in a Ju 52 plane. I could go home and I could see Gerda once again. In the meantime her father had arranged for her to stay at home. He had become sick and she was indispensable for his work. As a consequence of my wound, I was also no longer fit for work, but I willingly stepped into the unfamiliar paperwork that is associated with such a shop. After the end of my furlough, I would have willingly taken Gerda to my father, especially because the enemy fliers could not find our little nest and there was no worthwhile objective to bomb, unlike in the Rhineland where they constantly disturbed the night sleep of the good citizens there.

" 'Love me as I love you, and return again,' she sobbed as the train rolled from the station. A telegram had instructed me to report to a replacement pool at Horb.

"Ten days later, the letter that I had written right after my arrival was returned unopened. I stood with shaking knees and spoke with the mayor's office in her city. 'Enemy planes have destroyed the shop. The owner, family members, and employees are buried in the ruins.' The news shot like a flame from the receiver which I simply dropped and stumbled out of the booth. On the same evening I sat in a train headed north. But I came too late, much too late. The victims of the attack had been buried for days and among them was my entire happiness: Gerda."

Hocker's mouth closes hard and becomes silent in obvious pain. We sit petrified around the most sensitive, bravest, and hardest companion among us who had endured, suffered, bled, and sacrificed more than all four of us together. The passion still had not found an end.

"Since this morning German divisions have been on a fast march westward," spokesman Moehler screams into the tent and observes with gleaming eyes the open mouths of the unbelieving comrades staring at him. Like a sinew that has been suddenly set free, Briller jumps up, grabs Moehler by the shoulders. "Is it true, is it really true?" he gushes. "Yes," says Moehler, "X day has arrived."

The reaction of the men is undescribable. An almost heavenly light shines in the hollow-cheeked faces and an incomparable, joyous roar sounds in the half-dark tent. That which we have hoped for so long has come. German divisions are in a fast march toward the West!

As Allied forces reached the borders of Germany near Aachen, Hitler ordered a last great counteroffensive along the eighty-five-mile-wide Ardennes sector in Belgium. Known by the Americans as the Battle of the Bulge and by the Germans as the Ardennes Offensive, the surprise attack force of 250,000 men under Field Marshal von Rundstedt was launched on December 16, 1944, in the midst of fog, drizzle, snow, and haze. Pushing through the narrow valley called the Losheim Gap where German armies had passed en route to France in 1870, 1914, and 1940, the German offensive broke through an inadequate number of U.S. troops, pushing fifty miles westward toward the English Channel with Antwerp as the ultimate goal. German soldiers dressed in American uniforms created havoc as they changed road signs, cut telephone wires, and spread terrifying reports about the oncoming Germans. Thousands of American soldiers were taken prisoner and forced to march eastward toward Germany. The defense of the surrounded town of Bastogne under the acting commander of the 101st Airborne Division, Brigadier General Anthony McAuliffe, halted the offensive as the bad weather broke on December 22 and the encircled soldiers were supplied by C-47s. The Allies went on the offensive on January 3, 1945, and a month after it began, the Battle of the Bulge was over. While the First and Third U.S. Armies lost eighty-four hundred killed with sixty-nine thousand wounded and missing, the Ardennes Offensive was a costly gamble for the Germans, who suffered around ten thousand casualties and lost six hundred tanks and assault guns and over sixteen hundred planes. In his two-volume biography, *Adolf Hitler,* John Toland writes of the aftermath of the Battle of the Bulge:

> It reminded many of Napoleon's retreat from Moscow. Men shuffled painfully through the snow, feet encased in burlap bags with shawls wound around their heads like careless turbans. They plodded on frozen feet, bedeviled by biting winds, bombs and shells. The wounded and sick crept back to the homeland with rotting insides, ulcers oozing, pus running from destroyed ears. They staggered east on numb feet with despair in their hearts, stricken by dysentery, which left its bloody trail of filth in the snow.
>
> Their will was broken. Few who survived the retreat believed there was now any chance of German victory. Almost every man brought back a story of doom, of Allied might and of the terrifying weapon forged in the Ardennes: the American fighter. The GI who came out of the battle was the quintessential American, the man Hitler did not believe existed.[1]

* * *

Helmut Hörner shortly after induction in 1939.

Helmut on a military horse during training in early 1939.

Willi Hörner visited brother, Helmut, while on leave from the German Navy in 1939. Helmut was in training near Karlsruhe at the time.

Helmut Hörner with his unit during field training in the vicinity of Karlsruhe in 1939. Helmut is sitting in the front row on the far left.

Tension is high among the young men crossing the Shelde River in Belgium in 1940. Helmut was among those crossing the river to face his first battle of World War II, against the British.

By the spring of 1940, Helmut and his unit had become adept at crossing rivers. Here, soldiers cross the Lorie River in France.

Posing for a group photo in the field, Helmut (front row, second from left) and his unit prepare for battle near Dunkirk, France, in 1940.

By 1941, Hörner's grenade launcher group was in East Prussia, preparing for the German invasion of Russia on June 22, 1941. Helmut is in the back row, sixth from the left.

Helmut Hörner, still stationed in Russia, keeps watch through army field glasses.

Religious services in the field were not uncommon during World War II. Here, Catholic German soldiers receive communion.

German soldiers manning a mortar firing position on the Russian front in 1941 stand in front of their bunker.

Helmut Hörner at Bayeux, France, 1944.

The Chateau Breize Fraceise in Normandy was used as military housing prior to the 1944 Normandy invasion by the Allied forces.

Helmut at Saint Malo/Dinor in May 1944, shortly before the Normandy invasion by the Allied forces.

German soldiers from tank and infantry units gather in the town square of a French village just before the Normandy invasion.

Captured German soldiers in a French field are marched to a holding area under the guard of an American G.I. (Courtesy of National Archives)

German prisoners of war, captured in France, are transported by wagon to holding camps in American occupied France. (Courtesy of National Archives)

Captured German soldiers, several of whom are wounded, rest in a French town under the watchful eye of American troops. (Courtesy of National Archives)

German prisoners of war arrive at an American holding area in France. Note the piles of steel helmets and (apparently) rifles that have been confiscated from the prisoners. (Courtesy of National Archives)

A French girl refused to leave her German boyfriend and his comrades after they were captured by American forces. (Courtesy of National Archives)

A German prisoner of war enclosure in France. Note the makeshift shelters and the American patrol outside the fence. (Courtesy of National Archives)

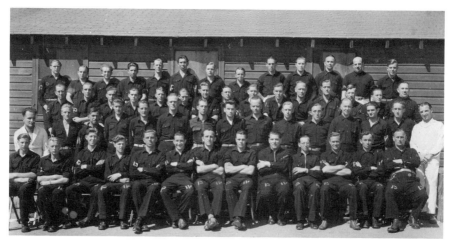

Once in the United States, Helmut Hörner's prisoner of war unit was photographed at the West Point, New York, camp in 1946.

Looking healthy and reasonably content, Helmut was photographed at the farm of Mr. Reuter near Glassboro, New Jersey, October 1945.

Helmut Hörner (standing, fourth from right) and his fellow POWs worked for area farmers while interned at various camps. This photo taken in October 1945 is at the Reuter's farm near Glassboro, New Jersey. Mr. Reuter is also pictured, kneeling at far right.

**BASIC PERSONNEL RECORD**
(Alien Enemy or Prisoner of War)

F. P. C.* _____

31G 678370
(Internment serial number)

HOERNER, HELMUT
(Name of internee)

Male
(Sex)

Height __6__ ft. __9½__ in.

Weight __186__

Eyes __Brown__

Skin __Fair__

Hair __Black__

Age __28__

Distinguishing marks or characteristics:
__None__

Reference* _____

INVENTORY OF PERSONAL EFFECTS TAKEN FROM INTERNEE

1. _____
2. _____
3. _____
4. _____
5. _____
6. _____
7. _____
8. _____
9. _____

HOERNER HELMUT 31G 678370

PW Camp, Camp Gruber, Oklahoma, 5 May 1945
(Date and place where processed (Army enclosure, naval station, or other place))

The above is correct:

(Signature of internee)

**RIGHT HAND**

| 1. Thumb | 2. Index finger | 3. Middle finger | 4. Ring finger | 5. Little finger |
|---|---|---|---|---|

**LEFT HAND**

| 6. Thumb | 7. Index finger | 8. Middle finger | 9. Ring finger | 10. Little finger |
|---|---|---|---|---|

W. D., A. G. O. Form No. 12-5
25 July 1944
(Old W. D., P. M. G. Form No. 2, 11 June 1943)

Note Amputation in Proper Space

* Do not fill in.
16—40965-1

Helmut Hörner's official "Basic Personnel Record" for his years of internment as a prisoner of war.

*20 December 1944*

An ice cold wind sweeps from the sea through the canvas quarters. The captive occupants of the tent lie upon the cold earth wrapped in their coats and blankets, but their dreams are filled with hope as Schulz and I quietly step into the open and look at the gray snow-filled sky. The machine guns stare from the watchtowers. The Americans have strengthened the guard. The German offensive must be the cause. Smiling, we make our way to the latrine for our appointment with Moehler.

"Good morning to you." He extends his hand from his throne and I immediately notice that he has not really been using the latrine, only waiting for us. But at this hour there is no one to overhear us. Not until after the coffee has been distributed is there a run on this place. Still we sit to the right and left of Moehler and let our cigarettes hang from the corners of our mouths. "To take all doubt from you, I brought the *Stars and Stripes* with me. Even if you cannot read English, it will not be hard for you to discern the German success," Moehler opens the conversation and pulls the small American army newspaper from his field blouse.

Shaking as though with fever, Schulz and I reach at the same time for the page. "Luftwaffe Like 1940," are the headlines printed in large letters over the report from the front.

"The Americans admit that the offensive was a complete surprise and express in the report their amazement at the firepower of the German divisions as well as their bold attack, although the weather, from their viewpoint, is most adverse to such an undertaking. While the German air force is whirling in the sky, they maintain that their own aircraft must be kept on the ground because of the weather." Moehler explains to us as we both attempt to decipher the report for ourselves. We are successful in getting enough from the black-and-white lines that the last doubts fall from us.

"An offensive which is carried forward with such force will not fail to bring about a successful breakthrough," is Schulz's commentary. "I was always of the viewpoint that the Americans must be grappled with during the winter. Unfortunately, they are better prepared with clothing than we were in 1941 before Moscow," I mumble, satisfied, as Moehler takes the newspaper back and puts it away.

"I must dampen your healthy optimism just a little," Moehler continues. "Whether you believe it or not, I do not consider this offensive the deciding one. According to my calculations it has been undertaken too early. It may be that it is something of a preparation to help create a more favorable situation, but the supply lines cannot be established in such a short time for a breakthrough." "I don't understand that, Moehler," I interrupt him. "The offensive is occurring in the Ardennes. Field Marshall von Rundstedt is an experienced strategist and I can imagine that he wants to drive a wedge between the English and the Americans and then turn to the north and south in order to encircle the enemy and at the same time push toward Paris with his tank companies."

"As far as strategy goes, you have thought it through carefully." Moehler laughs, slightly amazed. "But unfortunately you forget that we no longer live in the years 1940 to 1942, when we had enough matériel as well as men, weapons, and equipment. In the meantime the enemy bombs have significantly reduced our production. No, what does not please me is the absence of the new weapons. The reports do speak about a new kind of fighter plane, but there is nothing in the newspaper about what I have been waiting for."

"From my viewpoint that does not tell me anything." Schulz reaches in. "Just imagine what confusion this unexpected attack has caused our enemy. It is clear that the censors attempt to prevent everyone from losing their heads because of such alarming reports. These initial successes cannot be maintained only with carbines. I believe in the deployment of the new weapons." "We will have to wait and see how these things work out," Moehler indicates. "And now, coming back to us. You have certainly noticed that they assigned four men to each guardtower, with two machine guns. That is clearly connected to the offensive. I am afraid that when our troops reach a certain point, the Americans will load all prisoners of war on the ships as fast as possible. It is up to us to hinder it. I know for certainty that down in the Cherbourg harbor there are a large number of tanks outfitted with everything necessary, awaiting transportation to the front. Our assignment is to determine who among the noncommissioned officers are tank drivers, gunners, etc. Compile a secret list so that when the time is right we can get them all together. By the way, pay attention to the mood in the cages; try to suppress talk about an upcoming fight; and wait patiently until I know something definite, and then I will get back in touch with you."

"Listen, Moehler." I hold up the secretive camp spokesman. "If you believe that you can expect something like that from me without knowing anything about you, then you will be greatly disappointed. I am certainly ready to do everything that will bring us freedom, but I am not going to leave myself open to an adventure that results in useless bloodshed." "That is what I wanted to say," Schulz chimes in. "We are not dumb boys that you can persuade to join in a dangerous game. I would not think of setting in motion a mutiny by unarmed prisoners of war which would end in certain death and still not have any influence on the war."

"You must not look at it that way." Moehler goes on the defense. "It is clear that we are not planning a simple mutiny, but only in case of an emergency to hinder being shipped out, that is to help the approaching German troops to conquer the city and harbor of Cherbourg." "Until it is that far, we must eat quite a few American biscuits," I explain, "and then we will see what the hour demands of us. You are aware of the rumors that are coursing through the camp about marching the prisoners of war to Dunkirk or Lorient?"

"Yes, I have heard about them. I know that some idiots are exchanging tobacco for knives and spears with the neighboring enclosure. Unfortunately it is noncommissioned officers, whose naiveté will bring a heavy burden to the entire cage. But this matter does not have anything to do with that. I have revealed the goal of our plan to you. At present there are a thousand men in the cage, but including you two, only nineteen know about this plan, or in the meantime have you initiated your buddies?" "No," Schulz answers Moehler's knife-sharp question. "Then it is good." He calms himself and extends us his hand. "Let's leave it up to our comrades to create the circumstances and keep quiet in the meantime. If I get further news about any success I will get with you again," he says, cool, and leaves, headed in the direction of the kitchen barracks.

"There are several playing with fire in the most lighthearted manner," I whisper to Schulz on the way into the tent. "I find Moehler's conduct at the moment irresponsible," Schulz continues angrily. "He does not believe with his whole heart in the success of the offensive and still is trying to instigate resistance. I am in favor of keeping out of these things until there is some real promise of success." "And I am in favor that we watch out for ourselves until fate forces us to jump in and swim with the course of events," is my determined conclusion.

"Does that mean that you too do not believe any more in the final German victory?" Schulz remains standing, looking at me, surprised.

"Allow me to at least be honest with myself and my friends. This offensive will not bring the German troops to Cherbourg, that was clear to me from the beginning. Moehler is well informed about the German military potential. In his opinion, the offensive was begun too early. Why? Only because of doubt. But operations that are undertaken too early point to a war ministry that is nervous and carry the seed of failure within because the necessary preparations are not all completed. It may be that the Americans will lose their heads; I know from Normandy how weak they are when they come under a hard attack. But if we do not have any mysterious weapons to put into action which can lay waste to their divisions, they will stand up again and with their most courageous attackers smother us with their matériel. I think in the first place on the mighty Anglo-American airplane fleet, which can only be dragged out of the skies with a wonder weapon. 'Build them faster than the enemy can destroy them,' is the motto of the American aircraft- and ship-building industry. As prisoners we have already seen some of it, which does not lead one to doubt their power. Let's wait, Schulz, in a week we will know better; just don't get your hopes too high because they may never be fulfilled. I consider you to be the kind of a man that can endure the hard truth; that is why I let you know of my doubts."

Silently Schulz swallows the bitter pill and goes with me into the tent. " 'By Christmas we will be home,' is what they have said since the first of September 1939 to every soldier of this war every year again and again and now they do not even believe it themselves."

### 24 December 1944

"… and strengthen one another in the faith that next Christmas we will celebrate as free human beings in the homeland with our families." Spokesman Moehler ends his short talk as so many have done before him and distributes, like a Santa Claus sent from heaven, the Christmas gifts which the kitchen personnel have prepared for today after saving for weeks.

Yes, we really do celebrate Christmas. No organized Christmas with tinsel and electric lights on a Christmas tree, expensive presents, and a stuffed belly. No, we celebrate Christmas as in the original manner, from our inner impulses born in the moment of need and highest affliction.

As Moehler leaves the tent to go into the other quarters to take the other comrades the gifts from the kitchen, we sit on the earth deep in thought, staring at the impenetrable darkness. No word, no sound disturbs the silent night in the overfilled tent. While the weary heads of the imprisoned soldiers rest on their knees and the homesick hearts quiver with cramps, we hold in our limp hands the Christmas cake baked by our comrades until the sugar coating becomes sticky because of the warmth of our hands. The nibbling begins only gradually. "It tastes wonderful," we whisper to ourselves and pull ourselves and others back into reality.

For a few minutes gentle murmuring displaces the holy silence. Scraping sounds let recognize that the first are wrapping in their blankets and coats in mute dialogue with their relatives in far-off, death-threatened Germany to celebrate the most lonesome Christmas of their lives.

But suddenly there is a light in the tent. It is not the star of Bethlehem, but a can filled with wax painstakingly scraped from the provision boxes and an ordinary string as a wick. The flickering light brightens the windy quarters. Sixty pairs of eyes glimmer and stare for seconds at the light as a symbol of all life. "Silent Night, Holy Night ... " raw, and with shame suppressed, but more celebrated than in the Cologne Cathedral, the song of Christianity pours from the throats of the men up to the flapping tent roof and finally brings Christmas among those who have been overtaken by the war.

After the song has died out and all have wrapped themselves in their blankets, a mournful voice from the furthest corner of the tent begins the Christmas story: "And it came to pass in those days that there went out a decree from Caesar Augustus that all the world should be taxed. And all went to be taxed, everyone into his own city. And Joseph also went up from Galilee out of the city of Nazareth into Judea unto the city of David which is called Bethlehem. And so it was that while they were there, the days were accomplished that she should be delivered and she brought forth her firstborn son and wrapped him in swaddling clothes and laid him in a manger, because there was no room for them in the inn. And the angel said to them fear not, for behold, I bring you good tidings of great joy. For unto you is born this day the saviour. Glory to God in the highest, and on earth peace, good will toward men."

"It would be beautiful," Hocker whispers to me as the speaker ends and an icy silence spreads throughout the tent. "Even this day will come for mankind, Willi," I whisper back and in firm belief pull the blanket over my head.

### 27 December 1944

Since eight o'clock the American attendant O'Brion has been hammering on the kitchen barracks and he is still not satisfied with the results of his efforts. Lazily I sit on an empty box and wonder with the cynicism of a slothful fellow at the drive to work of this American. Why does this free man carry on with such work while hundreds of hands are carried around by their owners deep in coat pockets? What kind of a Yankee is he that comes into the cage and worries about the filth in the latrine and the cleanliness of the tents? No words of complaint, accusation, or threat have come from his lips during these seventeen days. Besides, he is red-haired and does not give the impression that he would be led around by the nose. But he conducts the roll call conscientiously, cares for the provisions, and has been hammering board after board on the shaky kitchen barrack for two hours.

"He is certainly your best worker," I speak to Moehler as he steps out of the kitchen. "You are certainly right about that." He laughs heartily and glances toward the American. "Is anything wrong?" The attendant grins at us and shoves the hammer in his back right pocket. "No, your work is OK," Moehler calls to him. "Unusual bird from the States," I indicate in passing to Moehler while I hope to get from him a message about the front.

"A decent fellow, this O'Brion," Moehler continues with the topic, "very intelligent, deeply religious, unfortunately a little too thick-headed. He is Irish." "Born in Ireland?" I ask. "No, only descended from Irish; his parents had just emigrated before he was born," Moehler answers.

"How does he feel about us?" I finally become interested in the man. "Not good and not bad. He is Catholic and believes that Hitler wants to dissolve the churches in Europe. They eat up everything that their propaganda ministers put before them." "We too." I laugh out loud. "That is really not so, or do you believe that Germany will finally be destroyed if we lose the war?" Moehler asks.

"Many kingdoms and principalities have already passed away in the long history of the people, but the people continue to live on. Poland has been divided often but still it exists today. Even Germany will continue to exist. You cannot wipe out a nation of seventy million people." I express my opinion. "Ireland is Catholic, and thoroughly hates England because they withhold freedom from them."

"One could believe that you have already spoken with O'Brion; then he offers the same viewpoint about Ireland as you," Moehler indicates. "Recently he told me that his father has half a heart for Germany. According to his viewpoint, America is carrying on the war only to get out of its own economic misery; then both father and son were unemployed in the USA until the outbreak of war."

"God knows how many times I have heard that. According to some, the war is only a business for the USA." I shake my head. "Also for us, every war is fought over money, that is, over power, which means the same thing." Moehler laughs. "Yes, yes, I know that too, but we always forget it," I snarl in remembrance of my own reflections.

"You can thank the propaganda for that, my dear. With it and the dumb ones is how war is conducted." Moehler slaps me on the shoulder with a ringing laugh. "But now I must see about the food. By the way, Aachen has been in German hands once again since Christmas. The fight continues in the Ardennes, but the Germans are slowly running out of steam. Didn't I say that the supplies would not be enough?" He turns abruptly toward the kitchen and leaves me alone in grief.

Sitting between my friends, I shovel the food slowly and thoughtfully into my mouth. The disagreement which has arisen since my open comments about the outcome of the war can no longer be kept a secret. Distrust has also arisen in our ranks. Only Hocker greets me as openly as always, while Schulz, along with Siegfried and Briller, apparently are practicing restraint. Still in doubt who I should take in hand without letting the present discord become known throughout the entire tent, an opportunity arises by itself when Schulz asks for my help in washing the dishes. Without hesitation I follow him to the water faucet, where we sullenly carry out the work in the midst of a crowd. As usual we go to the fence afterward and hang the cans upside down on the wire so that the water can drip out while we wipe our cold, wet hands dry on our pants.

"We will get some snow," Schulz says incidentally and rolls his head in the direction of the sky. "And we must part, Schulz, if we cannot understand one another anymore." I step close to him and force his gaze into my eyes. "It does not have to go that far, at least that is not what I wish," he explains very seriously. "Who wishes it then?" I want to know. "No one," he answers defiantly.

"Schulz, we are no longer children; if I am no longer agreeable to you, then I will face the consequences," I bluster to my confidant of earlier days. "That can never be the subject. But you have upset everyone with your change in outlook. I never would have expected it from you, that you would turn your back to our just cause," he stammers, unrestrained.

"You are distorting the facts. Am I somehow disloyal if I clearly believe what will become of the offensive?" I ask, becoming calmer. "You no longer believe in victory and that is why you disappoint us." He shows his colors.

"After our conversation with Moehler I indicated that the offensive would do as much good as hitting the water if no wonder weapons are deployed. With regard to Hocker, after long consideration I went further and explained to him that militarily the war is lost. My hope lies entirely with the intention of the Western powers or the course of a merciful fate. During the Seven Years' War, the Russian Tsaress died shortly before midnight and saved Frederick the Great from certain defeat. Perhaps Stalin will die tomorrow and through his death make all of the troops on the eastern front free for the western front. Only one of these possibilities, or both together, offer us salvation from the chaos. And if you do not see that, then I will tell you what I have just learned from Moehler: The offensive is running out of gas."

Coming to an inner peace with myself, I observe the harsh face of my friend after I have told him the bitter truth and expressed my unlikely hopes. Becoming contemplative, he nervously chews his spanking clean fingernails and stares at the rusty barbed wire.

"What you say cannot be simply dismissed," the stubborn Niedersachsen concedes. "That success is only possible with the new weapons is something I have been clear about for a long time. But it is not the only hope that keeps us going. And that is just what you are about to do, take everything from us. Let the thing run its course; in the end it doesn't matter what we are fighting about and making life difficult."

"You told me once in Alençon that it would be the intelligent ones that the barbed wire would finish off. Is that why you have joined with the fools? Are you now carrying on ostrich politics? It's all right Schulz, lay your hands in your lap and imagine that you will be a millionaire at the end of your days; that way you can more easily survive the rough years. Then it will not be so bad when at seventy you realize that you have deceived yourself. But don't expect that the world around you will participate in the swindle; otherwise you are not responsible since we are younger. We must start all over and we cannot begin soon enough." I tear the mask of camouflage from our faces.

"What do you plan to do now, based on your viewpoint?" he asks luringly. "Nothing. What can I do as a prisoner? We must wait through all the long months and convince ourselves that life will always go on. If the war comes to an end in the next few weeks, then we must make the best out of what the victors give us. But I fear that we personally will not see the homeland very soon; since after the last war two years passed before they sent the prisoners home," I answer without pathos.

"And what is with the idea of national socialism?" he asks. "Forms of government come and go. Perhaps they will allow the good achievements of this epoch to be carried into the New World," I ponder. "All right, then let's allow the events to run their course. What you have said often presses down on me during the long nights. But one does not willingly believe in what he doesn't want to have happen. You have aired your thoughts and I see that you feel better. We will stick together to the bitter end." He extends to me his hand. "And that is right, Schulz; because then we will need each other more than ever," I join in and at the same time congratulate him on his birthday. He looks at me in surprise and is obviously deeply affected as he mumbles, "You did not forget it."

### 1 January 1945

"Happy New Year, Happy New Year!" We shake each others' hands and wish one another a happy return home.

With old familiarity we listen to the crunching of snow under the boot soles. With the collars of our coats turned up and our hands buried as deep as possible in the pockets, I wander alone around the cage. It is about nine o'clock of the first day of the new year. I breathe deeply the aromatic air into my lungs and listen to myself: A year has fulfilled its destiny. It began full of hope on the snow-covered training grounds of Münsingen, and led me in the first days into France. I was happy that I did not land on the eastern front, but we underwent hard training in the beginning in order to be ready for the eventual enemy invasion. After being stationed in Bayeux, Caen, and Saint-Malo, we were transferred to the Cotentin Peninsula under a hail of grenades from the many Americans who had landed.

In addition to much misery and shortages was added the destruction of my brand new apartment in the homeland as well as the interruption of all contact with home. The month of August saw me leave the hospital healthy but in Paris I learned about the destruction of my division. Late summer brought imprisonment. Unnameable sorrow, both physical and spiritual, has been my companion since then. And the war still goes on. The sons of Germany condemned to death are now fighting their last doubtful struggle against all powerful forces in the icy cold. Afterward a graveyard silence will lie over blood-soaked Europe and only the cries of widows and orphans will be heard until the screams of the victors rise up and the blood and tears trickle away in shame.

"Check," I call to Schulz, very pleased with myself because I have driven him into a corner. "That was a well-thought-out move, Helmut. You have learned a lot in the last while." Siegfried presses himself as a kibitzer in the game. "You should not mix in, Siegfried. I don't like it." Schulz sets him straight and brings his king into presumed security. "Checkmate, Schulz." I tie him up completely as I bring into position the rook that he has overlooked. "It is a game for a king; however, it demands all one's attention," I excuse Schulz and make room for Briller. "Let's play a game, Helmut," the farm boy indicates, reaching for the figures. "I am too tired, Robert, and it is just about dark," I excuse myself. "Why don't you play with me anymore?" he asks, offended. "Because you are a poor loser," I answer him honestly. "Come on, let's at least go for a walk before dinner; the time passes faster." He does not let himself be repulsed and I step outside with him.

"During the last days you have been evading me, Helmut. May I know the reason why?" He immediately opens fire after we step onto the walk. "I do not avoid anyone, but you have spoken behind my back so that I could not defend myself." I reveal my disappointment. "I will not deny it, but do not believe that anyone has cursed you. You have changed your viewpoint, but that is your business. I mean the two of us and Hocker have known each other the longest and there must not be any contention between us," he speaks in an atoning voice.

"I am not interested in any strife, but I will not lie to myself and others any longer and whoever cannot bear the truth can continue to stick his head in the sand," I verbalize my wounded pride. "Do you really think we will lose the war?" he asks freely. "I really do not like talking with you about it because you lose your head so easily, old fellow." I smile roguishly into his jovial eyes. "That is behind me. It does not matter anymore. I did my duty and wanted the best. If we go swimming, I too will get wet. There is no escape," he comments, fully composed.

"Will you go back to Austria after we return home? Austria will once again be independent." I take part in his fate. "I will slip into any hole that gives off warmth when all this is over. As poor as I will be after this war, I can no longer afford to be a luxurious character. If my wife will no longer have me, I will lie somewhere else in a ready-made bed. In my profession there will be a shortage of workers since no painting has been done for years. Today we begin a new year; I hope that we will soon begin a new life." He spreads before me in his usual trust his plan for the future.

"Don't you think about the French woman with the paint store?" I joke with him. "That was a fantasy; you don't build a marriage on such a flimsy relationship. I tell you that everything that is in the past no longer matters to me." He stops in front of our tent as the food carriers enter. "I must admit that in your personal situation you have done much more planning than me," I acknowledge freely. "In the camp at Chartres I ridiculed your feelings. I am doing it again today. Use your common sense and think now about your home instead of troubling yourself about strategy and talk about the end of the world. Don't be a hothead and give other people right if they talk about dumb things; that way you have your peace from them and you still stand in high regard with them." He gives me a well-intentioned lecture. "One thing more, Helmut." He holds me firm as I start to go. "Is everything between us now like it used to be?" "Just like before, Robert," comes impulsively from my lips. "Then let's get at the dried corned beef so that we will have strength to endure." He laughs in his old way and scurries ahead of me into the dark tent where we are received in our reestablished trust by Schulz, Hocker, and Siegfried.

### 7 January 1945

The icy cold penetrates mercilessly through our worn-out uniforms. Even more mercilessly do the Americans conduct a raid and bring into the daylight, with mine-searching instruments, those items which the prisoners of war had produced during the many days and nights or acquired by trading in order to one day regain their freedom. Before our eyes lie, in a pile, many knives, picks, shovels, and iron bars which make for a wild tangle. We recognize the mental condition of the would-be escapees. Now foreign hands search our pockets in a familiar manner. But that is not enough. "Undress and lay all of your clothes in front of you," the command sounds from an American which causes our hair to stand on end. But it does not help; we must follow the order and we do so in blunt bitterness.

Wrapped in thick fur coats and overshoes, the searchers go slowly through the open rows and direct their instruments over the half-rotten clothing of their imprisoned opponents. And they have success. Nothing less than parts of two pistols with the necessary ammunition come to light. Not only are the Americans amazed, but we too stare in unbelieving wonder at the blue, dull-gleaming weapon parts. A light pride enters my heart and warms the blood for a moment. Faster than the much-feared costume ball in the German army barracks we jump into our clothes again. With stiff fingers we rub our numb limbs and tarry, awaiting further measures. But the Americans have time. After half an hour of useless standing around, they withdraw their soldiers and with them one-third of the inmates. Spokesman Moehler can no longer be seen.

"Wrap in the blankets, lie in a horizontal position, and keep your mouth shut, is the only thing that we can do at the moment," Schulz suggests to our excited tent, which returns intact but is carrying on a wild spectacle. "Such idiots in their childish simplemindedness dig a grave for themselves and others," the mob raves until the last one has found his place and fatigue and weakness bring sleep to the tormented ones.

We receive no food at noon, but at 3:00 P.M. a gloomy looking sergeant appears with his men to conduct roll call and introduce the new camp spokesman, who looks just as gloomy dressed in the uniform of a navy artillery sergeant. The kitchen personnel must be reinforced because more than half of them were caught in the search. To the great surprise of all Germans, the American asks naively who among us knew how it was possible for Moehler to disappear without being noticed. Of course no one admits to any knowledge of the entire affair.

As the Americans leave the assembled crowd to the new German spokesman and depart, an intense discussion rises within the ranks about the underground movement, which only a few suspected. The rumors that surfaced now and again about a march on the fortress at Dunkirk were considered by most as the pure fantasies of certain big mouths. Everyone is quietly happy that they did not have anything to do with the matter or at least were not discovered during the shakedown. But still it is apparent from the more or less open conversations of individual groups that the remaining eight hundred men still plan to be freed by German troops.

*11 January 1945*

After the scanty breakfast is behind us, we five friends step out into the cold winter morning with our blankets under our arms and walk across the hard, frozen assembly area ground into the school tent. Since some of the occupants of our cage have been transported away, there are some tents that are empty, and so the new spokesman is using the opportunity in conjunction with the available teaching staff to establish a school, which finds general approval among our comrades. And today we are attending the first instruction.

"English, as it is spoken, that is what I will teach you," the teacher, a sergeant we have known since Alençon, says, and begins with an ambitious method. "That's my hair," he takes hold of his hair and has everyone repeat after him. "And these are my eyes," he points to his eyes and continues further until all parts of the body have been identified and his teachable pupils can repeat them. In the second half hour he goes on to clothing and works patiently until the last person in the tent can say the English words, "pants button." At the end of the hour, the man has accomplished a great deal through his practical teaching method and finds grateful recognition from all the students.

The next class is philosophy, and most of the men leave. "It is too high for me." Briller laughs and hurries past us outside. I am just ready to join my friends when a sergeant speaks to me. "Stay here, Comrade. It doesn't cost anything and what I can pass on to you about life is of unmeasurable use." "I don't know," I attempt to break away, "whether I have the understanding for philosophy. To be honest with you, I don't know much about it." "Probably there are few here who know what philosophy is all about, but they are staying here to learn about it." He smiles shrewdly. "Good, I don't want to miss out on anything," I declare myself ready. "You will not regret it, if you stick with it." He shoves me back into the half-dark tent and stands on a wooden box.

"I see that some comrades feel sorry for me because only a few listeners have remained," he begins. "But that lies in the nature of the matter; since philosophy is a subject for everyone and no one. Even though nearly everyone is more or less his own philosopher, only a few know what it is and seeks. That is why, as an introduction, I will begin with the nature of philosophical thought, specifically that of Thales of Miletus, who lived in Asia minor about six hundred years before Christ. ..."

With stirring emotional words and summarizing sentences which are precisely formulated, he unveils the nature of thought and leads his listeners into a realm that hardly any one of us has ever entered before. Hanging onto every word that comes from the mouth of our teacher-philosopher, we sit on the rough-cut benches and experience a renewal of the spirit.

"Man recognizes the world as chaos. Philosophy comes when man rises in struggle against chaos."

After the philosopher has left the podium, we all remain listening in the following quiet. As though awakened from a trance, we slowly recognize our surroundings once again and thank our teacher with subdued applause.

"Was it boring?" the philosopher asks me as I light a cigarette in front of the tent. "Not one second," I acknowledge honestly and now observe the man somewhat more closely since during his presentation I did not have any time to do so. He is a small, square-built man about fifty years old, dressed in a worn-out navy coat and hat. His heavy eyebrows are grown together above his nose and stand like the wings of a bird above his black, shining eyes. The nose, slightly bent toward the mouth, reminds me of a horse. The mouth is broad, with the corners hanging almost to the middle of his angular chin. An ascetic.

"Come again," he says in my observation. "I will pass on to you the wisdom of the greatest souls of this earth and you will never find barbed wire the same."

"The stuff is so powerful that it threatens to crush me. I am now more confused than informed," I explain my inner thoughts. "That is good. You are already in search and will find it. The only thing that you lack is the will to think, I mean conscious thought and no thought games, but if you want I will gladly help you in your search for enlightenment. Not in gray theory, but from the pure light of history. Naturally it will be apart from my series of lectures, in little talks which will provide a slow but thorough introduction," he suggests to me. "Why are you going to all this trouble for me?" I ask in amazement. "I gain from it myself, in that I keep in practice and keep free through what is said. You have been in search of understanding for a long time and are awakened to conscious thinking. That is where philosophy takes its beginning. Use the time; it will never be available to you in such a rich measure," he counsels me and then departs quickly.

Philosophy! What a field and something so completely new to me! Or have I not been in search of understanding for a long time—world explanations and connections? The wind blows cold around my warm head. Alone, I make round after round. Suddenly I come to realize that we are no strange goods of the war, but simply laid on ice. Laid on ice to learn and to recognize, so that one day we have the ability to build a new, better world and to continue into the furthest generations. I will use the time, even though it seems to stand still for me.

*18 January 1945*

Days come and go. No authentic news from the front or the homeland penetrates the rusted barbed wire. There is no answer to all of the letters and cards that we have written. Daily prison life holds us unmercifully in its claws and only allows the hours and days to creep along slowly. Tormented by eternal hunger, strangled by the senseless, dirty existence, the comrades fall to their own burdens. Quarrels about nothing rule the long days, the dull doubt of the individuals, the even longer nights. Our life is an endless wait and death grins from the watchtowers.

"Now I must talk with you finally," a voice sounds in my ear. "For the entire time I have tried to read in your face what is really happening inside you. But I have not been able to. On the outside you seem to be so calm and in control, but still I feel that for the first time you are really unhappy. What is going on inside you, Helmut?"

"I will confide in you as far as I know myself," I answer him—a true, long-suffering friend. "I have come to a turning point from my life up to this time. You know yourself that we have never thought so much about it as we have in the last months. As soldiers we muddled through our deceived life and took everything for granted that was offered us by way of joy and sorrow. We lived not much differently than animals. Or have you given much serious thought about the suffering we brought with our march through the cities and villages of foreign lands? Not that we personally did anything to the people; in that case I cannot reproach myself for anything. But the many innumerable individual acts by people which the war in its totality has brought the most terrible suffering, is what comes to my consciousness as we now sit in our own misery.

"Today no one can convince me that wars cannot be avoided. Clausewitz defined this horrible word *war* as the continuation of politics with other means. He was the teacher of modern strategy and he must know for sure. But if war is the continuation of politics, that only tells me that incompetent politicians have prepared the way for war. Soon foreign soldiers will be marching through Germany. What kind of misery will they carry into the bombed-out cities! I have come to the recognition that war is nothing more than a crime. It is true that we always went into battle with a 'Hurrah,' but we were young, much too young to comprehend what kind of a wicked game we had been forced into. I don't mean just we Germans, no, all soldiers in this war are no different than misused creatures. What I cannot come to grips with, however, is the fact that our own fathers allowed it, even though they had this most bitter game behind them. One could say it was because of the propaganda which everyone succumbed to, but

I do not understand how grown men could allow themselves to be lied to again. Yes, it is true, that I am terribly unhappy with my new knowledge. Up to now I have believed, or at least imagined, that in a short time the war would end victoriously for us and we would soon be home. Now I know that the actual suffering is not behind us, but ahead of us—and that after years of front line duty. I can only tell you that those who lie inside the tents and think about nothing more than from breakfast to lunch are to be envied."

"I believe you worry too much, Helmut. You envy the others and you brood day and night over unlaid eggs. Why do you run like you are possessed into every lecture if you are convinced that we will be enclosed by barbed wire for a long time?" he asks, puzzled.

"Because despite everything I still hope that the sun will shine for us once again, not for those who can shoot faster and better than another, but for those who know more and can do more. In a school tent in Le Mans, a teacher said that knowledge is power and ignorance is weakness. Do you remember? This saying and its direction for a later civil life of creating and not destroying is what has guided my thoughts. Since that time I am no longer satisfied in believing what I hear, but I attempt, through logic, to see what the consequences will be. I soon realized that in order to do so, one must be free of the piles of nonsense from the propaganda mills as well as self-deception. That is why after a long inner struggle, I have thrown over all of the ballast. Perhaps it was a mistake to throw the whole thing at your feet, but I must do it in order to be free; then the lies are an inner prison, and bondage is the potential gravedigger for every true friendship. I know too about the inner struggles of Schulz and Siegfried. Both are much too intelligent not to know what is coming. Unfortunately they are too captivated by the fear they will lose face. Above all because they have never made a distinction between the Führer and the people. They harden in this epoch, without looking to eternity and seeing what is best for the existence of our people. Our generation is responsible for the continuation of our people. If you say I will deal with the situation myself, it is correct only so far as you believe that while we are behind barbed wire time will stand still. That is only apparently so. In reality fate has given us time for awareness and for personal renewal. From that comes the responsibility to use the time to keep our bodies, souls, and spirits healthy since later we will be the carriers of a new nation regardless of what consequences of war are laid upon us." I explain to Hocker everything that I have been wrestling with for weeks.

After lunch and a refreshing nap, we friends undergo a thorough bath, which is made possible by the soap and washcloths that were distributed earlier in the morning. We complete the bitter but necessary process in a turbulent whirl because of the cold weather. Exactly at 3:00 P.M. we sit as usual, in the school tent, as an unexpected shrill whistle from the camp spokesman disturbs the beginning of class.

"All sergeants are to report immediately with their blankets and personal possessions," is the call that brings us to our feet and presses us out into the open. "Is it another search?" we ask, noticing the guard detachment entering the camp. "Hurry up," the nervous spokesman encourages those who are lagging behind while the first ones are already in place with their possessions.

"Left face, forward march," a red-haired, overzealous, master sergeant orders, after roll call and the tents have been inspected, as he leads us out of the cage.

Silently the group moves through the narrow, barbed-wire-surrounded alleys.

Without a sound, the warm breath of the men meets the cold air and builds a beard of fog in front of their faces. From the left and right, eyes as bashful as those of deer glance from behind the barbed wire and follow our way out of the camp with sympathy. Where are they taking us now? But there is no use in asking this question. With difficulty the stiff legs carry the dulled heads over the abused high plain of Cap de la Hague.

Suddenly double rows of German prisoners under strong guard meet us coming from the opposite direction. In amazement we look at the fur-lined winter clothing and the fresh but mask-like faces of the prisoners. "Where did they catch you?" some of those in our ranks ask as they pass by, although the Americans are taking strict measures to prevent contact between the two groups. "The Ardennes," they whisper cautiously, and one can notice how strong they stand under the influence of their imprisonment.

"Look there," I say to Schulz, who walks beside me, "those are the survivors of the offensive." "And they do not know that fate has meant well for them." He surprises me greatly. "Do you understand where things stand and what assignment fate has decreed for the survivors?" I ask almost happily. "Yes," he answers with a hard face, "at the end of a lost war. I do not see anything more at least now; the rest is up to the victors what we can do afterward." "One day they must let us go home. Then the families must be brought in order, afterward the house, the city, and the nation. And new life blossoms out of the ruins." I nudge him from the door of the present into the future.

As night breaks, we friends lie with fifty-five other men, warm and reconciled on the hard floor of tent number 49 in the main Camp Cherbourg.

Apparently nothing has changed; only the fences are somewhat further apart, but they also enclose nearly three thousand men. Still the same salty wind blows over Cap de la Hague.

### 30 January 1945

The day Hitler seized power is inscribed on all German calendars and each boy knows that in 1933 on this day National Socialism began its rule in Germany. Perhaps it would have been better for me to creep back under the blankets inside the tent; then later if I am interested, I can read about this topic in the many books that will be written by the scholars. But I must remain true to my journal and preserve what happens as I experience, feel, and see it, so that later I can learn from my own errors.

### 10 February 1945

The sun shines with warmth over the tent city on Cap de la Hague. A sharp hint of the coming spring is in the air and fills the hearts of the prisoners with new hope. In the immense square near the right corner of the cage the hollow-cheeked, pale-faced men are waiting in the sun and wind. The tent walls have been rolled up on all sides. Primitive double bunks stand on the bare ground since yesterday. But we are happy that from now on we can sleep above the damp earth and that finally we have a place to lie on our backs. And today we get freshly washed shirts.

"Yes, yes, that is right." Siegfried laughs trustingly while Briller and I continue to play chess in unbelieving amazement at his declaration. "Come with me to the front of the tent and you can see for yourselves why the tent leaders were ordered up." He brings us to our feet.

But he is right. The prisoners are carrying armloads of olive green army shirts to the tents. After about half an hour genuine joy reigns in our quarters. Every man receives a shirt. Still Schulz has some trouble until he has distributed the riches entrusted to him, since even prisoners of war want to have the right collar size. It is nevertheless a sign that neither the Americans with their idiotic barbed wire nor the winter has brought them to their knees. On the contrary, the eyes lying in the deep holes radiate as if the possessors would dress themselves for the return home.

With the heavenly feeling of a child who after an evening bath pulls on the comfortable nightshirt, I slip into the wonderfully smelling fresh shirt and look with disgust at the raglike thing at my feet. It has been stuck to my skin for nearly six months and on only two occasions for a short time did it come in contact with the cold chlorine water in the camps of Le Mans and Cherbourg. It has served its purpose. If I would try to wash the shirt, it would fall to pieces just like my half-rotten underpants and socks that now seem to have grown together with my skin.

"The Nazi company is disbanded," the camp spokesman announces after evening roll call. "Now they are certain of victory," is Schulz's commentary as we return to our tents.

"And what will happen to us prisoners?" Briller asks tensely. "They will put a postage stamp on our ass and send us home by airmail," Siegfried comes up with an answer as he stands up to ringing laughter and climbs into his bed.

### 18 February 1945

"And whoever still does not believe that the next thing we will be doing is marching with the Americans against Russia, I will elevate him to an honorary citizen of Great Dummbach," a young sergeant screams into the tent and shoves a mighty spoonful of corned beef into his mouth. "Good, now he will have to keep his trap shut," Hocker moans with fever from his resting place.

"Willi, shouldn't we take you to the doctor?" I ask, for the second time today, our comrade who has been suffering with a fever since early in the morning. "Just leave me here; I will be better tomorrow for sure," he begs with a forced laugh. "I don't know if we can take the responsibility for that, Willi. If we at least had a thermometer so that we could know your temperature," I speak to him with concern.

"Do you believe there is any truth to the rumor that we will join with the Americans?" he asks with effort. "My God, how should I know that? In this damn war, anything is possible. We all know that America and Russia get along together like cats and dogs, but that it will come to an open conflict as long as the Third Reich exists I doubt very much even though that would mean our salvation," I explain, somewhat mixed up because I am more concerned about Hocker at the moment than something like a German-American effort against Russia.

"It is stupid that I had to get sick just now. If there is something to it, then you will leave and I cannot go with you." He frets over his misfortune. "It won't happen that fast. Keep yourself bundled up and sleep until you are healthy so that we can stay together," I say out loud and think in quiet that, even though there may be nothing to the rumor, at least it will give him the will to get better. "Yes, yes, I am freezing once again; lay your coat on top of me; I believe I will soon fall asleep," he mumbles through his closed teeth and rolls up.

"Listen up," Schulz thunders in his commanding voice throughout the quarters and with one blow ends every debate. "I will lay a complete outfit on everyone's bed. If they don't fit, then you have to exchange them with your comrades; otherwise we will never finish today. We are told that there is to be additional clothing in the next few days. Roll call is in half an hour. Afterward I need three men to pick up our allotment of soap. Afterward there will be something warm to eat." "And when will the hand weapons be given out?" a joker asks. "They will be given out, along with the newest shithouse rumors, at the latrine after supper," Schulz counters humorously and begins the distribution of the clothing.

At ten o'clock the dishes still have not been washed. We have all forgotten the first topic and have been busy with what has occupied our thoughts for months: the war and its possible consequences. But now we climb into our beds and wrap ourselves in our coats and blankets and lie on the hard bands of iron which are our substitute for springs and mattresses. And many thousand captive souls undertake their secret paths from Cap de la Hague into the air raid shelters in gravely wounded Germany.

### 27 February 1945

About seven hundred noncommissioned officers stand in front of the wide open gates of the main Camp Cherbourg ready to march out. It is ten o'clock on this slightly warm February morning. For over an hour ill-tempered Americans have been going through the long-ago plundered pockets of the men who have endured this hard fate together since Alençon. And people say there are no more wonders! Isn't it a wonder that we are standing next to each other in the best of spirits while here and there between the tents the first green from mother earth is ready to take its first big breath? Look around at your comrades and you will discover that God lives and his miracles are unending!

"Pick up your chest and don't daydream." Siegfried brings me back from my reflections as the column begins to move. Yes, I think, and follow in step out of this cage those who have shared my fate. You, Siegfried, I don't want to miss you. Downtrodden, your uniform in rags and smeared with blood, you arrived hungry and full of lice in Alençon. Then you were happy to have escaped from the revenge-seeking French and did not know that the suffering and hunger behind barbed wire were just beginning. But you have endured it like all of us and now you carry your body and soul healthy, your handsome face over the surrounding high plain of Cap de la Hague.

Our way takes us through the narrow alleys between the barbed wire past the misery of prisoners thrown together. Everywhere the same sad picture can be seen by the attentive eye. Only the many winter uniforms remind us that war still continues its mischief and, according to its own laws, separates its victims into three groups: the wounded, the dead, and ... the prisoners.

After a twenty-minute march another door opens. A repulsive pigsty receives us and the gate behind us is bolted shut after the last man passes through its portals. We are alone. No curious eyes blink out of the lonesome tents standing in the muck. "Halt," Schulz says to the lost crowd and we turn to the left. "Here we are, children." He forces a smile to his face and makes the tent assignments.

Later in the afternoon everything in this stall is in order. Schulz has been voted camp spokesman. Under pressure from the comrades, Hocker has given in and taken over the kitchen. Siegfried is in charge of the completely empty clothing room, while Briller functions as the implements attendant. I am available to Schulz as a clerk and man for everything. From now on our lazy life has come to an end.

"So, friends," Schulz says to those assembled in the kitchen barracks to help him, "here we will make a model example of society. The first one among you that is caught in any kind of dishonest act will be thrown out of the cage, regardless of who he is. Whoever cannot work under this motto can crawl back to his tent, because I can find replacements anytime. Now to work."

Exactly at 4:00 P.M. Schulz's group steps into the muck for roll call. A tall American with first sergeant stripes accompanied by five soldiers enters the compound and receives Schulz's report. Unintentionally he lifts his hand in greeting. Two sergeants, apparently from different worlds inspect each other with mutual respect. "OK." The American smiles, slightly off balance, and goes on with the counting.

A little later the American attendant, First Sergeant Bill H. Turner, assembles the entire German cage leadership with Schulz at the head. "In the first place I expect discipline and cleanliness from the compound inmates," the Yankee begins his lecture, which an American interpreter translates immediately. "It is easy to get along with me when my orders, which are given in the interest of everyone, are followed. In this cage the elimination of the mud is most urgent. Since there are only a few tools available for this purpose, they cannot, as the saying goes, be allowed to get cold until the night forces us to stop. Divide up into small work details which can be relieved after an hour; then tomorrow we can conduct roll call with dry feet. In three or four days I will have stones brought into the cage so that the roads can be built with a solid foundation. When I see that the work is progressing, then I have an open ear at any time for any special wishes in so far as I am able to fill them."

As night falls, the entire cage is provided with C rations and coffee. In the best of understanding, we five friends sit on our beds and eat, well satisfied with the passage of the present day except for the somewhat scanty evening meal. But Hocker will cook tomorrow and the incoming provisions will be honestly administered so that as far as the physical needs of the camp inmates things will continue to improve.

### 5 March 1945

After many hours of hard work, the entire cage is freed of mud. Now a gigantic pile of loamy field earth stands in the furthest corner of the enclosure. Since this morning rubble from Cherbourg is being brought into the compound. Briller is in his element. With a work detail of forty men, he begins the construction of the designated camp roads. There are only a few people who, for some reason, refuse to participate in the cooperative work. "Believe me Helmut, it was not easy to get this group to work," Briller says to me as I appear and wonder at his work. "And how does it taste to you, you old lazy bones?" I ask with a twinkle in my eyes. "It is fun for me. In fourteen days it will look differently here, you can depend on it," he explains, fully convinced that he can accomplish the work.

I go further and find Siegfried in his board shed sorting used American shoes. "Well, big shot, when can we get our civilian clothes from you?" I ask in good spirits. "You poor clerk, you have to submit a request for the stuff first." He picks up on my joke. "But you can have a pair of shoes from me." He winks at me. "I don't want to get in trouble with Schulz over that." I wave him off. "He has already given me trouble because I tried on a pair. But I believe he has a crack," the freshly baked chamber master complains bitterly. "You are only responsible for the slippers and they are not for your own use," I tease him and turn to the door.

Exactly at the appointed lunch hour, Hocker calls for the food carriers. The steaming food buckets stand in rows in front of the kitchen barracks spreading out their enticing aroma. It is impossible that we receive more raw materials than the other enclosures, and still Hocker's kitchen is able to fill up a two liter can for everyone with a thick soup.

After one hour of bed rest the assigned groups go back to work. I sit with Schulz on the handmade table and begin to write down the names of the cage inmates according to their tents while he puts together a request list for the Americans. But we are continually interrupted. Comrades come to Schulz with the most unbelievable desires. One suggests that Schulz request from the Americans boards to lie on the bottom of the tents. Another wants petroleum lamps in the tents. He is even asked to request flower seeds. Schulz listens to everyone patiently and accompanies each one to the doorway with a joke.

In this almost cheerful daily routine, suddenly a terrible report comes like a bolt of lightening from the sky and spreads quickly throughout the camp: French troops under de Gaulle have relieved the American guards and now occupy the towers.

Like Thor's hammer, Schulz slams his fist on the table made of thin boards so that it flies into scraps. With powerful footsteps he slides the pieces into the furthest corner and bolts from the tent like an angry bull. A little later the two of us stand five yards from the fence breathing heavily and look filled with hate at the comical young Frenchmen. "It makes you laugh, Schulz," I finally break the silence. "Just look at these pale children." "They put a dangerous toy into their hands," he snaps, staring enraged at the English automatic pistols in the hands of boys who are barely seventeen.

"They are going to turn the camp over to the French." Half of the camp sulks after they make their way to the fence. Grins beam from under the English plate helmets from the half-grown Frenchmen on the other side of the barbed wire as they slouch, unsoldierlike, against the posts of the watchtower.

Some time later an American officer accompanied by two sergeants walks past the juvenile guards, who remain unimpressive in their lazy conduct. "Salute," the dashing Yankee bellows with rage. But he has about the same success as if he ordered the watchtower. Slowly one of the boys reaches into his pocket and pulls out a cigarette, which he hangs with all smugness in the left corner of his mouth while another turns his back to the officer and begins to talk with his comrades in the tower. There is no salute in response to the second demand from the officer. Insulted in front of more than a hundred pairs of eyes and exposed to the bone to ridicule, the officer continues on his way uttering a flood of curses.

The dirty grins of the Frenchmen as well as the malicious laughter of the Germans will accompany this disappointed man from another continent until the end of his days. "When two are fighting, the third is rejoicing," Schulz quotes the saying and turns in disgust himself to go as the whistle sounds for roll call.

The first sergeant looks in amazement at the completely changed crowd, which for the first time in this cage does not fall into rank quickly. Even Schulz stares embittered and does not move a finger to speed up the formation. This breaks the good American's patience. Furiously he sends his interpreter to Schulz, where he delivers a hail of abusive words. Schulz lets everything pass by like an iron statue until the American catches his breath and stops his tirade.

"Tell your sergeant that under the administration of the French I am putting my position at his disposal, and from now on I am not responsible for anything," Schulz declares, ice cold. The furiously distorted face of the interpreter suddenly changes into a relaxed grin toward the first sergeant. In a few seconds the troubled waters are calmed. "Not one single German soldier will be turned over to the French unless he is guilty of some crime. The French guards are being used in an attempt to relieve the Americans," Bill H. Turner explains almost ceremoniously and goes ahead with the count of his erring sheep.

### 12 March 1945

"Veronica, spring is here, the birds are chirping tra-la-la," Siegfried sings in front of his board shed as he tears the cellophane wrapping from a package of Camel cigarettes. "Have you ever seen a bird here?" I ask him in passing. "No, but spring is in my limbs." He laughs happily and snaps two cigarettes out of the package in the American manner. "There, put one in your face and make some blue vapor for yourself." He holds me up. "Isn't this a burden for old prisoners to get eighty cigarettes with one blow?" He beams all over his face. "Certainly," I agree with him, "I am only fearful they will not last very long." "Haven't you noticed that the last little while you have repeated everything Schulz says like a parrot?" He whistles cheerfully. "What do you mean 'parroting'; it is my own opinion." I return the accusation but feel myself somehow still struck. "Man, stay yourself; then we are already laughing at the enthusiastic way you imitate everything Schulz does. Otherwise you will go home as a perfect Schulz the Second and no one will recognize you again." He slaps me on the shoulder and leaves me standing like a water-soaked poodle.

Damn it all, I think the monkey is right, I mumble to myself as I continue on. Am I really under Schulz's influence that much? It is undeniable that during the terrible long months he has become a flawless example. But do I want to be him? Oh, no! Even when I am not entirely satisfied with myself, I still want to be me.

"How's it going, farm boy?" I stop during my rounds by the sweating Briller. "Just fine." He supports himself with a roof rafter which also serves as a yardstick. "We are finishing up." "The area in front of the kitchen is to be covered with plaster, so I have heard?" I let fall as a matter of fact.

"They can kiss my ass." He furiously throws the rafter to the ground. "Do you believe that I am going to let those fools make a slave of me? I will build the camp streets and then I am finished." "Don't blow yourself up like a vain turkey! Who said that you would have to do it?" I brake him. "Do what you want; after this project is over I am going to lay myself in the sack." He calms himself further.

"Tell me, where did you get those beautiful shoes?" I stare surprised at the light brown American shoes on his feet. "Cursed be it, I stole them from Siegfried, of course. I am still from the Vorarlberg and not from Idiot City." He flies into a rage again. "Don't let Schulz see you, otherwise ... " "Tell your majesty, he can visit me this evening," he interrupts me and fingers for a cigarette. "Here, Robert, take one of mine," I hold out the pack to him. "Merci," he growls and takes it.

"It is still true that the stubborn buck is carrying on a circus here as though he was the Reich's governor in Normandy," he bleats forth, at the same time giving off smoke from the cigarette. "Understand Schulz, he is only trying to do right for everyone," I speak to him. "I know, I know. He is his own fool. He eats less than the biggest sluggard in the cage and half kills himself for these shirkers. And you, you are on the best way to becoming his asshole and accept everything," breaks out from him without restraint. "Take it easy, old man! You have had a bad day today; let's forget the bad words. Will you play a game with me after lunch?" I smile, reconciled. "I would like to." He grins broadly and goes to work with his rafter.

Is there something wrong with Schulz's position? Certainly not, I answer myself. He requires cleanliness from everyone in every situation. Who can accuse him? To do right by everyone is something nobody can accomplish. But nevertheless, in the future I will make sure that I paddle in my own lane without doubting Schulz's good intentions.

"You can see who has it easy," kitchen chief Hocker greets us again on this bright afternoon as we are enjoying a game of chess. "How does it taste?" he inquires of those who are eating. "You know, for me it is like with the women; she could be a little thicker, if she were only a little taller ... your soup I mean of course," Siegfried teases him. "You are an insatiable pig in the first place." Hocker finishes him off while he is already following the game. "I have nearly finished him, so that you can take me on, Willi," Briller extends an invitation without observing that my knight is threatening his queen, something which naturally brings grins over the faces of the kibitzers. See, it is about to happen, he reaches victoriously for his last rook and overlooks the knight. "Braggart," I laugh at him as I grab his queen. The figures fall from the board and roll on the ground. "Damn it all," accompanies Briller's blow to the innocent pieces. Briller remains a poor loser. "Idiots," he bellows, devoid of all good nature, and smashes the chess board into pieces.

"Our old friend had a bad day," I say to Hocker on the way to the kitchen. "This morning he wanted a piece of broiled corned beef. Can you imagine how

I had to chase him away? Later I regretted it, but if it begins with this then it will grow bigger," Hocker describes his dilemma to me. "That is why I do not enter your store. I don't want to bring either of us into temptation. And we don't suffer true hunger anymore." I relieve his concern. "If the bad times do return again and I am sitting at the source, then none of us will starve to death. Whoever excludes himself can peacefully die of stupidity." Hocker shows the same determined face as at Soissons and Alençon and steps into his fragrant realm. I think of the saying, "Who the gods want to punish, they give them an office," as I seize my pen.

"Ah, so you are doing some work! How long have you been squatting behind your list of names?" Schulz rumbles into the tent and disturbs me just as I am getting down to work. "For an unpaid clerk, I do plenty." I laugh. "Do you think I am paid?" he responds. "You owe it to your ambition," I continue without thinking. "So that too. Now you too are starting to cause mischief!" He glances, upset, toward the tent exit.

"Schulz, we are in the process of getting on each other's nerves. The general pressure under which you keep all of us because of your disposition for honesty is starting to work in the other direction. Briller already considers the cage a pen of fools and Siegfried complains because you cannot see any of the American shoes on his feet. Both of them describe me as your buffoon." I pour the pure wine into his cup.

"So, the dear comrades are only thinking about themselves. Do they believe that I will tolerate theft from the other comrades?" he hisses like an irritated lion. "Who has stolen something from whom?" I ask in unbelief. "You ask too? I requested Siegfried to sort the shoes by size and to get them ready for distribution as quickly as possible. Instead of going to work so that the poor devils outside would finally have a pair of shoes for their feet, he took all the time in the world trying on the best shoes for himself, even though he was working where it was dry. Briller has shown a completely different side in the last days and has worked like a horse. But that does not give him the right to ask the kitchen for an extra sausage. Hocker showed him the door, but so that I never hear of it again, I chewed him out myself. I will not tolerate that! That is theft from the comrades! We are the servants of the inmates and not their parasites. Whoever has a different opinion on this point can go to the devil. I will not cover up for a scoundrel."

The thunderstorm has passed. Now it is necessary to repair the damage. Threatening flashes still shine in Schulz's eyes, but he has caught himself again.

"You cannot judge so harshly, Schulz," I begin gently. "Briller may have thoughtlessly asked for a sausage. Naturally he would have eaten it if Hocker had given it to him. Believe me, it is much more painful for him than for you and that is why you should speak with him in peace. For Siegfried, it was certainly only harmless play. I do not believe he would waltz in here with new shoes before the last man in the cage was satisfied. Of course it was correct of you to interfere immediately. It might be that now everyone is aware of it and will proceed accordingly. But you should talk with them about it; otherwise, they will see in you the tyrant and the situation will become more difficult. It would be awful if work that has just begun would be wrecked because of our stubbornness. As cage spokesman, you owe it to the comrades." "I had planned to do that tonight, but you are right, I will take care of it right away," he replies and turns to leave the tent.

After dinner and a little chat, we climb reconciled again into our rickety beds and wait for the redeeming sleep.

*20 March 1945*

The hard days of work, that have changed the compound from the bottom up so that it now looks fit for human beings, are over. Along the two rows of tents runs a plastered road while in front of the tents small examples of the artistic talents of the inmates can be seen. Through the middle of the entire cage runs a twelve-foot stretch of green, which is the pride of the entire camp. Hunger, our truest companion, appears to have graciously abandoned us for the time being. Only once in a while does hate show its ugly grimace, when the Americans talk about the activities of the German submarines. The Yankees seem to have come to terms with the mentality of their prisoners.

Otherwise nothing has changed. Just like before, the most idiotic rumors run through the cage, and there are still plenty of ears who are willing to believe the most impossible lies. For days there has been no talk of a united effort with the Americans against the Russians. In its place are reports by some comrades, from the French children with the English helmets on the fence, that the Red Army has undertaken a crusade against the capitalistic West. But at the moment our hearts beat in thankfulness again for the Americans since Schulz has just passed out sixty cigarettes to each man. Since it was only eight days ago that we received eighty cigarettes, there is no doubt that the golden age for all smokers as well as traders has come. However, it must be admitted that the cigarette market has suffered a mighty blow today as the price for the cigarettes has fallen to rock bottom because of the new flood of stock which is now available. I too, must acknowledge that this time I have erred as far as the Americans are concerned; then I thought that they gave us the first cigarettes only to remind us how enjoyable smoking is, and then they would make it hard on us by stopping any more deliveries. Sometimes the mean enemy is not as bad as one thinks.

But I am not tormented by scruples; instead I sit with a Lucky Strike in my mouth behind the tent and watch the setting sun as my backside becomes uncomfortable because of the coolness of the evening. Still, I remain at my place so that I can think things over. Briller is threatening once again to tear apart our little band. Shortly before today's count, during a surprise inspection of the tents, the Americans found a third blanket in Briller's bed which the old chap had taken from the clothing room during Siegfried's absence. Since the discovery was made in the presence of a number of the tent occupants, Schulz is in a rage, knowing that the news of Briller's misdeed is spreading through the compound like wildfire. For prisoners of war there is no topic of greater discussion than the self-interest of camp leaders. Before you realize it, a mosquito becomes an elephant and you can find hardly anyone that will not confirm that he had known all along that the entire camp administration was made up of only scoundrels and strivers.

It is no wonder that when our good Schulz is haunted by a thousand devils he turns everything upside down to discover any other transgressions. Although I have no understanding for Briller's antics, I keep away from Schulz's exaggerated straightlaced complex but consider how we could break Briller away from these deceitful acts. I am certain of one thing: This is really not Briller because I know him too well. Everything has a cause and effect. Going from this acknowledgment, it is not hard to find a motive for his conduct.

Our friend is disappointed. It is true that we all are, but not in the same measure as he. Beginning with the naive simplemindedness of his parents-in-law about the complete failure of the wife he loved so much, to the unfortunate course of the war, there is a heavy load of disappointment which at some point must manifest itself.

"So you are making an appearance once again?" Schulz greets me, somewhat displeased, after I leave my place behind the tent and come in peace to get my evening ration. "Is something new, Schulz?" I ask without anger. "You are dreaming away too much time for me. I would like to have had you with me during the inspection."

"Take it easy," I say in jest in English and begin to eat. "At least speak German to me," he snaps, irritated, to which I become completely attentive and look more closely at the expression in his face. "Take it easy," I repeat in German, noticing his ill feelings.

"Unfortunately you have been doing that for days. You don't give a damn when we start to talk about affairs within the compound," he begins his lament. "That is not so, I have a clear conscience and if it is fun for the comrades, they can go right ahead and talk about me," I note, untroubled. "It does not have to do with you, rather the cage leadership and especially Briller's selfishness. If that happens again, he will be thrown out without any regard." He vents his spleen.

"Since you mention Briller, where is he?" I inquire. "In the neighboring tent, where he has joined up with another dissatisfied Austrian," he answers disapprovingly.

"Think about how it has come to this. We have treated Briller like a fool for weeks. Is it not to be expected that he takes revenge and in the end joins with other people?" I point to the beam in our own eyes. "It is his fault! He talks one way one day and the next day another. Why doesn't he have a firm position?" the hard man asks.

"Because he is swimming, he must simply swim because the bottom has fallen out of everything for him and we have missed giving him a solid hold in time. That is what comradeship is all about: The strong support the weak! But we were on the fastest road to shove him under the water completely. Let's think it over, Schulz, it is seldom too late to correct a mistake."

Schulz looks at me with awakened curiosity after I am finished. Then unceasingly he glides his hand over his forehead. A few seconds later he lays his strong arm on the brace at the end of Hocker's bed. "That is why," he whispers, "God gave comrades to the soldier."

### 24 March 1945

Radiant spring weather stands over Cap de la Hague. Divided into fifty blocks, nearly seven hundred noncommissioned officers stand in the immaculate camp looking with distrust at the interrogation officers, who have been at work for a half hour to determine the political views of their prisoners. But we have been behind barbed wire too long for them to bring it out of us. Only the purpose of this activity is unclear and that is why we discuss in the ranks the latest rumors that are being offered. Since the hearings are taking place far away from the group, no one in the ranks knows what the Americans are after today. And the rumormongers use that to their advantage in deluding the credulous dumbbells.

"They want to know if we will join them in fighting against Russia," scurries through the crowd. "No, they are interested in how much we still believe in Hitler since he will be replaced before the Americans do anything with us."

"That is all nonsense, you can see they are making notes today. They are going to organize us by branches of service."

Calmly I step in front of the American, who lifts his gaze for a second to my clean-shaven chin. "How long have you been behind barbed wire?" he asks sympathetically. How long? My God, how long has it been? Unbelievable! "Seven months," I hear myself say. "What do you think about us Americans?" his voice rasps as though coming to me from another world. "That is not possible to say in one sentence," I attempt to break out because my pride is swelling up and I am rebelling against the hearing. "The war can wait; we have time. But I would like to have you answer these questions." He remains firm. "What shall I say to you? They are people just like us, sometimes hate-filled, small, and vile, sometimes more than good-natured and concerned about easing our burden," I pour out in resignation. "What about the German master race?" he asks luringly. "That is only an ideal picture and exists with every people," I explain to him. "But your Nazi leaders are convinced that they have been called to rule the world," he counters. "There have been many statesmen from other nations before them that had to be taught better," I hold out to him. "Do you believe in the final German victory?" he asks, changing from a friendly voice to that of the interrogator. You can slide down my back, I will not tell you what I think, echoes inside me, but still I blurt out: "I hope for it."

"He only took notes with Briller," Hocker greets me as I return, somewhat crushed, to my friends, who have been following the interrogations with great interest. "What did he ask you?" are my first words, because I feel the distrust against Briller. "Apparently the same thing as you." Schulz laughs happily. "He wanted us to wish the Americans victory, but he was disappointed." "What did you answer?" Briller turns to me. "He made me angry and I was too proud to admit our defeat," I say to his amazed face. "I thought you would not give the Americans any satisfaction." Schulz beams excessively and slaps Siegfried then Hocker on the shoulder while Briller looks out to the ocean, disappointed. "Why didn't you tell him your honest opinion?" he asks, lightly dejected. "Because it is of no concern to them what I think. I could not do otherwise. Sometimes it is only seconds that make the difference for an entire life. But I do not believe that the hearings will have an effect on our provisions." I attempt to comfort him. "And if so," Schulz throws out, "that is why I do not talk with them for very long."

The hearing is over and lunch is distributed. United, we sit by one another and shovel into our hungry stomachs Hocker's tasty noodle soup. A radiant sun shines and a playful breeze blows to the delight of the inmates. But their hearts are hard. The hearing has left a bad feeling and brought distrust into the tents.

In nearly every circle of friends the Americans made notes from at least one man. Unsuccessfully I try to downplay the fact and turn the conversation toward a logical topic. But the old shadows will not be driven away. Again and again a hopeful beginning ends in a dead end followed by an oppressive silence.

Suddenly Bill H. Turner stands in the tent. Like fate itself, he waves a long list of names in front of Schulz's eyes, while the accompanying interpreter begins to speak: "All men whose names are on this list are to be ready at the gate to march out with their possessions at 4:00 P.M." "Fine," Schulz says only to the Americans and nods a tired acknowledgment. "Let's line up, Helmut." He turns to me after the Americans have gone, without looking away from the list.

At 4:15 P.M. I hold Briller's ice cold hand in mine and look for the last time in his eyes that once were so joyful and now are filled with tears. "Farewell, Robert," I manage to croak from my tight throat. "You have expressed yourself for Austria, for your homeland. That is certainly your right. Don't forget us and please forgive us if we have done anything to upset you."

"It is not what I wanted. Now you will despise me," the words shake from his lips. "We will do nothing." Hocker extends him his hand. "We have come a long way together and you have cleared away many stones for us. I will never forget you, Robert." "There is a kitchen in every cage." Siegfried forces a laugh from him. "Perhaps we will meet again." "Every man is the master of his own fate," Schulz says in farewell. "I hope that you will find what you are looking for."

Not until night breaks do Hocker and I find ourselves together in front of the tents. We walk over Briller's streets while the black rain clouds push toward land from the sea. But our silence sanctifies the hour. We have both lost a part of ourselves today.

## Chapter Five

# ATLANTIC CROSSING

BY THE TIME THAT Helmut Hörner and his comrades boarded the *Thomas Marshall* in April 1945 for transport to the United States, clearly defined procedures had been worked out since the first German prisoners of war were shipped from North Africa two and a half years earlier. Arnold Krammer writes: "The Atlantic crossing of the POW convoys was generally uneventful ... throughout the war not one ship carrying prisoners was sunk by the enemy. The most difficult problem with which the POWs had to contend was frequent seasickness and inadequate exercise and ventilation, a condition familiar to any American soldier transported overseas."[1] The usual variables that did have an effect on the trip were the time of year that the ships left Europe and which of the three primary ports—Boston, New York, or Norfolk—would be the disembarkation point.

\* \* \*

*3 April 1945*

A gray April day chases its cold, wet wind around the tents. It is the Tuesday before Easter in the Christian world, but that does not hinder the Americans from ordering us onto the camp road with our personal possessions. Angrily we pack our bundles and are ready to march out at the designated time. After the last filtering, which took Briller from us, there are less than five hundred noncommissioned officers left. And now we say farewell in silence from this field which has almost become a second home.

Yes, the Americans have time. It is already noon and we are still camped at the gate without any food. After the initial unrest which changed into blunt indifference the whole crowd now threatens to fly into a wild irritation. "They think we are fools," the first voices sound. "Let us go back to the tents," the impatient ones demand. But unstilled, the wind continues to blow its eternal song.

"Let's go," shouts Bill H. Turner after the hours of waiting and opens the door. We march in a southerly direction through rows of at least two hundred American soldiers, who stand on both sides of the road, past Poles, Czechs, and Austrians, a colorful collection of European nationalities. And all are in German uniforms.

We leave the collective camps of Cherbourg and reach the highway on which we were beaten here on December 7, 1944. How peaceful, yes nearly sympathetic, do the front soldiers march next to us today. All their weapons are shouldered. Not one hate-filled word comes from their lips. Silently friend and enemy enter Cherbourg. Even the French do not move a finger at our appearance. Unmolested, we reach the harbor and stumble over the boardwalk along the harbor until suddenly we are ordered to halt in front of three anchored U.S. ships.

Now an icy horror grips the thoughts of the prisoners. But we have no time. Immediately foreign hands are shoved against our will into our pockets and throw all the handmade knives, boxes, and cartons into the water while the accompanying officers go on board one of the ships and greet the captain like an old comrade. A little later we are shoved in double rows over a small gangplank and through an iron doorframe into the body of the American troop transport *Thomas Marshall.*

It is four o'clock in the afternoon when a voice over the loudspeaker calls our attention to the gigantic mountain of cartons of crackers stored in a corner of the large room in which we are quartered. "Everyone is free to take as much as he wants," the voice maintains and causes an unbelievable laughter to break out. Still, like pilgrims to a holy mountain, we make our way into the corner and the pile melts like snow in the March sun. Unbelievable confusion then breaks out. Soon the Americans appear and through their presence bring order back to the crowd.

The old tent groups find themselves in front of five-story bunks which are constructed out of iron bars and canvas. On each bed is a blanket and a life jacket which can be used as a pillow. While the bunks are located along the walls of the ship, in the middle of the room are tables and benches which remind one of a barracks mess hall. Right next to the room is the galley, where the cooks are busy. The washroom and toilets are below and lie at about the level of the water. The ship makes a splendid impression even though its facilities seem quite unusual for land rats.

At five o'clock two guards arrive; that is, they sit in our room at a table in the back between the stairs to the lower level and the entrance to the galley. They hold their weapons tight. Ten minutes later they recognize that their presence is ridiculous and they lay their weapons behind them. When the officer responsible for the prisoners enters the room with the captain and inspects his guards, he sends them away, satisfied with our conduct and the cleanliness of our quarters. With friendly words, he then explains that no one on board needs to go hungry; there are plenty of provisions. With this explanation he wins over all the prisoners, who express their enthusiasm by a spontaneous round of applause.

Shortly after six o'clock Hocker calls the first eaters to receive their food. Whoever thought that there would be a mad rush on the galley in response to Hocker's call is pleasantly surprised; then the comrades line up in rows without pushing or shoving. This can be attributed to the distribution of the crackers and the speech by the American officer. Besides, it is an old practice that when there are plenty of things available, no one has an overriding interest in them. Even though cooking is child's play for Hocker because all he has to do is to stir the prepared food into boiling water, he and his helpers are at work until eight o'clock in uninterrupted service as men from the starvation camps continue to reappear for God knows how many times with their empty plates.

Finally the biggest glutton lies on his cot with a full belly. As we four friends gather around a table, the electric lamps light the faces of the prisoners, who are satisfied with God and the world.

"Now we know the purpose for the interrogations," I open our first conversation since leaving the camp. "They are taking us away from firm land because we still present a threat to them," Schulz rasps, quite downtrodden. "If they just do not take us to England," Hocker joins in. "I do not think so, because we are on an American ship and our guards are apparently returning to the USA on leave." I brush Hocker's fear aside. "As far as I am concerned, they can take us to the moon; the main thing is that hunger has come to an end." Siegfried does not conceal his joy about the plentiful food on board. "If you ever get enough to eat, then I would like to finally hear something reasonable come from your mouth," Schulz thunders at him.

"That the war is as good as lost for us, does not change any of the facts with our long stay in France. But I don't see why we were not sent to America before, especially since the danger of being turned over to the French in the next little while seemed quite real. It is true that in the USA we will not be treated as vacation guests, but for whatever work we do they will at least give us enough to eat, something that never was and never will be the case in France. I have felt it myself and I am thankful today that fate has placed me on this boat. You know, I will not kiss any American's behind, but I like them a lot better than the French. For us prisoners of war it is very simple: we only have to survive the chaos unless someone intends to commit suicide. I am far from that. Just the opposite; I feel myself obligated to keep myself healthy so that later I can be of long service to my fatherland. That is our assignment from destiny and that is why I am going to get me a couple of crackers as long as they are in supply," Siegfried says and goes with a smile toward the greatly reduced mountain of cartons.

Impressed by Siegfried's viewpoint, we three stare at the linoleum-covered table top. With inner satisfaction, I admire Siegfried's insight and especially that he could express it so clearly in such few words after such a long time. It had taken me weeks to work through the issues.

"So Schulz, have you digested what I gave you to swallow?" Siegfried asks as he takes his place after shoving a carton full of crackers between us. "I have only determined that you are beginning to think. Eat another pot empty, and then perhaps you can imagine the map of North America. Then I will show you an area that is not far from Siberia, but is just as cold and thinly populated," Schulz explains in dead earnest. "I know what you mean. Still I would rather hunt bear in Alaska than stay in France and clean up rubbish on an empty stomach." Siegfried chuckles in satisfaction. "Perhaps he is right." Schulz turns to Hocker and me as he reaches for a cracker. "Siegfried's opinions are in complete agreement with mine," I explain, satisfied by this conversation. "I only need a recipe for bear meat. Actually it is really too bad that old Briller is not with us; he was an excellent shot." Hocker laments our lost friend, for which I throw him an understanding glance.

Around 10:00 P.M. a shiver runs through the ship. Unnoticed by us, the *Thomas Marshall* has left the Cherbourg harbor and steams under its own power toward the sea. The European mainland, our homeland, our families, everything that is important and dear to us, sinks in the night and fog behind us while the fury of this most terrible war slowly but surely eats at our hearts.

### 4 April 1945

... wild battle sounds rage around me. My eyes, blinded by the flash of grenades, are buried in the sandbags in front of my observation post. The murderous fire bursts from the fighter planes and cracks into the steel helmets of the attacking soldiers. A dreadful-looking enemy grabs my wrists and says tranquilly ... "Come, Helmut, wake up, otherwise the coffee will be cold."

"Are you crazy?" I stare angrily at Siegfried and realize immediately that I was dreaming. Around me hums the noise of the ventilation system. The life jacket indicates the impression of my forehead where I sought refuge from the unaccustomed electrical lights. The room rings with the tinny sound of dishes! "Damn it all," I say and climb out of my bunk to drink my coffee while Siegfried looks at me, shaking his head.

"Is this can standing still?" I ask Hocker and Schulz, still completely confused but feeling a fearful pressure around my heart because at the most the ship could only have reached England. "Did you just notice that, you sleepy head?" Hocker smiles comfortably. "Don't you have any idea what that could mean for us?" I ask, amazed at their satisfied faces. "So, what could it mean?" Schulz shrugs his shoulders indifferently. "We will be unloaded in England, you fools." I slowly become unfriendly.

"Blessed are they that sleep a long time; then they first notice later what has been tormenting the others for hours," Schulz explains in good humor. "Drink your coffee, Helmut, and calm down. We don't have to get out here." Hocker pats my heated cheeks. "Why is the ship standing still?" "The guards say that we are waiting off England and will join a convoy, probably tonight, for the States." I finally get a plausible answer from Siegfried and can eat my breakfast in peace.

While we friends are in the washroom to shave and wash ourselves, a voice sounds through the loudspeaker and announces that after eight o'clock we can go on deck for an hour in groups of one hundred men. Feverishly we try to wash the soap we have brought from Cherbourg from our bodies, but we are unsuccessful. Finally we notice that only saltwater comes out of the pipes and it does not react to the usual soap. But there is enough ship soap around that the problem is quickly solved.

Exactly at eight o'clock the door through which we entered yesterday is opened and a flood of one hundred interested spectators pours onto the deck. Shoved toward the railing, I lift my gaze; yes, over there, wrapped in a gentle veil of fog, lies England.

In the meantime the sun has broken through. There is great excitement all over the ship. Crew, guards, and prisoners stand for the first time shoulder to shoulder. With a typical seaman's gait, Siegfried comes toward me. "So, my faithful Eckehard of the rag foot squadron, how do you like it with the navy?" he asks, full of pride now that he finally feels the deck under his feet. "Up to now, excellent, you unemployed coolie," I respond in the best mood. "There are a lot of people among us who have suddenly become world travelers against their own will." He calls my attention to several gloomy-looking comrades. "You are right. It is the older ones who are worried, while the younger ones are obviously carried away with the spirit of adventure," I add to his observation. "What do you promise us in America?" he asks with a clouded forehead. "It is hard to say," I respond and gaze out over the endless-appearing sea. "Oh well, it cannot be any worse than we have had up to this time." He comforts himself. "Certainly not. America is no closed group of people. It is the melting pot of the entire world. We will not be greeted exclusively with hate, especially since the country has been untouched by the war and has plenty of citizens of German ancestry," I confirm my agreement. "Let's be surprised," he suggests confidently and pushes me back down below since our time on deck has run out.

After a restful afternoon nap, we assemble at four o'clock around coffee. Despite the mass production, Hocker understands very well how to get the best out of the coffee powder. "Tastes like mom's," Schulz says. And that means something, because on this point he is a real connoisseur. There are plenty of cookies to go with the coffee. "Among the Americans on board, it is said that the Germans not only know how to conduct war but also how to eat," the man next to me, a tall Bavarian, reports.

"Funny people, these Americans," Schulz continues. "When I first came into their hands, they immediately gave me something to eat. It was a strong chicken soup with a lot of meat. The man who brought it to me was so moved by his hospitality that I was afraid he was going to burst into tears. Just as I finished the soup and wanted to start on the precious meat, another came and kicked the cup out of my hand so that the scraps of meat flew through the air. Afterward it was three days before I got anything more to eat. Now we can eat until our belly bursts but I think once we land we will go hungry again."

"You should have eaten the meat first, but I can imagine that you sat for hours stirring the soup and that had apparently made the American angry. Therefore eat now Schulz, so that you have something on your ribs when we go hungry again," Siegfried counsels him lustily. "Later we must exist on the fat in our intestines." "Damn right you are, pass the box of crackers here." He follows this advice without delay.

Two hours later Hocker passes out the evening meal. The door to the deck is closed tightly and two guards sit again at the table. Now this unusual precaution by the Americans does not bother us. Everyone regrets that he does not have a buckle on his belly because the food tastes so good. Even Schulz shows what he can accomplish with eating. Again and again we three step to the doorway of the galley until Hocker raises a warning finger: "That stuff will stir up your stomach. Be careful, you eating machines; otherwise you will explode."

Strangely enough after the fourth helping we cannot eat anymore. "Are we full?" we say in amazement to each other. "Impossible," everyone says to himself; then we still have the desire to eat. "That's enough, friends." Schulz gathers up the dishes. "The stomach must get used to it again. If you demand too much of it, then you will have to pay the price."

Tired and filled to the top button on our shirts we slip into our bunks. At 8:30 P.M. the engines start running. The ship shakes and water splashes on board. Farewell Europe. Dear homeland, may God protect you.

### 5 April 1945

Right after breakfast certain sergeants are ordered on deck. A rescue maneuver is underway. Foggy weather greets us as we push through the small door into the free air. All around us boats of all types are steaming to the west. A convoy, a feast for the submarines.

"We have a long way ahead of us and there is the possibility that we must abandon ship without reaching our goal," a scrubby member of the crew begins his address, which is translated immediately by an interpreter. "For this purpose you must be instructed how the life boats that are assigned to you are to be lowered into the water. I call your attention to the fact that in an emergency no one can worry about you and therefore I ask you to pay close attention how things are to be done. In addition I would like to recommend that the entire maneuver be so organized among you that everyone will know to which boat he is assigned. There are enough ships around us that if necessary they can take care of all of us. By the way, our people are in the process of putting rope ladders all around the ship. We cannot do anything more for your safety. Now please follow my instructions carefully."

"That's all that is missing, that the good Admiral Doenitz sends his gray wolves after our throats," Schulz whispers to me after the maneuver has ended and we are once again on our way below. "If they find us, they will go after the largest vessels. Our little steamer belongs to the Liberty class and is not worth a torpedo." I comfort myself and him. "Aren't your brothers in the navy?" he asks me, remembering a conversation from an earlier day. "Yes, but not anymore in these waters since my oldest was killed," I confirm. "Oh well, then you can sink into a watery grave and don't have to trouble yourself with thoughts that it was your own brother who sent you to the bottom of the ocean," he says.

"Man, that is pretty bad. Why isn't this ship marked with a Red Cross?" The first offense by the Americans against the Geneva Convention comes to mind. "I don't understand it either. They could make these little ships immune from German torpedoes," he says as we arrive at our bunks. "We must send the interpreter to the officers; perhaps they will at least raise a Red Cross flag." I see a possibility to protect ourselves. "I will speak to the man afterward about it." Schulz nods and climbs in the direction of his bunk.

At 2:00 P.M. Hocker is among us once again. As curious as the first people, we stand on the deck of the ship and look out at the armada which plows through the quiet ocean in a zigzag course as though led by a magician's hand. Siegfried does not grow tired of offering explanations. "We are coming into a bad weather zone" he says, turning his eyes in all directions. His ears are pointed slightly ahead and there is a furrow between his eyebrows. His rust-red hair flutters in the wind. "It does not look good for at least half of our comrades," he indicates somewhat dramatically, with a grin of ridicule in his good-looking face. "What do you mean for half of them?" I ask, disturbed. "Because they certainly will have to throw up when the dance starts," he explains calmly. Slowly the ship lifts its nose and then slowly lets it sink. "The vessel does not have enough springs." Schulz swallows suspiciously and follows with a sour smile. "The chest has just taken a deep breath." Siegfried grins maliciously.

My eyes glide across the water desert, somewhat disturbed, while a slight nausea creeps up inside of me. Small gray-black hills pass by the ships. Sometimes they spray up as in shock in front of the deck.

"What a mess," Schulz growls as the first spray comes over the rail and throws salty drops of water onto his freshly shaved skin. "It is just the beginning." Siegfried can no longer withhold a wide grin. "Look there, the first are already starting to throw up," he shouts in unrestrained, malicious joy. "Keep your mouth shut, you damn ... Aa ... , oh ... no," Schulz crows and then suddenly leans over the rail.

I too am sick as a dog. And the others laugh. "Is it that far, Helmut?" Siegfried asks in ridicule. "You will know then the first load is going in your face," I reply, disgusted with everything. "I am going to lie down, perhaps then I will feel better." Schulz turns from the rail and stumbles as though he is drunk and I follow him without delay.

Hour after hour I am tied to my bed. Only in the horizontal position is the rocking bearable for me. But my head pounds. A thousand little devils sit in my stomach pushing up into my throat as soon as I try to stand. I have no desire for food and every conversation is unpleasant. In bad spirits, I stare at the iron ship walls and listen to the rustle of the water until sleep takes this vile sickness from my consciousness.

*6 April 1945*

A restless night lies behind me and the other seasick victims. But this morning I feel somewhat better. After I wash myself in the filthy washroom, I go to Hocker to receive my breakfast.

"Man, your face is as white as the wall," he greets me, concerned. "That is quite a feeling, let me tell you." I wave as though I have been beaten. "Wait a moment, I will brew you some coffee. In the meantime take these frankfurters and don't let anyone else see you." He shoves a long, slender can into my pocket.

I give up and sit down on a stool. Hocker flits around his kingdom as though the life of a dear brother is at stake. Indifferently I look around the room. There is a plentiful supply of spinach cans and meat cans stacked in a corner. Four men are busy opening the cans. Even without being seasick, this kind of life would make me throw up. Now that we have plenty to eat, it does not taste good. Is this the way it is for rich people who have sick stomachs?

"Now drink this." Hocker hands me a large cup from out of which the strong smell of coffee rises to my nose. "And if you have any other wish that I can fulfill, you know I will handle it."

"Thanks Willi, and you stay healthy. Don't you feel anything from this damn rocking?" I wonder about his apparently normal situation. "Not in the least. Send Schulz in so that I can also take care of him. By the way, Siegfried has been put to work by the Americans, since some of the dishwashers are absent because of seasickness." He gives me the latest news as I leave and I feel very thankful for his friendship.

But Hocker's coffee is not meant for me. I have hardly swallowed it before it turns around and comes up and over the deck into the salty element. Schulz does not have any luck with it either. Together we kneel to the north and offer everything to the water gods. Everywhere, on all corners and ends, men are hanging over the deck throwing up everything but the soul in their bodies. The guards disappeared long ago and exchanged their weapons for washcloths. Friend and enemy are united under the same misery: seasickness.

When Siegfried comes on deck during his break at 2:00 P.M., it seems that the fun over our condition has left. "Come on, get away from the railing and go to the middle of the ship," he says with a voice that does not tolerate any opposition. "Sit down here. I will get your blankets and coats, wait for me," he commands like a concerned father who has about had it with the nonsense of his children.

Shaking from the cold and sickness, we lean against a chest of tools at midships while the *Thomas Marshall* bounces over the hill-sized waves. The wind's velocity has increased. The mountains of clouds hang low and darken the day.

"So," says Siegfried, returning with our blankets and coats, "wrap up and put on your life jackets. Don't look forward nor backward, but straight into the sky or else close your eyes tight. This is the best place in the entire ship. There is vomit all over down below. That makes even the strongest sick."

Without contradiction we follow his advice. But this unusual sickness will not leave us. True, after an hour it is somewhat better, but perhaps we are just imagining it. In any case, there is no longer joy in living. All around us is the same misery. Only small groups stand here and there as commentators. "Throw up everything, comrade, then you have your peace," I hear the suggestion from some wise guy. "But be careful." Another raises a finger in warning and shows his horse-face grin. "If a brown ring comes up, then you must swallow it again immediately, because it is your asshole."

The evening meal proceeds in a manner unworthy of human beings. Swallowing and vomiting follow in a senseless rhythm. The men squat deathly pale before their dishes, out of which the soup spills and tables and benches are covered. But no strife develops. Every other man is sick as a dog and robbed of his will.

At nine o'clock the ship's captain announces that during the night the storm will hit. "That means number-ten-sized waves, gentlemen," Siegfried comments, looking at Schulz and me with regret. "I will get tin biscuit cans with removable lids for you," Hocker thoughtfully suggests.

Provided by Hocker with an empty and a full biscuit can which are squeezed between the ship's wall and the bunk's diagonal bars, I await sleep as the savior from distress and torment.

### 13 April 1945

For days the *Thomas Marshall* has squeezed through the storm-tossed sea. Mighty waves roll over its deck and tear away everything that is not nailed or tied down. Night-black rain clouds push against its main mast and pour streams of wrathful tears unmercifully upon its body of steel. Heaven and hell, storm and water have united in a wild inferno of nature's power. The brave ship totters westward, moaning and groaning, and threatening to be torn apart at the seams, while inside the most complicated creations of an almighty God have been humbled to the most pitiable creatures. While they seek a hold, they spit the last juices from their bodies.

Weak and miserable, a listless bundle of flesh and bones whose inner functions have been turned around and who is unable to bring any resistance to this ridiculous sickness, I lie on a small piece of canvas throughout the long hours of the endless days and nights, totally exhausted, until I am ready to exhale what little bit of life remains inside me. It is not much different for Schulz and the rest of the seasick. The exhaust system does not function because of a technical problem and the air is a mixture of oil, fat, soup, coffee, cigarette smoke, and the vomit of the seasick. The tables, benches, pots and pans, and boxes have broken loose and clatter around the room as though they are under the influence of a magnetic power. Now it is finally clear to us that the weathertight quarters is an evil, windowless cellar under whose iron floor the ocean rages. And whether we want it or not, there is no escape, because up above the sea bellows as though judgment day had begun.

At the same hour a message spreads around the earth's globe which could serve to turn the world around. It even reaches us in our deep cellar: The president of the United States has died of a stroke. This report hits like a torpedo in our room in the ship, but we are not now able to ponder the consequences or discuss them.

It is 3:00 A.M. Over the loudspeaker comes the order to put on our life jackets. The storm has become stronger. The *Thomas Marshall* is, for all practical purposes, a toy for the unfettered elements. Completely apathetic and driven only by a gnawing fear from the most remote corner of my heart, I act according to the order and pull on my life jacket. Hocker and Siegfried swing out of the bunks and stand on the floor ready to help Schulz and me if we fall. "Prepare to die," Hocker comments with a serious face about the situation.

In the process of leaving the bunks, the furiously rolling ship takes a thundering hit against its bottom that must be a torpedo or mine exploding. Immediately complete disorder develops. Panic-stricken, those in front dash up the stairway and bang with their fists against the closed bulkhead. In the next moment a voice over the loudspeaker hinders the chaos: "Attention, there is no reason for excitement. A swell has simply pushed the front of the ship out of the water and let it smash on top of a huge wave. In five hours the storm will be past and we will be in a calmer zone. Again, no reason for excitement, no reason for excitement, in five hours we will be in a calmer zone."

With hanging heads and slightly ashamed, but freed for the moment from the pressing fear, everyone reels back into his bunk. But outside the storm and ocean rage and bellow undiminished.

### 14 April 1945

It is eight o'clock in the morning of this laudable day, the fourteenth of April. Schulz and I sit with our backs against the tool chest on deck in the wonderful sunshine, looking relieved over the endless but finally calm desert of water. Our brave *Thomas Marshall* has proven itself to be a tough fellow in the last stormy days. With a bearable rocking movement, it heads westward again today in the company of its brothers and sisters while its strange human freight of prisoners comes out to recuperate. Naturally it is quite fresh so early in the morning, but it is a clear day. Only a few single shreds of clouds chased by the spent wind pass over us. A harmless series of waves rolls ahead. The ship is running with the wind.

In the meantime Hocker is busy as a cook for the Americans and is in competition with Siegfried to help the two of us failures to get on our feet again. One tries to outdo the other in stealing delicacies. Condensed canned milk and wonderful bread rolls with jam make up our breakfast. Hocker has promised salmon and mayonnaise at ten o'clock and Siegfried plans to take care of lunch. Considering everything, we have every reason to be satisfied with the way the day is going. But we are not, at least not Schulz.

"It is bad enough to tear out your tail," he observes, using a vulgar expression I had never heard from him before. "Now, when we are finally free of the eternal worry about food, we have to vomit the intestines out of our belly. Why didn't they spare us the food?" he asks, upset. "In that case they would keep it right away," I explain with a sneering laugh. "You cannot make them responsible for the storm. That would be unjust." "Just look at yourself! You are well on the way to kiss the Americans' asses because they do not let you starve on their garbage can," he hisses at me.

Surprised, I take a closer look at him. He is very pale. Isolated red spots lie on his protruding cheekbones. The deer-brown eyes lie nearly extinguished in the sockets and deep, furrowed wrinkles radiate out from the corners of his eyes. Deep blue shadows lie under the eyes. The temples seem to be slightly fallen in and are suddenly covered with gray hairs. The man appears very sick and dreadfully exhausted. My God, I think, what he must have suffered, as an undescribable feeling of sympathy enters my heart.

"But Schulz," I say with good intentions, "what is wrong with you? I don't know you this way." "Neither do I. Excuse me, but everything is distasteful to me. If they had only left us in Cherbourg."

At 2:00 P.M. Hocker and Siegfried join us. The American cooks have given them the afternoon off. "Do you notice it is becoming colder?" Siegfried asks sympathetically as he sees us shivering. "I have felt it for a long time," Schulz rasps. "Do you know why?" he asks, full of excitement. "I have already said: we are headed in the direction of Alaska." Schulz wants to outdo him. "But this time you are completely wrong, Chief. Our march route will take us to Boston, where I have relatives, or direct to New York. I have seen the maps. By the way, they are hanging below the upper deck on the starboard side where the officers' and the steersmen's berths are located, directly between the third and fourth bulwark on the wall. You can see for yourself. No one will say anything. This can is almost in German hands. We have some pretty bold dogs among us. They run around as though the ship belongs to them ..."

"Stop your seaman's tales. I want to know why it is colder." Schulz interrupts Siegfried's glibness. "You are unthankful for good news, but I will still tell you. Today we had an interesting and unusual encounter ... " "Don't make it so dramatic," I join in. "Are we going to meet the ice cold Stalin, perhaps?" "More icy and without a moustache: Icebergs!" he says with awe. "So what?" Schulz asks. "Perhaps we will bump into one of them and then our asses will be on vacation." "Then I must disappoint you if you are so ready to leave this life. No, all joking aside, there are supposed to be two gigantic pieces of ice. The captain is well oriented. There will be nothing of mermaids, Schulz." Siegfried rejoices, thankful for the change.

"If you have looked at the map, how far is it to the New World?" I ask with interest because I still long for firm ground despite the fine care on board. "We have completed about half of the trip," Siegfried notes, downcast. "So, how is that possible? We have already been underway for ten days. I know that it is over four thousand miles from Cherbourg to New York and a ship can make the trip in fourteen days at the most," I express my doubts.

"Exactly, you said it, a ship. But we are traveling together and only go as fast as the slowest ship. Besides, we are still at war and because of the submarines we are following a zigzag course. Furthermore, we have lost time because of the storm. You see, my calculations are right." He tries to convince me.

"If we only had good weather, I mean just for the two of you; as far as I am concerned the ship could take us all around the earth," Hocker confesses and looks shyly to the side, awaiting a barrage of protest. But neither Schulz nor I are upset about it. Just the opposite; one could agree with him if it were not for the awful seasickness.

"Iceberg in sight!" the call sounds throughout the entire ship. "Starboard, ahead. Iceberg in view ... " and everything else is forgotten.

Friend and enemy stand in thick clumps pressed together on the starboard railing, staring with the same feeling to the west. It is a natural iceberg which melts, at least for the moment, the artificial icebergs in the people on board the *Thomas Marshall.* But there is nothing more to see than a blinding white mass which is not bigger or higher than a sugar loaf rising out of the dark water. But still people now speak happily in different languages to each other. Iceberg! What a magical word. ...

It is three o'clock. The sun stands in the southwest fantastically lighting the continually growing crystal colossus which, because of the imposing view, awakes in us memories of the gruesome shipwrecks of earlier days.

"That was in our fourth grade reading book, the story of the emigrant who found a four leaf clover and wasted so much time that he did not pay attention to his ship that he ran into an iceberg and everything was lost," I hear someone behind me say. "He must have really liked that story if he can still remember it today." I nudge Hocker, who turns with a grin to look at the speaker.

"That was around 1912, in any case shortly before the First World War, that an English luxury ship on its maiden voyage collided with an iceberg and sank with the richest people on board." "Yes, yes, that is right, I have heard about it," his neighbor remembers. "Didn't that have to do with the Blue Band?" a third voice chimes in. "No, my friend," a fourth mixes into the topic, "it was a millionaire on board with whom the captain was in love, but did not have any luck with her. That is why he steered the steamer with full intent into the iceberg ... " "Not with power," I interrupt him to pull his leg. "Idiot," he mumbles arrogantly and goes on. "He wanted the whole brood to drown like rats."

"Stop, that is not quite right," the first one contradicts him. "What is not exactly right?" The romantic defends his newly discovered love story. "I know, because I am older than you. The ship was named the *Titanic* and at that time was something of a world wonder in the realm of sea travel." "That's right, just leave love out of the game. As far as rich people are concerned, the only thing that matters is money."

"In this case it was the Blue Band of the shipping trade. I read the book, so I am informed about the matter," another listener states bluntly. "So, you read the book. ... Do you believe you always find the truth in books? I know better, you can count on it," the hard-headed one insists on his fairy tale. "Keep your mouth shut; otherwise the iceberg will sink in front of us out of shame." The reader finishes him off.

But the iceberg does not move because of the nonsense spoken by its observers. Proud and unapproachable, it follows its course while on the horizon two more appear. Seized by respectful awe, no one can take his gaze away from these giants of ice.

At 5:40 P.M. we are parallel with the two majestic mountains to our north, about four miles away. "Only a third of its mass sticks out of the water," Siegfried explains to us and thereby unleashes a big discussion. "Then you can figure out exactly how tall the cold wanderers are." Another one behind us picks up the topic. "For that you must know how high the part is above the water," another interested commentator adds. "That is garbage with gravy! If two-thirds of it were under the water, it would have hit bottom long ago," the old know-it-all reports and we four quietly decide to pull his arm.

"Look there," I scream like I am possessed, "on the middle glacier in the crack a polar bear is climbing up." "Man, she has her cubs with her," Hocker follows my bellowing. "Where, where?" Everyone pushes to the rail. "Don't push so carelessly," Siegfried growls; "the beast is big enough to be seen from anywhere." "My eyes are old; I cannot see it very well. But I feel sorry for the poor bears; they must have missed the chance to jump off when the colossus was formed in the North Pole." Schulz joins our ring of liars, which stimulates the intensive search over the immense ice mass even more.

"Only the devil knows where they are," someone complains behind me. "Man, don't you have eyes?" we hear the voice of the fairy teller. "There on the left projection by the big crack. I discovered them long ago," the man brags with the same bravado and conviction that he dished out the captain's story. But Hocker cannot keep up the falsehood. Roaring laughter drives the tears from his eyes and mucus gushes from both nostrils. Immediately Siegfried and I join him in malicious laughter until it becomes uncomfortable because those we deceived are furious with us.

*15 April 1945*

Today, the third storm-free day, the *Thomas Marshall* steams through the blue floods of the Atlantic with a beautiful and magical red dawn back to the east. Trusting dolphins accompany the ship and make the hearts of those on board happy with their presence. Generously the comrades throw biscuits into the never-satisfied mouths of the great gray-black fish, which seem to know how to give their thanks with their entertaining dives. Groups of prisoners have been formed which consider certain dolphins their own and even give them names. Again and again the faithful sea animals show their attractive backs before they dive and swim under the ship to feed on biscuits from their sponsors on the other side. Leaning on the rail, I think, what poor fish: a few weeks ago these same men who now feed them would have risked their necks to snatch one of your fins.

"Why so deep in thought?" a familiar voice sounds in my ear. "Oh, what a pleasure, Doctor Braun personally, so early in the morning," I greet my philosophy teacher. "The doctor is hanging in Flensburg in his closet," he clappers with his large false teeth. "The main thing is that your mind is here and still intact. The hat is only for show." I comfort him. "That's exactly right. Otherwise, did you survive the seasickness?" he asks and throws a biscuit to a beautiful dolphin.

"They are the first animals that we have seen for a long time, and I love animals very much," he excuses his frivolity as he notices my surprised expression. "Yes, we have them." I nod with double meaning and look somewhere over the endless water. "I see that you don't enjoy the game. But you are right. We can never again join up so easily with human fools." He comforts me. "People forget easily. Perhaps it is good that way, at least in most cases," I explain, reconciled. "In some cases, yes. But that they have forgotten to mark this American ship with a Red Cross is not only punishable idiocy, but a blow against all international agreements. I have just read in a magazine that someone lent me that the victors will sit in judgment over us and find us guilty of war crimes." He steers into political waters. "Let them write what they want. Paper is patient. When the killing is over, they are just as much murderers as we."

"I hope that I am not disturbing you," Schulz says respectfully as he joins us. "No." I comfort him. "Braun is also upset because the ship is not marked." "The interpreter spoke with the Americans about it, but they did not give him any explanation. It is best if we do not make a state issue of the matter; otherwise we will harm the good feeling in our ranks. As long as no one is aware of the danger in which we swim, they will not worry about it," Schulz says, always concerned about keeping others from becoming upset.

"Do you think that we are unnecessarily exposed to danger?" Braun becomes lively. "This Atlantic Ocean is a war zone. According to the Geneva Convention, the Americans are responsible to inform the German navy headquarters through Geneva about the transport, just as with the transportation of wounded. Unfortunately none of the warring powers inform their soldiers about these provisions. The reason is obvious. Some soldiers would choose imprisonment over a hero's death if they knew what kind of favorable conditions awaited them behind barbed wire because of the Geneva Convention."

"What use are these agreements on paper when no devil pays any attention to them?" I throw in. "Don't say that," Braun indicates. "I had the opportunity for four months to watch what was going on in a prison camp. The inmates were mostly English fliers, seamen, and commandos. I can only tell you, they lacked nothing. The German camp leadership stood on its head whenever a big shot came for an inspection or whenever a neutral control commission showed up." "Did they also have a brothel?" Siegfried jumps into our serious conversation, which brings a look of disgust from Braun. "Oh, well," overlooking Siegfried's rudeness, "we will soon see how far the Americans live up to the international agreements in their own land."

As Braun is called away by his friends, we three are alone. In the meantime the sky has become cloudy and a strong wind blows over the sea. The *Thomas Marshall* slowly begins to vibrate. Its masthead bends as much as thirty degrees forwards and then back. "A storm is coming, I am sorry to inform you," Siegfried says, giving thoughtful attention to the whistling of the wind. "Then let's go to our bunks," I suggest to Schulz, as he already seems queasy. "I have some delicate intestines for both of you. Are you hungry?" Siegfried grins like a rascal. "Bring the delicacies to the bunks so that they are digested when the great vomiting begins," I wave to him as I make my way below deck.

Around four o'clock, the cooks have trouble keeping the coffee in the pots. They quickly look to get rid of the hot drinks in order to keep from getting scalded. Meanwhile the ship steams courageously with its hard-working machines through the broiling sea. In my bunk I follow fearfully the irregular rocking movements, which up to this hour have remained bearable. But in time the ship starts to roll. Tired, I close my eyes.

*20 April 1945*

As much as the pen may resist writing down this lunacy, still, to respect truth: on board this American troop transport, which this morning escaped the merciless stormy sea and is now being carried by soft waves as it approaches the American continent, we German prisoners of war celebrate the birthday of our Führer and highest commander.

Since lunch was distributed, a small group of fanatics have been agitating for this paradoxical birthday celebration. There is no argument that will deter these men from their intentions. With mixed feelings most of the prisoners follow the subversive work of these last Mohicans, but these are unable to prevent this mistake since those who know how to handle such critical situations are still lying in their bunks seasick. Finally those who resist are able to influence the fanatics to wait until the last hour of the day for the celebration in order not to provoke the Americans and upset the good relationship that has developed.

Now it is time. While a fair number have assembled around the tables and benches, a sergeant from the air force approaches the makeshift podium and greets the meeting with the German salute. "Comrades," he begins in a skilled voice without digression. "Following an old tradition, we are assembled here to celebrate in a modest way the birthday of our supreme commander of the army and leader of the German people, Adolf Hitler. We all know in what a fearful situation the Führer, our people, and our fatherland find themselves. But it is not the first time in history that a people has stood on the brink of destruction only to gather itself around a leader for one last immense effort to beat its enemy and make them sue for peace. It may appear impossible to believe in victory, given the situation on the fronts, but as soldiers we have the obligation to remain true to our oath, to arise from our defeat, to trust the Führer in this highest hour of need, and to believe in the victory of our weapons. It is true that we are prisoners and have no influence on the course of events. But that is all the more reason to remember the truth of the Führer's words, with which I end my speech and call to our German brothers and sisters all over the world: 'Woe to the people that gives up its weapons and delivers themselves to the mercy of their enemy.' "

With a devotion seen only very seldom in people in unusual situations, the men roar in song, "Deutschland, Deutschland, über Alles." Then the celebration is ended.

### 24 April 1945

For three days and two nights wind and rain have whipped the *Thomas Marshall* through the raging sea. Without interruption heavy breakers lash over the deck and threaten to drown all life. The entire ship cracks and groans as though the devil himself were on board. But again and again the brave ship rights itself and unmercifully slices through the weak bodies of the oncoming waves. In only two more hours this terror trip is to be completed and then we will be near the coast and in calm waters, according to the ship's captain.

But now there is no breath of relief in the stinking room. Like imprisoned rats, we hop around the cellar of this dancing ship with our fearful eyes on the thin steel walls which separate and protect us from the wet, raging elements. For a long time now, the most stiff-necked have become tired of this insane Hell dance and long for land. For land? Which land? The recognition hits me hard that we are rejoicing over something that we do not know awaits us. Yes, one land can be like another, but people are not always human beings. But in the first place we have been delivered to them. Body and soul are being delivered to them. As prisoners and members of a people near destruction we will set foot without protection on the land of the victors. A victor who has already demonstrated all the faces of humanity from an understanding smile to a merciless grimace. We have stood against the murderous bellow of his cannon, the hail of bombs, and his machine guns. We have waded through misery and need, accompanied by terrible hunger and thirst, filth, and meanness. Almost unprotected, in ice cold, gray-filled days and nights, his barbed wire held us with iron clamps. We were spared nothing, nothing at all, until we were loaded on this little ship and required to leave Europe without receiving any news from our families. And finally we met human beings, people of goodwill without reservation, who filled our hungry mouths, exposed themselves to the same fate, and allowed us to vomit the souls from our dishonored bodies. Who can measure the feelings and perceptions of this lost heap of captured German soldiers on board the *Thomas Marshall* as they near the American mainland? Who will judge us because of the many misunderstandings dictated by the barbed wire which makes one more confused than the other one? Whose fault is it that we ended up in this situation and now stand with a fettered mind in front of problems that cannot be solved without compromise?

We are trained in our parents' houses and in the schools to be truthful and to fear God. As youth we learned to love the Führer and fatherland. The loyalty oath and the weapons training for the alleged defense of these ideas complete the young man and seal on him for time and all eternity his individual bondage. But war needs him that way. Even though in other lands the same thing is happening, it is not the same in their eyes. Suddenly the imprisoned soldier is treated worse than a criminal. Everything that was sacred and holy is trampled in smut by his keepers. And they notice nothing—that they carry around the same ideas in another coat and in their name trespass against other people. The gallantry and respect for the vanquished foe is reduced in value and exists only at the fringe of the war as a few hopeful blossoms. Instead of the beginning fair fight, naked violence is practiced. And these are the facts with which we will embark on this strange land tomorrow. But despite it, I will leave all the ballast and every prejudice on board and take my first step into the New World with light baggage. Still, I will stand by my faithful companions, ready to help them at any time until destiny guides us once again back to the beloved homeland.

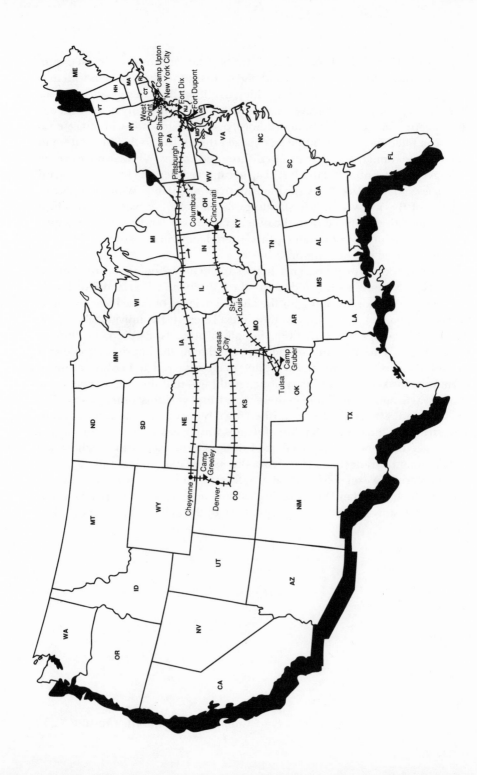

ME

NH

MA

RI

CT

Camp Upton
New York City

West
Point

Fort Dix

Fort Dupont

VT

NY

NJ

DE

Camp Shanks

PA

MD

VA

NC

Pittsburgh

WV

SC

Columbus

OH

Cincinnati

KY

GA

MI

IN

TN

AL

St.
Louis

IL

MO

AR

MS

LA

WI

Kansas
City

IA

Camp
Gruber

MN

Tulsa

OK

KS

ND

SD

NE

TX

Cheyenne

Camp
Greeley

WY

Denver

CO

NM

MT

UT

AZ

ID

NV

WA

OR

CA

## *Chapter Six*

# THE UNITED STATES

*25 April 1945*

A RADIANT BLUE heaven covers the metropolis of New York City like a giant canopy. In the upper bay of the Hudson River the *Thomas Marshall* docks as the German prisoners of war assemble on deck to disembark. Greeted by the small island with the Statue of Liberty, it works magic as smiles break across the faces of us foreign soldiers—soldiers who despite all our efforts are conscious that we are prisoners of the freest land under the sun. But our hearts beat in unhappiness, despite the impressive display that comes from all sides. Our amazed focus is on the mighty monuments of stone. The skyscrapers of Manhattan, weathered gray, cold, and foreign, completely impersonal, towering in the American sky. Then in deep shame we glimpse at our worn uniforms whose color can no longer be distinguished. Even when everyone had done their very best with what was available not to frighten the unknowing citizens of this war-spared land, our clothing is nothing more than rags. Our appearance depresses everyone at the moment.

On the other side of this great harbor, we four friends stand and take in together the impressive view of the unequaled city. "Why," I ask myself and friends, looking toward the skyscrapers, "have the Americans built such gigantic structures?" "It is as easy to explain as the pyramids of the ancient Egyptians," offers Schulz; "then I can imagine that the land here must be extremely expensive and so they simply built in the direction of heaven." "But I would not like to live in those beehives; I like the cottages on the other side of the river much better," declares Hocker. "I agree with you," Siegfried chimes in. "As impressive as those cement piles are, I wouldn't live in them even for free." "We will not have that dilemma, but look at the cars going down the harbor road." I call the attention of my companions to the endless line of automobiles traveling alongside the Hudson River. "I thought there was also gasoline rationing here," Hocker notes just as a ferryboat with the marking "New York Central System" comes alongside.

A civilian, who has been on board since early morning instructing us on filling out all the forms, calls out, "Attention, only three men at a time on the gangway. In your left hand have your *Soldbuch* and in your right hand the forms. Give the papers to the Americans, move onto the gangway, and go over to the ferry. That is all. Move out and no shoving. You all may go on land."

While the deck of the *Thomas Marshall* slowly empties as the ferryboat takes us on, we see some distance away other ferryboats which also have German prisoners on board. Apparently we are not the only prisoners that the convoy has brought here.

An hour later we leave the *Thomas Marshall* with a quiet sadness in our hearts, we turn our backs on the brave ship and its fair crew. Awaiting our fate, hundreds of eyes stare at the land of unlimited opportunity that we are quickly approaching.

It is exactly 12:18 P.M. as Hocker and I set foot in the New World. Like lightning my thoughts speed back the more than four thousand miles to the homeland and search without success for my dear loved ones. As a consequence, an impatient U.S. soldier shoves me in the ribs with a red-lacquered stick and brings me back immediately to reality.

"Let's go!" bellows the soldier, thereby introducing us to the American tempo, something that hits us like a whirlwind. In an unbelievably short time we are separated into groups of fifty and marched to gigantic barracks just as the captured freight of another steamer from the convoy disappears. Faster than we can comprehend, we are in a room, and in obedience to the commands tear the clothing from our bodies while blacks with gleaming white teeth throw net sacks with two brass tokens down onto our heads. Seconds later our clothing is in the sacks on the way to the delousing chambers. The only exception is our leather boots, which we carry into the shower room.

The Americans have organized things well, and we think of nothing until after we have showered, dried, been sprayed with delousing powder, searched for skin disease, weighed, measured, put on our damp rags, and are herded together into a large room. But there is no time to rest. After the last of our group of fifty stumbles into the room, the wall behind us opens to make free the ninety-foot distance to the end of the barrack. We line up in rows, fifteen feet apart, and make our way out of the room. As we go around the corner, there is a line of guards with their backs to the water apparently stationed to prevent a freedom-loving prisoner from jumping in. These soldiers, however, demand little attention; instead it is a single fat individual, with the characteristics of a specific race that has good cause to hate us, who becomes the focus of our interest. He shoves a long needle into the buttocks of each German who passes by and, although far removed from every battlefield, carries out his own kind of war. Immediately I stop running and limp on past him, looking at my wound as he yells and claps his hands for joy over my pain. Once I reach the end of the barracks, I turn and grin at the narrow-minded jerk. With his fleshy face and belly hanging over his belt, he repeats the malicious applause and I respond by giving him the finger, then quickly slip weasel-like around the corner, but not without first stealing a glimpse of our furious oppressor.

In the next moment I reach a room lit only by a skylight and in which my comrades and I look, like caged apes, at the railroad tracks that run through the building. But here there is no wait. In thirty minutes we find ourselves in a building adjacent to a New York railroad station and within another half hour at least twelve hundred German prisoners of war are assembled and once again subjected to a search. For this purpose containers are set up which look just like our food barrels in Le Mans and Cherbourg, but here they are used as garbage cans into which the black soldiers throw the last of our possessions.

Using my total knowledge of English, I speak to a soldier in an attempt to recover my earlier diary notes. Even though they are severely damaged, I am successful thanks to Dr. Braun, who tries to explain to the black soldier that the notes are necessary for his study. As the man turns his back to the garbage can, I reach in quickly and lift out my notebook and my shaving kit, in which I find my cigarette case.

We are not the only ones who recover lost possessions. Actually it is not so hard since the blacks consider it all trash that their white countrymen pull out of the pockets of strangers to throw in front of their brooms.

At 5:35 P.M., as we climb into the train cars, another wonder of the New World occurs along with those we have already experienced—the skyscrapers, auto traffic, and exemplary demonstration of organization. The entire train is made up of first-class Pullman coaches on whose fine upholstered seats we are to sit.

But there is no waiting or pushing here and there. The doors are barely closed behind the guards, who get on with us, when a signal sounds and the train begins to move. Only two things trouble us: that we can only raise the windows a short distance since small pieces of wood have been nailed to the outside frame, and that armed guards are assigned to each coach. But in reality we are prisoners of war and not the sons of millionaires going on vacation.

While my pen scratches over my paper recording what I have experienced today, the last houses of New York flash past and an officer enters our coach and reads the five rules for travel. "You will stay in your seats in this coach until we reach our destination. You will eat and sleep here. You will raise your left hand when you must go to the toilet and wait to be recognized by the guard. You will raise your right hand when you want a drink of water and only one will be permitted out of his seat at a time. Who feels sick should indicate to the guards by raising both hands."

The officer has barely left our wagon to continue his litany in the next when two blacks in snow-white jackets appear and pass out cups and paper plates. They are followed by two others who bring a canteen of heavenly smelling coffee, serving the costly drink in the cups we have been given. A few minutes later the plates are filled with a meager serving of baked ham, eggs, and fried potatoes. It tastes much better than the fare on board the ship and we gulp it down in terrible hunger.

It is too bad that our plates are empty, but there are no second helpings. To our disappointed faces, the guards simply tell us to throw our cups and plates out through the crack in the window. "Throw it away, you will receive everything new." It was something we had heard before, but sorry to say had not yet been fulfilled.

Finally we are left to ourselves. Our tired arms and legs stretch out while our eyes take in the foreign landscape through which the train hurries on its way.

"Now what do you think of America?" Siegfried asks, yawning, with his mouth open so wide that you can see the two gold crowns on his back teeth. "I like it," I laugh, free of the fear that had been troubling my soul. "No reason to complain; I do believe that all of them here are filthy rich," offers Hocker, who sits next to me as the train thunders through Chester.

"The organization in the harbor was impressive, but when you think that everyone here is rich, you have been asleep, Willi," Schulz instructs. "I noticed, by the way, at the train station, how a pair of women in uniform made the sign of cutting our throats. It is clear to me that even in this land there is much that we will have to face."

"But Schulz, I did not expect a beauty queen to throw her arms around me. By comparison with Russia for example, the difference is like Heaven and Hell."

"There is no doubt about that," he agrees, "only … look for yourselves." He interrupts himself, pointing to some shabby houses that we can make out in the dusk. "That's bullshit," Siegfried proclaims. "We have dilapidated houses at home. In any case, I have already seen some girls with legs up to here. One must consider the beauty, Schulz, and overlook the rest." "I'll recite something for you, which although not by me is still valid," Schulz declares as though taking an oath and begins:

> Many lands I have not seen,
> But in everything I strive for the best.
> May evil follow me,
> If my heart is ever ready,
> To feel a need for foreign lands.
> Even if I wanted to lie and even if I could,
> German cultivation surpasses all.

"You presented that very well," laughs Siegfried, while Hocker and I, impressed but quiet, look out the window. "These two verses from the 'German Song' by Walther von der Vogelweide say everything that distinguishes us: love of the homeland, loyalty to the fatherland, and a brave character. That is what I want to remind you of before the so-called New World turns your heads," Schulz adds and falls back, dead tired, into the soft benches as our train rolls into Baltimore.

Immediately all the sleepers are awake. The train stops on track 3 and we have a clear glimpse into the life of a city that has not been touched by war. People come and go like in all railroad stations throughout the world. But it is another picture than what we have known for years in Europe. "Just like it used to be," someone sums up the impression of us all as the train begins to move and we fall back into our seats.

The trip continues. In a racing tempo we speed through the fields. Only here and there the black night is torn by the light of a small town. The bone-weary figures turn their heads into the cushions and immediately fall into an unconscious sleep.

*26 April 1945*

As night turns to day the cities of Harrisburg and Pittsburgh are behind us. The land appears gigantic and virgin as the sun shines in the unending distance. Here and there a farm lies in the sparse vegetation of early spring. In contrast to Europe, it takes an hour before the train reaches another inhabited place. Weary and hungry, we look bleary-eyed at the unpopulated stretches. Finally a black porter appears and serves coffee, ham, eggs, and fried potatoes. If there were not fourteen hours' difference between this and our last meal, one would believe it is a continuation of the first because there is no difference in the food that is offered.

"Didn't I say that hunger would be our true companion in America?" asks Schulz as we, in disappointment, throw the empty cups and plates out the window. "Yes, Schulz, that's what you said, and that's why I ate all my reserves." Siegfried laughs without concern in the early morning.

"I certainly understand something about cooking, but I must admit that the stuff does taste good even if we have to eat the same thing again," Hocker honestly concedes. "Only too little, way too little," Schulz adds. "You were always satisfied. What's the problem that you find a hair in everything?" I search out in Schulz's closed face.

"Nothing's wrong, absolutely nothing. Everything is in the best order. We travel in Pullman coaches through the United States, permit blacks to serve us, and imagine that we will end up in some resort. There's a half-breed Indian with a rifle and when we want to limp to the back, we have to first get his permission. You make a great show for the little food we get and act like ham and eggs were discovered here. Therefore I must look into your radiant eyes when such a war profiteer stands at the railroad crossing in his luxury car. But just wait and see how thick we come in the ink."

"Are you completely turned around?" I ask in amazement. "In no way," he replies with scorn. "Schulz, I hear from you only envy. Be honest, you imagined America would be different," Siegfried throws at him. "You thought for sure we would be transported in cattle cars and land someplace in the deep forest. Then you would have been able to complain, and it would have been better for you. Instead we are going through a cultivated land sitting in a first-class coach and you are disappointed because you can't see the forest for the trees."

"You are stupid," challenges Schulz. "Don't you know that everything here has been cut down and that they carried out such a pillage that even the climate has changed? Have you forgotten that this country is at war and it's easier to make first-class coaches available than freight cars?"

"Congratulations, Schulz, your memory still works," Siegfried responds with mischief. "Perhaps I don't know enough about this country." "How should we know anything about it?" I question. "I know that it was discovered by Columbus in 1492 ... " "Look out there, the city is called Columbus," Hocker yells.

"See, I'm right. Columbus was certainly here." I join in the general laughter and look out the window at the city as the train roars on.

"And what else do you know about this country?" Schulz once again picks up the topic. "As I already said, not much. After the discovery Europeans came and settled the land. New York was called ..." "There were people here before Columbus's discovery," says Schulz sharply. "Clear, the Indians," Siegfried quickly adds. "That's right," as Schulz pushes on. "And where are they now?"

"I suppose the young ones are in the army and the old ones hunting," Siegfried offers in simplicity. "You know very well where they are, my friend!" Schulz snaps. "Then say so; they were exterminated just like they will exterminate us. That's what you were leading up to," Siegfried continues in scorn. "Let's forget the nonsense, boys; it doesn't lead anywhere," I break in once again. "Why shouldn't it lead somewhere? It's a fact, or will you argue that this country belongs to the Indians?" Schulz continues, unwilling to leave the fruitless topic. "Naturally you are right, but that is a long, long time ago. Later they had to bring in black slaves and so on and so forth." "It is always the might of the powerful that will rule the world. What else do you want to know?" I ask in disgust.

"Nothing more, because you are already blinded by the glitter and riches of this land," Schulz responds, feeling misunderstood. "Don't be so dumb, Schulz," Siegfried brings from his reserve. "I am impressed with the people here. Their forefathers had enough of Europe's oppression and fought here for their existence. As the land-grabbers tried to implement the eighteenth-century European methods of oppression, the citizens here turned to their weapons. The first shots were fired in Massachusetts that led to the War of Independence with England. In Boston they preferred to throw the English tea into the ocean rather than pay taxes to a distant king. Even Goethe was impressed with the result of this struggle:

> America, you have it better
> Than our old continent.
> No fallen castles
> And no basalt.
> Nothing bothers you internally
> At this lively time
> Not useless memories
> And past strife.

"That's it, Schulz, that also impresses me, in contrast to the European hairsplitting. And I recommend that you open your eyes. Throw away all your prejudices. It is never too late to learn something more. In Baltimore last night your poem from the twelfth century closed your eyes. The city has nearly a million inhabitants and over a thousand factories. Now you are worrying about Indian wars instead of looking out to the land to see what's happening."

In anger Siegfried chews on his fingernails after his admonition. Schulz is upset and withdraws in the corner of bitter truth. It was the influence of our sumptuous meal, I think to myself, and am ashamed of my own lack of knowledge of America.

While the train thunders in a southern direction out of Columbus, most of our comrades are asleep. Even the guards are no longer as attentive as at first. Wearily they are posted between the door casing and gape sleepy-eyed at the other prisoners. In their slumber they are not disturbed by any thought of escape. Since there is nothing special to see out the window we also close our eyes until the train rolls into Cincinnati and the black caretakers put dishes in our sleeping hands.

Immediately everyone is awake. Even the guards press on the windows. "Cincinnati," says one of the guards, without thinking, to a German, who immediately answers "No." "Yes," says the guard, staring at the wobbly Schwab. "No," he gushes again as the American starts to wonder himself. "Of course," he tries his luck once more. "Kiss my ass, you dumb fool," is the reply in German. "What's wrong?" I ask quickly, to try to clear up the misunderstanding. "That guy is crazy," the honest Schwab dryly answers. "He continues to ask me if I am a Nazi." (*Sind Sie Nazi?*) Everyone shakes with laughter as the guard looks at us, perplexed. Quickly I explain to him and he understands. Forgetting his orders, he stumbles out of the wagon, rolling with laughter. A moment later he returns with his fellow guards and the laughing does not stop. Finally Cincinnati is behind us, but the guard continues to come and see the man who provided the best joke of the day.

### 27 April 1945

After a long stop at night, the train continues into the third day with its long and by now uncomfortable trip westward through the broad land. The two meals a day and lukewarm drinking water do not help to make the trip very comfortable for us. In all ends and corners of the wagon grumbling is in full force. Seldom does a fleeting village offer any change. But the Americans conduct themselves properly toward us in all places. Not one false statement or threat can be registered. Although it is easy to see the surprise in their faces when they see us, quickly they fall back into indifference, and in part sympathy for us. But hate, visible hate, is not there.

Even our friend Schulz appears to have lost his initial rejection of everything American. "Do you believe that we will be herding cattle in Texas?" He laughs after a meal of hot dogs, potato salad, and coffee. "It would be wonderful to ride a stallion over the prairie," I say, looking out at the sparse landscape. "You read too much Karl May." He kindly winks at me, at which Siegfried joins in the conversation. "In Texas it is hot and lonely, nothing but cattle, cow herders, and no girls."

\* \* \*

A native of Dresden, Karl May lived between 1842 and 1912, and though he never saw the American West, he wrote over thirty books about the American frontier which influenced the outlook of millions of Europeans on the American West. Ray Allen Billington wrote of Karl May's characters, such as Winnetou and Old Shatterhand:

> All were reincarnated Germanic Galahads, bent on clearing the West of desperados and bad Indians, and glorying in their missions of mercy. They bore slight resemblance to the rough-and-ready plainsmen of actuality, but they won the hearts of Germans as did the creations of no other author. ... Karl May's books were purchased over the next years by over thirty million people, translated into twenty languages, and read by an estimated three hundred million persons. Karl May was Adolph Hitler's favorite author—and Albert Einstein's.[1]

\* \* \*

But before we reach the city, the train unexpectedly rolls across a bridge under which the dirty brown flow of a mighty river drifts southward. Missouri River or Mississippi River is the question, and regretfully no one is in a position to answer for sure. Even the guards shake their heads. But quickly the scene changes and we forget the wild unregulated river as the train comes to a stop on one of the many tracks in the railroad yard in St. Louis.

A large and old city lies hidden from us in the haze. We have a great desire to visit the city, to glimpse inside the houses, simply to be with people again, but we are prisoners shut off from life. Instead we watch the railroad workers and especially the children on the nearby street. We observe that nearly all of the men are wearing military pants, shirts, and jackets while the children, in comparison to Europe, are more practically clothed. The boys wear simple blue or khaki-colored pants and a colored shirt. The pants on the girls reach only to their calf and they wear blouses in dazzling colors. In their play they are just as active and dirty as everywhere. When they notice that we are watching them, the little ones stick their fingers in their mouths while the bigger ones hop the tracks and come to our wagons, where they stand in shock. Although they do not stop gazing at us, they do seem a little more trustful. Certainly they think we are the damn Nazis who come from legendary old Europe about whom their teachers have told so many horrible things.

Since the train does not appear to be ready to leave, a large group of people gathers around the window. The prisoners look with lustful eyes at a group of sumptuous young ladies who are loading packages into a transport close by. They throw flirting glances toward our windows. When one of the railroad workers starts up a conversation with us, even the girls come closer. Not one of our usually adventuresome group moves from his place even though the girls generously make their way to us with blouses filled with risk and desire. It's not that we are not taken with the charm of their hills and valleys, but it is our neglected clothes, long, unkempt hair, three-day beards, and the whole shitty situation that keep us in our places. But even the workers are not in their evening dress and when we are addressed in German by one of them through the crack in the window, everything seems to happen naturally.

"How are you, my countrymen?" an old and quite worn worker asks us in a Schwabish dialect and looks compassionately through the dusty window. "Let me wipe the dirt from the window so that we can see each other better," he begins and goes right to work. "So," he says with a nearly toothless mouth, "now, how are you?" "Good, as far as someone in our situation can expect," I answer him quickly. "Be glad that you are out of that crap. I was in the last war with the Prussians and I know the swindle. No one needs to tell me about it. I was a noncommissioned officer and I'm happy that I am too old for this one. You are so dirty, did you come right out of the trenches?" "No, we spent the winter in a French field behind barbed wire." Hocker laughs.

"Even worse, I did the same thing. I was captured in 1918, released in November, and came to the States in 1924. Stay here, boys. We have enough girls who want to marry industrious men. Take a look for yourselves." He laughs, pointing to the girls. "What is the matter, pop?" one of the bold girls asks as she comes up to the window. "Just my type," growls Hocker.

Boy, you have good taste, I think to myself. She is really a nice dish. Her well-formed breasts press against the thin blouse and their round form is easy to discern.

"She is a race track," snaps Siegfried hungrily. "Just look at those danger-ous curves." "Don't you have a souvenir for the young lady?" the old man asks over the noise at the window. "Yes," says Hocker and lightninglike tears a star from his shoulder and passes it through the window crack to the old man, who in turn gives it to the good-looking girl. Blushingly she thanks Hocker and goes back with swaying hips to her girlfriends, holding the star over her charming head like a victory trophy. Siegfried grouses: "What a damn thing to do to come and parade something like that in front of us after such a long time."

"Here boys, a few cigarettes." The old man appears once again before the window and shoves three packs of Lucky Strikes through the crack, something that is happening at the same time all along the train.

"That's the goddam Germans!" bellows a fat, recently arrived Yankee, shaking his head and nervously chewing his cigar as he sends the men back to work.

A short time later the train moves out again. Accompanied by the friendly good-byes of the girls and children, we fall into the dreams of an endless night.

*29 April 1945*

Early in the morning on the fifth day of our journey we reach Tulsa. It is Sunday throughout the world and once again we have the opportunity to see well-fed citizens in their Sunday best streaming into a magnificent church. How that can pain an innocent prisoner's heart only those who have been in a similar situation and who have had to look in the uncomforted eyes of their comrades can know. But it is useless in the spring of 1945 to complain of injustice when we consider how unjustly millions of others have been treated. Then others are concerned every minute with the necessities of life while we journey toward a safe but unknown fate.

As the temperature rises we leave the city and an hour later we are immersed in the loneliness of the hilly landscape. As the heat in our wagon climbs to an almost unbearable temperature, the train stops at an open station. Outside the window stand white-helmeted American soldiers holding their rapid-fire weapons at ready. "Get out!" rings in our dust-covered ears and all the doors open.

With well-practiced precision, the entire transport is assembled in three lines in only a few minutes. Slightly irritated, Hocker, Siegfried, and I notice that Schulz, in the confusion, was shoved by the military police into another group. But he waves to us, unconcerned. We look calmly toward the camp that lies about a mile in the distance and whose green-and-white painted barracks glimmer in promise under the southern sun. Surrounded by military police, the first column, in which we three friends find ourselves, begins the march toward the camp.

Within twenty minutes we reach the gate, over which stands in large letters: "Camp Gruber, Oklahoma." We don't know whether to laugh or whether we are just dreaming about the blade-sharp creases in the khaki pants of the prisoners strolling around the compound. Once again we are counted, searched, marched toward the apparent heavenly kingdom through lanes formed by former North African veterans, and welcomed by the German camp spokesman.

\* \* \*

Located one mile north of Braggs in east central Oklahoma on the west side of Highway 10 and across the road from the U.S. army camp, Camp Gruber was one of the first prisoner of war camps established in the United States, and many German prisoners of war, like Helmut Hörner, passed through it en route to other locations in the south, southwest, and west. The camp operated from May 1943 until May 1946. A large camp, with a capacity of 5,750, it served as a base camp for a number of surrounding branch camps. The greatest number of prisoners of war confined in the camp was 4,702, on October 3, 1945.[2]

\* \* \*

"I greet you in the name of the comrades in the prisoner of war camp Camp Gruber in the state of Oklahoma and offer you our hearty welcome," the German camp spokesman begins his speech as we, the veterans of the slime camps of France, sit in the dining hall. "Judging by your appearance, it does not take many words to know what lies behind you, but you can be sure that inside these barbed wires everything will be done to make your heavy burden lighter. And now I wish you a good appetite."

Quietly and with everyone busy with his own thoughts, we grasp the eating utensils. In the nickel-plated trays are piles of roast beef, spinach, potatoes, and pudding. Because we are not used to such a feast, we begin slowly, then with greater enthusiasm, and finally with great pleasure to enjoy the tasty meal. But the dining room is boiling hot and thick, unending drops of sweat pour from our bodies.

Finally, like refugees, we leave the hospitable room and go back toward the barracks. "This heat is terrible," stammers Hocker and, like me, rips the dirty uniform from his body. Strangers, with whom we must share their living space, observe us with obvious disgust. "In fourteen days you will be used to the climate," a large, blond-haired soldier lying on his bed advises us with a friendly laugh. Surprised, I look at him. On his nightstand, next to the picture of a black-haired girl, no one other than Adolf Hitler looks out from a homemade frame. Now I notice that nearly all of these former members of the Africa Corps have small swastika flags over the head of their beds. It dawns on me that in truth we are in a different world.

After two hours of a death-like midday sleep, I roll out of the sweat-soaked cover onto my feet and, with Hocker, follow the call to get our clothing issue. As we come back I notice with astonishment that someone else has apparently taken up residence in our places, because lying on the beds in careful order are brand new toothbrushes, fine soap, shaving equipment, and wood sandals.

"Did someone make a mistake?" I ask with contained anger. "The stuff belongs to you, comrades. Thanks is not necessary because it is from what we have extra," the blond-haired finally moves himself to explain. "Yes, but we can't …" "Yes you can," he cuts me off. "You can actually do more, that is go into the shower room and change yourselves into human beings. We know how you feel. We traveled halfway around the world before we could finally have a shave."

By evening roll call most of those from our transport stand in tip-top form, clothed in the khaki uniforms. Only the long hair and pale faces separate us from the old-timers, who, for the most part, wear the field caps of Rommel's army.

Before dinner I have the pleasure of greeting an acquaintance from my neighborhood. "We'll drink a bottle of beer together in the canteen tonight," he says as we say good-bye after a chat just like we had run into each other in a German barracks. "I wish you could say that." I laugh at him. "Oh yes." He remains standing, "There is beer in the canteen."

At 7:00 P.M. we meet each other at the bar in the canteen. Generously my acquaintance buys a variety of things for me. In amazingly well-stocked shelves lie cigarettes, tobacco, billfolds, and other toilet articles. There are also underwear, wood sandals, socks, and towels. It is impossible to describe with what feelings I take the whole thing in. But I do not have any time to spend with my thoughts because my companion pushes me into another room, where we find a free place and sit down behind our bottles of beer.

At 9:00 P.M. the lights go out and I know nothing anymore. Have I really experienced this day, or am I lying in a tent in France crazy with fever?

*30 April 1945*

After the most thorough cleansing ordeal of my life, I am in the shower dressing room and slip into the white underwear and the khaki uniform of the American army with the painted letters, "P.W." In a cloud of perfume mixed with after-shave lotion, Hocker and I leave the bath facilities with a regained consciousness and go into the mess hall to eat breakfast. We take milk and cornflakes from the counter and sit down at a table. "It's too bad that Schulz ended up in another compound," I say to Hocker as I bend over my milk bowl. "Perhaps it would be possible for him to change with someone," Hocker suggests. "Possible," I agree. "Let's give it a try. But look, here comes Siegfried."

"Hello! How are the two of you doing? You brothers smell like French whores." He grins all over and sits down by us. "Schulz was unlucky," he continues. "We were just talking about him," I answer. "Oh, well, let's not spoil our appetite. This is a stinking good store," as he turns to his cornflakes. "Do you like your barracks?" Hocker asks. "Not exactly. I am not with any of the old group. Do you know that the idiots here think we are all traitors and deserters?" he says bitterly. "That's not possible," I insist. "Listen to me, keep your mouth shut and don't talk about the lost war here," Siegfried advises. "They will throw you into the barbed wire. In my barracks everyone has Adolf hanging over his bed. By the way, supposedly someone was tried here for high treason and hanged." "Just where did you dig up these cock and bull stories?" I ask in unbelief. "You can hear it all in my room." He nods back and forth while spooning the milk from his bowl.

\* \* \*

Nazi prisoners of war did carry out retribution against certain prisoners they felt were guilty of treason. Usually this was in the form of beatings. Despite the rumor of an execution at Camp Gruber, there is no record of any such event. However, at two other camps in the vicinity, Camp Tonkawa in north central Oklahoma and Camp Chaffee, just east across the state line in Arkansas, Germans were murdered by their fellow prisoners. At Camp Tonkawa on November 4, 1943, Johannes Kunze was beaten to death in the company mess hall by a number of prisoners for allegedly disclosing information about factories in Germany and military positions in Hamburg. Eventually five men were hanged for the murder of Kunze. On March 25, 1944, at Camp Chaffee, a twenty-one-year-old prisoner of war, Hans Geller, was killed by about a dozen other prisoners. One prisoner was tried and found guilty of the murder; however, his death sentence was commuted. Geller was a paratrooper who had been wounded twice and had lost three brothers killed in action as German soldiers. He spoke and read English well and, in the eyes of ardent Nazis in the camp, cooperated too much with the Americans. At least five other prisoners were executed in other camps: Felix Tropschuh at Camp Concordia, Kansas, on October 18, 1943; Hugo Krauss at Camp Hearne, Texas, on December 23, 1943; Franz Kettner at Camp Concordia on January 11, 1944; Werner Dreschler at Papago Park, Arizona, in March 1944; and Horst Gunther at Camp Gordon, Georgia, on April 6, 1944. Other deaths, considered to be suicides, may have been the result of activity by pro-Nazi extremists.[5]

\* \* \*

"It is understandable." I try to place myself in the world of thought of these men of the Africa Corps. "Part of them have been prisoners since 1942 and don't know about the situation in Russia or France." "But they have newspapers here, for Hell's sake. They must know what is going on." "They don't believe it," Siegfried interjects. "The best thing for us to do is keep our mouths shut. Otherwise there will only be trouble and that doesn't help anyone."

"I don't criticize anyone that still believes in what we all once hoped. The day will come when everyone will have to correct his outlook. But I do condemn those who scream that they knew what was going to happen ever since 1933 and then trample on others while they buddy up to the Americans."

"I'm of the same opinion," Siegfried adds. "But it doesn't matter at all. If you went along, you are condemned. The Americans don't care what we think or don't think. They are only interested in victory." Hocker ends the discussion as we gather our dishes together.

After morning roll call we are sent to the barber while the work groups go out to pick cotton. In a conversation with the German camp spokesman, we learn that not all of us will necessarily stay in this camp, but that all noncommissioned officers will be transferred to another camp if they elect not to work. Although he is of the opinion that we should be of as little use to the Americans as possible, the camp spokesman recommends that in our own interest we should go to work. The days will pass more quickly and we can earn twenty dollars a month, which in purchasing power is about the same as twenty Reichsmarks. Otherwise we receive only five dollars and are denied the right to purchase tobacco. He also thinks that things are a little confused at this time and we will have to wait and see how everything goes. That answers the question about Schulz. With the hope that in a few days we will be reunited, the three of us enter the barber shop and finally are rid of our long manes.

During the course of the morning we are not bored. The time is taken up in filling out registration forms, a doctor's examination, shots, photographs, and fingerprints. Finally, about 1:00 P.M., we are once again assembled in the dining room. The well-prepared noon meal consists of sauerkraut, mashed potatoes, and mutton chops. It tastes wonderful, but the terrible heat makes us sleepy. The change in climate at this time of year makes it especially hard for the body to adjust. In order to prevent the loss of body salt, salt tablets are distributed and the doctors encourage us to drink at least two quarts of water a day. After we have drunk one quart we disappear into the barracks. We lie on our beds in our underwear and wait for the coolness of evening.

Shortly before the return of the work details, we friends undertake a tour of the camp. The rectangular barracks, built of plywood, remind one at first of the twelve-man army tents with which we became acquainted in Alençon. Painted green on the outside, they are very comfortably outfitted. The bright gray walls help the small windows provide excellent light to the interior. On the somewhat larger side walls there are single iron-frame beds painted black. The nightstands are built by the prisoners themselves and, for the most part, decorated with pictures of family members. The shelves hold toilet articles and writing materials. The prisoner's wardrobe consists of a khaki shirt and trousers, an olive green suit, underwear, and two pairs of shoes. Stated simply, it is the same outfit as that of the U.S. soldier. In addition every man possesses the obligatory sea sack, in which all of our old things are stored. The barracks are heated with natural gas. Everything is there for the prisoners of war. In comparison with what we have experienced, it is very comfortable.

But that is only secondary, since we are mostly interested in the garden plots in the camp. All barracks are surrounded by green grass. The streets and sidewalks are spick-and-span clean and framed by small, bright limestone pillars. In the middle of the compound is a miniature obelisk with the insignia of the paratroopers, a plunging eagle. There is also a relief of the entire continent of Africa with a miniature of Rommel's tanks pushing as far as El Alamein. Then we stand before a wonderful creation that charms us all: the mill in the Black Forest Valley. It is an authentic model on which nothing is missing. Even the clapper of the mill wheel is easy to distinguish. It is true, and what ability and what love was necessary to create such a masterpiece. "Black Forest, my homeland, you are so beautiful ... "

\* \* \*

The romantic Black Forest occupied a special place in Helmut's heart since his birthplace, Karlsruhe, is located on the northern edge, and he made numerous outings into the area both before and after the war.

\* \* \*

"How do you like it here?" a gray, crippled Africa fighter asks us as we watch a group of turtles and admire their lovemaking. "Very good," I respond, still under the influence of what I have just seen. "Yes, when I came here, it looked pretty bad," he says as he sits down on a curbstone. "Nothing but sand and a few barracks, I can tell you."

"Were the Americans in agreement with everything that was built here?" I ask. "Yes sir! The boys were enthused," he remembers with glee. "They even helped us. Everything was different than now. Shit! We should have gotten to know each other earlier, the Americans and us. We would have complemented each other very well. You can believe that the English would have had to fight their lousy war alone. Now we both sit in the ink. We are on the ass of the prophet and the Yankees have the Russians at their throat."

"The whistle has blown for roll call, we'll see you again, comrade." We nod as we toddle to the parade ground, still thinking about what the old fellow said. "A queer codger," Hocker notes as we line up. "Children and fools speak the truth," Siegfried adds.

### 4 May 1945

"All the newly arrived noncommissioned officers are to report immediately to the American orderly room to prove your rank," the camp officer of the day announces throughout the camp. "Are you crazy? We had to give up our *Soldbuchs* when we left the ship in New York," someone screams from under the shower. "Then you were lucky, comrade; the Americans took them all from us when we were captured," another comforts us. "Man, I am lucky that I hid mine in the last minute," Hocker announces happily. "Mine is lying in Paris in the prison," Siegfried reports, uncaring. "Oh, well," I comfort myself, "I have two photographs and a telegram with my exact address, which should be official proof." "You can wipe your hind end with them," an old timer counters. "All that stuff doesn't matter. The Americans want a *Soldbuch* or a document like the orders promoting you to sergeant."

"I sent those documents home a long time ago," I explain. "Then the only possibility is to write to Geneva. Many of us did that and we were able to receive verification of our rank," another counsels me. "The Americans should worry about that; my *Soldbuch* is in New York; they only need to ask," I conclude.

"Everyone can say he is such and such a rank and a picture or letter is no documented proof," the American technician explains as I fight, with others, for the recognition of our rank. "I have another witness who was in the same unit as me," I try as a last resort. "I'm sorry." He shrugs his shoulders. "I have my guidelines. As long as you cannot produce any documentation, your rank will be listed as undetermined and you must work. Please sign here." "I hold the rank of sergeant and will only sign in this condition." I remain firm. "It's up to you, then sign as a sergeant," he says calmly.

An hour later all those who do not have their *Soldbuchs* are called to the dining hall by the camp spokesman. "There is no other possibility but to compile a list and request verification of your rank from the International Red Cross in

Geneva. But that takes weeks. In the meantime the Americans will require you to work and assign you to work groups. The trick in New York was successful," he concludes sarcastically.

\* \* \*

It is understandable that Hörner and others who had to give up their books were upset since it was a document that verified who they were and would be very difficult to duplicate. According to Arnold Krammer:

> The *Soldbuch*, a contraction of the German "soldier's book," was a 15-page booklet carried by every German enlisted man and officer, infantry or air force. In effect, these booklets were condensed Basic Personnel Files and contained not only such personal data as weight, height, birthdate, birthplace, parental information, vaccinations, and eye examinations, but also information about military training, units, transfers, duties, and promotions. The inside cover of the *Soldbuch* carried a photograph of the owner and his signature. More than an aid in the registration of the prisoners, these booklets often contained helpful information for interrogators and intelligence analysts; at the very least, these documents could prevent a high-ranking prisoner or potentially dangerous captive from intentionally slipping undetected through the registration net. The random confiscation of documents and of *Soldbuchs* was not in any way condoned by the American authorities. Military documents of any nature came under the control of the intelligence services and were sacrosanct. The *Soldbuchs* in particular, were to be confiscated only by interrogators and used for screenings, after which the documents were sealed in envelopes and passed from commanding officer to commanding officer to accompany the prisoners as they were shipped to their final camps. In the end, however, the random confiscation of these booklets by souvenir-hungry American guards needlessly made the War Department's efforts more difficult and led to registration problems whose results would continue to crop up even in the American camps.[4]

\* \* \*

"That is the most awkward net I have ever fallen into," I say angrily to Hocker and Siegfried on our way back to our quarters. "It is all shit." Siegfried waves in resignation. "Let's just go together and pick cotton." "You really want to have your fun with me," I swear in anger.

"No question that I will go to work too." Hocker tries to comfort me. "It doesn't bother me. I wanted to speak with you about it anyway. I am tired of lying around here. Besides that, I am impressed more with twenty dollars than five. It's just the way they do it that stinks. To take your *Soldbuch* and then demand later that you have it to prove your rank, that's just a damn swindle." The anger returns to me again.

"I have even worse news." Siegfried raises his eyebrows. "Perhaps you will cool yourselves on it." "Out with it, let's take care of the whole mess at once," I say, not knowing what he has in mind. "The Russians are in Berlin. The Americans in Munich. The war is completely lost," he says, fighting back the tears.

Hot, unbearably hot shines the sun in Oklahoma. But much hotter burn the hearts of the people. By the mill in the Black Forest Valley in the prisoner of war Camp Gruber in the American state of Oklahoma, three German soldiers sit and listen to the clattering of the mill wheel and feel they have lost the world. Our thoughts go out to the furthermost corners of Germany, but are continually reduced until they encircle only a handful of people who at this hour offer the only bond.

"We knew for a long time; why do we squat now, like when someone has hit us on the head with a hammer?" Siegfried breaks the silence. "We have known for a long time that we all must die and still are sad when it comes," I explain mournfully. "Didn't you always say that we will go on afterward?" he offers, undistracted. "All the time," I concur. "Or perhaps the mill will not clatter anymore?" "Then let's see if the uniforms are dry. I want to put mine on when they are ready," Hocker says and stands up stiffly.

"Prepare to die," Hocker and I are greeted as we enter the barracks and lay our cleanly washed uniforms on the bed. "Do you know the latest?" the blond asks. "I'm satisfied with the old," I rejoin. "Hitler has abdicated." He laughs idiotically. "The Americans claim he shot himself." Another grins. "Do you believe that nonsense?" the blond questions. "No, I want to have the documentary proof just like the Americans want it from me," I say with double meaning, at which they break out in roaring laughter. Harmless fools, I think, your awakening will be terrible.

### 9 May 1945

On the streets of the compound inside Camp Gruber, German prisoners of war stand in rows of five. It is 8:00 A.M. Officers of the American army appear.

Taking a deep breath, the oldest unfolds a sheet of paper and after looking in earnest over the heads of the prisoners of war he begins. "The war in Europe has ended. The German army has surrendered unconditionally. The German Reich has ceased to exist. The German army is no longer bound by the oath of loyalty to the Third Reich." With considerable satisfaction, the officer raises his head briefly and continues: "From this point on the wearing of the German uniform is forbidden. The same goes for the wearing of all emblems, insignia, and medals of the German National Socialist regime. Conduct against these directives will be met with severe punishment. The German prisoners of war in the United States of North America will be returned as soon as the necessary transports are available."

Without a word the Germans return to their quarters. In silence Hocker and I unbutton our shoulder straps from our field jackets, roll up our German uniforms into a bundle, and step outside.

"Here, I think, is the best place. What do you think, Willi?" I ask in dead seriousness. "It doesn't matter, anywhere," he answers and shoves the fire shovel that we have brought from the barracks into the sand.

A short time later a hole about three feet deep lies before us. In an instant our uniforms are thrown into the hole and quickly covered. "When I had to put it on in November 1938 I was proud," Hocker says softly. "A long time," I answer, all ready to leave. "Forget it now." "I can never do that. I met Gerda in it," he says with a face from which all hope seems to have disappeared.

As dusk lies over the land, it is as still as the grave in the camp. Like an unbearable load, the unbounded hopelessness lies on the souls of the sons of a people God has forsaken. And no light shines in their despair. For no purpose! Everything was senseless. Every offer of blood and possessions from everyone is looked upon as useless. Finished!

The Reich of the Germans, our fatherland, has ceased to exist.


*16 May 1945*

On the seventh day of the year zero, Hocker, Siegfried, and I stand on the edge of the turtle run and watch their intensive lovemaking. We have overcome our depression. In its place is a boundless longing for the homeland and our loved ones. We want to go home. Without delay.

"What will they do with this beautiful camp when we are gone from here?" Hocker thinks out loud. "Perhaps they will erect a bordello for the training division on the other side of the street. In any case we don't give a hoot. The war is behind us," mumbles Siegfried while he pokes with a stick to hinder a male turtle as it tries to mount a female turtle who has opened herself to receive him. "Let the two of them have their fun." I knock the stick out of his hand. "There are old ladies who will not have such a pleasure for very much longer; he should take care of them first," he says as though it is the most serious thing in the world.

"How do you think the German women are acting toward the occupation troops?" I toss out lightly although I have long been busy with such thoughts." "Are you worried?" asks Siegfried. "Personally no; I just mean in general," I answer self-righteously. "They certainly have other concerns," Hocker offers, truehearted. "It is because they have other concerns. Do you remember the situation in the hotel at Soissons? Now it is that far. This time we have failed. No one knows better than I what was going on in France and how bad the French were," I hold up to him. "Our women are not French women." He tries to dismiss the issue. "Do you believe they always did it for love? I am of another opinion. Often it was not only their sexual need that was the mainspring," I explain to him. "If a woman did it for money, then she is a whore." He waves contemptuously. "That's right," Siegfried chimes in, "but often women combine both the pleasurable and the useful even in these things."

"Now I want to go home," Siegfried says abruptly as we go to roll call. "The return transport will occur as soon as the necessary space is available." Hocker comforts him. "Do you know when it will be available?" I ask. "Yes," says Siegfried. "When the victor wants it to be."

After roll call the three of us find a comfortable place in front of the sick bay and sit down in the grass. Like a glowing ball, the sun hangs over the woods to the west. Sharp orders of the drill sergeants ring from the U.S. training camp in our direction. "The war is not yet over for them." I break the beginning silence and turn my neck in the direction of the nearby city of Muskogee just as a convoy of trucks moves toward the camp.

"The Japanese will take a big bite out of their ass," Siegfried suggests with inner satisfaction. "They know that. There is a good reason that they are accompanied by the MPs on the trains." Hocker laughs maliciously.

"It's too bad for those who must bite the dust. The poor devils are certainly worse off than we." A feeling of sympathy for young American boys condemned to death rises in me. "I wouldn't want to be in their shoes. The Japanese soldiers are at least as dangerous as the Russians," Hocker admits. "Perhaps even worse," Siegfried adds; "then those idiots really believe their Emperor is a true God and a hero's death will stand them in good stead in the hereafter." "They are dumber than we," I say angrily as the whole infamy of the ruling class of this world becomes obvious to me.

*18 May 1945*

Shortly after 3:00 A.M. I notice that my friend Hocker is not asleep. The gods may know how many times in this fate-filled night the path we have trod together continues to parade before my spiritual eyes. Paris, Le Bourget, Soissons, Chartres, Alençon, Le Mans, Cherbourg, the trip across, New York, St. Louis, and Camp Gruber, Oklahoma, are the stations of our forever preserved friendship. Providence brought us together. But now an incomprehensible fate has willed we must separate. The unexplainable fact that while in New York Hocker followed the sudden impression to hide his *Soldbuch* and did not give it up as he was supposed to is the cause of our separation.

There are 450 unverified noncommissioned officers, including Siegfried and me, who leave Camp Gruber today for an unknown location. Hocker and apparently Schulz remain, although separated. All our efforts to remain together are for nought. Fate has decreed differently. But we approach it with the conviction that we know how to bear the burden.

After breakfast I stuff my things into my sea sack with unending sadness in my heart. Hocker sits worlds away at the head of my bed. "Stop that chain smoking. It makes me nervous," I order him as once again he holds a match to a cigarette. "There," he mumbles, returning to his senses, and throws a tin of tobacco into the sack. "Pack that away. I will give it up when I don't have to see you any more." "Then you can send me your ration," I tease without looking at him.

"You had better look for another dumb fool who will take care of you," he answers, puffing excitedly on his cigarette. "I'll have Siegfried with me. He will swing with me." I try to cover my sorrow. "He is worse than you. Both of you will suffocate in your own filth. I can see it coming," he gamely teases as the whistle blows for assembly.

"Should I try once more to convince the camp commander? I get afraid when I think about eating the sweet desert alone." I pull his leg in playful meanness. "Stop all that nonsense and get out of here. They are already waiting for you," he says, grabbing a handkerchief because something bothers him in his eye.

The prisoners of war selected for transfer stand in five columns ready to march. Although the khaki uniforms carry a knife-sharp crease, they appear somewhat grotesque because of the printed letters "P.W." on them. The sea sacks have already been loaded. Only the clerks with their lists, which they continue to compare, keep us from departure. It is a mood like that at a train station. You have already said good-bye to your loved ones and talked about everything that matters, but the train does not leave.

"OK, who gets home first will immediately visit the families of the others," Hocker says already for the fourth time within ten minutes. "And when we all get home, we will have a big party." We confirm our plans for the first days of freedom. "You all will have to visit me." "And me." "And me."

"Yes, yes, and me," says the German camp spokesman, "but now you two have to do a right face like the others." And then: "Forward." Quickly we fly into each other's arms. "Be good, Willi," I say softly. "You too," he laughs bravely, and "March," is the order that tears us apart for God knows how long.

Twenty minutes later we are sitting in the blue seats of the Santa Fe railroad pullman coach. They are mostly the old faces from the starvation Camp Alençon around us. Now they are well groomed, well clothed, and well fed. Siegfried and I are not the only ones who had to leave dear friends in Camp Gruber. Such is the mood in the wagon. But the American pace does not allow anyone time for sentimentality. We have barely sat down before the train rolls into the hot day.

"That we could not say good-bye to Schulz stinks all the way to the Stone Age and back again," I say to Siegfried while my unpracticed fingers try to roll a cigarette. "If you keep it up, you will have more tobacco on your pants than in the paper." Siegfried grins. "But with regard to Schulz, you took the words right out of my mouth. He is a man of stature, like I have seldom met before. Perhaps a little stubborn, but completely clean on the inside." I grasp in remembrance. "For me he was too straight, and I'm afraid it will be trouble for him in this land without prejudice," Siegfried thinks. "I do not believe he will become acclimated. Do you remember at Cherbourg and someone told him to carry up the honey bucket? He did not refuse but gave an example," I contradict him.

"I don't mean that." He offers me a burning match for my rolled cigarette. "But his honesty with regard to the hearing officer." "He only needed to tell the truth. In the meantime it became clear to him that some had terribly misused the truth and the faith of a German who loved his homeland." I comfort him.

"That's why I am worried that he will come across as a bum to our former enemies when he sees that everything he held sacred is soiled and he therefore also considers himself dirty," Siegfried means. "Do you think it will be different for us? It takes courage and truth and that is the least that he lacks."

"Is there something wrong with his marriage?" Siegfried asks. "What marriage?" I ask, not altogether there. "Schulz's, naturally. I'm not very smart about such things, but something wasn't quite right." He chuckles to himself. "His wife was a little slut earlier, someone's mistress, that's all," I say, not wanting to go into all the details.

"And he married someone like that; who can understand it?" he wonders.

"We don't understand everything about love. She was suddenly there and demanded her rights. Hocker told you in Le Mans that this shortcoming of Schulz is better than none." I peck at his thoughts. "I wonder what Hocker is doing?" He turns sleepily to the second single man from our circle. "Certainly he is sitting by the Black Forest Mill hanging his thoughts on the wheel," I say and also close my eyes.

As darkness falls, we pass through the ocean of lights in Kansas City and are busy preparing the coach seats for the night. What seemed an unbridgeable cleft between guards and the guarded during our first train ride, has, for the most part, vanished. The guards are young men like us and don't concern themselves at all with what is going on in the wagon. In fact, one offers some good advice on how to best divide up the seats so that everyone of us has a place to lie. Only the food could be better, but in the end, we are used to much worse.

By about 11:00 P.M. the last talkers are quiet. Night has dipped the land into deep darkness. Even our thoughts lose their sharpness and finally we glide into unconsciousness.

### 20 May 1945

On the third day of travel our train continues to speed in a westerly course through the seemingly unending loneliness of the state of Kansas. Since we wear the uniform of American soldiers, we are hardly recognized as Germans in the towns unless they happen to see the "P.W." on our backs. And so we are greeted by the citizens of this land, as we are always used to—as soldiers. Especially the children and cute young ladies catch our attention. Naturally here and there something goes wrong at the small train stations where we stop. The tracks are not closed like in Europe and everyone can walk right up to the train. After they greet us and start to speak to us, the people who were initially excited usually leave in disappointment.

But sometimes they are even more curious about us and appear to be looking for the horns on our heads which the war propaganda has spread about all Germans. "They look like us!" one can hear and that brings a sorrowful laugh over the lack of knowledge by people of the twentieth century. This happens only once in a while and we are honest enough to admit that in Germany there are people who know only their own manure piles.

What causes us to wonder, however, is the fairness of the guards, who never try to drive the people away from our coaches, not even when they are young ladies who joke with us. It must be because of the much-praised freedom of the Americans. Only during a stop in Fort Wallace can we see long faces at the Red

Cross station. Our guards return, loaded like pack animals, with long boxes of pastries over which we are extremely happy. Not only are we joyous, but also the guards and the friendly sisters, because giving by good people always releases a special kind of joy. But still the American ladies seem annoyed when they discover that their dear offerings are being enjoyed by German prisoners of war, something the guards were silent about when they picked up the delicacies. As the train begins to move and the complications dissolve, the women show their happy faces and wave a cheerful good-bye, but it is not clear if they mean to include us. In any case we enjoy the sweet pastries without concern and the guards appreciate our thankful glances.

Shortly after 2:00 P.M. we reach Denver, the capital of the state of Colorado. As usual, the train does not halt in the busy main station, but rather between two freight trains in the switching yard. Still we have a glimpse of a small part of the city that glimmers in the sun at the foot of the Rocky Mountains and whose tall buildings offer a scene typical in other large American cities. The difference between this beautiful city and the others we have seen so far is not the tall buildings which catch the eye, but the small dwellings, often built of stone, that look like they are set in parks and bring out a feeling of home in the onlookers. In the background the Rocky Mountains rise and on the highest peaks snow and ice glisten in the sun like polished silver.

After this city is behind us, the train goes north a respectable distance from the Rocky Mountains until it rolls into the small farm city of Greeley. An hour later we are all loaded into transports and rattle out of the peaceful little town on a wide road through sugar beet fields for three miles to a barracks camp with guard towers and surrounded by barbed wire.

"Camp Greeley, Colorado," stands over the gate around which the U.S. soldiers swarm as we leave the transports. With the usual precise organization we are counted, searched, and received by the German camp spokesman, who leads us directly to the dining hall. After a short welcome the familiar red cards are distributed, personally signed by each of us, and collected. "I have been taken prisoner and I am fine. My new address is Camp Greeley/Colorado, Box 20, New York," is what those in the homeland will read should the card reach anyone.

* * *

Camp Greeley, located seven miles west of Greeley, was opened in March 1944. Constructed to house three thousand prisoners of war, the camp was described

... as pleasant and well-organized—located in an attractive area where Long's Peak "looms beautifully" and where the men seemed satisfied. Newly planted shrubs and trees lined the gravel roads and walkways. Prisoners took an active interest in beautifying the grounds with flowers. Buildings were covered with tan siding and they all had concrete floors. ... A double graduated hog wire fence and eight guard towers enclosed the camp. Each tower had a machine gun, siren, search light, and electric heater. Kennels housed twenty guard dogs for use in patrolling camp boundaries.

The primary purpose for the prisoner of war camp was to provide workers for the sugar beet fields. Others worked in potato and onion fields while some went into the mountains to cut timber. The camp was formally closed on February 28, 1946. Eighty-three of the camp buildings were purchased by the cities of Greeley and Loveland. One guard tower and light was acquired for use at the Greeley municipal airport. "Today a cornfield lies where POW Camp 202 had been. Only portions of two cement posts that mark the former camp's entrance serve as a reminder of northern Colorado's prisoners of war."[5]

* * *

After eating the tastefully prepared pea soup, we shoulder the sea sacks that were unloaded and disappear into our assigned barracks.

After a refreshing shower, Siegfried and I wander though the barracks city, Camp Greeley. The streets are all asphalt and wide, as is the entire camp, but as such there is nothing of note. Here there is a division into compounds and all internees are assigned to companies which are housed in barracks next to each other. Camp Greeley is a pure work camp and only the company leaders are noncommissioned officers. The comrades here have not worried about how the camp looks, which is easy to understand given the work in the sugar beet fields. But the camp is clean in every corner. There is a reading room with good literature and table tennis, and other games for our entertainment. There is also a movie theater available. Everything considered, it is very comfortable for us prisoners of war.

"How is the work?" Siegfried asks an acquaintance who enters the reading room. "There is no lack of work," he answers, "but we watch out that we don't work too hard. Since the end of the war they demand more and more from us and still the food is less and worse." "How is it at the workplace?" I ask with interest. "The daily quota has to be reached before we can leave the fields." He laughs with amusement at our concerned faces. "But they will tell you all of that, and besides you will see a film in the morning which shows how the work is to be done," he adds and gives us a copy of a German prisoner of war newspaper, *Der Ruf*, published in the United States.

"That will be a lot of fun when we are the next to hack sugar beets in Colorado." I laugh in Siegfried's face as he despondently grasps the newspaper. "You say it is fun when they assign you how much to do?" he strenuously disagrees. "We will see how it goes, old boy." I soothingly pet his rust-red hair. "It won't matter to us how the field looks when we are finished in the evening."

At 9:00 P.M. I throw the newspaper onto the table. "Come Siegfried, let's go, otherwise I'll get sick," I tell him, obviously upset. "The way they write is like manure in the cheesebox," he offers and follows me outside. "It's best if we forget about newspapers in the future," he suggests while we are en route to our barracks. "I wouldn't say so," I contradict him. "Only this *Ruf* I will never pick up again." We finally know how badly the Third Reich lied to us. "Where do prisoners of war in America suddenly develop a knowledge of things that were only possible in the dark Middle Ages?"

"Do you seriously believe that this newspaper was produced by German prisoners of war?" he asks. "Only the devil knows who really writes it, but in the future I will only pay attention to the public American newspapers," I decide. "We will have to learn much in this land. I have previously read an American paper. They contradict on page three what they proclaim in headlines on page one. We will have to first learn how to read American newspapers." He slaps me on the back and opens the door to the barracks.

"Have you heard that we are to hack sugar beets?" an old acquaintance calls to us. "We have," I say as I make my bed. "So," he takes my arm, "are you going to participate in the swindle again?" "What do you mean, again, so far we haven't done anything?" I laugh unsuspectingly, trying to avoid the subject. "So you haven't done anything?" A well-known hothead mixes in." "Didn't we hold our necks out for Hitler and his cronies? Shall we now do the same kind of slave work for the Americans?"

"Complain to Adolf. Now comes the consequences of his thousand-year reich over us," I say, uncaring.

"Consequences you say? Is it a consequence when they take away your pass and then demand we prove who we are?" he screams, rising to his feet. "I don't really care." I turn away. "And I say it must finally stop that they continue to make us work. If we decline to work there is nothing they can do. We are noncommissioned officers and according to the Geneva convention are not required to work," he blows out. "And I tell you, we should have stopped much sooner because it is the curse of a wicked deed that the evil that follows must be born." I laugh from my double-decker bunk in order to provoke.

"What evil have we done?" an old-timer questions. "When given the command to march, we marched. Therein lies our entire guilt," I explain. "And if we didn't march, they would have stood us up against a wall," he responds. "And if we don't hack sugar beets, the same thing will happen to us," I laugh. "Then the swindlers are the same here as there." The hothead ends the day as the light goes out.

*23 May 1945*

Monday shortly after 7:00 A.M. we are dressed in our blue-and-gray work clothes and partake of the sparse breakfast in the dining hall. A carton of milk and two slices of bread, skin thick, is all that is offered us. With only this we are to work. But the mood is unusually good. "We will hack them good today," Siegfried says happily and sets his cap on his head as we leave the hall just as hungry as before.

\* \* \*

As of April 1945, the suggested daily caloric level for sedentary prisoners was twenty-five hundred, with a maximum of thirty-four hundred calories daily for prisoners engaged in moderate activity. A month later the caloric level was reduced to three thousand calories a day; however, many argued that the ration reductions were much more severe than suggested. Red Cross officials concluded that the rations had been cut too severely and offered as evidence statistics for a camp of 240 men: Coffee reduced from twelve to fourteen to three to four pounds; margarine from ten to five pounds; lard from twelve to one and one-half pounds; sugar from twelve to sixteen to four pounds; condensed milk from forty to seven cans. Prisoners felt that the rations were cut because the Americans no longer needed to worry about American prisoners in the hands of the Germans and saw the cut also as a measure of revenge against the German prisoners. Three reasons were given for the cut in rations in May 1945: the prisoners were receiving more food than they really needed—most had gained weight since arriving in the United States; there was a shortage of foodstuffs in the United States because of the amount of food being sent to Allied countries; and food would be needed to continue the fight against Japan and to help prevent, or at least reduce, starvation in Germany and other war-torn countries.[6]

\* \* \*

At 7:20 A.M. the company stands in front of the barracks. The poor company leader has trouble until the individual work groups are assembled. Twenty-five men are assigned to a farmer, who picks them up at the gate with his own vehicle. Our noon meal is sent with us and consists of a slice of bread, sausage or cheese, and an apple or an orange for each man. The farmer provides the drinking water.

"About face," the company commander orders with an expression of concern for the first work day of this group of revolutionaries. But then an astonished laugh breaks out when we start to sing, "No woman has betrayed me like you," as we march in step to the gate where the farmer is already waiting for us.

Moments later we climb onto the truck owned by Mr. Miller, a gray-haired man with a well-meaning face. The guard assigned to us is about as thick as he is tall and apparently has found no time to tie his shoelaces. Laughingly he helps the farmer close the tailgate and swings up to us on the bench. The old crate rolls out backwards toward the road. From now on we are costing the farmer money, and "time is money," is the saying which describes the pace in this land.

Twenty minutes later we stand before a field and no one can say where it begins or ends. Everything around us is green. Twelve inches high of green sugar beets. Only between the rows, through which the machine has already apparently gone, is it grayish gold. Grass is hard to discover. The ground is well worked, but the beets are too thick together.

"I want good work to be done," the farmer says, turning to his conscripted helpers, who encircle him grinning while the disinterested guard smokes, leaning against the truck, his rifle hanging on the door handle of the truck. "I do not require a lot of work, only good work, do you understand?" he asks in his difficult German.

"Yes." We laugh and observe the funny little hoes whose handles are only about thirty-five inches long. "I will show you how to do it," he says as he begins to hack out the extraneous beets in one of the rows until only one plant remains for every twelve to fifteen inches. "That's all there is to it. Who is a farmer?" he asks, looking into our uncaring faces. "We are all students or shopkeepers," Corporal Kunze explains in dead earnest while the rest of us struggle to suppress the laughter.

"Bullshit!" the good man spits out and looks searchingly in the circle. "You know what I want?" He goes to a noncommissioned officer from Bavaria. "I am a pastor, but I understand something about garden work," the trained locksmith and former tank driver explains. "Pastor?" he finally stops and scratches his head. "Well, I can't do anything more. Please begin."

Like a pack of young dogs we bound out into the beet field and the fur starts to fly. With a face that God must have mercy on, the farmer looks at us. "Stop," he calls after a while and points helplessly to what resembles a battlefield. "Don't do any more; you will destroy everything," he babbles and shows us the secret of hoeing sugar beets for the second time. "Do it this way and it will be good," he says patiently. "All your comrades have learned how."

"We are thirsty," the bogus pastor groans and looks with radiant eyes into the sky. "I'll get some water," the farmer says, ringing his hands. "Please start again."

After a short and silent agreement with the eyes, we go back to the rows. The small hoes play lightly through the vegetation. The farmer watches us excitedly. "Excellent work," he praises us happily. "I am a Volga German," he explains to Corporal Kunze, when he asks about his forefathers. "Then bring us milk instead of water and you will be well satisfied with us," he offers as an inducement. "It's forbidden, everything is forbidden. I'm sorry," he swears. "Bring milk and do it fast. It is terribly hot." Kunze remains firm. "OK," he finally agrees and goes toward his vehicle.

\* \* \*

The Volga Germans of Colorado had originally emigrated from the Rhineland at the invitation of Empress Catherine II to populate the Russian Empire's newly acquired Volga and Black Sea territories. In 1763 they were offered generous grants of land, religious freedom, and exemptions from involuntary military service and taxation for thirty years. A hundred years later, the privileges granted the German settlers were eliminated by Tsar Alexander II. In 1874 the Russian military began conscripting German youths and in 1880 the Russian language was made mandatory in German-Russian schools, and Germans feared there would be further efforts to force them to adopt Russian ways. The most intensive period of German-Russian immigration to the United States was between 1873 and 1912, and Colorado became a primary area of settlement, with most Volga Germans arriving in Colorado during the first decade of the twentieth century with the advent of the sugar beet industry. By 1909, of the 10,724 beet workers in northern Colorado, 5,870 were German-Russian, with Japanese and Spanish-American workers numbering 2,160 and 1,002 respectively. Some of them reached Colorado after stops in Nebraska and other midwestern states; others came directly from Russia. According to Kenneth W. Rock,

> Descendants of Germans from Russia constitute the second largest ethnic group in contemporary Colorado. Only Spanish-speaking people number greater. The United States census of

1920 enumerated 21,000 Germans from Russia residing in Colorado. By 1930 it was estimated that there were nearly 50,000. Between 200,000 and 300,000 of their descendants reside in the Centennial State today ... [7]

* * *

"I believe we will do better with the old man if we don't cause any trouble. You know he has to pay fifty dollars for the day and he willingly gives us something in addition. If he is willing to get milk for us, then we will get something from him to eat. Are you all in agreement?" Kunze asks after his comments. "What do these stupid beets concern me? If it gets any hotter, I will not take another swing," the Bavarian complains to him. "Let's work until noon as we have been and see what the old man springs for." Kunze finally reaches a unity after some debate.

When the farmer arrives with the milk, each man has finished two hundred yards of well-hoed beets. The man appears very content with his field. "Good work, boys," he reports and turns to the guard, who sits in the shade of the wagon stewing in his own misery. Unconcerned with them, we continue to work lustily. But the negotiations take too long for us. Even though it is only ten o'clock, the sun burns hot in the sky.

"He can either bring the milk now or he can take the dirty beets to the man in charge himself," a man from Mecklenburg sighs. "First he has to convince the guard. Otherwise he will have problems," Kunze warns with reason and the work goes on.

At exactly noon we are sitting on the truck and traveling for our noon break toward the mountains, where about two miles in the distance a lonely farmhouse stands in the shadow of trees. The breeze cools our heated bodies. Work, when you are not used to it, how painful it is.

In the shadows of a weeping willow we distribute what little bread we have. Regretfully the farmer shrugs his shoulders as Kunze explains to him that we can't work with so little to eat. "If I give you food, then I won't get any prisoners," he says, looking with anticipation at the guard, who gets up and goes into the farmhouse. With a dexterity that no one would have thought possible, the farmer hurries into a nearby shed and throws five long loaves of white bread out the window. "The bill is correct," says Kunze tranquilly. "A loaf of bread for every five men."

After 1:00 P.M. we are hoeing beets again. Yard for yard, hour after hour we slash our way through the plants. "This work is the shits. If I only had my *Soldbuch* with me. Hocker certainly made the right choice," Siegfried begins to lament.

"Think of it as a sport, and it is easier," I suggest to him, friendly. "Sports in this heat; I wouldn't last very long," he says quite apathetically. "Pull yourself together. It will pass. We will get used to it." I try to encourage him. "How long do you think this swindle will last?" he asks, taking a break. "I believe I said once before it took two years after the last war."

"You must be crazy. Do you believe I will hoe sugar beets for two years?" he spits out. "Not in the winter; the things don't grow then as far as I am informed." "Idiot!" he says and begins again to hack away at the sugar beets.

"OK boys," the guard calls as the sun nears the Rocky Mountains. "Is it already five o'clock?" Siegfried asks, slightly wounded. "Isn't it too bad. Ask him if he will allow you to work overtime." I shove him toward the truck where two contented Americans wait for us.

As the truck travels back toward camp, we observe our blistered hands. Everyone earned sixty cents today, I think, and raise my view to the glaciers on the mountains. "I can buy a toothbrush in the canteen with what I have earned," I grumble. "Or a bottle of after-shave lotion."

Yes, I can do that. Could you do that in Germany? Probably not, and they have prepared a warm evening meal for us in the camp. We will stand under the shower and a good bed awaits us. Shouldn't we now be content?

After a refreshing shower, the two companies who now have their first work day behind them eat dinner in the best of spirits. Parsnips, potatoes, roast beef, and pudding are prepared by the cooks with the usual quality. We only wish there was more. But the chief cook comforts us with an extra slice of bread and as we leave the mess hall our stomachs are busy with digestion.

When we arrive in the barrack, Siegfried and I are dragged into an unpleasant conversation. "The International Red Cross has given up the care of the German prisoners of war. All complaints are to be directed to the Red Cross in Washington," says the philosopher Braun with raised eyebrows that spread like the wings of a bird.

"Well," says Siegfried, "they haven't worried about us much anyway." "That is a pigsty," Braun reacts. "Now you can complain to the devil's grandmother." "What do you want to complain about, Braun? Has anyone done anything to you?" I ask, although I am not enthused about the change of events. "Not yet, my friend, not yet, but in the future we will have reason to complain," he contends. "You are a good philosopher, but we will have to see if you are as good a prophet." And I think I have found a way around him.

"Just read the newspaper; then your eyes will be opened. They encourage hate and revenge and you can watch and hear it happen." He hits me on the shoulder. "Why do you read them? Don't go crazy over the carelessly written words. If it becomes reality, we will experience it soon enough." I smile at him. "Then it will hit you all the harder because you are unprepared," he says.

"Who told you that I am not prepared? Believe me, I am used to everything, and have been for a long time," I explain.

"So are you of the opinion that Germany will become communist?" His eyes gleam at me. "It would be a logical conclusion to come from the denials and selfishness of the leaders, not only of Germany, but also of Europe, and by the way, America not excluded," is my answer. "And what do you imagine a communist Germany would be like?" he asks, upset with my point of view. "I don't imagine it at all. Only our hate for the rich Americans could make us communists, if they happen to set up a terrible regime," I interject.

"That may be right if you apply the present political sentiment of this camp to all of Germany. Unfortunately we know nothing of the attitudes of other Germans. For example, those in the Russian-occupied sector. I do not believe the Russians handle the population there with kid gloves," Braun explains. "It would be in the interest of the Russians to do so," Siegfried chimes in. "We will see who the smart victor is. If both happen to be smart, then the final outcome will be bad for us." I bring my quick fears into the open.

"You mean they will eat us up together? I don't believe it," Braun declares. "No, I know they won't," he continues. "You see, America must have war because war is their best business. That's what I read yesterday. I emphasize business. No one could read that in Germany, but still the wire pullers mean the same thing. World domination is in Russia's program. If America continues to think businesslike, then she will secure Germany's industrial potential and dictate the price to Russia. For that they need skilled workers, who can only be had if there is a chance for them. If the Americans leave Germany in misery then it will become communist without question. In that case Russia alone will have won the war; then Russia would not need to buy anything more from the Americans because she could find everything she needs in Germany."

"You concede that Germany and Russia would complement each other the best." Kunze mixes in the conversation from his bed. "Wouldn't that be a second way out of this dead end? I mean, we have lost everything, so what is there to keep us from communism?" "The Americans," Braun laughs, "in that they will help us to acquire new possessions so that their own business will blossom."

"Why did you take up this damn topic, paint the devil on the wall, and then give the Americans the last word?" I ask Braun on the way to the latrine. "Because the nihilism is so rampant," he explains. "They talk themselves into becoming communists tomorrow, but do not expect anything from it. Now they simply hate the Americans. They also hate the Russians. Yes, they even hate themselves. But they no longer believe. One has to turn a light on for them, otherwise they will fall into the morass."

"And what do you really believe?" I ask anxiously. "That we are not yet completely lost," he whispers into the night on his way to the wide street, where he makes his lonesome rounds night after night.

### 31 May 1945

As on just about every Saturday, the washroom of the third company is a beehive of activity. All the men are busy washing and scrubbing their work clothes. In this promised land there is no shortage of wash soap and washing is child's play. But still you have to be there, and that is what drives us to haste. It is already 2:00 P.M. on this free afternoon. Drying is no problem since it seldom rains in Colorado. You just hang your clothing on the line behind the washroom and take it down completely dry an hour later.

"So," says Siegfried to me when we have our uniforms on the line. "We've got that behind us. Now let's go shower and then afterward go to the recreation room." "I have made plans with Braun for the afternoon; don't you want to join the party?" I ask courteously, although I know that he is not very enthused about philosophy. "What is the topic of study today?" he asks. "A commentary on Nietzsche's 'Zarathustra,'" I reply. "Is that where he says when you go to your wife, don't forget the whip?" He laughs like a naughty boy. "You know that for sure, but what you don't know is that he rejected democracy," I throw at him. "And why did he reject it?" he asks in interest. "That is what I expect to learn from Braun today," I explain.

"I must finally tell you my opinion, Helmut." He pulls out a sack of tobacco and paper. "You are all the time running from one wandering preacher to another, believing one thing one day and something else the next. Don't drive yourself crazy. Don't believe anything you don't see for yourself. What good is the old Nietzsche, when he rejects democracy and the Americans are still determined to institute it in Germany?"

"In the first place we aren't sure what the Americans will do, and in the second place, I want to see how it is all connected," is my response. "I admit that at the moment nothing is firm because I saw things during the Weimar Republic that stuck in my bones: unemployment, lack of authority, decay, and their sorrowful companions. The egotism of the rich, the confusion of the middle class, the workers driven to murder their brothers, and the crimes of the flotsam of all classes. We know that all of it centered in National Socialism, and logically we conclude that its downfall must take us along the road to communism. All I know about Marx and Engels is that they wanted to help the workers enjoy the fruits of their labors. But I was in Russia and saw how, in practice, it really was. I admit that the country still remains at least fifty years behind the West in its development because of the feudalism of the tsar; however, now they can catch up quickly. If the masses can accomplish something, such as better clothing, housing—in short what we Europeans understand as culture—remains to be seen. In any case, inside I don't feel that I am a communist, not yet."

"Here, smoke one, perhaps I can help you a little more," Siegfried says, passing me his tobacco. "You know I was not in Russia, so I don't have any disturbing pictures in mind as I consider the situation. But still I am convinced that for Germany Russian communism or bolshevism is out of the question. We are an intelligent and industrious people that must live together in close quarters. I can imagine that if we were to develop a system based on the teachings of Marx or Engels in which one does not rob the other. Instead the fruit of everyone's work would be thrown into one pot and then, based on production but with an eye to maintaining a minimum level of existence, redistributed to everyone. I believe we could develop a form of government that would lead us out of chaos."

"That would be an ideal solution, Siegfried," I agree, "but unfortunately you forget that not all people are idealists. Imagine what would fall under the pot when the wrong people had their fingers in it." "Naturally they would have to be watched," he interjects, "and the watchers must be watched and so on until we are all watched, who will then produce anything and where will we find any free time?"

"Here behind barbed wire," answers Braun, who joins us. "Where have you been? I thought you were coming to the round table," he asks, disturbed. "We wanted to take our dry clothes," Siegfried quickly answers for me. "No Braun," I admit, "we were discussing the future and forgot about the time." "Every discussion is fruitful, unless it is just gossip. Are you coming with me now? It is just about 4:00 P.M.," he says, turning to go. "Naturally." I get up. "But I want Siegfried there too." "I'm coming." Siegfried laughs and toddles behind.

After Braun's interesting lecture and following dinner, I play a very fun-filled ping-pong match with Siegfried and then go to the reading room while Siegfried brings out the sweat in another partner. Somewhat bored, I leaf through an old magazine, amazed at the advertisements for automobile companies and feeling pure envy toward the Americans swelling up in me.

I am hindered by the advertisement of a photo company. Even a second translation shows there is no other conclusion. There it stands under a photograph by an amateur: three American soldiers with their helmets in their hands on the grave of their fallen comrade and nothing more and nothing less. "You can make these same kind of pictures with our camera, you just have to buy one and so on and so on."

"Yes, is there really such a thing?" I think out loud. "Yes," says Kunze behind me. "Even that too is America." "Don't they understand the lack of piety?" I shove a stool toward Kunze. "They are realists and make business even with sorrow. Even mortuaries advertise for their caskets." He laughs, untroubled.

"What is right and what is wrong?" I ask. "It is nothing more than pig swill from the photo company. But the government cannot do anything about it because they respect the freedom of everyone. It is up to the individual people what they do with their freedom," he explains.

"What is your occupation, Kunze?" I ask and ponder the sympathetic face of the thirty-year-old corporal. "Industrial salesman. I had just finished training and wanted to begin to earn money." He scratches himself under the chin. "Let's have a smoke, Kunze, we have much in common. Are you married?" I ask and pass him my tobacco sack. "Thank you." He reaches into his pocket. "I don't care for the Arizona dust. No, I am not married. But I do have a fiancée waiting for me in Germany."

"Will she wait for you?" I begin to be interested in him. "Possibly, that is, I hope so." He laughs, somewhat uncertain. "But you should know that." "Calm yourself, I know. But you can't say that to everyone, otherwise they will consider you an idiot. For most men the girls and even wives are only there for their pleasure. When they become old, then they make them cleaning women until they die," he pours out. "You still have parents?" I ask quietly. "Yes," he readily answers. "My fiancée is with them since her parents were killed at the beginning of 1944. We are from Schweinfurt, you know, ball bearing industry, the thorn in the eye of the English." "Then she is well cared for and you don't need to worry about her." I rejoice for him. "No, my father's job was decentralized in 1943. They are all together in a small town in Bavaria." He laughs happily. "They too are subjects of the Americans." I close the topic and we retire to the barracks together to go to bed.

*6 June 1945*

The work detail of students and salesmen rolls out of the camp. It is Wednesday and just like any other day the sun stands in the east full of promise.

They will put it to us today, I think, as the truck of Mr. Roy Watson heads toward the city of Greeley. For the first time the way to work goes through the city. As always we have our bread in the box, while a small shadow in our stomachs longs for the time to eat. But now we have reached the first houses of Greeley and we forget our hunger. Really a very nice farmer's village. Framed by well-cared-for lawns and weeping willows stand cute, white-painted family houses whose small windows look out through the screens like blinded eyes. But otherwise they are inviting and in front of every house on the well-kept asphalt street stands a pretentious automobile such as we never saw in Europe.

"That would be something, to take a wagon like that into the Rocky Mountains for the weekend." Kunze nudges me. "And one of the pretty little kittens in a colorful sweater who can drive you wild with desire." "That would be something for my father's son," Siegfried exclaims so that even the weeping willows shake.

"We are only slaves, you idiot, how can you express such wishes." The pastor cuffs at him. "Take your eyes away from the backsides of these dolls, when you speak to me as a pastor." Siegfried pulls his leg as he actually stares at a curvaceous being as we depart the city.

"Mr. Watson said you should hoe out the small ones and leave the large ones," Siegfried translates the farmer's wish to the pastor. "Tell him he can smell my behind. It is always that the little ones must die. But now I have control of the situation and this time the large ones are going to have to pay the price." The former tank terror forgets his role as a priest and actually does hoe down the large beets, at which a hail of curses escapes the farmer's mouth. "You fire me when my work does not please you," the pastor screams in anger.

"What did you say?" Watson asks, upset. "You can fire him when you are not pleased," Siegfried translates quickly. Without a word, the farmer turns his back on the prisoners and stomps toward the guard. Together they come back along the pastor's row. As they reach the former tank driver, pandemonium seems to break out as twenty-four men surround them with their hoes. "OK, take it easy, it is all right. Take it easy and continue," the guard says, lowering his weapon and going back to his old place. Cursing, the farmer looks back. There is strength in unity, also in this land, is the conclusion of this episode.

At lunch time Mr. Watson is a changed man. We have worked hard for him. In thanks he treats us to an ice cold orange soda. The guard sacrifices his cigarettes. Contentedly we doze in the shadow of the cool barn. How soon it will be 1:00 P.M.

"If we have reached the irrigated section by 4:00 P.M., the farmer will take us home," Siegfried screams across the large field and scares everyone out of their groveling in the sugar beets. The eyes of the men wander along the deep green rows assessing what still needs to be done. "That's nearly two hundred yards," the first offer their guess. "We can do it." A few are already excited. "We cannot show what we can really accomplish; otherwise tomorrow they will expect more of us," warn the cautious. "Dig in, you lumpheads; before the others get back to camp, we will have showered and eaten," they respond convincingly.

Ten minutes before four o'clock the truck rumbles from the field. Greeley lies like it is dead in the gleaming sun. Whistling, we return to the camp.

"Water is the gift of God," Kunze says as he hurries under the shower. "But to drink it continuously is no good," the pastor instructs. "We learned to treasure it in Alençon; what do you think, Helmut?" Siegfried shoots out like an arrogant youth. "I don't remember; otherwise I have bad dreams," I reply through the thick soap suds. "I came from Marseille to Cherbourg; no one needs to explain anything to me." Kunze winks. "Shut up, or tomorrow I will go wild and tear out the sugar beets," someone cracks from the corner. "America be praised, the land of water and sugar beets," the pastor says, festively wrapping a towel around his hips and tapping out a few rumba steps with his wooden sandals.

A few minutes later in the dining hall we sing the song, "I am in love with Erika, just like Columbus with America." "You won't be in love any more," the mess sergeant mumbles, depressed. "Why? Did you put too much salt in the soup?" we ask, untroubled. "Today we received only two small potatoes and one herring for each person," he answers, proceeding to dish it out. "The bums, the swindlers, we won't do one thing tomorrow," swells the anger immediately throughout the hall. "It is worse," as the cook throws the herring onto the plates. "The canteen does not have any more tobacco and in the future one pack is to last us for fourteen days." "Then we will refuse to work," is the total commentary.

"Be reasonable," the camp spokesman warns us that evening as the majority vote to strike. "What can they do to us? No food, no work, that's logical," say our hotheads matter-of-factly. "They can't do anything more to us if we are united because the farmers need us," is my view. "Then the company leader and camp spokesman should go to the commander and lay out the situation. We are willing to work, but we want something to eat," Kunze joins in. "That is a suggestion that we can get a hold of," agrees Siegfried. "That's the way it should be," concludes the entire company.

At 9:00 A.M. our company leader reports the results of the discussion with the other companies and the position of the camp spokesman. "It is not possible to form a united position with all the companies. The Austrians in camp are opposed to any threat of strike. The majority is also against refusing to work at present. The camp spokesman has guaranteed that in the morning he will speak with the commander about the possibility of a strike and indicate what that would mean for the farmers. He urges us to go to work, explain our situation to the farmers, and try to do the best work we can. He believes if the colonel is unwilling to agree with them, then the farmers themselves will persuade him. In this region there is no work force to replace us except a few Mexicans that we meet here and there in the fields. Every day the beets will grow longer. The next thing they need to do is water them with the stored water from the Rocky Mountains. All of the advantages are on our side. Even if it comes to sending us to a punishment camp, they will have to bring in other prisoners from far away. But that will cost time and money and if they are not given anything to eat, then the whole circus will start again. So, comrades, go out tomorrow, make the farmer angry, and you will see that we will receive our food," the company leader ends his wise counsel, and, comforted, we all retire to bed.

### 16 June 1945

The pressure on the farmers has worked wonders. Not that we have had a great feast, but at least a minimum for existence is assured. But in return, the quotas are raised, something that cautious people could see coming. The incentive to return earlier to camp resulted in a number of groups returning to camp by 3:00 P.M. The Austrians, who normally were quite lazy, are especially industrious. No wonder then that the Americans, with their keen sense of business, reach such conclusions.

In the meantime, the newspapers have poisoned the whole atmosphere with their reports of the German concentration camps, about whose existence we had no idea. We knew that Hitler locked up those who spoke against him, but the gassing and complete destruction of the Jewish people in the lands controlled by the Third Reich was not known to anyone among us. But now we have to bear the consequences of the inhumane crimes, even though it surpasses our understanding to believe that these atrocities happened.

To help us understand, today we do not go to work, but must view a film that was made by the Allies as they liberated the German concentration camps. If one had been able to film the rage of the plague or cholera in the dark Middle Ages, then every mortal person on this earth would be inclined to doubt the reality of what we saw and pass it off as hate propaganda. Some among us maintain that they saw such burned corpses in Germany after the attacks with phosphorus bombs. Also the Polish officers that Germans found in Katyn are supposed to have looked like that.

Personally, however, I distance myself as a German and a soldier from now on through all eternity from this Thousand-Year Reich with all of its lies, inhumanity, and accomplices who knowingly carried out and covered up these beastlike atrocities. But as an individual, I am ashamed to my bones to be a human being.

* * *

All prisoners of war in the United States were required to view a twenty-five-minute film on German atrocities. While many, like Helmut, were obviously shaken by the portrayal and accepted the film as a truthful depiction of inhumane crimes committed in the name of Germany, other prisoners could not believe their countrymen were guilty of the mass murder depicted in the film and were convinced it was the work of Hollywood propagandists. Some felt that the atrocities had been committed by Russians on Germans or, as suggested in this passage by Helmut's comrades, by the Russians against the Polish officers at Katyn.

After the Soviet Union moved in to occupy eastern Poland when Germany attacked Poland in 1939, Soviet forces took approximately 250,000 Polish prisoners of war. In the spring of 1940, 10,000 officers, approximately 45 percent of the total of the Polish land officers' corps at that time, and 5,000 Polish intellectuals and others disappeared. They had been held by the Soviets in camps in Kozel'sk, Ostashkov, and Starobel'sk until April 1940; however, their trace ended several miles west of Smolensk in the Soviet Union. After Germany invaded the Soviet Union, German troops found mass graves of the Polish officers and others executed by the Soviets. Some of the graves were twelve layers deep with bodies. Photographs of the exhumed bodies were taken and Germany publicized the finding in an attempt to drive a wedge between the Soviet Union and its allies. The pictures of the bodies of Polish officers killed at Katyn do resemble pictures of dead victims killed at such concentration camps as Dachau, Auschwitz, Bergen-Belsen, and other locations.[8]

* * *

*27 June 1945*

The uncertainty continues to hold body and spirit prisoner. No glimmer of hope penetrates the frightened hearts of the misused creatures. A lamentable horror burdens the days of the prisoners. Only the work saves us from doubt and insanity.

For the second time today we climb off the truck of the farmer Miller and follow Kunze, who carries our box of lunch provisions into a shed while the farmer summons the guard inside the farmhouse. Silently each one of us takes our bread from the box and crouches in the dim light of the shed. Beaten down, we stare after a few minutes with hungry eyes at our blistered hands. Suddenly the farmer stands in the doorway. "I have meat and bread for all of you in the cupboard," he says, pointing excitedly to the darkest corner of the shed where a dust-covered wardrobe stands. "Divide it up and eat quickly; the guard is drinking a beer," he stammers and then disappears as suddenly as he came.

With a turn of the hand, the wardrobe is opened to reveal a large bucket on top of which lies a fork. As hungry as wolves, we quickly divide the tasty meat among us and stuff in the bread afterward. A pitcher of cold orange juice comes at the end of a wonderful meal. As the guard looks after his charges, we are all grunting contentedly.

"Are the provisions better in camp now?" the farmer asks me as he takes a pack of Camels out of his pocket. "There is simply too little," I answer as I reach into the package. "The commander said that the reduction in the provisions is an order from Washington and must be strictly adhered to. If we farmers give you something to eat, then we run the risk that we will not get any more prisoners," he says trustingly. "We know that, and for that reason we are not angry with the people, but who works should eat," I say bitterly.

"At the beginning, we believed that it was our captured soldiers that Hitler allowed to starve. For that reason, the entire country was in an uproar because we would see German prisoners here everyday that were well fed and well clothed. Did you know anything about these atrocities?" he asks anxiously.

\* \* \*

Farmers were given specific written instructions from the camp commander at Greeley on how to handle German prisoners of war.

### INSTRUCTIONS FOR PERSONS USING PRISONER OF WAR LABOR IN YOUR COUNTY— APPROVED BY CAMP COMMANDER, GREELEY, COLORADO

1.  Prisoners of War are accustomed to orders. Give your orders to the German leader in charge of the detail. In giving these orders don't be rough or abusive about it. If the Prisoners of War don't do the task assigned or are troublesome, call the Camp Commander or his representative. Merely call him and ask him to come out. Don't state you are having trouble. Most of you are on party lines.
2.  Have the work to do. Have the equipment to do it with. Have the work

laid out. Don't have the prisoner waiting on you. If you can't do the above, Prisoners of War will be pulled out of the field and given to somebody who will.

3.    In using Prisoners of War, keep your mouth shut. Don't explain trouble over the telephone. Don't explain it to neighbors or other people. Don't permit newspaper reporters to gather information. Send them to the camp commander or his representative for information. Any person found releasing such information will have Prisoners of War removed from the field. In all cases, call the camp commander or his representatives.

4.    Don't try to gain information from Prisoners of War.

5.    Don't talk to Prisoners of War except in line of duty. You should not fraternize with Prisoners of War or allow a third person to do so. If you do fraternize with them and then there is an escape, your action might tend to make it appear you had helped him to escape. Helping a Prisoner of War to escape is a criminal offense.

6.    Everyone must understand that Prisoners of War are enemy nationals. What might appear to be innocent conversation and small favors may in reality prove to be actions of treason.
DON'T EVER BELIEVE A PRISONER OF WAR LIKES YOU. HE DOESN'T.
DON'T BELIEVE THAT A PRISONER OF WAR LIKES TO WORK FOR YOU. HE WORKS BECAUSE HE IS ORDERED TO WORK.

7.    Do not try to discipline Prisoners of War on the job. That is the camp commander's job and right. (Refer to section 1 above.)

8.    Do not take any written letters, slips of paper or packages from a Prisoner of War. All this matter must be censored by the Armed Service.

9.    Don't think a Prisoner of War won't escape if he can. He will. YOU ARE RESPONSIBLE FOR THE SECURITY OF THE PRISONER OF WAR AS THE ARMED GUARDS.
You should make your telephone available to the guard so that he may phone the camp commander or his representative at any time.

10.   Do not give Prisoners of War anything.

11.   Inform your civilian employees and others who may come in contact with your Prisoners of War labor of the instructions you have to follow and insist that your instructions be followed.

12.   The War Department expects your cooperation in the above matter. Failure on your part to follow these instructions and other instructions given by the military authorities may result in the cancellation of your contract and a refusal of the War Department to furnish Prisoners of

War for labor on your farm.

13. If you want your detail, be on time. If you are late, your prisoners will be assigned to somebody else. Prisoners are as anxious as anybody else to start work on time.

14. Get your Prisoners of War labor from your labor manager not the Prisoners of War camp commander. The camp commander cannot assign prisoners to anyone.

15. All farmers hauling Prisoners of War to and from work daily should be very careful to follow all traffic regulations. You are expected to use reasonable precaution in hauling prisoners. An injured prisoner is unable to work.

16. Use horse sense. Do not allow this memoranda to fall into the hands of Prisoners of War.

17. No woman, under any circumstances, will be allowed in any field where there are Prisoners of War.[9]

* * *

"These revelations came like a bolt of lightning out of the blue sky for us. We really had no idea about these horrors. It is even hard for us to believe these things because we were soldiers abroad and had to conduct ourselves properly." I explain to him our situation. "Something like that would be impossible in this land." He shakes his head. "And if tomorrow you laid a board fence around the camp and would allow us to starve to death slowly, who would then know what happens to us?" I offer as an example. "It would not remain buried to us because as free citizens we have the right to stick our noses into everything, even where it stinks," he says proudly. "In Germany we only had the right to elect the scoundrels. Afterward the people had no rights."

Around 5:00 P.M. the guard calls us to the truck. Ten minutes later the truck rumbles through Greeley. A young lady completely clothed in white—hat, dress, and gloves—steers a magnificent Packard behind us. For us prisoners, a picture from a dream. As we cross the railroad tracks, we must stop. She pulls the Packard up close to us. "How are you, my landspeople?" The lady smiles as she lifts her hand. While nearly everyone nods to her friendly, the pastor speaks. "We are hungry, mother," he says with a face that could move mountains. "Hunger?" stammers the nice lady, in shock as though someone had hit her. "Don't you happen to have a piece of dry bread for us?" the pastor continues, even worse than before. "I don't have anything at all with me," she responds, confused, as the truck begins to roll across the tracks.

"Aren't you ashamed of yourself that you scared that nice lady so badly?"

A number jump on the pastor. "You are all stupid," he defends himself. "She will tell other people about it and when there is really something as far as freedom and democracy is concerned with the people here, then the good citizens in this beautiful town of Greeley will make sure that in the evening our plates are once again full."

After this sermon in the wagon, no one doubts the wisdom of the pastor and everyone seems to be busy with their own thoughts as the lady continues to follow us in her automobile until the truck turns right from the road into the camp. Once again she raises her white-gloved hand. Thankfully we wave back for this friendly gesture. "Mother," the pastor says, "ja, if only mothers ruled the world. ..."

Out of the shower streams hot and cold water so that everyone can mix it as he pleases. The bodies of the men under the shower shimmer like old gold. Our flesh and bones are healthy, but our souls are sick, unbelievably sick from the many disappointments of an untruthful world.

"Scrub my back, Siegfried," I ask my friend because it is more comfortable and because we have always done it this way. "Once again we have skin like leather," says Siegfried. "We can thank the American water and last but not least the comrades from Camp Gruber who provided us with such a rich treasure of toilet articles." I laugh, proud with our well-cared-for look. "So," says Kunze, "we are clean. Now pass me the jar of Pond's Cream and the after-shave lotion so that we smell good." "Do you remember, Siegfried, how we smelled in Alençon?" I say with a changed face.

"Do you know, Helmut, if you had not gotten us some extra food by selling those rings, I believe I would have starved to death." "Now that is all past, Siegfried. So bad as we had it then, we will not experience again." I set free the terrible memories. "It could not have been any worse there than in Marseille." Kunze fastens his belt. "But I hear that you secured food by selling rings? Did one of you have diamonds?" Kunze asks. "And what for diamonds." Now the joy over our success returns. "Tell me friends, I am as curious as an old woman," Kunze pushes, and we are very willing to accommodate.

As we enter the dining hall, Kunze continues to laugh. "That was quite an accomplishment." He finally quiets himself and reaches for his utensils. "This is good ham," says Siegfried and licks his tongue on the thin strips of ham with fried potatoes and lettuce salad and an apple that constitutes our evening meal. "They only give us enough of these good things that we must leave the table half crazy." I shove the empty plate away from me in anger.

"That is the method of punishment of the primitives! And in doing so they cut their own fingers. Otherwise we would have worked twice as fast and twice as good," is Siegfried's opinion. "We still work more than the Mexicans. Did you see how far back they were last Monday? The farmer is very envious of Mr. Bean because we leave his Mexicans behind," Kunze interjects. "We are dumber than they," Siegfried comments and collects the empty plates.

After two chess games we leave the recreation room to go for a chat. The sun has just disappeared behind the highest peaks of the Rocky Mountains but there is a gold tint still on the glaciers. "We had a real great guard with us in the field," a man from our barracks opens with a well-loved prisoner theme. "First of all everyone received two cigarettes; then we went to work while he drove the farmer's truck to the city. At noon he appeared in the farmhouse with a large basket of bread. Mr. Jonson, the farmer, donated three gallons of milk and let us lie under his porch until 2:00 P.M." "The guards are by and large good fellows," a command sergeant from Alençon concurs. "Recently we had one with us that got a kick when the bull in a neighboring pasture looked at a cow," another remembers with fondness. "Boys, I can tell you when you come to Tomson you will pop your buttons off your pants. He has a daughter that otherwise you would only meet in a dream," another says lustily. "Yesterday I saw one in Greeley that nearly took my breath away. Such a pair of breasts," another exclaims in ecstasy. "Let's go to bed, otherwise it will get thicker," says the command sergeant. "Let us at least talk about it." Siegfried grins, enthused about the theme. "Save your strength, you can use it at home." Kunze laughs at him. "In the meantime others will comfort them." Another winks cynically.

"At the moment it looks pretty shitty for us. On Saturday they will show us a film about life in Alaska. It may be that we will land there." Another paints the devil on the wall. "What are we going to do during the winter?" asks Siegfried in the circle. "In the Rocky Mountains there are branch camps; perhaps we will be transferred there to cut wood," says the command sergeant. "Then good night, gentlemen; in the meantime we are still thinning sugar beets." The crowd separates and each man goes to his own bed.

### 1 July 1945

As we climb onto the trucks, a surprise awaits those who sailed on board the *Thomas Marshall* from Cherbourg to New York and had to surrender their *Soldbuchs*. The *Soldbuchs* have arrived in Colorado and will be distributed to their owners by the camp spokesman at the company office.

I thumb through the book, whose absence in Oklahoma caused me to be separated from Hocker and Schulz, left Siegfried with me, and finally brought me together with Kunze, whom I regard quietly for days as my friend. Nearly every day he demonstrates his affection for me in his own reserved way and I too am very sympathetic toward him. Last night he confided to me that he is a former member of the SS. I promised to help him remove his blood type tattoo from under his arm with a needle and condensed milk, if possible, or if necessary, a razor blade. This binds us even more closely in these days of dark secrets.

Naturally Siegfried is initiated into our closed group, but only after I am able to allay Kunze's doubts during the course of the day. It would have been simply a breach of trust toward Siegfried, since he, like me, cares for Kunze; I need his help; and finally there is no fear that he would betray Kunze.

When I return to the barracks, I carry my *Soldbuch* in my hand. Still lost in thought, I make no move to take my swimsuit from the window sill as usual. This seems to bother Kunze and Siegfried.

"Are you thinking to make use of your passbook?" Siegfried rasps after a minute of silence. "Do you want to get rid of me when you ask something like that?" I respond with a twinkle in my eye.

"You have the possibility to spend the rest of your time as a prisoner without doing any work. No one would blame you. In fact just the opposite. Why should we hack sugar beets for the Yankees? They give neither us nor our families in the homeland enough to eat," Kunze suggests with a shrug of the shoulders. "I will tell you something, men. The work in the fields is good medicine for us. If they had not pulled that trick on us with the *Soldbuchs*, we would all be in Oklahoma picking cotton. But fate chose another course for us and we already know why. I am very sorry that I lost Hocker and Schulz, but did I really lose them? Certainly not! The time we were together has only ended. Our hearts and souls are always together, just like with our family to whom we are even more bonded the greater the distance we are from them. Siegfried, we have not forgotten Briller, even if we don't speak of him everyday. But why should I make a big speech? They have just whistled for our pay and I need a few things very badly from the canteen. That's why I am going to thin sugar beets on Monday, not because of your beautiful eyes, that now stare so dumb." I laugh from the bottom of my heart and shove my easily confused friends out of the barracks.

At 4:45 P.M. I am a rich prisoner of war. I now possess $21.60 for thirty-six workdays. Naturally they are not real dollars, of which half of mankind dreams, but coupons for which I can only purchase things in the camp. But no beer and no cigarettes. Since the end of the war tobacco ration cards have been introduced, just like in old Europe. Still there is a brisk business in the canteen, since there is still plenty to buy. And what brave soldier does not think of his suffering loved ones when he looks at it all. It is a paradox that in our present camp, when our return home seems so remote, every comb, sewing needle, fine toilet soap, skin cream, and such things are purchased in great quantities. But in the first place, what else can we do with the hard-earned money? And in the second place there glows a flame of hope in the furthermost corners of our hearts that one day we will see our homeland again. That is why on payday everyone goes shopping and those items meant for the dear family members are buried in the bottom of the sea sack like a treasure. Even we three friends are no exception.

After dinner thick clouds of cigarette smoke hang in the barracks so that it is nearly impossible to remain inside. A glance in the recreation room is enough to quickly close the door. The table tennis is occupied and surrounded by those waiting. Because of our unnecessary chatter, we have missed the opportunity to find a suitable location. Only the latrine, in which is located the shower and washrooms, lies lonesome in the dim glimmer of the camp lights. The moment is right. The operation can begin.

While I sterilize a needle over the flame of the alcohol containing after-shave lotion and Siegfried stands ready with the salve, Kunze works on bringing the condensed milk we took from breakfast to a simmer. His heater is next to mine in the shower room and consists of a can into which is poured a bottle of after-shave lotion and in which a smaller can holding the milk is placed. The can is wrapped with wire and stretched out long to serve as a handle. Finally we are ready. Kunze stretches out on the damp floor of the shower room, his head resting on his underarm. I work the stone into the shape of a zero and cover the arm with a linen cloth soaked in the milk. I stick the needle through the cloth into the skin, following the dark circle so that the milk can dissolve the mark of Cain. After some time the whole process is over. Now we wait to see if it is successful. It is important for Kunze that no one notice the plaster under his arm which, in these depressed days, if discovered by a half-crazy could lead to serious trouble. After our work, we try to ease our nerves by walking around the camp.

"What shall we do in Greeley?" Siegfried asks theatrically. "You like to watch the young girls." Kunze, who has once again found his good disposition after the recent torture, nods. "Perhaps you don't?" Siegfried demands. "Yes, indeed," I reply. "Even more than I should." "So," he snorts, almost insulted. "I feel sorry for you. It's about time to finally know for what reason a man is a man." "You always speak about men, Siegfried. Don't our girls have to go without?" Kunze censures him.

"What do you mean ours? I don't have any firm relationship, thank God. We told you something about Briller and Schulz before, but were completely still about Hocker. Women bring only sorrow. You are hardly gone and then the devil is loose. With some, the bed is not even cold before another is already lying in it," Siegfried maintains.

"You are crazy. It is obvious you have only associated with whores." Kunze sets the record straight. "Knock it off. What does that have to do with it? Let's be honest. When we are away, we are not happy alone in bed," is Siegfried's opinion, and I do not make any effort to contradict him. "You have not known true love; otherwise you would not talk such nonsense." Kunze shows his understanding of Siegfried's position.

"I don't want to cause you any pain, but perhaps you will remember my words. I can imagine that a young lady who has not heard for a long time from her fiancé takes the opportunity when it is offered. And you can be sure that they do come about." Siegfried wipes away every illusion.

"What do you think, Helmut?" Kunze turns to me and forces me to express my opinion. "Basically Siegfried is right. Only we are making the matter too light. We don't want to believe it about our own wives, but still we believe that it is possible with all the others. They are no better or worse than us. It takes both a woman and a man to make a whore. If I can use Briller as an example, we know that it was a woman who ruined him. He took revenge on her type every time he had the chance. Why shouldn't a woman take revenge when she is disillusioned? And they will be disillusioned even more than men because they are more dependent. You know how first we desire them, but how, in most cases, afterward we forget them. I say, in most cases. And now you, Kunze. Only when we are really in love, when two souls become one, is when we never forget it. Then it is love. Everything else is idle magic, which immediately flees as soon as we have our pants on again." I end my explanation.

"Even though I am abroad and across the sea, if I still did not feel certain that my Brigitte loves me just as much now as before, who knows what I would have done the evening of May 9, 1945. After the most bitter hour of my life had struck, that I can still hoe beets, I owe alone to this knowledge. She gave me the strength to want to live. If someone tries to convince me that love is purely physical, then I feel sorry for the poor wretch, because he follows his instincts like an animal without enjoying the highest pleasure, which comes when the souls and bodies of two people who share real love melt together."

After Kunze ends, we all three look up to the canvas of stars in the heavens just in time to see the light from a falling star and experience the impression that the Almighty has underscored Kunze's words with a flaming stroke. As we silently return to the barracks, I muse that Kunze is right and everything else is filth or senseless, misconstrued theories.

### 11 July 1945

"I require from you that the assigned sections will be hoed," the farmer Bousac blares threateningly around 3:00 P.M. after we have lost all desire to work and now sit on our haunches. "Do it yourself," the pastor suggests, which causes the farmer to charge off in a fit to try and stir up the guard. He simply shrugs his shoulders while a cigarette dangles from between his lips. After the farmer realizes he cannot pressure us to keep going, he offers to take us home as soon as we are finished. "Shall we show him what we can do?" Kunze asks the sweat-covered faces.

"He only gave us water which has been warm for a long time. He can hoe them himself; he had plenty to eat for lunch," is the majority response. "If we don't make the quota, we will still be sitting here at nine o'clock tonight," someone calls us back to reason. "That does not matter; what do you want to do in that pen? Here you can look as far as the eye can see and there is no barbed wire to destroy the view," our weather beagle says, who owes his name to the fact that he spent most of the war at a weather station. "What the Hell, let's get it done; otherwise they will bring in spotlights like they have done with the other groups," another suggests. "Let's go," the pastor joins in and everyone picks up his hoe.

At 4:00 P.M. we climb onto the transport while the grinning farmer closes the tailgate. Immediately we are under way, rolling away from the sugar beet fields that shimmer as though struck by a thousand bolts of lightning.

"We served the skinflint." Siegfried laughs maliciously. "We handled him today like we did the drunken Polinsky last Tuesday." The pastor rubs his hands together as the wagon leaves the road and follows a path through the field. "What does that mean?" the rest of us wonder.

After a short trip the guard says, "Start work again," pointing to a badly overgrown sugar beet field. "Sit still," bellows the staff sergeant. "We are not dumb boys who are promised something and not given it." "Come on." The guard waves, pointing to his watch. "You have to work until five o'clock." "Kiss our asses," the pastor screams. "Shut up and start work right now," replies the bored guard as he plays with his rifle.

"There's no reason to resist. Others put us into the mess and now we have to deal with it," I warn them so as not to allow the matter to come to a head. "I suggest we get out and thresh the field short and small," Siegfried offers. "Good," is the rumbling threat rising out of the pastor's breast, "but where I touch, no beets will grow again."

Shortly after five o'clock the hoes are thrown onto the wagon as the farmer watches with a hamster-like grin. "You worked hard, you stupid krauts," he mocks us as we follow the hoes. Still we laugh, satisfied because tomorrow when the sun is shining his first glance at his sugar beet fields will be an eye opener.

Dinner consists only of sour milk and three boiled potatoes. The dissatisfaction mounts quickly. "Either something to eat or no more work," is the sentiment of the noncommissioned officers, and it infests nearly the entire camp. Only the Austrians give it the cold shoulder.

"The Americans told us if we work hard, they will soon send us home," is their argument against a strike. "If we don't work, then they will send us home even sooner. They won't get rid of good workers," is the opposite point of view offered by the noncommissioned officers. "Neither good nor bad work, neither strike nor submission, instead following the golden middle road will lead us to better food and to home," the cautious maintain.

The camp leader suggests to our barracks, "If you listen to me, you will go to work this week. I do not believe the commander is to blame for the sparse rations even though it is maintained that he can direct the camp however he wants, the barracks are his private possession, and he is the kingpin of the sugar beet factories. There is no proof for all of these rumors. We know that there are farmers who hate the factory bosses because they are dependent on them. But that is none of our business. They carry water on both sides and are free-born citizens, while because we lost the war, we are booty for our former enemies. A united action against the hunger rations is not possible in this camp, and if we pursue it we will be the stupid ones. The camp leadership is of the opinion that the prisoners whose service grades are unconfirmed are sympathetic to a meeting. We can be sure that they have already thought about what they are going to do with us. Personally, it is my opinion that now we are experiencing the consequences of the German concentration camps and therefore we should respond only with less productive work which we can attribute to poor nutrition. That is the way we can achieve what we want: more to eat."

"I am still as convinced as ever that we have to show the Americans that we would rather be destroyed than be enslaved," our rabble rouser begins another speech. "It is clear that the camp commander has to submit reports to his superiors. When he writes that the German prisoners are quiet and productive despite the shortage of food, then the Americans will think they can experiment with us anyway they want. We have already seen the third film about fishing, timbering, and fur trapping in Alaska. The thought will not leave me that one of these days we will be, like the Afro-Americans, second-class American citizens. In the grand scheme of politics, it looks like the Americans and the Russians will come out very well. If it stays that way, then the victors will depopulate Germany and scatter us to the four winds. History will then record that they and those who came later sanctioned how we were handled. Man has a right to his homeland. That is why we must never tire of taking every opportunity to further that right. In the reading room lies a newspaper which contains a small notice: 'Send the threat home, they don't work, only eat our food, and stand united with the German officers and noncommissioned officers regarding what should happen in the States.' You see out there, our conception is right when we maintain that they will never release a good worker. In about three weeks the beets will be hoed. Then we have missed the opportunity. If we simply disappear in the wilds of the Rocky Mountains or Alaska, then there is no sense for rebellion. No rooster will crow if they allow us to starve. That is why I am in favor of an immediate strike. Tomorrow evening it will be reported in the local newspaper and the next day in all newspapers. People will talk about us, reporters will come, the churches will join us, and you will see that they must serve us chicken for breakfast. Comrades! We are in a free land! Throw off the yoke of subservience. We deserve the sympathy of this free people; we are industrious, clean, and reliable, which the farmers confirm every day and which our guards can underscore."

Impressed by the speech of the paratrooper staff sergeant, the noncommissioned company is all the more disposed to refuse to work. But while we are busy drafting a resolution to the commander, a rumor makes the rounds that transfers will be made from the camp in the next few days. The camp spokesman confirms that he has seen a transfer list and that a sergeant confided in him that the disruptive element of the camp would disappear. There is no doubt who will be sent into the desert.

### 17 July 1945

After we deliver the work clothes and bedding to the clothing building, Siegfried, Kunze, and I return to the barracks and tie our already packed sea sacks. Travel fever simmers around us. In the rafters of the barracks hangs the dense and sweet smell of countless cigarettes.

"I wonder where we will land this time," Siegfried says and twists himself a cigarette. "If we go north, that will be bad," Kunze mumbles while his moist, deep blue eyes look over my bed and out the window, which seems to flitter because of the heat. "Maybe we will meet Schulz and Hocker in Alaska." I play with the possibility as it sends a shudder up and down my spine. "Damn it anyway, don't drive yourself crazy. And if so, bread will be baked in Alaska. Perhaps in the meantime Hocker got the recipe for bear bacon, then nothing can go wrong," Siegfried snarls and grabs his sea sack since the whistle for assembly has just blown.

"Get out of here," screams the pastor. "I have to clean out the room. That today of all days I have barracks duty," we hear him cuss in the room for the last time as we follow Siegfried outside.

Thirty minutes later 350 noncommissioned officers climb onto the transports. "Take care and greetings for the homeland, if you should see it again," the inmates of Camp Greeley call to us as the wheels begin to turn.

At 4:00 P.M. we exchange the hard seats of the truck for the soft upholstery of the Pullman coaches. At 4:20 the train rolls out of quiet Greeley. With ever-increasing speed, we travel through the land that has drunk our sweat, while our eyes scan the green sea of sugar beets. "We do not have a permanent location anywhere," the words of Schulz come to me, which he cited during the many changes of camps in Cherbourg.

"We are headed north." Kunze rips me from my silent contemplation. He is afraid it is Alaska, I think, and choose not to look into his sad eyes since the sound of his voice has already upset me.

"That doesn't mean anything. We have been traveling only for an hour." I laugh out of the window as I stare at the eerie forms of the Rocky Mountains, along whose foot we travel. "A wonderful mountain range," Siegfried praises in his carefree manner, which does make my heart lighter. "It is because of Brigitte," Kunze registers after a pause, as he takes a photo out of his wallet and stares at it like he has lost the world. "You will see her again." I force a smile and open my tobacco pouch. It is funny, I think, this Brigitte is not actually pretty in so far as one can judge from her photo, and yet he hangs on her like a blind man.

"Cheyenne, Wyoming." He points with his index finger on the window as we look out at the gentle view of a city after the train makes a sharp right turn. "Now our course is eastward," Siegfried offers, as the golden beams of the evening sun lie in his rust-red hair, lighting it like hammered copper. "So nothing will come of a meeting with our old friends. If we were going to Alaska we must go west over the mountains to the Pacific Ocean," I say to Kunze's relief.

"If they would only take this damn uncertainty away." He cracks his fingers. "They probably don't know themselves what they are going to do with us," Siegfried titters. "They know for certain. They will work us until we break," another mixes in unnecessarily from the seat across from us. "Dead workers have no value." I laugh at him. "If it has to do with Germans, then yes!" He nods rapidly. "Don't talk nonsense," Kunze snaps at him, and he turns away, insulted.

"A black picture is always painted. It twists a person when there seems to be no end," Kunze sulks. "They say such nonsense only for people to convince them otherwise. Or do you think they believe it themselves?" I shake the returning feeling of discomfort from me.

"Then they should keep their mouths shut." Kunze gives a hostile glance at the blabber mouth, who responds by giving him the finger. "They are three conceited apes," he snaps to his neighbor. "They will have their asses ripped off when the trees fall." He looks with dumb cow eyes at us as the light in the coach is turned on. "Do you mean that nothing can happen to your wood chopper's face?" Siegfried jokes with him. "The buzzards will eat you because you will destroy yourself through your presumptuousness." He spoils it for all of us. "But only because of the smell of your ass," I throw at him. "You perfumed bastard," he responds loudly enough to bring silence throughout the entire coach. "I know that you are saving your money instead of buying soap, so that you can enlarge your manure pile at home," I hit back since it is known the man was thrown out of the barracks in Oklahoma because he never washed.

"You had your red feedbag in the Le Mans Nazi company. Now where do you stand?" His bitterness overflows. "You were in the party yourself, you vulture," the pastor comes unexpectedly to my help. "I was forced to," he defends himself and everyone laughs. "Thank you, pastor." I wink at the Bavarian. "Keep an eye on him, that sort talks too much in order to cover their own filth," he says so loud and clear that the others crawl inside themselves.

In the meantime night has fallen. Stars blink in the blue heaven over the silent plain. Only here and there in the distance the lights of a lonely farm shimmer. The heads of the tired men fall on their breasts. Sleep demands its rights and gives the confused soul rest.

*21 July 1945*

On the morning of the fourth day of our trip we detrain in Fort Du Pont, Delaware. Thank God, the monotonous train ride is behind us. Nothing, absolutely nothing of note occurred. Only a gigantic land from the Rocky Mountains to the Atlantic Ocean, from Camp Greeley to Fort Du Pont. Now we stand next to the track and look at the white-painted, two-story barracks of a U.S. training camp where young soldiers assemble in ranks.

"We are finished with that nonsense forever." I watch the men who respond automatically like robots to every command given in the sweltering heat that practically takes our breath away.

"If we had won the war, we could be in Russia commanding lice." Kunze turns his back on the recruits in training. "How we have changed our outlook," Siegfried observes and wonders himself about the realization. "We went to a hard school, Siegfried." I laugh at him almost joyfully.

"If we were to be released, you could hang my diploma in the latrine for all I care," he responds dryly. "We are once again on the Atlantic; all we need is a boat. In twelve days we could be in Germany." I build a dream castle.

On the grounds in front of the two-story barracks of the prisoner of war camp—Fort Du Pont—we stand in five rows with shirts soaked with sweat listening to the greeting of the obese camp spokesman. "Consider yourselves embraced, you millions from Adolf's army, and enjoy yourselves with us. In the mess hall is an egg for each of you, potato salad, and all the peanut butter you want. Don't forget the salt tablets because sweat is cheap here. Watch out for the mosquitoes because they carry malaria; that is the reason for the screens on the windows. I will show you the barracks after you eat."

"This spokesman is a lusty noodle." We nod to each other as we enter the shady mess hall, receive the small portion from the mess sergeant, and find a free place to sit. Large cans of peanut butter are on every table.

"Boys, boys, this is a humid, hot climate," Kunze moans and strips off his khaki shirt. "In the sweat of your brow you will earn your daily bread," I quote from the Bible.

"Unfortunately more sweat than bread." Siegfried laughs and helps me off with my dress shirt. "I wonder what kind of work they do in this camp?" "You can't work here, it is just like a sauna." Kunze refuses to believe. "Just wait, they will whisper it in our ear." Siegfried wipes the theme from the table and stuffs his mouth with peanut butter.

After we have found a place in the second story of the barracks, we look up our friends in the washroom and find a recently vacated basin where we can shave. Then we shower and wash off the dust from our journey. A half hour later we lie in a deep sleep on the beds while the hot sun nearly brings steam from the ocean water.

In the evening we assemble for roll call and the veil around our future activity is lifted. "The newly arrived people have been sent here to fight mosquitoes," the German camp spokesman reveals to us in the presence of a U.S. officer. "We have permission for a rest day tomorrow, so that the work will not begin until Monday. Saturday is inspection and the entire camp must be cleaned. After roll call is dinner, and afterward I need your names, etc. Come to the office in groups so that we can take care of it without any friction."

After dinner we lie behind the barracks in the grass and Siegfried says out of the blue: "I don't like that fellow at all with his stupid talk about the Nazi company. There are perhaps a hundred men among us who were not in Alençon. The transfer here came not without a reason. We will soon find out if they have sent informants with us."

"I hope you are wrong; it is no secret that we were the agitators in Greeley. Do you think the Americans are asleep? I am not concerned that we were members of a Nazi company because other German officers and noncommissioned officers were assigned to them. No one can expect of us that we knew personally those to whom we gave our oath of loyalty. It is not a crime to be a German. I freely acknowledge that to a specific time period I believed in victory. Whoever denies that today is a coward who lowers himself even in the eyes of the victors. The victors would dirty their own hands if they seized those who have been misused and are not personally guilty of anything. We blamed the blabber mouth on the train because he could not find any other method of escape. That is why he wanted to shut us up with these memories. By the way, he was in the Party. That is all too filthy for me. If the Americans also think that way, they will kick everyone in the behind that comes to him to implicate a comrade." I open my thoughts to Siegfried.

"The transfer cannot be a punishment. I like it better here than Camp Greeley. We will get used to the climate." Kunze also disagrees with Siegfried's point of view.

"You mean it is more beautiful here? In Colorado we had dry air. The Rocky Mountains were a daily joy to look upon and the work was healthy sport. Here it is damp and sultry, nothing to see, and the work is dangerous. I am afraid there will be a stink," Siegfried contradicts him. "I am not happy with the work either. To fight malaria-bearers can cause us to be infected with malaria," I agree with him. "We will see what fate has prepared for us." Kunze rises and goes into the barracks as retreat is blown in the training camp.

### 25 July 1945

After a boring Sunday, most of which we spent sleeping behind the barracks, we climb on board the trucks without any concern. The spray cans and containers of poison have already been loaded, a fat sergeant confides to us.

As the convoy starts to move, I glance at the fresh faces of those around me while a quiet anxiety troubles me. "What if we catch the dreaded malaria?" I grumble without interruption until Siegfried shoves me, asking, "What's wrong? Your face looks like you are going to a funeral," he says with laughter. "I don't like it," I continue, and look at the poor huts of the Afro-Americans, which stand between the trees almost ready to collapse. "They look hopeless." Kunze follows my eyes. In front of the huts young boys romp while the heavy-set women hang washed shirts on the clothesline. But we have reached our objective. The trucks stop at the edge of a thick woods which reaches to the edge of the village.

"Here is where the Atlantic Ocean begins." The pastor shoves his hands into his pants pockets, spits into the shallow, dirty water at our feet, and then stretches out his arm as though he is trying to pull the horizon toward land. "Over there lies Germany," he screams like an actor on stage and many pairs of eyes look out toward the line where sky and water seem to unite.

At 9:30 A.M. we fill the spray cans with the liquid poison from the containers. Like unknown beings, we speak from under the mosquito nets. Practically nothing can happen to us as long as we use the gloves and nets. There is nothing to see that is flying. We are to destroy their breeding grounds, which are on the edge of the countless ponds. We go to work.

"President Lincoln had a German in his cabinet. Schurz was the brave man's name." Siegfried grins as Kunze and I look at him in amazement after he has stretched out in the grass. "So what?" Kunze asks. "What does that have to do with your laziness?" "It has a lot to do with the situation." He nestles his head in his crossed arms. "He was opposed to slavery. That is why I am so sympathetic to the old countryman. I am also against it."

"You were not lazy in Colorado." Kunze still wonders and shakes his head in confusion while I lie down. "Get up, there are snakes, black widow spiders, and whatever else I don't know," he bids us without comfort. "Lie down, you earned your pay long ago," Siegfried encourages him. "If the guards come, then we are the stupid ones." He hesitates. "They are not that stupid that they put themselves in danger." I close my eyes and finally Kunze decides to do the same.

Around us is a quiet like we have not enjoyed for a long time. Finally alone! Finally no glance of the guard or cry of the concerned comrades. Our only witness is the silent wood in which an unknown, secret-filled life goes on that is sympathetic to us. Quietly the branches of the slender trees bend to frame the joy of three friends, who are in difficult circumstances but are drawn from consciousness into dreams.

As the sun rays slant through the roof of leaves from the west, a shrill whistle rips us from our heavenly rest. "Quitting time, gentlemen," Kunze says and springs to his feet. "Is it so late?" I ask. "It may be four o'clock," Siegfried suggests, fingering his tobacco pouch. "Don't smoke now; we have to go to the vehicles," I insist. "Good workers are the last to leave their workplace." He grins, but shoves the tobacco in his pocket and trots with us to the assembly place, where everyone arrives within ten minutes.

"We left the spray cans lying there," Kunze whispers in my ear as the guards count the group. "We must get them," I say, shocked; "otherwise we will have trouble with the sergeant." "Calm yourself, we dropped ours in the water long ago." The staff sergeant grins at me. "Are you crazy? There will be trouble for sure," I declare. "That's what we want! Do you believe they will do something to us?" the staff sergeant asks. "We slept like young Gods!" I reply with satisfaction and climb on the first truck.

The camp is busy as the returning work details turn in their equipment. "Where are the spray cans?" the sergeant screams at us in English as we push by him. "We don't understand." We laugh and pick up the tempo to get to the barracks while he is busy with others.

At evening roll call the situation comes to a head. It is not possible for the Americans to say which group did not turn in their spray cans and so they want to know from us. But 350 German prisoners of war stand as silent as the grave. "It could not be the intent of the guilty parties to bring punishment to all of you because of their foolish action." The German camp spokesman tries to change our fate after all of the efforts by the Americans have proven fruitless, including taking away our dinner. "Be calm and keep your mouth shut," is whispered through the rows until everyone realizes that there is nothing to be learned from this crowd and we are ordered to our barracks, where instead of dinner chess or cards await us.

At 7:30 P.M. the camp spokesman and the sergeant go through the barracks to try and shed some light on the matter. But everywhere they run up against icy resistance. "We returned everything we had," is the response on all sides. "Be reasonable," he begs. "The kitchen will serve the food immediately as soon as the Americans know where the spray cans were left." "He can take the snake feast to the mosquitoes," is the response to his good intentions. "You are cutting your own flesh, because you won't get anything to eat until the matter is resolved," the sergeant goes over the spokesman to play his last trump. "Tell him that we are used to hunger and while we are afraid of him, we are not willing to submit," a self-appointed spokesman responds—a man who in Alençon would slip out of the camp at night to steal milk from the French farmers and return to his comrades in the morning gray, satisfied, and loaded with rich booty.

"That is nonsense; you can't hold out. They will punish you with hard labor. Men, be sensible. Don't make the situation extreme. The Americans have enough of a sense of humor to close their eyes one time." He tirelessly continues to press the matter. "In this climate dinner is already spoiled. If we don't get any breakfast in the morning, no one needs to imagine that we will work," is the last answer to the begging and threats of the camp leadership despite the desperate situation.

"We have maneuvered ourselves into something for which we cannot take responsibility," I open the conversation after the camp spokesman and the sergeant have gone. "That's right." Those who traveled with us from Alençon nod to me.

But there is no return. We have suffered so much injustice that we simply no longer know who in the future will be right. They should send us home and stop this eternal rape of the little man.

"Do you really think we should not work in case they withhold breakfast?" is now the determining question in the sweltering room. "I am of the opinion that everyone should be allowed to decide for himself what he thinks is right; otherwise injustice would be found on our side," Kunze throws into the discussion. "What do you consider right?" asks the pastor anxiously. "As the provisions, so the work." Kunze laughs into the serious faces. "According to that I understand no food no work. Is that right?" booms the bass voice of the staff sergeant. "I have been understood," Kunze offers, satisfied.

"What will the consequences be?" Dr. Braun asks after a pause. "At the most hunger, and that we have become acquainted with again since the ninth of May," the pastor expresses, uncaring. "What do you think?" Braun turns to me. "This time I don't have an opinion, but I am willing to follow any decision like a good soldier." I dodge the responsibility.

"Then I will tell you something." Braun jumps to his feet. "I have, to this point, never been mixed up with the business of forcing people to obey. It has usually turned out right how the group has responded to the pressure of the Americans. But we cannot forget that this is possible only because of their mentality, which is prone to respect the freedom of the individual in general. You know without a doubt that this does not have anything to do with the equipment. Instead you feel yourselves misused and as human beings you resist it. Since we as the weaker also are in the wrong, it is not cowardice or crawling if we assume responsibility for what is personally explainable to me. It was a spur of the moment action born out of fatigue and hostility. If you are in agreement, I will go with the camp spokesman and explain it to the commander. He will understand and will find a way out without insisting on learning the names of those responsible for this idiocy. But I will do it only if the majority is in agreement. Otherwise I conduct myself as before and suffer the consequences with the rest of you."

"Let's go to bed, friends. At this hour no one is available anyway. 'Take, therefore, no thought for the morrow: for the morrow shall take thought for the things of itself,' " the staff sergeant closes the fruitless discussion as "lights out" is sounded.

### 26 July 1945

A cloud-filled sky accompanies the brutal heat of the assembly area at the prisoner of war camp Fort Du Pont, where at exactly 8:00 A.M. on this fate-filled day we German prisoners of war are assembled. With an unpenetrable countenance the camp spokesman stands in front of the group glancing at the gate through which the decision in the form of American officers must come. And they do come, but not alone. Nearly half a company march into the area, make a column left, and stop across from us in front of the barracks. The camp spokesman reports smartly to an officer. He returns the salute, tells us to sit on the ground, and turns to his sergeants. Minutes later they send the brash young soldiers into our quarters. "A raid," we mumble, upset, and worry about the belongings in our sea sacks.

At 9:30 A.M. it is over. The Americans have gone and we go to the mess hall for breakfast. "That went well," I say to my two companions, after we have a carton of milk and two slices of white bread smeared with orange marmalade in front of us. "Yes, if those boys didn't rob us," Kunze offers for thought and then concerns himself with the food. "Now what will happen?" Siegfried asks with full cheeks. "We will soon know," I explain as the camp spokesman enters the hall and asks for attention: "The commander has informed me that he will not seek reprisals, since he has other methods at his disposal," he begins. "Your stay here was to be temporary from the beginning. Still I will not shed a tear for any of you; then I have never met anyone as stubborn as you. My countrymen in this camp speak only with admiration for you because you have shown that you have backbone, but I consider it a folly in our camp. But it was not all in vain. After breakfast please be so good as to wash your work clothes so that other comrades will not be given them soiled. After 3:00 P.M. the room will be opened for you to turn in your bedding and other items. I will be pleased if during the day you will give the others a hand. Also, in the barracks there is some work for you to do. Early tomorrow you will be sent away, as far as I have been informed. Take care of yourselves and see that you return home in good shape. I can't get rid of the feeling that there is a shortage of men there."

After he has ended, the barracks threatens to collapse from the stamping of feet which accompanies him as he leaves the hall. "The spokesman reminds me somewhat of Schulz," I scream in Siegfried's ear. "And me of my father when I broke a window in the neighbor's house," he responds happily as the noise slowly dies down and the dining hall empties.

Right after lunch we three friends take the clean, dry work clothes from the line. We fold them neatly and take them to be collected by comrades who will turn them in later. Satisfied we lie on the beds and eavesdrop for a while on what is going on inside the mattresses.

At 3:00 P.M., the refreshing listening duty is at an end. A cold shower revives the blood, after which we help the work details to restore the camp to a new glow. During the daily inspection we see only satisfied faces. The sergeant appears during dinner to observe the tranquil serving of the food, but his mouth starts to water and he leaves in order not to be overcome by his desires.

We lie in the cool grass in the shadow of the barracks after our day's effort and wonder about where we will end up. "Perhaps for a change we will work in a factory," I comment and thereby dislodge a mighty discussion. "That is out of the question, to be a coolie in a stinking sweatshop," the staff sergeant begins. "I could work as a locksmith, since that was my civilian training," the pastor interjects. "They could use me in the factory canteen because my father-in-law had a bar that I am to take over one of these days," a young noncommissioned officer jokes. "I'll go to the office," Siegfried adds. "And I will go home," says Kunze, who has had an especially difficult day.

That brings silence to the group. The thoughts rush across the ocean, climb over the dunes on the shore, follow various directions along the railroad tracks, and are lost in the confusion of the cavernous streets of the destroyed cities until they find a well-known house and simply know nothing more, because in the meantime the world which once was understood as the homeland has collapsed. Not until a bugle blows retreat from the training camp do we finally search out our beds. Alone, terribly alone is the man in spiritual need, unless he has God with him.

\* \* \*

It is not clear why Hörner was sent back to the east coast in July 1945. In any event, it seems that his stay at Fort Du Pont, one of the 150 major or base prisoner of war camps in the United States (as was Camp Greeley), was to be for only a short time, despite the conflict over the "lost" or "forgotten" equipment. If the plans were not already in motion to send him on to Glassboro, New Jersey, then he and the others would have been subjected to disciplinary action, or, presuming that they would have been treated with a measure of magnanimity on the part of the Americans, simply given a new assignment at Fort Du Pont. As it was, five days after his arrival on the east coast from Colorado, he was sent to the camp at Glassboro, New Jersey, approximately thirty miles from Fort Du Pont, Delaware.

\* \* \*

### 27 July 1945

The voice of the camp spokesman is drowned in the noise of the engines. Laughingly we wave good-bye to him as the wheels begin to turn. Fate takes us away from people who were well disposed to us.

The guard passes around a pack of cigarettes while his eyes shine with what is best in people: sympathy for others.

"Where are we going?" Siegfried asks when he offers him a light. "I don't know, perhaps to Fort Dix," he offers while the convoy moves through the heavily populated area.

Late in the afternoon we reach the small town of Glassboro, turn left off the main road, follow a lane lined with bushes, and stop in front of a small camp. The entire camp is surrounded by barbed wire. If it was not for the watchtower in the corner, one could imagine that the area in which a few apple trees stand is nothing but a boy scout camp or youth hostel. After we leave the vehicles, we assemble in front of the rail gate and march past a primitive washroom into this island of peace. Since there is no one to lead us and as a consequence no command is given, we come to a stop like a herd of sheep and glance around helpless.

Aside from the U.S. soldiers who brought us here and who sit in front of the barracks, no other soul is to be seen. We explore through the barracks and our first impression is substantiated: the camp is completely empty. There are not even any beds in the barracks. There is nothing to do but seek refuge from the grueling sun under the apple trees where, because of fatigue, we fall asleep in a few minutes.

After a good hour has passed, the crashing voice of an American wakes us from slumber. "Does anyone speak English?" he asks, friendly, and glances enthusiastically at the group. "Yes," answer many voices in chorus, at which he selects the best ones with a wave and calls them out for a meeting which is immediately translated by our comrades.

"You are now in a branch camp of the main camp, Fort Dix, New Jersey, and are under the command of Captain Brown. In order to get things going, I need a camp spokesman, translator, two clerks, a man for the clothing room, a mess chief, two cooks, two dishwashers, a medic, a man to handle the heat, and one for the sanitary facilities. All who feel inclined to one of these positions, please step forward."

While the amused American watches the group debate, transports arrive at the gate loaded with bedding and mattresses. After some back and forth, he finally identifies the necessary men who are willing to take on the assignments temporarily. Immediately afterward the camp springs into activity. Transports arrive from the main camp loaded with provisions, clothing, and bedding. In less than two hours the barracks are set up, work crews assigned, bath water brought to boil, and dinner prepared. Praise the German-American talent for organization.

"I have received so many raw vegetables that I believe I can satisfy all of you," the mess chief greets his would-be eaters and fills the white porcelain plates to the top with green peas and bacon. "We will be happy if in the land we can finally get this eternal hunger out of our guts," Siegfried jaws between Kunze and me, but in the next moment he incautiously burns his mouth and tightens up like a stabbed ram.

"Idiots," he screams above our laughter and soothes the burned lips with his tongue. "Didn't you hear there is plenty of food? Why do you push it so much?" I go after him. "Because I only believe what I know." He laughs, sticking out his chin and winking with the left eye.

"Did the mess sergeant really promise you so much?" I return to the theme on the way to our quarters. "If it stays like this in the future, I will be a good worker," Siegfried says with the sound of a vow. "What kind of work do they have for us?" Kunze asks. "Perhaps the peach harvest?" I joke, explaining that during the trip I noticed a number of well-cared-for orchards. "They will not make the goat a farmer. I will eat everything I pick." Siegfried shoves the barracks door open.

These quarters compare in no way with those in Camp Gruber. It is a long barracks, whose plank floor gives a strong impression of comfort and homeyness like those in Colorado. In addition, the walls are covered with a white-painted plywood, which was not the case in Camp Greeley. Our only complaint is the iron bunk beds since fifty men must live together in each barracks. Naturally it is only habit; in a few days we will think nothing more about it. In general I feel much at home as I now lie full but tired on my soft cot.

At 7:00 A.M. Captain Brown wants to count his wards. If he knew how unwillingly we climbed out of bed to meet his wish, he would probably forget about it, because in the first place no one is locked up, and in the second place he is a fine fellow, whose goodness radiates from every pore. But so that he will not be disappointed with us, we hurry out and stand in rows under the apple trees at the designated hour.

"I am pleased that we were able to get everything under roof and put away in such a short time and I am convinced that in the future we will get along very well when my orders are carried out in a like manner. I will provide good and abundant food but I expect that you will do a good job on your work assignments. You will help the farmers here in the state of New Jersey with the peach harvest. The farmers are instructed to handle you properly and not to demand more of you than their own farm workers. The workday is eight hours. Lunch will consist of sandwiches which will be passed out to the individual groups before work. The farmers are allowed to add something extra, but you do not have the right to demand it. Inside this enclosure you can enjoy every freedom, but you must obtain permission from me for every special event. That is all."

After this speech full of hope, the captain and his entourage leave the camp. "At ease," the newly designated camp spokesman, Sergeant Klunge, laughs, and begins his own speech.

"I won't keep you long, just long enough to cover the important items. First of all, I want to make it perfectly clear that I am not eager for this position and that I am here for everyone who needs me. If someone believes he can do a better job, he is welcome to it. If I keep the position, I will be most grateful for any good suggestion. Now to specifics. We have the entire day tomorrow at our disposal to finish settling in. The camp is, by and large, clean, and what is still to be done will be finished tomorrow. After 9:00 A.M. the clothing store will be open. Only work clothes will be given out at first. The exchange of bedding, etc., will be announced later. There is not much here for recreational activities. We have a barracks with a stage. The performers among us will be allowed to perform for the men without restriction. The assembly area can be used as a soccer field. Later the captain will arrange with a planning group to acquire land outside the barbed wire where we can burn up any extra energy. That is all for today, good night."

"Are you comfortable, you old sleeping beauty?" I bend down to Siegfried, who is on the bottom bunk. "Yes, you raccoon, pull your claws in," he mumbles, half asleep. "Put the picture away now; you will certainly see your Brigitte soon in the natural." I turn my head to Kunze, who lies at the same level, with only three feet of air separating us. "Maybe you are right," he giggles. "Sleep good, the day after tomorrow it is into the trees."

\* \* \*

There is little information available about the temporary prisoner of war camp established at Glassboro, New Jersey. It was a branch camp of Fort Dix, New Jersey, located to the northeast about thirty miles away. All German prisoners of war assigned to Glassboro were considered privates. According to labor reports, the camp contained between 350 and 400 prisoners of war. It operated just over three months, or the entire time that Helmut Hörner was there, from July 27 to November 6, 1945. Most of the prisoners were employed in the orchards around Glassboro, a city in 1945 of less than 10,000 people located in southwestern New Jersey.

\* \* \*

*29 July 1945*

The gate of a prisoner of war camp is the central point around which all hope and also all the disappointment of the single day and night revolve. One day a man can step through the gate into freedom and, in a certain sense, completely change his life into a different person when he goes into new surroundings with the determination to carry out his intentions. But it can also be that a free man comes through the gate to the prisoners and destroys all hope and good intentions. Yes, this free man, who by chance or what you could call providence, has been given power over the prisoners, is in the position to, with only a few words, make resisters out of the willing, bad out of good, and bitterly disappointed out of the hopeful. The opposite can also occur, because prisoners do suffer, but they are always ready to change. That is why it does make a difference to whom they are entrusted, unless they are considered only objects. If that were the case life would be meaningless, every hope self-deception, life a lie, and the nihilists would be right.

But there stands Captain Brown, exactly in the center of the gateway of this branch camp of Fort Dix. The hand of his wristwatch is moving toward the eighth hour of this young day, while his own hand again and again guides a cup to his mouth and his eyes lie with good intentions on the fresh faces of the work details who are in the process of getting into the trucks of the waiting farmers. And now from this moment on the three groups of people which fate has brought together have the future in their own hands. On this playground that our creator has set up for us everything can turn toward good or bad.

Captain Brown has demonstrated his goodwill from the first moment on, although it was probably known to him that we, for good reasons, were inclined to rebellion. If he did not happen to be an experienced man, who knows with what words he would have greeted us after one glance at the papers which accompanied us. As the saying goes: "As you call into the woods, so will it respond back to you." But he called out something good, and I am certain that it found a good response. Now we will see if the third group in the league, the farmers, will consider us as objects of war booty or see us as human beings that should be handled as such and not expect more of us than our heavily laden nerves can endure. If fate is good and we all understand one another and each one's situation, then we can make the best out of what the times require of us.

"The group for farmer Ritter, please come to the gate," calls the American executive officer, a friendly man who has a tolerable understanding of the German language and who finds time to eat a sandwich while he works. "Be good." Spokesman Kluge says good-bye to the group which includes Kunze and me. "Don't forget the peaches," Siegfried, who has been promoted to a clerk, reminds us as we march through the gate and are received by an older gentleman who would have been at home on any German farmstead.

"Judging by the truck, we are going to a respectable house," the pastor says and makes the effort to be the first one on the truck.

"I would not pick up my countrymen in a manure wagon," the farmer stammers in awkward German and unleashes the first surprise for us. The second soon follows. The guard sits in the cab and not with us as has been the case up to now. They trust us, we concur, while the truck follows along the road leading from the camp. The wheels have hardly touched the road before the new Ford hurries through the little city of Glassboro and fifteen minutes later reaches a magnificent farmhouse lying in the middle of a green space shaded by well-grown weeping willows and encircled by a low wall. Happily we jump from the truck into the farmyard and wonder at this place of obvious well-being.

"Sit down on the benches; I will see how far my people are," the good-natured farmer indicates and goes into the house. Before we can sit down and make ourselves comfortable on the benches which stand around a table under a weeping willow, a young girl in a fine outfit appears on the steps leading out of the house. "The old gentleman could be well taken care of by her," slips out as my eyes go from the snow-white gloves over the entire figure clothed with a flower print dress to try and read the pretty face under the white hat. But the cosmetics have changed the face into a fashionable mask. Life comes into the doll. With quick steps she goes from the house into a shed where, after a moment, a motor howls and a dreamlike picture of chrome, red-painted sheet metal, and glass on wheels rolls slowly into the yard. The girl sits like a sovereign at the wheel of this cloud of a vehicle, which in the next moment disappears with her out of the yard and out of our view. Never before have I found poverty so shameful as now at this minute.

But we are in America and the farmer reminds us of that. A young man comes out of the house toward us who is no better or worse clothed than we. "This is my son Bill." He introduces his son. "We will load the baskets there and some ladders on the old Mercedes." He points with his hand to a shed completely filled with round baskets. We go to work a little depressed from what has just happened.

Just as we finish, the poem of a vehicle with her grace at the wheel stops right next to the old Mercedes. "Get this woman out of our eyesight," I growl in silence to the farmer as I take a pack of Camels from her hand. Amazed, the others also receive cigarettes and do not recover from this fright before the being from another world disappears into the shed with its automobile. We stand smoking in the yard while the father and son go through various work buildings, apparently looking for something.

Finally they are ready and we can take a seat on the Mercedes. But before we drive off, the young lady appears again on the steps. And once again she amazes us with her image. This time she is dressed in work overalls and a scarf. Idly she pulls on the large chrome-colored leather gloves, and then goes through the yard with great charm to the tractor and starts the motor, then rattles through the yard.

"She is not such a fancy doll," the pastor murmurs, but he is the only one left cold by all the magic. After a few minutes the Mercedes begins to move and we soon reach a grove of peach trees. "So, here we are," the farmer says, and we jump down from the vehicle and wonder at the magnificent fruit on the trees. In the next moment our teeth sink into the juicy fruit that lies on the ground. "What is on the ground belongs to the pigs." Mr. Ritter laughs and picks a fine example from a tree, breaks it in two, and studies the degree of ripeness like an expert. "We will start here," he says after a while and begins to direct us.

"This is just the right job for us, Werner," I say to Kunze, sitting on a branch. "Eating as many peaches as we want, seeing this work as sport in the fresh air, an honorable farmer, and in the camp a fatherly commander. What more could we want?"

"To be home by winter," he answers somewhat sadly while his hands reach mechanically for the fruit. "Did the girl also awaken the homesickness in you?"

I ask with sympathy. "It is a pity when someone like that is paraded before your eyes; how they have betrayed all of us." The painful misery overcomes him again.

"Look, Werner," I try to comfort him, "the people here also have their worries. A single tornado could ruin them. It is correct that they are free, that they can eat as much as they want, and come and go as they want. But whether they are happy, I mean really happy as in being completely satisfied, that must be found on another page."

"Certainly I do not want to be called Ritter or be an American. After the whole swindle is behind us, I just want to build my own existence, marry my Brigitte, and live our life as human beings are entitled to do," he says forcefully.

"We must be content, Werner! We must absolutely be content! Think about all those who marched out with us and will never return home. When you think about it, then you know it is very unjust of us to haggle about our fate," I present to him. "Excuse me, Helmut. Naturally you are right. Sometimes, unfortunately, I forget it. But listen, the guard is whistling for lunch," he notes and climbs out of the tree.

In the shade of the weeping willow, we assemble around the table and take the bread out of the basket while the farmer pours coffee that he has donated. Even the guard sits at the table and unpacks his sandwiches, made of a thicker pile of corned beef than ours. Otherwise there is no other difference. Certainly this harmony would not please the warmongers, if they knew. But the little people are beginning to come to their senses while the big ones are busy dividing their profits.

"Apparently there is conflict in Berlin." The farmer folds his newspaper together, gets up to go into the house since he has not yet eaten. "The Russians ..., oh yes, I am not supposed to talk about anything political with you," he interrupts himself with a laugh and strides toward his house just as his wife comes to call him.

We look at him with grins until our eyes come to rest on the motherly figure of the farmer's wife. There she stands, nodding to us, friendly, the mother in her blue-white, striped apron on which she drys her hands. Why do men listen so little to their mothers? It would simply not be possible to be sitting here in prison and millions of young lives resting in the earth snuffed out forever.

At 1:40 P.M. we climb into the trees again. Basket after basket is filled with the delicate fruit. Pleasantly surprised, the farmer observes his willing helpers. About 4:00 P.M. he no longer puts out any empty baskets. "Now we will drive our blessings to the house," he says and nods to us in complete satisfaction.

"Can we take a few peaches back to camp with us for use there?" I ask the farmer timidly before we climb aboard the truck for the return trip. "How many men are there?" he asks, friendly. "Actually I was only thinking about a personal friend of mine." I am concerned about filling Siegfried's wish. "Let's do it this way; every day you can take a full basket with you. Is that enough?" He delights, looking into our happy faces. "That is very nice of you," I thank him. "We will show our appreciation for it." "I am very satisfied with you; now let's take you back to camp." He lays his hand on my shoulder and herds us onto the new Ford.

After a refreshing shower, Kunze and I slip into the barracks, where we meet Siegfried at his favorite activity; then we cover his entire bed with peaches. "Did you have good fortune on the farm?" he asks with both cheeks full. "Very good." We laugh together. "Then we are enjoying good times. The captain was out today and was full of praise for everyone." He turns again to the peaches. "And how do you like the clerk's office?" I ask. "Typical office work, but there is an advantage in that I can practice typing. All the work rosters are issued in triplicate. I am busy, I can tell you," he offers and looks skeptically into our faces to see if we believe him.

Even though the count agrees, roll call is a waste of time because there are a number of stragglers still in the shower room. Afterward the hard-working peach-pickers assemble for dinner. Green beans in a white sauce, mashed potatoes, and sausage are added to the innumerable peaches in our stomachs. It is enough. Suddenly everyone has the desire to put on some fat. The cooks continue to haul out gigantic aluminum pots from the kitchen and fill the plates of those who remember the hunger of Alençon and Marseille.

"I hope it stays as beautiful as today ..." a couple of high spirits sing as they return to the barracks and bring to specific expression that which we have so long desired for our life as prisoners in America. "Why was it not like this in Colorado?" Kunze asks. "Because America is so different," I respond and hop into bed. "No," Siegfried hits the nail on the head while he is rubbing Ponds Cream into his brown, burned face, "because the man who has the power in this camp does not misuse it and is simply a human being."

### 8 August 1945

Like on every workday, the farm details stand at the gate. The guards on the outside present an unrestrained spectacle. Like after a night of carousing, nothing seems to go right. One searches for his hat, another his weapon, whereby they curse continuously with the most vulgar expressions they have learned as soldiers. Naturally it all occurs as a joke and a number make sure that the confusion increases in that they exchange the weapons for a fire shovel attached to the barracks. It is understandable that the captain is not very excited about the theater—the hair of his underlings stands out in all directions and their entire get-up leaves a great deal to be desired. But he tolerates the disorder good-naturedly, especially since the farmers who wait outside observe the confusion good-naturedly and take the whole affair quite lightly.

\* \* \*

The guards were celebrating the detonation of the first atomic bomb dropped on the Japanese city of Hiroshima on the island of Honshu on August 6, 1945. The bomb inflicted 130,000 casualties and destroyed three-fourths of the buildings in the city. A second bomb was dropped on Nagasaki three days later, and on August 15, Japan entered into a cease-fire agreement.

\* \* \*

Finally, the first group is called out and marches through the gate to the vehicles. We greet Mr. Ritter and a friendly guard helps us into the truck. After he helps the farmer close the tailgate, he must share the secret with us. "We dropped an atom bomb on Japan," he sputters and awaits anxiously the reaction which his words were intended to produce. But he looks at us with disappointment.

"So," says Kunze, who stands next to him. "Where is the chain reaction?" "What do you mean with that?" the guard, apparently a German-American, wonders. "In school we learned that when the atom is split a chain reaction will occur that will destroy all life on this earth," Kunze explains since he obviously does not believe the words of the guard. "I don't understand anything about that, but the bomb was really dropped and exploded. Japan faces capitulation," he says somewhat more contemplatively and gets into the cab.

"Is that fellow trying to pull our leg?" the pastor asks after some time as the Ford speeds through Glassboro. "There is something to what he says," Peterson, a quiet bookworm and former sergeant major at the division level, concludes. "I know that German scientists worked on the project in Norway. I remember hearing that an English commando group blew up the heavy water which is an essential part of the undertaking, and through their deed caused a tremendous setback for the project." "Siegfried, didn't Moeller speak about a new type of bomb while we were in Cherbourg?" I now recall.

"Between Christmas and New Year's it was printed in the *Stars and Stripes* that the Germans had the atom bomb, but did not have any aircraft with which to transport it," says Siegfried, who has volunteered to go with us to the farm. "Why didn't you say something before?" I wonder. "I didn't think the matter was very important since there was so much nonsense in the paper and you and

Schulz were sometimes silent about what was said between you and Moeller." He recalls the former situation. "So there was something true about the talk of a secret weapon," the pastor ends the topic as we come to a stop in the farmyard.

* * *

When Germany conquered Norway in May 1940, she obtained the only major source of heavy water in the world—the Vermork hydroelectric plant in south central Norway. Germany stepped up the production of heavy water by over 300 percent. Bombing raids were carried out by the Allies against the plant and an unsuccessful attempt was made to sabotage it in November 1942. Three months later, in February 1943, a sabotage team of Norwegians put the heavy water works out of production for an estimated twelve to eighteen months.[10]

Albert Speer notes that two primary obstacles stood in the way of Germany constructing an atomic bomb. First was the concern by leading German scientists that successful nuclear fission could not be kept under control but would continue as a chain reaction, setting the globe on fire. The second was ideological:

> Hitler had great respect for Philipp Lenard, the physicist who had received the Nobel Prize in 1920 and was one of the few early adherents of Nazism among the ranks of the scientists. Lenard had instilled the idea in Hitler that the Jews were exerting a seditious influence in their concern with nuclear physics and the relativity theory. To his table companions Hitler occasionally referred to nuclear physics as "Jewish physics"— citing Lenard as his authority for this.[11]

> Albert Speer goes on to note that even if Germany had been able to concentrate all of her resources, she could not have produced a German atom bomb until 1947—much too late to be of any use in defeating the Allies.

* * *

After the usual loading of the baskets, we take our places on the old Mercedes, which is driven by an old black permanently employed by the Ritters as a farmhand and whose well-ordered hut, where he lives with his family, is located on the other side of the farmhouse. On the way to the orchard, we have the privilege of seeing the farmer's daughter plowing with a tractor. We are long aware that the daughter and also the farmer's daughter-in-law put in eight hours a day of hard work. For that reason we have had to radically change our rash opinion about the women in this land. However, we have not yet been able to discover the daughter-in-law anyplace. We find no value in meeting women since they only make us restless, especially when they are good-looking, and don't lonesome men find everything beautiful about a girl?

"You apes into the trees," commands the pastor and stands the ladder upright. "Yes, we are ready," Kunze indicates with an understanding side glance toward Siegfried, who picks from the ground up and seems to stick everything in his mouth. "Last night we emptied several bottles to celebrate the victory in the Pacific," the loquacious man expresses while Kunze and I busy ourselves filling the baskets. "Were you in Germany?" Siegfried asks and lifts his eyes to the soldier's ribbons. "Not since my childhood. I was assigned to Italy and I'm waiting here for my discharge," he says happily. "Are your parents German?" Kunze wants to know. "They were," he lifts his head, "but of Jewish descent." "So tell us what they did in Germany to harm you," I ask him urgently.

"My parents took off at the right time," he begins. "We lived in Berlin and had a men's store. When the Nazis came to power they put a placard on the shop door, 'Don't buy from Jews.' The people obeyed because there was a danger of being photographed and having their picture published in the newspaper. So we immediately packed our suitcases and left for Austria. The atmosphere was already poisoned in Vienna, so my parents decided to immigrate to the States. We were luckier than those of our faith who came later and had to leave nearly every single possession behind. What happened to those who stayed in Germany, you learned about when the war ended over there."

"Do you hold the German people responsible for these crimes?" I continue. "Who else?" his voice sharpens. "You did give your consent to the persecution of the Jews, didn't you?" "They encouraged the hatred because your business practices ruined so many poor devils. Naturally that is no reason to put a noose around your neck, but the Nazis used it to win quite a few voters," I express in defense. "They were only a few that you find in every herd," he responds.

"Would you think it in order if the people here were punished for the misdeeds of Himmler and his cronies since we are only indirectly guilty because we happen to be German?" I inquire. "They will make you collectively responsible, like the Nazis did with us. You all screamed 'Heil' as long as you had the advantage. Don't whine for mercy. It won't do any good. This time you will be finished. And completely so that people can finally live in peace," he says without any pathos.

"Why are you so friendly toward us if you believe we are all murderers?" Kunze asks after his response has quieted me. "Because I don't know for sure that you are some of them, and I regret making any false judgments," he explains quietly. "Have they judged us already?" Siegfried questions. "Well, there is the Morgenthau Plan, which will condemn you to thirty years' forced labor if it is approved." He stuns us. "Do you find that to be in order?" I laugh, half-crazy from shock. "No, because it would be a continuation of what Hitler began." He distances himself from this frightful consideration and walks conveniently away.

* * *

The Morgenthau Plan, named for Henry Morgenthau, secretary of the treasury in Franklin D. Roosevelt's cabinet from 1934 to 1945, was designed to reform the German national character and society more than carry out revenge against Germany. It contained twelve provisions for dealing with postwar Germany:

1. The demilitarization of Germany—to mean complete disarming of the Germany army and people; destruction of all war matériel, the total destruction of the whole German armament industry, and the removal or destruction of other key industries basic to military strength.
2. The partitioning of Germany—Poland and the U.S.S.R would get East Prussia and the southern portion of Silesia; France would get the Saar and territories bounded by the Rhine and the Moselle rivers; the rest of Germany would be divided into two autonomous, independent states—a South German state comprising Bavaria, Württemberg, Baden, and other smaller areas, and a North German state comprising a large part of the old states of Prussia, Saxony, Thuringia, and several smaller states.
3. The Ruhr area, the heart of German industrial power, would be stripped of its industry and prevented from becoming an industrial area in the future and would be governed by an international security organization established by the United Nations.
4. Restitution and reparation would be carried out by the restitution of property looted by the Germans in territories occupied by them, the removal and distribution among devastated countries of industrial plants and equipment from Germany, forced German labor outside Germany, and the confiscation of all German assets outside of Germany.
5. Education and propaganda would be controlled, with all schools and universities closed until an Allied Commission of Education formulated a reorganization program. Also all German radio stations, newspapers, magazines, etc., would be discontinued until adequate controls were established.

6.  Political decentralization: Germany would be eventually partitioned into three states, with strong emphasis on local autonomy.
7.  The military control of the German economy would not deal with the usual economic issues of price controls, rationing, unemployment, consumption, housing, or transportation, but would serve only to facilitate military operations and military occupation.
8.  For a period of at least twenty years, the United Nations would maintain tight controls over foreign trade and capital imports.
9.  War criminals would be punished.
10. The wearing of insignia and uniforms would be prohibited.
11. No military parades would be permitted and all military bands would be disbanded.
12. All military and commercial aircraft would be confiscated and no German would be permitted to operate such aircraft.

Following the death of Franklin D. Roosevelt on April 12, 1945, support for the Morgenthau Plan began to wane quickly, and on July 14, 1945, President Harry Truman accepted Morgenthau's resignation as secretary of the treasury. At the Paris Economic Conference in July 1947 a plan proposed by Truman's secretary of state, George Marshall, was adopted. The Marshall Plan called for an increased amount of aid ($11 billion) above what had already been given to Europe and the Far East from 1945 to 1947. The massive, systematic American economic aid sought to revitalize Europe's economy in the belief that an economically healthy Europe would be more effective in withstanding communism.[12]

\* \* \*

The farmer provides coffee, cake, and cigarettes for lunch. We choke down our food without enthusiasm. Our conversation with the guard had quite a few listeners and now they are also informed. Afterward we lie in the grass that also serves the farmer's family as a lounging area and which is located behind a white-painted wooden cottage. I am oppressed with the brooding recollection of what I once read in the German newspapers about this plan. They even talked about castration, but we knew also that Goebbels made elephants out of fleas. Now there seems to be something to it.

Confused, I rack my brain, always asking if people are really capable of such action. But the film from the German concentration camps confirms my fears. If up to now I have considered us Germans better people because others had convinced us it was so, and we have then sinned against others, then those who seek revenge will make sure a plan is worked out to deal with us. And this would not be the first time in history, either. Even the English are considered the discoverers of the concentration camps, as they sought to exterminate the Boers in Africa in a similar manner. We still have very difficult times ahead, I conclude, and once again I see the homeland disappear in the unending distance.

During the afternoon the farmer is a riddle for us. Our output is less than half, but he does not complain. Only once in a while his eyes glide over the empty baskets. Then he distances himself further. About 4:00 P.M. he selects several men to bring the fruit to the farm. Siegfried and I are included. Silently we load the Mercedes. The previous fun and joy from the work has disappeared from our faces. "Take your time, comrade; then we have thirty years' time," is now the catchword.

When the farmer hears it, he takes the pastor firmly by the arm. "What does that mean, we still have thirty years' time?" he asks, disturbed. "You know what they have planned for us," the pastor answers and leaves him standing. "I don't know anything," he calls to the group. "What is going on?" "The Morgenthau Plan," I say in passing and bend over to pick up a full basket. "That is nonsense." He becomes indignant. "That guy is crazy. We have something to say about it. We are a free country. Don't believe all the manure that you see in the newspapers. Here everyone writes what he wants. You will be home for Christmas, count on it."

But his words are lost in the wind even though they are honest and given with good intention. However, we work quickly out of anger, even though everything has become meaningless for us.

At 5:00 P.M. we return to camp. From the shower room to the barracks the indiscretion of the guard is told in many variations until Kluge comes to Siegfried after dinner.

"Is it true that your guard told you we would be deported this winter to Alaska for thirty years?" he asks, extremely upset, but which sets off a salvo of laughter from us. "Did you want to pull someone's leg?" he presses anxiously while feeling insulted. "Neither," says Siegfried, and wiping his wet forehead goes on to explain.

"These crazy guards. First they drop an atom bomb on Japan which causes a chain reaction that destroys the entire world and now they gossip about deportation. That is quite a bit all at once, gentlemen." Kluge calms himself and quickly leaves the barracks to take the wind out of the sails of the rumors. By bed time the atmosphere is calm. The atom bomb was exploded, but Japan is very far away. Besides, wasn't a captured German responsible, so they won't do anything to us? ...

*29 August 1945*

After a record production during the morning, we sit contentedly at the table in the farmer's yard for lunch. The long-haired daughter-in-law, who we now see quite often, has just served us sweet potatoes, peas, and pork, then disappeared into the garden behind the work buildings while we enjoy the well-earned food.

"They try even more to show their recognition and acceptance," the pastor mumbles and begins to distribute the meat. "Certainly they must know that I am celebrating an anniversary today," I say with mixed feelings. "Anniversary? Which one?" everyone asks. "Today I have been a prisoner for one year," I explain and cannot believe it myself that it is a year already since I put my hands in the air for the four Americans in the grove near Soissons. "Yes, the time flies by." Kunze lets out a deep sigh. "Unfortunately not fast enough," the pastor offers. "Otherwise we would be home already." "But would we be sitting at a table set like this one?" Peterson asks, but no one stirs. "We didn't ask for that, or did we?" Kunze furrows his eyebrows. "Certainly not," confirms Peterson and rubs his hands over his eyes as though he is trying to dissolve a picture.

"You can help us with the sorting, Helmut." The farmer holds me tight as I start to climb on the Mercedes with my comrades. "OK." I laugh, reserved, because the others throw glances at me. "Go into the shed; Bill will show you what needs to be done," he says and gives the black the nod to start. In the shed, I observe the sorting machine with the various-sized holes. Finally Bill comes with the mother, daughter, and daughter-in-law. Now I need to keep my ears open since the young ones are not very good with the German language. But we are able to understand one another. What I do not understand about the technical aspects, I learn by doing as Bill explains how the sorting is done under the cheerful watch of the ladies. I make a concerted effort not to look into a certain pair of eyes, and I am successful until their owner directs a specific question to me.

"How do you like this job?" the daughter of the house asks. "Very well," I answer her in English, although I don't like the job at all because the situation is too agonizing for me. "You didn't get a letter from home?" The mother turns to me. "No, I have not received any mail from home." I answer, painfully touched. If I had only told the farmer that I would rather be with my comrades, I criticize myself and spill half a basket of fruit next to the machine, over which the ladies break out in amused laughter. "Don't worry about it," Bill says and hurries to my help, after which we continue with the work. I only feel the glances of the women, but with time I get used to it.

At 4:00 P.M. Bill turns off the machine while the mother serves coffee. "Is the coffee OK?" The daughter concerns herself with my welfare. "It tastes very good." I offer polite praise. "Thank you," the mother responds happily and starts to bring the pot to me but the daughter saves her the trouble although Bill shakes his head disapprovingly. "Thank you very much." I hold the cup under the stream and glance at the ring that builds up on the rim while the coffee is poured. I wonder if they know what that means for girls in Germany and notice the tight vibration in the girl's voice as she responds with, "You're welcome."

Ten minutes to five o'clock, I nod farewell. "Good-bye," a voice rings out joyfully as I leave the shed with the farmer and climb into the Ford, where the fellows greet me with grinning faces.

"The little one most certainly threw a glance at you," Kunze suggests after we get to the barracks. "The charm of a young lady's heart," I explain and strip off the work clothes. "Did you feel anything in her presence?" he asks cautiously. "Thanks for your concern, but sympathy would be very uncomfortable for me." I pick up my swimming suit. "I'm nearly ready," Kunze's unusual voice sounds across the bed. "Don't you think it is more than sympathy that they feel?" "No, I am a married prisoner of war," I explain bluntly and hurry to the shower room to stand under the ice cold water.

After evening roll call and dinner, we assemble in the barracks theater. The artists among us have been busy for weeks preparing a variety evening. Tonight they will demonstrate their talents as they entertain all of our comrades. Even some Americans who have mastered the German language attend. Among them is the dispatch sergeant, a Jew, as we have learned in the meantime, but a man with a golden heart and a demeanor that moves him to tears if a harsh word is spoken in his vicinity. But now he sits in front of Kunze and me and relishes with joy as though he were attending tne Metropolitan Opera in New York City. My fatherland, which is also his fatherland, has done him a great injustice, I think as the curtain goes up.

The emcee, a fun-loving, imposing comrade, springs onto the ramp and opens the program with a beaming and sparkling face and an exuberant cheerfulness. The enthusiastic applause has barely ended when three artists appear who demonstrate extraordinary power, body control, and supple elegance with their vaults, somersaults, and formations. After them, two musical clowns appear on stage and present a wild spectacle in their long gym shoes until they begin to play the tragic melody to the song, "Rosemarie, Rosemarie, my heart has called to you for seven years." The sad notes penetrate to ring in the most hidden corners of our hearts. After they finish, a full minute passes before the absolute stillness is broken by tremendous applause while bitter tears of homesickness roll over the cheeks of many. After a short pause, Jimmi Pony, called the Ice King, makes his appearance. A magician from the old school, he deftly turns a stiff cord into a necktie which he puts around his collar and then tears a solid chain into pieces and concludes, leaving all doubters in amazement by bending an iron horseshoe. The excellent program ends with a short sketch, "German invasion troops on the New York pier." We leave the theater with thankfulness in our hearts and return to the barracks, where every one immediately snuggles into bed.

One year as a prisoner penetrates my consciousness and the past experiences spin past my eyes in the darkness of night. When, I ask the Almighty as so often before, will the rays of freedom shine on me and my comrades?

### 9 September 1945

"Barracks one through four, fall out," sounds the sergeant in the dewy fresh September morning and calls the first half of the camp inmates to the mess hall. But we are not ordered there for a happy feast. No, white-helmeted MPs and strange U.S. officers arrived in the camp early in the morning and now stand with earnest faces in front of the kitchen barracks, dangling red-lacquered nightsticks from their hands. After roll call, we march in rows into the hall and are led by the guards to tables.

It is indicated that four men are to sit across from each other at the tables and we comply without resistance even though we do not understand the purpose of the ceremony. But all that changes quietly as soon as the last have found places and a guard is positioned at each table. The officers now pass among the rows of tables and lay between every four men an illustrated magazine somewhat in the form of the well-known *Life*. "You will now carefully study these illustrated documents of the crimes of the Nazi regime and discuss them among yourselves for a full hour," an officer brings to the surface the secret of this unusual arrangement. "Begin immediately!" he commands most sternly. We stick our heads together and stare at the shocking pictures. There is Göring, with his Reichsmarshal's badge given by Hitler's grace. At his feet lie rows of shot deer at the edge of the woods which, in the next picture, are transformed into the human sacrifice to the bombs of his air force. In addition there are Hitler, Himmler, and Goebbels. All are identified by the consequences of their terrible deeds, the brutal destruction of human life.

There we are, ourselves sacrifices, staring at the head leaders of the thousand-year Reich, whose demonlike spirits misled an entire people and in the end led it into destruction. The condemning eyes of the soldiers of the revenge-seekers observe our shocked faces. Finally, after an hour, we are ordered outside and squint confused at the young and innocent day whose glowing sun stands ready to banish the dew from the grass.

At 1:00 P.M. we are sent out to work. Whatever consequences may have been intended, the crimes that were presented to us have caused a mightier discussion and thereby the Americans have apparently achieved the hoped for goal.

The work suffers in no way from the events of the morning. The weather is simply too beautiful. Whoever is sitting in the trees, picking the colorful peaches and once in a while opening his eyes to the world of birds, caterpillars, and butterflies that shimmer in all colors, does not consider at all that at the same time there are people who seek to destroy the lives of others.

*18 September 1945*

"Happy birthday and a good trip home, Helmut." Siegfried and Kunze shake my hand just after we awake. "Thanks, friends," I offer with a cramped feeling in my heart, but I am pleased that at least they are thinking about me. "The next one you will celebrate at home for certain." Siegfried tries to comfort me. "I think so too." Kunze agrees. "My birthday is on December 28 and I am sure that by then there will be a silver lining on the horizon."

After we pass by the gate with the good-natured Jewish officer, we are greeted as usual by Mr. Ritter and escorted to the Ford. Today, a guard, who arrived yesterday and wears numerous ribbons on his breast, helps him close the tailgate. I wonder if he was in Germany. We travel to the farm and a short time later spring from the truck. The black has the Mercedes running already, which indicates that a major effort will be undertaken and the peaches will be delivered directly to Philadelphia. That's why today there is no time on the farm for our usual conversation, but instead we are taken immediately to the orchard where there is a great amount of fruit to be picked. A few minutes later we are hanging between the branches and busily gathering the blessings of nature into the basket while the guard enjoys the peaches.

"Good." He laughs intermittently and allows us to toss him the most beautiful of the beautiful from time to time. "Who is from Frankfurt?" he asks in English after he has developed trust toward us. But there is no one from Frankfurt among us, so that we only shake our heads in response to his question.

"Is Frankfurt badly destroyed?" I ask him to keep the conversation going. "There's practically nothing left," he explains without feeling. "How are the people doing?" I explore further. "Very bad." He nods in thought. "They have nothing to eat and hardly any place to live. The women are all alone with the children since the men have all been killed or are sitting behind barbed wire. The Nazis have been placed behind bars and the military regime governs with the strictest regiment. Germany will never recover."

"How do our women bear this misery?" I ask him anxiously. "I don't know. But those with whom I came in contact sold themselves for cigarettes." He grins cynically. "That is a lie or else you were in a brothel," I snap back at him. "Certainly not. They were, for the most part, respectable soldiers' wives. Also included were the daughters of former party bosses," he coldly maintains. "I don't believe it. You are forbidden to fraternize with Germans," I counter while at the same time I feel the blood pound in my temples.

"That's what it says in the newspapers, but in practice it is much different." He laughs indulgently while fingering a leather wallet in his back pocket. "Here, look at this." He looks me in the eyes and holds my arm tight just as I change baskets. "I don't want to see anything." I turn from him to the tree where Kunze is working like he is possessed while the guard holds a photo in his outstretched hand. "Take a look at what is in the picture," Kunze calls to me, and I turn around again and glance at the photo.

"That's from France, my boy." I laugh, relieved. "The French sold these kinds of pictures to us earlier." "Then look at these," and he suddenly has another in his hand, from which I recoil as though hit by a whip. In a German living room a naked woman lies on the couch with spread legs. Laughingly she holds a long American cigarette between fingers on one of which is a wedding ring. On the wall above the couch is the picture of a German sergeant with the Iron Cross Second Class and Infantryman's Badge on his breast. At the living room table, on which stand wine bottles and full ashtrays, a U.S. soldier is sitting, apparently asleep. Everything is there in one view and there is simply no possibility for the observer to escape it. For that reason I give him back the picture without saying a word and climb dejectedly with my empty basket into the tree with Kunze, while the meaning of my conversation in the hotel in Soissons has new relevance. Each generation brings the women to the fore that they deserve, is what Herbert said then. The French failed in 1940 and in the end their women surrendered too. And in answer to my question, how it would be for us, not one iota better!

You handled that well, Herbert, I concur with him and automatically reach for the innocent peaches, whose delicate outward appearance do not mirror any false magic, but keep what they promise all the way to the center.

"Was there anything special to see in the photos?" Kunze asks again for the second time and thereby tears me forcefully from any thoughts. "Nothing important. A depraved whore selling her body, otherwise nothing." I lie to my friend to spare him the worry.

For lunch the farmer provides chicken and congratulates me on my birthday. The farmer's daughter sits at the table dressed in a tight-fitting, audacious dress and has a friendly smile on her well-made-up face. But I have lost my appetite for everything. The spiritual load strangles at my throat while the unknowing companions converse loudly and enjoy the tasty meal.

"What's wrong with our birthday boy?" she wonders after a while when my disturbed character no longer goes unnoticed and I am otherwise one of the most lusty in the group. "Homesickness, leave him alone," some say. "Love sickness because he does not have the courage to ask the little one to come to the camp," the others answer. "Keep your stupid mouths shut and mind your own business." Kunze sets them straight and pours me a cup of the farmer's strong coffee. "We will soon be home, then everything will be all right." He lays one hand on my shoulder and, with the other, holds a burning match to light my cigarette.

The afternoon is spent working hard. I politely turn down the farmer's request for me to help on the sorting machine. Under no circumstances do I want strange people around me today. My place is here with my comrades until the light of freedom shines for us all. It is not the faithfulness of my own wife that troubles me. No, it is the disappointment with the German women for whom we suffered everything that was demanded of us to the end by our insane leaders. We have also lost them. That is the hardest blow which the war has brought me to this time. And especially on my birthday. That's why there is complete quiet in my heart.

In the evening it goes around the camp. Other guards also showed pictures. The debates go on endlessly and stretch our fatigued nerves to the breaking point. As night descends on each individual in camp, it does bring a comfort that makes it possible to bear up under the light of a new day.

### 8 October 1945

Time passes but our fate does not change. Day in and day out we are busy with the farmer's peaches and exist from the small hope that we get from time to time that our return home is nearly in view. Tonight the good Mr. Ritter sent us away again with the comforting words that we will certainly be home for Christmas. At the gate the Jewish sergeant with the golden heart greets us. Nowhere is there strife and everything follows a peaceful course. The roll call is conducted as a formality and only seldom is it correct since there are usually some in the shower room or changing clothes in the barracks. The Americans just laugh after they have signed the roster and the latecomers appear. There is no need to worry about the food since what the kitchen provides is plentiful and good and the extra provisions from the farmers are a change and insure us even more healthy, nutritious food. Our present appearance is testimony of our good care: young, strong-muscled, tanned brown, and alert. So at least we appear to those on the outside looking in. But in these healthy bodies still live sick souls; then they alone are without nourishment.

After dinner Siegfried, Kunze, and I sit in the clerk's office engaged in a lively discussion with the camp spokesman, Kluge. The theme is the usual and in general uninteresting—the mentality of the Americans, their rational agricultural practices, high politics. The conversation finally splashes in the insipid water of our sexual needs, and mixes with the omnipresent question of our return home, where it sinks in the hopelessness of the late hour of our return. A gnawing feeling rises in us that we have senselessly squandered even this day of our young lives, when a man enters the room and reports the following to Kluge: "The dishwasher Anton, who since the revelation about the Morgenthau Plan has been susceptible to light derangement and sometimes greets the Americans with the Hitler salute, is distributing his belongings to his comrades in the barracks."

"If his condition does not improve, we will have to send him to a hospital," Kluge says, considering the situation carefully. "Take the items, but in the morning bring them to me in a sea sack. It is nearly time for lights out and after he goes to sleep, he will have forgotten it all by morning." Kluge turns to the men.

"The fools in the room are laughing themselves half dead over his crazy talk. He is a member of the party, he says, and does not intend to see the homeland again. That is why he no longer needs his ring and wallet. Someone can take the things to his family," the man reports further. "They should stop it immediately. I will look after him a little later. It is 10:00 P.M. and immediately the lights will be turned out. See that he goes to bed," Kluge instructs the somewhat flabbergasted man, after which we leave the clerk's office and seek our quarters.

"Perhaps he is playing the crazy, so that he will be sent home early," someone proposes as we get ready for bed. "It's possible, but it would have to be quite a good act," another interjects. "If so, he is making a mistake, by appearing normal too often," maintains Peterson. "Go to sleep, the whistle has blown," Kluge concludes and turns out the light.

Ten minutes later I sit up. Kluge is standing before me upset, explaining that Anton has disappeared. "Come and help us search," he whispers. Quickly my friends and I get out of bed and put on our pants. The rubber soles muffle our steps as we slip out of the barracks. "Where will you look?" "He has certainly hidden himself," Kunze mumbles, lightly shaking from the cold because he forgot to put on his shirt. "After retreat he went to the washroom with his shaving kit," Kunze reports. "Two men from our barracks observed him and they went to check and see if he was shaving, but they did not find him. He left the washroom by the back door. The two returned while I was standing by his empty bed. They are looking for him behind the barracks. Come, let's look by the apple trees. I feel something terrible." Kluge startles us even more.

We separate quickly and look in every nook and corner. He is nowhere to be found. Even the two men from his barracks come back discouraged. "What do we do now?" Kluge asks, perplexed. "If I report to the captain that he actually escaped, then we have betrayed him. But if it is something else, then we are losing precious time."

"Do you think he is mentally ill or only pretends?" I ask the men from his barracks. "He could not pretend that well. Sometimes his eyes flitter like the village idiot at home," is how the possibility that he is only pretending is set aside. "Then I will go to the captain. Kluge! You cannot take the responsibility to assist a lunatic to escape. Imagine what he could do out there," I say determinedly. "Perhaps he only acted that way so that if they catch him he can simply continue to play a crazy." Kluge still hesitates. "Now you are duty bound to report the escape. He can't expect anyone to cover for him when he seems to be crazy," Kunze also emphasizes. "OK, but please don't you ever accuse me. I am going now, but look everywhere once again. Who knows ..." he gathers himself up for the first difficult step, then runs to the gate.

"Let's continue to look," Siegfried says in resignation and we separate. In the meantime, nearly half the camp is up. While some search in every corner, others pursue the trivialities. "Anton, where are you?" they call in firm belief, but he has long since gone. Suddenly a scream hits my ears. Immediately I rush from the tool shed in the direction of the barracks theater where the scream came from. Like me, all the other searchers hurry to the theater building.

"He is lying inside. He is dead." Two men point at the same time. "Light," we all shout, "turn on the light immediately." But the camp is asleep, including the guards.

Finally Kluge arrives with the Jewish sergeant, who holds a long flashlight. "Did you find him?" Kluge asks. "Yes, here in the bushes. He is dead," a broken voice asserts in the night. "The captain is not in camp. What should we do?" The good Jew rings his hands, his whole body shaking. "Give me the lamp," says Kluge and pushes with us into the small clump of bushes. Shocked, we stare at the sunken figure on the ground, who is lying against the wall with both legs outstretched, bleeding in the yellow light of the flashlight. Both wrists have been severed with a razor blade. There is also a long wound on the throat. The bleeding has just stopped. Any help is too late.

"It took too long." Kluge finally breaks the unbearable quiet and ends his inspection of the dead man. "He first opened the blood vessels in his wrists and then the artery in his throat," he adds and wipes the blood from his hands with a handkerchief. "Yes," the recently arrived medic confirms. "If he had cut the throat artery, he would not have been able to cut his wrists." "Get in touch with the captain." Kluge turns to the dispatch sergeant. "He is in the city, but we don't know where," he answers helplessly. "Then everything must remain as it is," Kluge orders. "The MPs will undertake an investigation even though it is clearly a suicide."

"I will inform the main camp, Fort Dix, immediately." Life slowly returns to the Jew, who was scared to death. "That's right," says Kluge as we follow him out of the bushes to the assembled crowd which has gathered in the meantime.

The self-inflicted death of a comrade has set loose a burning hatred against the Americans. Everything good is forgotten for the moment. The most idiotic curses are expressed in deep anger until Kluge intercedes: "Be quiet comrades! What has happened here lies apart from all hate. The man lost his nerve. His spirit was disturbed. Who do you want to make responsible for that? Take your own heart into your hands and guard your own nerves from internal strife. We must go home, men! That is, return home healthy, to protect our own loved ones from doubt. Go to your quarters and sleep. In the future help the weak ones to be strong again so that we are all spared from our own self-destruction."

After Kluge's words the crowd disperses and returns peacefully to the barracks.

During the night our dead comrade is transported to Fort Dix, where he will be treated with proper military honor. German prisoners of war from the main camp will stand at his grave, the captain ceremoniously informs us. Kluge and Siegfried, however, sit behind the typewriter until morning in order to finish the report for the investigators. Now death has struck for the second time among us.

### 22 October 1945

The peach harvest is over and the long-promised return home seems imminent. Only a few apples and pears remain to be brought in. Work on the farms begins to go against all employment theories. The farmers no longer know what to do with us for the entire day.

Today we are partly busy collecting the half-spoiled fruit from the ground which will be used to feed pigs. A nearby pig farm might make use of the fruit. But since we consider the work about as important as do the farmers, we and the guards engage in little battles in which one group attacks the other, throwing peaches until they begin to resist and suddenly go from the defense to the offense, accompanied by wild Indian yells each time. Often these games cover wide distances within the plantation. Today by this activity we meet a group of black women, who with their white foreman are working along the edge of the plantation in a cornfield. Naturally the game is immediately interrupted. These people, different from us in every way, react to us immediately with curiosity as though they had met us on a different planet. The women lay the heavy machetes with which they cut the corn stocks in their arms while we scramble for the half-rotten fruit that we want to use as missiles.

"We hear that you will soon be going home," the friendly workers approach us. "Are you German?" Peterson asks, surprised. "Ja," the woman laughs with a careworn face in which we can see that life has not been easy for her. But still she looks at each one of us and then says warmheartedly, "You all look so good. Hasn't the war or imprisonment caused you any sorrow?" "We have adjusted to everything, dear lady, and we are too young for our faces to reflect what lies behind us," I answer with a light touch of melancholy. "Aren't you happy about your return home?" She laughs, motherlike. "So much that words cannot express it," Kunze quickly explains.

"Who would know that better than I. At age twenty-one I left beautiful Dresden and followed my bridegroom to Philadelphia. In two years he had risen very high. So it was with a light heart I left Germany since it was just after the First World War and over there the future for a young lady was very dim. We married shortly after my arrival. It was a wonderful time. Then the depression came in the 1930s. My husband, like many, became unemployed. In Germany he was sympathetic to the communists but here he forgot about it. As an occasional worker, he landed in the same channel. In addition came the alcohol and with that my happiness was completely destroyed. I had to go to work in order not to starve. That's the way it still is today." She ends her account and glances at us sadly.

"Are you sure that we are the next ones they will send home?" "Certainly. The churches and women's organization will not tolerate that the Germans be held much longer," she says as the guard admonishes us back to work. "Hopefully we will be home for Christmas," we stretch out our hands. "You will; stay brave," she encourages us while wiping her teary eyes with her apron.

At noontime a jeep from the camp pulls into the farmyard. After a brief conversation with the guard and farmer, the driver turns the vehicle around and speeds away. "What did he want?" we ask the farmer when he comes to the table. "Just eat. When you are finished I have to take you back to camp," he answers, somewhat disturbed. "Will we be released?" we all shout and jump from our seats. "I don't know. I couldn't get anything out of that fellow. Eat first, otherwise you will insult my wife," he says nervously.

Excited, we inhale the rest of our meal. Going home, going home—it hammers in our temples and gives us no peace.

As the Ford rolls out of the farmyard, the farmer's family stands on the steps waving to us with mixed feelings, "Good-bye." Even the black steps out of the shed and raises his hand in farewell.

The truck speeds to the camp after it reaches the main road. In front of the gate already stand the trucks of other farmers.

Most of the work details are already back. We say good-bye to Mr. Ritter with a handshake and go through the gate. In the barracks, confusion reigns. All are taken with going home fever. Many are already organizing their possessions on their beds. Then it is popped like a soap bubble. "A hearing will be held," Kluge calls fatefully in the barracks and brings all the activity to a stop just as though he had cut through a power line. Our disappointment is gigantic. After a minute-long silence, the comrades spew poison and gall. "This is the reward for our work," someone bellows and throws a full bottle of after shave lotion that shatters in a thousand pieces against the wall. A shrill whistle ends the tumult. "All occupants of barracks one through four, come immediately to the dining room with a pencil," the sergeant of the day orders.

Ten minutes later a questionnaire lies in front of us on the table. Strange officers instruct us to answer the questions on the forms to the best of our ability, keeping in mind that all the answers will be reviewed in Germany and everyone will be called to account for any false responses.

Quickly I skim though the individual questions. Not one holds any danger for me. None even for Siegfried. Only Kunze seems to have a conflict with his conscience. "Shall I admit it?" he asks quietly and thereby brings Siegfried and me in distress. "Stay with your earlier responses; they have a lot to do if they want to review everything. You don't have anything to feel guilty about; you were a soldier like all of us," I whisper to him. "I would rather indicate it. I was in a music choir." He takes up his pencil. "You are crazy," Siegfried warns him. "It may be, but not a coward," he mumbles and writes with a calm hand his SS division after the relevant question. Shortly afterward I sign my name to the completed form.

Now you go for the interview in the clerk's office, the officer to whom I give the form indicates, and I walk across the grounds to the clerk's office. After I answer the questions in person, the interrogator lifts his head slightly and carefully watches me though glasses framed with black horn: "Do you believe in the continuation of the German people?" he asks and presses with his tongue against his uneven teeth. "Yes," I respond honestly. "Are you of the opinion that Hitler could have led Europe out of the chaos of the time?" he asks anxiously. "I think he is dead." I wonder at this strange question. "That is not a matter for debate. I'll ask the questions. Answer the questions." He overrides me. "The German people will no longer give him the possibility," I explain matter-of-factly. "I didn't ask you that, so please," he says, somewhat quieter. "No," I answer hard and suddenly see before my eyes the film of the concentration camps. "Have you developed a political outlook?" is the next question, which he introduces in a very quiet manner of speech. "Not yet, but I would like to see the German people enjoying the same freedom that the U.S. citizens have," I answer honestly. "Would you work with the military government?" he asks, excited. Now I can obtain my freedom. I search my conscience and my heart answers loudly, "I would be happy to, as long as my activities did not go against my people." "Do you believe that America would help the German people?" he asks. "At the moment, it does not seem to be the case as far as I am informed, but I hope they will," I explain. "That is good. You can go," he releases me with a friendly nod.

As I trot back to my quarters, a sharp, cold wind blows the silver leaves of the apple trees to the ground. An old woman's summer, perhaps the last nice Sunday of the year, I think, and brush away with my hand a swarm of tiny insects that dance around my head. The interrogation might be connected to our release, my thoughts jump to conclusion. Naturally, that's the way it is. They will be confirmed when we are sent home. But that is all nonsense. Who can guarantee that everyone else says what he thinks? There is even the possibility that the turncoats will be sent home now. But I cannot change it. We all want to go home and every method has its problem. We will leave it to fate, I comfort myself, and as I reach the barracks I roll a cigarette while my thoughts wander homeward.

During the evening the hope of our return home swells like house-sized waves and washes all doubt out of the camp. We only have to go to work for a few more days and then we will be loaded on ships, is what some guards have supposedly confided to some. "The Gods were pleased with us," we tell each other around the barracks as we happily go to bed.

### 6 November 1945

A raw wind blows the last leaves from the apple trees and scatters them in the empty, spotlessly clean barracks, whose doors stand open to let the wooden floors dry. At 9:00 A.M. all the men are busy loading the bedding onto trucks, cleaning out the clothing room, and packing the kitchen equipment. It must be a true eye-opener for the captain and his guard personnel to observe us at work; then everything is going like clockwork. Naturally it is no wonder; then we are to be at Fort Dix at twelve o'clock for lunch and from there we will be taken to the New York harbor. Who should be in a greater hurry than we?

Yes, it has come at last, we can go home. Much earlier than I had thought.

With overflowing joy we have said good-bye to the farmers. We had our pictures taken and had them quickly developed so that everyone on the farms could have a permanent souvenir of our joint work during the past months. There were many words expressed on the farms whose only witness was the autumn sun. But it is difficult for someone who carries an unquenchable yearning in his heart to accept even the good-intended suggestions, and soldiers from the great battles know that happiness is not dependent on the size of one's purse, rather, in the end, from a satisfied heart and an untroubled soul.

That's why at 10:15 A.M. we climb onto the trucks with a couple of bars of soap and a few other useful things in our sea sacks and travel unconcerned to Fort Dix without turning around once or without a feeling in our hearts that hangs on what has basically remained foreign to us. But we will never forget the land and the people because both have given us so much that we will never be separated from it.

"Fort Dix, New Jersey," stands over the door through which we roll into a gigantic camp with white, two-story barracks that are separated into many compounds. The camp spokesman who receives us in our compound unfortunately does not have any personal word for the newly arrived comrades, but follows like a rude drill sergeant throughout the area until he finally directs us to the barracks. "Maybe and maybe not," he answers our question if we will be sent on board ship in the next few days.

"He is a stupid old goat," Kunze declares and goes with Siegfried and me up the stairs to the upper sleeping room.

"I don't want to eat half a pound of salt here." Siegfried glances around the large room after we lay our sea sacks on three unmade beds. "Salt is cheap here, comrade, if you are unlucky, you may eat a whole ton of it," a man with a moon-round face comments from his bed. "How long have you been here?" I ask curiously. "Nearly half a year," he moves toward us and rolls a cigarette with well-trained fingers. "When are you going home?" Kunze asks. "I am no prophet. Until now they have only brought the postal workers together. They are supposed to be sent on board ship soon, apparently so that we can finally get mail from home," he indicates, unconcerned. "I would like to have your nerves." Siegfried laughs. "We are indeed here to be put on a ship." "Go take a long look around. The transport home will take a long time." He grins and wrinkles his round face.

"Aren't you aware that we are going home?" I ask impatiently. "That's good to be going home. ... I should also go home. Why do they ask about it? Don't get your hopes up. In the meantime you will be permitted to slaughter stinking chickens in Philadelphia." He unfolds an olive green handkerchief and wipes his nose. "You are poorly informed." I lay my hand on his shoulder. "We will sail in the next few days." "With your hand on your ass by way of Alexanderplatz." He laughs heartily and moves his left hand in circles on his large butt. "Either you are full of nonsense or we are." Kunze turns to unpack his sea sack.

"Be reasonable. You were brought here because there is nothing more to do on the farms. At this time all the prisoners from the branch camps are coming here. At present I am on the sick list, and I know what is going on. Perhaps around Christmas, but I am not counting on it," he tells us so specifically that it nearly makes me sick. "Dammit, I want to know for sure," Siegfried storms and stomps out of the room.

"It is possible that they lied to us." I sit on a bed and stare spiritless at Kunze, who covers his face with both hands. With a shrug of the shoulders, the man goes back to his bed to continue to sew his clothes. After a while Kunze pulls himself together. Tired, he sits next to me and takes his tobacco can from his pocket. Silently we roll the cigarettes. "Now the world must stink," he mumbles after the first draw. "Now a wonder must occur," I change the beginning to the well-known hit, "and I want to drown in your kisses, Brigitte." He jumps up and hits himself in the forehead. "We are idiots. ... We are triple idiots! They can do this only to us. We always believe!"

"Be quiet, Werner. For heaven's sake be quiet or I will go crazy," breaks out of me. "You are right. It's useless. We must endure it," he says bitterly and sits down again just as the whistle sounds to eat. "Go alone, Helmut, I don't want anything now," he bids. "That's out of the question; we won't give them anything." I take his arm. "I don't want anything and I can't eat anything," he refuses. "Then neither do I." I stretch out on an uncovered mattress and lay my arms under my head.

Silently the blue-gray smoke clouds rise to the ceiling. Even the cigarettes don't taste good when one's consciousness works feverishly. Such an underhanded, mean trick. How can people fill you with hope and have no thought to see it fulfilled? Or didn't the people themselves know any different?

"Why didn't you go eat?" Siegfried rattles us unceremoniously out of our useless groveling. "They can smear it in their hair," I answer, angry at everything. "That is stupid. Listen to what they say," he says importantly. "We are not going to stay here. Perhaps we will go someplace else today. But the group will be torn apart, that is, for technical reasons. It probably has to do with the transportation. It doesn't matter; the main thing is that the three of us are on the same ship. In any case we will stay together."

"Are we in an insane asylum?" I assert. "Yes, are we going home." Kunze slaps himself on the thigh. "They talk about many foolish things. Don't let yourself be confused. Everything will come out. At 1:00 P.M. is an assembly; then we will hear more," Siegfried says, satisfied, and lies down on his bed.

"In the first place I want to make clear that we are not in an insane asylum," the camp spokesman opens his speech shortly after 1:00 P.M. while he nervously organizes a bundle of rosters. "You are not little children who howl because someone has mistreated you. We are all going home, but not now. Let the postmen get out of here first so that we can send a telegram from Bremen; otherwise those at home will fall dead from shock if we suddenly appear at the door. That's only secondary. All those who I now call out repeat your prisoner number immediately so that no mix-ups occur and move to the left of the group. I have seven transport lists that are finalized. Every attempt to try and change these is futile because the Americans have two carbon copies and are ready to move those to be transferred immediately. So let's begin."

After the lists are read, I am standing by a little group of twelve men. Siegfried was not called out, but Kunze was assigned to a group of forty men. I know for certain that this means our final separation, but I am simply not able to comprehend it. I believe I have reached a state of painlessness, that I can sense nothing. I cannot think and I have no feeling. Perhaps I have a little fear, but that is all. I stand and stare intermittently from Kunze to Siegfried, to whom as well there seems that nothing can be done. The words of the camp spokesman do not reach as far as my understanding. Not until they are all gone do I comprehend that they have attended my funeral and wonder to myself why Kunze and Siegfried do not realize that I am dead. But I can hear Siegfried's voice very clearly. He stands in front of me and next to Kunze. Then finally I come back to reality. A buzz hums in my ears as though two valves have opened. "Yes, I believe that we will see one another again," I hear myself answer. "Then come, you must get your things," Siegfried says. "The others are already in front of the company office." "OK, I'm going now." Life finally returns to me.

"How comfortless November can be," Kunze insinuates as we stand a short distance from the truck that will take me away from here. "Now the asters are blooming in Germany," I remind myself. "Yes, on the graves," Kunze adds. "Cut it out." Siegfried stamps with his foot. "Life goes on. Doesn't it, Helmut?" "For certain just like before, betrayed and unmerciful," I am compelled to respond.

"You will get hold of yourself. Think about your responsibilities to your family and say yes to everything they may ask of you. The day will come when we will be free; then we can take our lives in our own hands," he encourages me. "It's time to get on the truck." Kunze chokes and goes to his truck that is parked in front of the gate. "Yes, it's time." I go from one foot to another and hold Siegfried's hand. "It is for certain that we will see one another again," he says and holds my hand tightly in his. "Then, I'll see you later, Siegfried. Take care," I say and turn to Kunze. "Good luck, Werner, to you and Brigitte. You both deserve each other." I press his hands. "Stay the way you are; the stars do not lie; we will get married on your birthday," he stammers as Siegfried lays his hands on ours.

"Have a cigarette," the guard hands us his pack after we leave Fort Dix and race along the open road. I am not acquainted with any of the men in the truck. Naturally I saw one or the other before, even in Alençon. But to really know them, so that one does not feel alone in a time of need, is not the case. That is why I crawl into my coat and try to sleep. The entire day has been too much. Perhaps I should ask the guard where they are taking us, but I don't really care. Finally, as the truck travels through wooded hill country, I begin to take some interest in the area. Impulsively I ask the American whose cigarettes we have been smoking our destination. "West Point," he announces, which I remember I have read the name somewhere in connection with a military academy. "What did you ask him?" my neighbor wants to know. "Where we are going. We are going to West Point," I explain, somewhat unfriendly. "Ask him what we are going to do there," the man presses me. "It doesn't matter, for all I care train apes." I lean back and look through the slit in the canvas at the mature stands of trees in the forest.

As night falls we reach our destination. A small but clean camp surrounded by a thick forest takes us in. The German spokesman greets us in the clerk's office with heartfelt words and accompanies each one personally to the assigned barracks. Someone has made the beds for us. They are wooden, green-painted bunk beds whose brand new mattresses are covered with a white linen sack. A second sack serves as a sleeping bag in which we can put two blankets, like the Prussians with their blue-and-white-checkered bedding. We do not have to wash it ourselves, we are immediately told.

After we have placed our shaving equipment on a board fastened to the wall, we are called to eat. The mess hall is located on the other side of the camp so that we have to go across the grounds which, with goal posts at both ends, also serves as a soccer field. "It looks like it's a training camp for a future national soccer team," I say bitingly. "It's possible; the people here in the barracks are certainly young enough," someone says in a Mannheim dialect. "Are you from Mannheim?" I ask before we enter the dining hall. "Yes," he answers and lets me go first.

"Take plenty, there's more than enough," the mess sergeant says in a Schwabish dialect after we have spooned empty the first plate of a tasteful green pea soup with pork. "Then we can be friends." The Mannheimer grins and takes my plate without asking back to the counter. "Eat, comrade, and call me Ted. I'd like to call you Helmut. Unfortunately I have known you since the bad days." He laughs a few moments later and places my full plate on the table. "I am pleased, Ted, that I am not completely among strangers." I pull the plate thankfully to me. "There is still a full pot of this stuff in the kitchen. Let's keep going, it really tastes good." He does not let up until I strenuously refuse to take another spoonful.

"I ate eight platefuls," he comments, satisfied, as we waltz across the sports field stuffed like garbage cans the day after Christmas. "Hopefully we will be able to sleep with our filled bellies," I register my thoughts. "Much better than if they were empty," he says and shoves me into the barracks.

After a short conversation with my new comrade about where he is from and the prospects for the future, Ted and I get to know each other better. The homeland has once again retreated in the far distance. Tomorrow we will go to cut trees on an old shooting range to make a ski area for the U.S. Military Academy at West Point. But the food and treatment could not be better, the long-time inmates report. Even the work is not taken too seriously. With this knowledge I snuggle into my warm bed and reflect on the day. A great deal can change in twelve hours, but hope makes it possible to endure everything.

\* \* \*

Also known as Camp Popolopen, the West Point Prisoner of War Camp was located in the hills approximately six miles from the United States Military Academy at West Point. The camp received its first prisoners on January 16, 1945. W. H. McCahon, who inspected the camp on May 18, 1945, noted that the camp capacity was three hundred prisoners and that "the buildings are all wood constructed, the barracks being of CCC [Civilian Conservation Corps] type huts measuring approximately 20 x 120 ft. Sixty men are housed in each of the 5 barracks." The camp made a very favorable impression on McCahon, who noted that in May, at least, the sick rate was exceptionally low and that there had been no escapes and no serious trouble with the prisoners. Most of the prisoners worked to clear land in the surrounding woods, with a detachment of about fifty assigned to West Point. As far as leisure time activities were concerned, he wrote:

> ... its program is very well developed, consistent with the needs of the prisoner group. A sports field is available and sports equipment has been obtained. There are two radios in the compound and a small orchestra has been formed. An adequate library containing German books is available. In addition the usual American newspapers and magazines are on hand. Regular religious services are conducted for both Protestants and Catholics by German-speaking civilian clergymen.[13]

\* \* \*

### 10 February 1946

I have overcome myself and today I resume my diary. The reason for the break lay in my deep depression, during which I simply let everything happen to me more or less as a bystander and without really being conscious of what was going on. There was nothing special that happened to turn me from my lethargy. The Christmas season was full of meaning, uplifting, and not the least, the Americans did demonstrate brotherly love in good measure, which brought everything to a certain high point. But for that reason it seemed to push me and others into a new kind of misery.

The new year saw us without hope and came and went very quietly. We passed the days out in the woods in snow and ice without anyone concerned whatsoever with what we accomplished. Sometimes we were sent to West Point as snow shovelers, where at the gate George Washington with his drawn sword seemed to reprimand us from his pedestal. But the living guards let us enter the holy shrine of the American army without any trouble, simply glad that we were there to help make the streets passable. Hunger, our greatest enemy, remained far away since the kitchen provided more than enough for everything. Should we look at it correctly, every complaint would be a lie, if we only knew when we would see our homeland again.

What I missed the most was my friends. Naturally, it was my own fault when I could not find replacements for them among the many men. But I was afraid that sooner or later I would lose them too, and therefore I closed in around myself rather than be disappointed once again. But still I am not considered a loner because people here don't know me otherwise and I am friendly to everyone. Ted is a good comrade, but unfortunately does not have the same background as I.

Since there is a good library in the camp, I spend the long winter evenings with good literature. Schopenhauer, Nietzsche, Goethe, and Schiller are now my indispensable teachers. Through them I have finally been able to build things up again. In addition, for some time I no longer spend my days in the woods, but instead I am working with a group in the personnel kitchen in West Point.

But all of this did not make me completely healthy because there were certain assumptions that were not met. While nearly every one of my comrades were from the western occupation zone and had received news from their families, I was just about the only one still waiting for mail. As a consequence, my morale was reduced to zero. Although I comforted myself from one day to the next, every evening brought only disappointment until it ate away my confidence and I concluded something was not right with my wife. It was not that I sought her among the war dead. No, I often clearly felt in the long nights that she thought about me, but still something was not in order. Despite the unending rumors about the shameful conduct of the German women, which were nourished daily by the American soldiers' talk, I could never connect the lack of mail with it. At least not as the last consequence. Because of the eternal doubt and being torn here and there, I vegetated and finally denied my inner voice any attention until my existence no longer held me in the present or pulled me toward the future. I had nothing to counteract the unknowing which, with its secret working within the soul in the dream-filled nights, laid everything bare and barred any new hope. So the real consciousness by day was in continual struggle with the incomprehensible power of the night while on the outside I more or less automatically did my work. Then suddenly everything changed with one blow.

As today, like on all other evenings in this camp, I climb indifferently from the truck that brought us back from West Point every day to the barracks. The duty officer lies on my bed grinning in anticipation. "Since when is it the practice for the drones of this camp to misuse the beds of the workers?" I respond, annoyed at the man. "For once I would like to have a nice sausage like you bring the others from the kitchen," he says, unashamed, grinning at me." "I am only willing to give people something if they also earn it," I explain and take what I have brought today from my coat pocket and lay it on the nightstand. "You will soon see that I deserve all the sausage in West Point, when you have read what I have in my possession." He laughs, self-assured. "I can buy my own books or check them out of the library," I continue indignantly and yank the thick olive green sweater off. "No bookstore in the world offers what is on this postcard," he says with a light vibration in his voice and hands me the card on which months ago I had written my address and sent to the homeland for a return response.

Hesitatingly my fingers take the red card. While I glance at it all the men in disbelief stand in a half circle around my bed and share my fate with me. "We are all healthy and well. Don't worry about us. Love Elly," is inscribed in the handwriting of my wife in the blank space on the card. Only the street name and house number are different, I determine in my bewilderment, and plunge outside.

After the second time around the compound, it finally becomes clear to me. They are alive! They are healthy, every nerve pounds like they are bound while my hands let go of the rusty barbed wire and in the milky night of the moon my eyes seek the heavens.

* * *

Helmut had waited months for Elly to write; however, because of a misunderstanding in which Elly was told by another soldier who had seen Helmut in France before he was sent to America that he would be home soon, she thought that there was no purpose in writing. It was not until she received a letter from Helmut in America and mail service was restored following Germany's collapse that she wrote.

* * *

But like always, nothing reveals itself to whom I can shout my warm thanks, except the same stars that were over me in my deepest sorrow and which did not allow me even a partial answer. I do not have God in me; otherwise I would not doubt. But didn't He always whisper to me in the many nights of inner dissolution that they were alive and only unusual circumstances kept the news from me? Miserable worm that I am, why did I not listen to the good inner voice but instead gave heed to the whisperings of the devil? Yes, yes, we want everything in written proof, even from God; and that has made us nihilists.

Finally, after hot and cold shudders wrench my body, I find my way back to the barracks. Shaking, I undress and fall under the covers. "You have a fever, Helmut." Ted takes his hand from my damp forehead and goes for the medic.

### 5 March 1946
The flu epidemic, which laid low nearly one-third of the camp for weeks, is receding and the afflicted are on the road to recovery. Even I am in convalescence and today I am permitted to leave the quarantine barracks. The

snow has disappeared. The athletic field lies dry in the warm March sun, while behind the gates the first green of spring is visible as I wander in the open.

Days and nights full of confused, fever-ridden ideas are now behind me. A spring rejuvenation, just like in nature, now controls my entire being. In the meantime they have dyed our uniforms black for the return home, so that it can only mean in a short time we will begin the return trip home. But I still cannot believe, even though this time it does really appear to be true since they have on hand zone maps of divided Germany with the home address of every man carefully identified and noted in his papers. Preparations for the return home are in full swing throughout the camp. Naturally not on the part of the Americans. What is taking place in the clerk's office remains for us a book with seven seals. But the purchases in the canteen by the comrades, getting sea sacks that are now inscribed with home addresses ready, packing and repacking, are all sure signs of the general change. The work in the woods has slowly come to a halt without raising any concern from the Americans, and is a further sign of a coming event.

And the prices rise, not in the canteen, but in the items traded by the prisoners of war. While many artists among us spent the long winter nights and quiet Sundays creating genuine works of art such as paintings and carvings, which for the most part they gave away, now there is hardly anything to be had unless one has something special to offer himself. There is one especially gifted man who should be noted, who, despite his dubious appearance, produces the most amazing creations. He built machines out of wood that worked perfectly, carved wonderful wooden fruit pieces and wall plates, even figures in natural colors from the cedar wood in the forests around West Point. Before now, the good man had given his masterpieces more or less to his admirers, and now he must experience how they are sold to others for enormous prices. But it does not bother him; instead he continues to work unannoyed, living in the glory enjoyed by true artists.

The same is true for others who craft masterful jewelry boxes out of cedar wood or the shells of turtles that they found the previous summer in the woods. People who possess a rarity, such as the skin of a rattlesnake, or the rattles, are offered enormous prices for their treasures. Even the small, fourteen carat gold cross with chain which during the winter could be purchased in the canteen for eight dollars has doubled in price in the sea sacks of the speculators since the Americans have no longer made them available.

Since I have received mail and thereby life now has a purpose, I also begin, after a long time, to make purchases in the canteen with the sixty dollars that has grown in my account. In opposition to my indifference of the past months, I feel a real buying frenzy inside me. Actually what we are experiencing is something on the order of a closeout sale, since already the shelves are quite bare. But the storekeeper is a friendly man, and for someone who was sick and unable to do anything, he still has something under the counter. In any case, within thirty minutes nearly all my dollars are spent and I return to the barracks to admire my new treasures.

The little gold cross with the neat chain that I was lucky enough to acquire I continually slip through my hands with unrestrained joy. A complete outfit of woodcarving knives is to be my son's inheritance and help me to train my hands, while a chessboard with pieces will be a relaxing pleasure for the entire family. In addition to these presents, I have thirty pieces of the finest toilet soap, which all of Europe has been without for years. Still there is not enough. We think about everything that our dear ones in the homeland now need. Therefore, while in my heart the holy flame of love blazes, my hands caress the lighter, combs, toothbrushes, toothpaste, powder, perfume, razor blades, skin cream, towels, darning needles, and good supply of darning wool. How wonderful is giving, especially for those who have acquired their entire wealth as a slave!

As the work details return, my sea sack is also packed. Now, if God will permit me to unpack it first when I am home once again.

### 16 March 1946

Even though for weeks the inexhaustible theme of our return home has dominated all our being, they still send us to our workplaces every day. And that is good. Even though not much work is being done in the forest, just being there is a good diversion for the men. Others are busy with my group in the kitchen at West Point. There everything goes as before like clockwork, since the soldiers, mostly truck drivers, horse, weapon, and equipment handlers for the academy, want to eat. That is why today I climb into the small truck with complete enjoyment and travel to West Point, where as always we arrive at 7:00 A.M.

"So, you are finally healthy," the sergeant—a product of a Polish maid and a German master—greets me, friendly, as he notices me among his helpers. "Yes, Sergeant, I am doing very well." I take the hand he offers me. "I am very happy for you, but you look a little thin to me. But that will change quickly, won't it?" He laughs like a schoolboy because he knows that I look out for only the best leftovers. "You can be sure, in my condition I certainly will not pass up your stew." I grin with an old familiarity.

"That's right, I don't want you to say that old Boda let you go hungry.

Come, let's have a cup of coffee first. Today we are having ham and eggs." He leads me to my old eating place. "You are a good fellow, Boda. I am going to cry when I have to tell you good-bye," I explain without moving. "Not that; I can't stand tears; I would rather have a case of beer. But tell me, you got a letter, so I heard," he expresses his interest and puts a cup under the coffee machine. "Yes, Boda, finally," I explain and pour condensed milk into the coffee. "Then everything is fine. You will soon dig up a bed for the two of you. Everything else is unimportant," he says in dead earnest.

At eight-thirty the first good-natured soldiers appear for breakfast. Nearly everyone has a joke for us while they hold their plates under the egg scoop. We know them all. That is, we know just how much this one or that one wants to eat and what each individual likes the best. We distribute the portions accordingly.

Weeks ago when we first entered the kitchen, we sensed immediately an uncomfortable animosity on the part of the American personnel. It was worse when the soldiers had to receive their portions from us. They brought us here because the army was being demobilized and every unneeded man was being sent home. It was a bad beginning and we wanted to forego the new assignment. But Sergeant Boda and the responsible officer made sure that we were not harmed. After three days the soldiers calmed down, especially after we prepared chicken German style. Even the cleanliness, which we took great pains to maintain, impressed them. With time we became well acquainted. When once in a while a rube left his chewing gum on the table, the day came when he was ashamed himself and cleaned it up. Sometimes we helped ourselves because we knew our friends and enemies. Our foes received chicken necks and a shrivelled apple while those we liked got drumsticks and bananas.

Today that is long forgotten. Wild Jack is still here. He would prefer a whole cow for breakfast. He gets a heaping plate of ham and eggs and is satisfied. Johnny, the long, skinny clown, eats no ham, only eggs. That's fine, and Mike, the always-sad eyeglass-wearer, says thank you, a cup of coffee is enough. All the men have their peculiarities, which we try to take into consideration; then it is untrue that all people are alike, at least in the small everyday things.

After all have left the dining room satisfied, it's time for us to roll up our sleeves and go to work. All the tables must be washed. The parquet floor must be waxed. The dishes washed. Work in rich measure. But it is a joy to work in an American kitchen where everything is done mechanically. Naturally, you have to know what you are doing. The electrical polisher, for example, causes trouble for every beginner because when it is not handled correctly, it does not polish, but instead hops over the parquet like a wild ram.

Now we are familiar with everything and know when the potato peeling machine has to be turned off before all that is left inside are small balls of potatoes. And Boda has great fun with us. Now he doesn't have to worry about inspections anymore. Therefore he allows us every freedom, especially in the large refrigerator where all the delicacies are kept. Everyone can eat what he wants. That is why by lunch I have put away two pounds of cooked ham. From now on I will avoid the potatoes and only take in strong nourishment, since the happiness in me stimulates a mighty appetite. Since Alençon the Americans have owed me a great amount of provisions and now it is up to me to even the score. But today I am convinced that if we are the next to be sent home, then we can call it equal.

At 7:00 P.M. we leave our workplace. The kitchen and dining room are polished to a high gleam and everything is ready for tomorrow's breakfast. Sergeant Boda now has a little worry because we are taking a five-gallon can of chicken fricassee for our comrades in camp and he doesn't know for sure if the driver will keep quiet about it. But life is a risk; that's why it doesn't bother our conscience, especially since the good food will only be fed to the pigs. Naturally everything is supposed to follow regulations, but crack-brained restrictions must always be corrected by those they impact. That is only successful if none of the participants are possessed by a subservient spirit. One can say much against the Americans with regard to their concept of freedom, but still all people can learn from them. That is manifest again when the driver is happy as a clam to put the rule-makers in their place and makes it clear what will be done with the chicken fricassee. "People come first; the pigs will still get their feed," he says, nearly angry, and shoves the tarp aside so that we can sit down.

A little later we reach camp. A soft spring breeze moves the first green leaves in the ancient trees of the forest through which we travel. The guard at the gate wants to know what is in the can and wonders why we are hauling food into camp, but he understands that it is a delicacy for the prisoners and lets us in. In the barracks Ted is pleased and samples the food after we heat up the can. "We also have a surprise," he says, licking the spoon. "We are leaving here." "So, leaving here, is that all?" I ask skeptically. "By the way, we are not going home." He turns his face to the wall. "What do you mean, damn it all." I glance into the round, disappointed faces. "We are to attend a school in a camp by New York," they finally explain. "How long does the course last?" I ask, unaccented. "That is not known. In any case our return home is once again on ice and we can unpack our sea sacks," a clerk implies who usually is well informed about everything. As a consequence my inner spirit drops back to the freezing point.

After a quick shower, I circle around the barracks until shortly before retreat and finally lie down exhausted in bed. Before I fall asleep I am convinced that we have reached a new turning point and now stand before the last stage of imprisonment. Unusual enough, I feel the old confidence and trust grow inside before sleep lays its gentle hand on my consciousness.

### 11 April 1946

"By and large it was the most peaceful and refreshing camp during our long sojourn," I say to Ted as we light cigarettes and take one last look at the small, sparkling clean camp. "We are healthier than before. We won't find a situation like this one again very soon," he contemplates and carefully brushes the cigarette ashes from his sharply pressed black pants. "In the new camp they want to teach us democracy, Ted. Don't forget that one comprehends a new form of government much better on a full stomach." I try to eliminate the fear of the new unknown for him; then this is the first time I am leaving a camp without any regrets. I don't have to leave my friends behind and I carry the hope that we are coming closer to freedom. "Then why don't we get on our way instead of them making it so suspenseful," he mumbles, displeased, as the camp spokesman appears at the head of the convoy and bids farewell with humorous words.

"The course lasts only four weeks, as far as I have been able to learn. You will still be home before us," he calls as our truck begins to move and rolls out of the camp at the end of the convoy. A warm April morning has already dried the road and permits the vehicles a quick trip along the winding road through the woods in the direction of New York. Sometimes the trees, with their boughs, wave to us trustingly when they are moved by the wind from the truck. Spring is already in their branches and has freed them from their winter slumber so that they, like us, are anxiously prepared and await only the starting signal which will allow them to unfold freely.

We will take a reeducation course, then board a ship, and fourteen days later set foot on German soil in Bremen. How simple it all suddenly seems. Actually too simple to be true after so many disappointments. But it cannot be otherwise! It must finally end something like this. Have I anticipated it too long so that now my heart does not rejoice? Or is there still something that will make my return home a struggle? But no, I am glad. It is only the eternal fear of the incomprehensible power of chance, providence, or fate. The fear of the doubting Thomas, who is punished by the Almighty because he only calls on God in the deepest need and affliction and expects an immediate answer. How naive I really have always been. Again and again I try to push my way into the secrets that life sets down, even though I know that I am knocking on the wrong door.

* * *

The two-week reeducation program which Helmut attended at Camp Upton to learn more about America and democratic ideas was a modification of two different reeducation programs. The first was a sixty-day course at Fort Getty and Fort Wetherill, Rhode Island, between May and October 1945 which graduated 1,166 prisoners considered to be the most promising and cooperative anti-Nazis as identified by the intelligence officers and assistant executive officers in prisoner of war camps around the country. The graduates were returned directly to Germany to take over minor German government posts. A shorter, more intensive six-day course operated at Fort Eustis, Virginia, from January 4 through April 5, 1946. With ten hours a day of lectures, discussion, films, forums, and English lessons, over 23,000 prisoners went through the Fort Eustis program, which revolved around twelve major topics: (1) The Democratic Way of Life; (2) The Constitution of the United States; (3) Political Parties, Elections, and Parliamentary Procedures; (4) Education in the United States; (5) American Family Life; (6) The American Economic Scene; (7) American Military Government; (8) Democratic Traditions in Germany; (9) Why the Weimar Republic Failed-I; (10) Why the Weimar Republic Failed-II; (11) The World of Today and Germany; (12) New Democratic Trends in the World Today.[14]

* * *

But there is New York. Slowly we travel into the jungle of this world city. Our way goes over Washington Bridge along Broadway, then off a bypass road and later past Manhattan with its mighty skyscrapers and on to Long Island. There are too many impressions to hold them all, but we will never forget the scenes, since it is no picture show, but New York as it really is, a witch's pot without comparison. Gigantic and phenomenal. A city of which mankind can be proud, I believe; then I have not seen anything greater created by the hand of man.

We roll past the happiness of this world and a short time later Long Island spreads out before us. "You are here in Camp Upton, New York," a good-looking American in an elegant civilian suit greets us in the camp theater in a German that suggests he is a Rhinelander, while the German camp spokesman stands next to him beaming cheerfully. "You will stay in this camp and attend a school which will give you a good foundation in democratic thought to take with you when you board the ship to return home. Naturally there will be work details in the nearby hospital. The work there is not overly demanding, but it is necessary.

The provisions here are abundant and through your own incentive they can be improved from the hospital kitchen. Whoever is caught stealing, is himself guilty; besides I don't think the punishment will be very heavy. In any case, to this time no one has wanted to catch anybody. I am available for all difficulties that may come up for any individual. I promise to be here for everyone and when possible to ease any problem. Whoever follows orders will never have a reason to complain. That is all. And now we will elect a company leader who brings with him the necessary prerequisites and will be responsible for the care of 250 men."

\* \* \*

Camp Upton, named for Emory Upton, was established in 1917 on land donated to the federal government. In August 1946, two months after Helmut Hörner left the area, the military reservation was designated for atomic research and subsequently became known as Brookhaven National Laboratory.

\* \* \*

At 10:30 P.M., about an hour after the unusual welcome speech of this even more unusual American, I enter the orderly room as a newly baked company spokesman, accompanied by the clerk that I have selected. While our quarters consist of tents like those we had in Alençon, floor boards have been laid down, heat is available, and splendid beds are there for us. The orderly room, kitchen, mess hall, and other buildings are regularly constructed barracks. We are greeted like comrades by the other company leaders and the other company personnel and immediately introduced to our new assignment. The entire responsibility includes practically the functions of a sergeant major, from the paperwork to evening roll call, which is set for 5:00 P.M. daily except Sundays and holidays.

After a plentiful lunch, which consists of spinach, potatoes, and roast beef, my clerk and I sit behind the typewriters and clatter out the names and work rosters in four copies while our comrades pick up bedding and work clothes. When we have finally completed our work and reach into the pack of cigarettes offered us by the very polite company leader and begin to refresh ourselves with a little talk, the gong sounds outside, calling us to roll call.

Roll call goes in perfect order. Every company leader has a board with numbers on hooks above his desk on which every man in camp must hang his token. With these tokens and the work detail rosters, he can determine the company strength in the orderly room. The U.S. sergeant on duty does the same thing, so that roll call can be completed, even though some details do not return until about midnight.

No problems arise when the officer and I halt at the end of the company and compare lists. The numbers agree. The officer greets the company, friendly, and then retreats again. After I have explained to the group that I don't feel I am cut out to be a company leader, but I am thankful for the trust they have placed in me and will play the boss as long as it is bearable for all concerned, I assign the work details. In the end, everyone seems content since nearly all are assigned to the hospital kitchen, even though some don't understand that we can't spend the entire night redoing the lists so that they can work with their friends.

After dinner I finally have the opportunity to get acquainted with my new quarters, which Ted and two others share with me. I stand in front of my bed reflectively considering a pinup girl, scantily clothed in a teasing nightgown, whose photo is pasted on the tent wall. "If I did not meet your taste, you can move into my place." Ted grins at me unashamedly because I apparently spend too much time in front of the picture. "It's in order, Ted; in any case, this kind of wallpaper is not the worst, but in our situation they do stimulate sordid fantasies," I explain, amused, and sit on my bed while my eyes take in the other nine pictures in a row.

"Our predecessors, who had hungry eyes for women and undressed them in their thoughts, are now swimming toward home," number three in the tent laughs—a true-hearted Schwab. "Then I hope that is a taste of what is ahead for us." I point with my hand to a sumptuous doll. "I will not meet anyone quite that beautiful, but what is there is genuine," indicates the fourth one, a school teacher from Stralsund named Karsten. "That's the most important in any case. There must be a heart sitting under the bosom; otherwise you can keep them all. Something like those can be bought, like a glass of wine. Sometimes it tastes good, other times it doesn't. But you still have to pay for it." The Schwab claps his large backhand against an innocent picture. "What do you hear about the return home?" I ask abruptly.

"That is good. I imagined that we are in the news center and now the company leader asks us what is going on." The school teacher rings his hands theatrically. "Do you believe I have had a minute's time before now to chat?" I become irritated. "Oh, it is always the same with the orderly room gang. They work themselves to death and then squat at the table and sleep with open eyes," Ted laments and continues, "so let's instruct the company leader. In this camp everyone is completely convinced that in the next few weeks we will be shipped out. The schooling consists almost exclusively of lessons in American history, while the work in the hospital plays a secondary role. According to the opinion of the know-it-alls, they are looking at us under a lens in order to distinguish between those who are ripe to return home and those who are future werewolves. So it doesn't matter at all if one was a Nazi before or not; the main thing is that he has given up his former outlook and in the meantime has come to a better understanding, at least that is what they say in camp, and this Mr. Kohlenblau, the American gentleman in the camp, is supposed to have found his closest friends among former members of the SS. That is, in a broad stroke, a picture of this so-called reeducation camp."

"We will be numbered among those returning home even though Nietzsche warned us against transplanting Americanism to Europe; the foundation of this viewpoint is that individual freedom is better than the lockstep of Nazism," I confirm in closing. "It's too bad that no listening device is in the tent. With those statements you would certainly have earned your ship tickets, if Mr. Fox had heard you." The school teacher looks at me in amazement. "Then do me a favor and go tell him what I said; those ship tickets are very valuable to me," I suggest laughingly. "And the price, that you have to lick his boots?" he asks lightly. "No, if only spit-lickers could go home, I would rather stay behind barbed wire; then I would consider that as a mark of distinction," I explain forcefully.

"Then I am in agreement with your election, although I voted against you," he expresses candidly. "And why were you against me?" I ask, slightly irritated. "Because at West Point you were such still water, and the reasons were obviously deep," he brings into the open. "I was sick up in the mountains, emotionally sick, do you understand that?" I lay my hand on my heart. "Yes, very well, then I had to wait for mail nearly as long as you." He nods in full understanding and leaves the tent.

During the course of the evening, my hope for the upcoming return home increases. In conversation with the American gentleman and the German camp spokesman in the orderly room, I learn of the departure of a part of the camp inmates who have just received their diplomas and are to go to sea in the next few days. I especially accept the openness of the long-time inmates from whom the burden of a long, uncertain stay as prisoners appears to be lifted. This I attribute not in the least to the work of this unusual, good-hearted, and intelligent Mr. Fox.

The man has the gift to radiate a power of persuasion which is very difficult to ignore. But still something warns me about him that I cannot explain. Perhaps it annoys me because he has the habit when he asks a direct question to avoid looking directly at the individual by covering his watery blue eyes with sunglasses even though there is no sunlight in the barracks. In the same way I do not understand the complete lack of concern by the German camp spokesman. He is supposedly an educated former head of a German university and now accepts every word of the American with a demeanor bordering on mindless worship, even though his words from the most obscene theme to high politics contain many contradictions. Or has the German intellectual seen through the other and plays a magnificent role to assure his return home? Already in bed, I break my head over those two. I plan to watch myself, to exercise caution and keep my eyes open. One thing is clear to me: the physical well-being of my associates is in need of no attention since the kitchens offer excellent fare which can also be supplemented with the permitted thieving in the hospital. But the future for each one of us certainly lies in the hands of the civilian caretakers who, like magicians, control not only the masses, but also the intellectuals of the camp like marionettes. And that is what does not allow me to sleep; then I feel in me the fear of a weakling against the power of the incomparable strong ones.

### 23 April 1946

Today, the seventeenth day after our arrival in Camp Upton, I find time to take up my pen to indulge my hobby and continue with my writing. I pull out of my sea sack the many pages I have written and spend an hour leafing through them. I am seized with a vision that I have in my hands a contemporary document of our violated generation which will provide my descendants with a glimpse into an occurrence that has become history and will make them aware of the entire epoch. But that was not my intention. It was to be assumed that one could read about it in the history books that will be written by professional historians who seek authentic documents in order to make possible the actual connections. From the beginning on I held fast to all of the developments in my immediate neighborhood, what I heard, thought, and felt. If here or there I have gone too far in my contemplation, saw things false, judged them wrong, I am still not ready to strike them out. I came to the conclusion to preserve everything— how the little infantryman, the courageous German soldier with all of his prerogatives, weaknesses, and errors, experienced, endured, and in nameless sacrifice to the terror of a horrible regime, the terrible conflict of total war, and the interminable suffering of imprisonment, has carried it all patiently to the edge of personal doubt. To him, the German soldier, the hero against his own will, and the brave mothers, wives, brides in the faraway burned and bombed but still-treasured homeland, is this record dedicated.

Still it is not so far. Still it is not for sure that the many pages I have written will reach the homeland with me. New rumors, spread by the hospital personnel, report of deportation to France and England. Because some Americans are not familiar with our mentality they unknowingly and thoughtlessly seek to stamp out the last sparks of the flame of love for the homeland and for German women in that they boastfully expose their dirty sexual orgies in Germany. They are eager to hold before the shocked eyes of the poor wretches the pictures that they took so that for the prisoners the tortuous nights once again threaten to pulverize their souls.

But now the great personality of our civilian guardian is made manifest to me. With persistence and tenacity he moves against the rumors, using his mid-day lecture on active democracy in that he stands by the weak, excuses the whisperings of his countrymen, makes them seem like trifles, and becomes something of a psychiatrist for those suffering from prisoner psychosis within the camp community. Furthermore, he knows how to fill the evenings with improvised variety programs so that the masses begin to tear themselves from their initial lethargy and, in fact, become enthusiastic.

The next program is for the entire camp to go to the ballot box. In certain regards it is to be a practical example of democracy as the camp is to elect a new spokesman. The candidates have been nominated and busy hands paint scream-ing placards which put forward the strengths of each. Although it is clear that the incumbent will be elected again, nearly the entire camp is caught up in the electioneering. But Mr. Fox reaches his objective. The people are diverted. The hate-filled rumors are silenced. Only in a limited sense is the mistrust still awake. But it is silent, like me, then I have seen through this American Goebbels and recognize his nearly boundless power over us. Only when I set foot in the homeland will I be ready to forgive him. Still, I do not shut myself off from his entire racket since the hullabaloo is good medicine for all of us. The more one can believe in it, the better he overcomes the time. Because those who swim against the flow waste their strength and will be destroyed, I remain quiet in the belief that my opinion cannot influence fate.

As far as Mr. Fox is concerned, I don't believe one word. A silversmith who comes from Pforzheim and is now a wealthy American now living in New York spoke to me at the fence and told me that the man is paid by the American Information Service. The same assertion has been seeping through the tiny canals of the camp for days. And the aged colonel, the military commander of the camp, carries beneath his friendly mask secret grief in his heart. Lies, to young people at his age, is a torment. But today you are already forgiven, Mr. Colonel, in case you must act according to procedures which affect my fate.

*7 May 1946*

The rumors of the first transports to the homeland have proven true. The day before yesterday two hundred men were brought to Camp Shanks for shipment, with all the best wishes for the future not only from their German comrades, but also the Americans as well. The men were not searched. It is indescribable—the resulting good spirits and trust in anticipation of the return home. The people of the United States of America are praised as the most humane under the sun, and woe be to those who might be of another opinion. Yes, I am of the same viewpoint, even though the inner devil encourages me to be careful. Naturally that is because this is not the first time I have rejoiced in the promised return home.

Even the election of a camp spokesman is behind us. Nothing has changed because the old one was elected again and a new one was not necessary. In camp everything is in good hands. It simply cannot be better. We live like maggots on bacon. The work details return to the tents with large quantities of meat, eggs, butter, milk, and cigarettes. The work details in the hospital have access to all the provisions, which they pack in clean kept garbage cans which are brought into camp by the removal details who pick up our garbage where the food barrels are exchanged for the garbage cans. It all works like a fine watch. The Americans have no interest whatsoever to look into the secrets of the prisoners and it causes me to wonder why. But it is difficult to find an answer. Perhaps it can be explained that officially they do not want to seem like they are fattening us up, but in reality they are pleased if we do gain weight; then no one in starving Europe will believe that we suffered any need while in the American prison camps. At least that is my opinion on the matter. But in general that does not matter to us. In any case from evening to evening a smell hangs over the tents from secret recipes, frying steaks, bacon and eggs, and who knows what all. And the Americans are silent.

But today, on the eve of the anniversary of the announcement of Germany's capitulation, the civilian guardian proves again his integrity with regard to the recently concluded preparation of packages. For days every hour of our free time was filled with packing packages which will be declared as our personal possessions and will be sent by way of Geneva in advance of our return home. Nearly everyone has three large packages lying in the storehouse ready to go which have been approved by the censor even though I continually wonder at what my comrades consider their personal possessions. But the guardian is a gentleman, I must admit, since he has generously overlooked everything even though he discovered a considerable amount of U.S. army property in the boxes.

Even the officially forbidden and only superficially disguised packages of cigarettes are quietly overlooked. Even though I do not express it, I still wonder if the packages will ever get to our homes and the whole camp shares my view. That's why our guardian arranges with the commander that at least two Germans must accompany the packages when they are delivered to the post office in New York in order to confirm for the rest of the camp, everything is in order.

Now I have the opportunity to see with my own eyes where the cartons are taken since the gentleman has assigned me and another company leader to be the witnesses. That is, today I am traveling to New York to see the city for the third time and to attend the delivery of our jointly stolen packages. Again, heaven may forgive me if I do this man an injustice, but I am tossed and torn by doubts as the two trucks roll out of the camp in the direction of New York with their freight and the two of us as witnesses.

The sky looks down on us somewhat unfriendly and we sit uncomfortably among the cartons, but the motor hums its song through the land which the nearness of the city does not disturb. Suddenly, the picture changes. Barely have the first houses appeared than the traffic swells to a river and slows all the drivers. At the first post office we are sent away because it is overfilled. Cursing, the responsible sergeant climbs back into the cab and once again we submerge into the bustling traffic without passing a particularly interesting spot in these canyons of streets.

Sometime later our truck reaches the black section of Harlem, enters a terribly dirty street, and stops in front of a tall postal building. Shortly thereafter an elevator lifts all the freight to the dizzy heights of the building where, in a gigantic hall, numerous blacks handle and stamp the packages. No doubt anymore; the personal belongings of the German prisoners of war in the USA will reach the homeland. This same program is carried out in all the camps. Packages from many states are stored here, well packed with clearly written addresses, the appropriate stamps of the Red Cross and the U.S. government, all ready for shipment.

Ten minutes later we drive over bananas and orange peels out of the residential district of the blacks, New York's most unfortunate people. Where there is much light there are many shadows is what we say in Germany, and that applies absolutely to this one-of-a-kind city.

Tonight we can report to the camp that the packages were delivered to the right place. Now it is up to the postal service when we, that is our family members, can make use of the goods out of wealthy America. With this, another chapter in the camp is closed. For the moment there is nothing at all to complain about. The night will be peaceful and give everyone a healthy sleep.

### 9 June 1946

The slanting golden rays of the setting sun fall on the mess hall as the comrades who are designated to be shipped out press through the entrance to take part in an improvised farewell party. Two hundred men, including Ted and me, and nearly all my company, will go to nearby Camp Shanks early in the morning to be shipped out. Now I stand tired and worn out in front of the orderly room, in the circle of those who helped me complete all the necessary paperwork during the day. My thoughts take the way that lies before us. I wait in vain for the exalted feeling that should be in my breast on the eve of our departure for home. Although a happy shock went through me when I found my name on the transport list early this morning, a little later I was overcome by paralyzing doubts because of the unusual circumstances. One of the bosom buddies of the American guardian was also on the list but the American ordered his name removed. As others asked to be able to return home with those friends who were to stay behind and even provided substitutes, he rejected it with such a definite scruff that it blew ice cold from his personage.

From that moment on I tried throughout the entire day to read his face. But he was stronger than I and will always be so. In his well-groomed face, there is, to this hour, no trace to be found which can give my mistrust any new nourishment. But unusual enough, there is also no sorrow in my heart until the colonel, in the accompaniment of two lieutenants, comes through the door with leaden, taciturn face, to take part in the celebration. A light melancholy comes over me. Does the man, who has been like a good father to all of us, know where we will land? How it must pain his old heart when he is forced to lie.

"I greet all of the homebound in my position as commander of the Prisoner of War Camp Upton," the colonel begins his speech through a translator to those of us assembled in the decorated dining hall, "and I am happy with you that this disgraceful time of imprisonment is coming to an end. I know that great hardships lay behind, but also in front of you, and I wish you the power to overcome the past and strength for what comes. Your return home is now a reality. Tonight, for you the last in Camp Upton, brings us together once again for a meaningful hour. A worthy conclusion to all the good instruction you have received. I hope that never again among the peoples of this earth will it come to the shedding of blood. I wish you all a happy return home."

After we Germans have thanked the honorable commander for his unbiased speech with unrestrained applause, the German camp spokesman rises and turns to the assembly: "It is for me, tonight, a special need, and I know I speak for all to express my and the entire camp's sincere and heartfelt thanks to our commander, the officers, the guards, the hospital administrators as well as the entire personnel within Camp Upton, and not in the least our guardian, Mr. Fox. Thanks for everything which we prisoners of war in this camp, and I would like to add in this land, have experienced for the good and for the hope-filled future. But after we have all left the land, the freest under the sun, we still carry in us the knowledge that its people have also learned to know and treasure us. Not every one of us had the opportunity to come in daily contact with the leaders of the camp. But they showed a high measure of tolerance for us. Even the last among us realize your boundless goodwill and that you did everything you could to lighten our burden. Therefore I would like to thank the Americans, but also to attach to this thanks, the wish that they will never grow weary until the last soldiers of this most terrible of all wars is carried back to the homeland."

After the applause for the speaker's words end, we all help ourselves to that which the kitchen personnel have prepared for us. Coffee and artistically decorated cakes in plenty adorn the long tables, and are praised by everyone. It is true that in view of the richly provided fare many are conscious of the hunger in the homeland and the happiness of the upcoming return home looks somewhat dubious. Certainly there is not one among us who would not rather be eating potatoes with his loved ones instead of these cakes. It is also not the case that the Americans through their own initiative made this farewell banquet possible. Nearly everything which can be found on the banquet tables was provided by our comrades in the hospital. It may be that our American guests wonder quietly about the richly provided tables, the paper napkins, etc., but it still tastes good and they act as though they had delivered it themselves. And we find that to be more than proper. Every uninitiated observer would simply never imagine that here prisoners sit at a feast with their captors. United and without dissension, we share the joy of this hour.

After an hour passes, the officers leave, as etiquette dictates, and we are by ourselves. Mr. Fox approaches us with the wish of the few soldiers who are still here. They want to hear the song "Lili Marlene" and he encourages us to sing. Somehow this melody must touch the Americans just as it did us since we heard it for the first time over the German soldier program from Belgrade, and we do the favor for him. The spirit is so good that a number of harmless soldier songs go out from the stage until even the guardian is tired and he directs his uniformed comrades to conclude it. As they exchange a few words with the camp spokesman in front of the orderly room, a wiry fellow who works in the commander's office as a clerk comes back to us in the mess hall and wants to hear the "England Song" from us. Because for good reasons I try to obstruct his wish, he encourages my comrades himself to sing the song, which they immediately do without thinking and so from the hall a loud chorus breaks into the night, "Then we sail, then we sail against England, England."

"So that's it," I say to Ted on the way back to our quarters. "We are sailing to England." "You are crazy, Helmut," he answers, shocked. "It may be that I am the next to go off the deep end, but now I see it all very clear, too clear my friend. But I must ask you to be silent. It is in the interest of all to be silent since they are all so happy and I may be mistaken." I laugh wearily and throw the door to the tent open.

Under the glaring light of the electric lamp, Ted still shakes his head in unbelief. "That can't be. There is no person so base and underhanded as you suggest," he says with conviction. "Perhaps they lie because they are not so base as to tell us the truth. I am ready to lie to myself because I don't want it to be true and I want to be sure you have a good night's rest," I explain as we undress.

"What are you two talking about?" the teacher asks just after he enters the tent and catches the last words of our conversation. "About the return home, naturally; Helmut is afraid that he won't get us to the right ship," Ted answers before I can find an excuse. "He can leave that to the Americans; they know the way to England," the teacher Karsten says so tranquilly that I jump out of bed, my mouth wide open like Ted's. "What do you mean?" I ask with no inflection. "Nothing, keep your mouth shut. I want to go to sleep," he responds very quietly and turns the light out so that it is night around and in us, as we lie already like in a grave.

### 10 June 1946

The sun overhead stands ready to blow its hot breath on us as it watches the black homeward bound uniforms with their preciously filled sea sacks get into the buses that stand at the camp gate. While Mr. Fox, the American gentleman, stays out of sight, the commander concerns himself in a fatherly way with our well-being. He continues to come to the windows to ask if everyone has a seat, to take roll call, compare the count, and finally to say good-bye with a military salute as the motors begin to whine and the vehicles are set in motion.

The farewell occurs quietly and painlessly. Despite the fine care, or perhaps because of it, no close comradeship came about. Mr. Fox interceded far too much in the personal life of each one. He had all the strings in his hand and everyone danced the way he wanted. That is why I am now happy to be separated from his presence. After some time, we enter a section of woods and the steep, sloping way slows all travel, but we arrive safe and sound in Camp Shanks, which now, in its mighty expanse, stretches before our eyes. The sight of the many Germans, all clothed in the black uniforms with the bright "P.W." initials on their backs like us, standing around inside the wire fences, makes it clear to me that today we will board no ship. That is confirmed immediately when we leave the buses and are received by the camp leader. It will be between two and seven days before we board the ships, is the information that this man has already given to thousands before us.

\* \* \*

Camp Shanks served as the port of embarkation for U.S. troops headed to Europe during the war. Helmut Hörner was one of the last German soldiers to leave the United States. Prisoners of war were sent on every available ship, so that by the end of May 1946, 90 percent of the German prisoners had departed the United States and only 37,491 German prisoners remained. The last group, 1,388 prisoners of war (not counting 141 serving prison terms, 134 in hospitals or psychiatric wards, and 25 escapees) left Camp Shanks on board the *Texarkana* on July 23, 1946.[15]

\* \* \*

Thirty minutes later we are already in the barracks and indifferently place our sea sacks on the unmade beds. Immediately, however, I am surprised by a development which borders on the impossible. The man who enters our barracks with the roster in his hand is none other than Master Sergeant Boger, whose acquaintance I made in the hospital in Paris. But I restrain myself and remain sitting on the bed; obviously he has grown older, and it is possible I am mistaken. Since he must check with everyone to see what they need, our paths will soon cross and we will see if he remembers me.

But it has already happened. "Ja, is it possible?" He beams at me. "Helmut, right?" "You've got it, Boger." I shake both of his hands until we notice that his list is flying all over the barracks. "I can't believe it. The world is indeed small." He cannot recover from his amazement. "Yes, wonders and signs are occurring, old friend; but I have a question for you which has troubled me for some time and for which you, in your position, can perhaps answer for me. But there is time. Take care of your duties after you tell me where I can find you in this jungle," I say very seriously and quietly because our reunion has caught the attention of many.

"Man, I believe that you did put into practice the suggestion I made in Paris." He laughs like a school boy. "What do you mean?" I ask cautiously. "Ja, man, have you become a professor here? You are so puffed up when you speak to me. Damn it again, everyone has gone crazy in this land. Everyone is an academic; apparently all the normal soldiers have died," he storms like before his first outing in Paris when he did not know the address of the girl telegraphist.

"You are unjust in your opinion, but who in the meantime has learned something does not need to be crazy. Have I changed for the worse?" I ask jokingly. "I didn't mean that, but I have experienced that every time the comrades changed camps they became more educated, and naturally more conceited. Finally, I was only with people who had declined to be officers because they knew from the beginning we would lose the war and I know for sure what kind of bootlickers they were earlier and how, during the time of hunger, they clamored for victory. Or did you know in Paris that we would lose?" He hangs his bitter words on this question.

"No, Boger. Then I still believed in Germany's victory and I am not ashamed of it, but I don't worry about it now and I do not trust any discussion about it. That is why I have a question for you," I continue, keeping to the point. "Then I am not disappointed with you. I believe I know what you mean and I will try and answer with as much certainty as I can. Come after lunch to barracks 72; it is quite small here. I am free until 4:00 P.M." he says in farewell with a knavish wink and presses two meal tickets in my hand.

As I lie in the bed and think about the unexpected meeting with Boger, the rumors spin in masses around my ears. No wonder. Prisoners of war from all the states in the United States come to this camp. In and out. Ted is now on his haunches and has his ears tuned in to every conversation. But he makes things easy. He only believes the positive rumors which substantiate that we will soon be on our way home. He rejects all the others that suggest transport to England or France. Naturally spirits are stimulated and the clowns are at work spreading their nonsense. I am nearly thankful to Mr. Fox because he acted with such prudence; then it is clear to me that whoever lands in England or France will not soon see the homeland. And too bad for us if we had known for sure.

After we eat, which ended up being quite meager, I look for Boger and meet him as he is lying on his bed. "Sit down, my boy," he says with an old familiarity and sits up. "You are worried, I know. But at the moment I cannot help you. The situation is this: as soon as I know with which transport you are going to sea, then I can find out to which country it is going. But I will tell you up front, there are transports that go to Le Havre that are taken on to Germany by train.

Even under these circumstances everything is possible and there is no reason to be upset. I have been here since January and I know that not all who went happily on board ship arrived in the homeland. It is quite an indecent thing that the Americans have done and it can come up bitter for them one day if the Russians handle things better. Still, we won't let them get the best of us, will we?"

"I won't mess my pants if it doesn't go right, even though the thought of it makes me nearly sick. I have been preparing myself for everything for eight weeks, but one does not believe the worst very well. How long do you think the others will be held in case they reach the wrong harbor?" I ask with an ache in my belly. "It can't be very long; then the Americans are already thinking about the next war. The Russians are making the victory a conflict for them, something we have known for a long time. There is a worm in this victory, I tell you. The bear has been killed and now it is the fight over his hide. Unfortunately we are caught in the middle. It is a dumb situation, but tell me, have you received mail from home?" He changes the subject. "Yes, shortly before Christmas. Everything is fine at home, at least they are all still alive," I explain. "That is the main thing, my parents are also alive," he says happily.

"Did you hear anything from Inge at the time?" I ask, remembering his previous hope. "No." He reaches for his cigarettes and offers one to me. "I ended up in prison shortly after I was released from the hospital. I was taken to a racetrack near London where I nearly starved to death. Then I came to America in August. Here it was not too bad; at least the Americans make sure you live even though after the end of the war they hung the breadbasket damn high. I was then sent to a lumber camp. By the way, the trees are still standing that I was to cut down. Still, I earned my twenty dollars a month and bought this watch. The boys took mine while I was in France. But I am satisfied; this one is better than my old one. Fourteen carat gold, and I have got other things. But stop, I am talking only about me. I see you have taken good care of yourself; how was it for you?"

When I leave Boger at 4:00 P.M. because he must go on duty, I feel much better. The provisions for Ted and me in this camp are insured. Boger gives us as many meal tickets as we want. Naturally it is not right. Schulz would have turned them down flat. But I am not that dumb anymore. We know nothing at the moment about when we will be shipped out, but Boger will do some reconnoitering for us. So I go back to Ted so that, with regard to the provisions, he does not need to worry any more as long as we are here.

In the evening we make the rounds with Boger on the camp streets. We will be on the high seas in three days, if Boger's information service is correct. Three more days then the *Empress of York* will carry us to Bremen. Perhaps. ...

## 14 June 1946

The veil of a delicate early mist lies above the water on which the wide and stout *Empress of York* sits ready to receive us. She is not docked in a harbor with dock walls and loading cranes, but on the other side of New York, two hundred meters from a lonesome beach from which a primitive wooden gangplank leads to the ship. At one time, Camp Shanks and this lonely beach served the American invasion troops, which used this location as their springboard for their victorious push into Europe. Now we stand here, German prisoners of war with the same goal in our hearts, but instead intended on a peaceful return home. After they have pushed us around for years into all corners of the world, young Americans, our guards, stand with us also on the beach and shall return to the land of their fathers to keep the peace there. But the same joy is not to be seen in their faces as in ours. For them it means good-bye to a homeland that was untouched by the war, which gave them a life of freedom and unconcern while we Germans marched through Hell and now are finally ready to return to our exit point.

Yes, Boger's information has sealed in all of us the belief we will be going home. So we say good-bye in silence to the land in which we experienced the deepest sorrow and highest joy. Without a word, we obey the order to pick up our sea sacks and follow the officer and his soldiers on the swaying gangplank on board the *Empress of York*.

"Hopefully we will have good weather," Ted says after we have put our sea sacks in the bottom of the ship. "Now it is June; then it was April, Ted." I catch my breath and look around the room. We find ourselves again on a troop transport of the liberty class. Only the canned rations are missing. Ted notices it immediately since he was also on board during the stormy trip. "Let's look for a bunk." I turn to those who are the last to be with me from this terrible time.

"That's not so important. We will be in Bremen in twelve days. I will sit on the back end, if it is necessary." Ted laughs and toddles with me along the bunks where shaving kits have already been placed to indicate that they are taken. "Here are two that are empty." I stop. "Then I will take the lower one," Ted says, satisfied, and rolls his massive body into the bunk. "Are you comfortable," I grin at him. "Who can feel his bones when he lays down was simply too lazy to eat," he bellows in a baritone voice his conviction and brings all those in our vicinity to laughter as I also test my bunk.

But I should not have done it. I should not have selected this bunk. Why did I have the misfortune to climb into this bunk which sends so much fear and shock into me that I am not able to utter any noise while over and under me the good humor of my comrades spreads out. But I soon know; everything has its purpose and meaning. They simply cannot read what is written above me on the canvas. I may not tell anyone, I realize; otherwise a tumult will break out if I open my mouth or show anyone what is written in capital letters. "10 March boarded in Camp Shanks. Goal Bremen—Hunger—Disembarked 22 March in Liverpool, England. Everything is only lies!!"

What should I do? Jump overboard. It is not far to shore. The ship has not moved. But they will either shoot me or capture me and it would all be for naught. As the engines start up, I take the cup myself and taste the bitter drink for the reason that whispers in me, everything is up to fate.

"Come, now we can go on deck." Ted shakes me. I willingly, but without feeling, follow the gangway up and approach the railing with him. In the meantime the sun has dispersed the mist. The tops of the trees sway gently beyond the shore and wave to us good-bye with their dark green leaves as the ship gets underway. Silently I turn from the land and look eastward where the gigantic water desert of the Atlantic seems to blend in with the cloudless blue of the sky. Homebound? Not yet, but time will work for us.

*Chapter Seven*

# ENGLAND AND HOME

TIME DID WORK for us. We unloaded in Liverpool, England. Our dismay was beyond measure. The English knew it and they handled us like one would try to comfort angry children. They put us on a train in Liverpool which we quickly compared with what the Americans had spoiled us. The German prisoners of war in the USA were transported just like the citizens of the immense land—in highly modern, very comfortable private company trains. Served by waiters in white jackets, who brought our food to us where we sat. That was one of the first American wonders for us. But in England we sat on very old wood benches and traveled across London to Colchester, a city in southeast England. Immediately that brought us poor fools to the thought that we would be loaded on ships and sent from there to Germany. We all shouted "Hosanna!" until it was made clear to us when we reached a very large camp full of German prisoners that we would be sent out to work camps. Then followed howling and gnashing of teeth.

\* \* \*

In June 1945, the United States held 2.1 million German prisoners of war in Europe in addition to the approximately 375,000 prisoners in the United States. Under agreements negotiated during the war, the German prisoners of war were slated to help with the reconstruction of England and Europe. Of the nearly 2.5 million prisoners held by the United States, France received 700,000 prisoners; Great Britain 175,000—one of whom was Helmut Hörner; Belgium received approximately 50,000 prisoners; and an additional 50,000 were divided between the Netherlands, Scandinavia, Czechoslovakia, Yugoslavia, and Greece. Another 600,000 were to be kept by the United States for work with the armed forces in Europe. The last German prisoner of war held by the United States was released on June 30, 1947, a year after the last German prisoners of war left American soil. Helmut Hörner was one of the last German prisoners to leave England. Among the Western powers, the French held German prisoners of war the longest, with the last being released in the summer of 1948. In the east, German prisoners of war were held in the Soviet Union until the early 1950s.[1]

* * *

While our new guards went through our well-filled sea sacks under the strict supervision of officers, we observed the terrible, depressing, filthy huts which were to be our quarters.

Our new caretakers were good people. They knew how to turn a disappointed, obstinate, conspiring herd into a purposeful, but powerless and harmless group. After a few days I landed with four other comrades in Work Camp 95 in the vicinity of the cities of Watford and Saint Albans in the green belt around London. From this main camp we were sent to a nearby hostel with a company of German prisoners gathered from all corners of the earth. The barracks were acceptable, though primitive compared with those in America. But there was no bedding or blankets. Still, the Germans kept it sparkling clean. The unwritten rules of the German army were in force, which obviously the English did not oppose.

The English divided the food they had with us. We know that for sure because we could look into the pots of the workers daily, and they in ours. We were satisfied. I was used as a translator. My only work was to pass on the instructions of the English to about fifteen comrades. I did not have responsibility to oversee their work. We did not need any. Relatively speaking, things went well for us. Naturally we were homesick, concerned about our families and homeland; no one was spared that since we knew, as far as we could imagine, at least, what was going on in Germany. We had official stationery that hardly anyone used. Instead, we German prisoners of war used airmail letters sent through the public mails with money we earned for our work.

I, along with others, used the mail to send the money which we earned, about thirty-two marks each month, to our wives. For comparison, my wife paid twenty-five marks a month in rent. The money I needed for cigarettes, good toilet articles, to purchase a fish dinner on the street once in a while, I earned by selling toys on the street made by others who did not have the time or who were bashful about selling. There were plenty of buyers, since they had money but nothing to spend it on.

I spent the time from August 1946 until January 1948 in poor Great Britain. Looking back, I do not consider it lost time. It was very informative.

We were loaded in ships at Hull and transported to Hoek van Holland and from there by train into Germany to a camp where we were released by the English. It was on January 5, 1948, my wife's birthday. I immediately sent her a telegram with birthday greetings and an announcement that I would soon be home.

On January 8, about twenty-five of us former soldiers were transported to Stuttgart, where we were carefully examined by doctors and had the necessary paperwork completed. The people who took care of us were all German civilians and were very considerate and friendly. We did not find any trace that they considered us "war criminals," as the rumors circulating through England had proclaimed. Even the food was reasonable. We stayed overnight, and early the next morning received our train tickets which took each one of us to our hometown. At the train station in Pforzheim I had the opportunity to travel by truck to Karlsruhe, which offered the fastest way to get home.

Since the arrival of my telegram, my wife and son had gone to the train station every day with the handcart to carry my sea sack. We missed each other, since I was practically driven right to my home. However, I did not know it because our old dwelling had been bombed and I only had the new address from a letter sent to me by my wife while I was in England. I started carrying my sea sack in the wrong direction until some women noticed me and knew from my telegram that I was expected home at any time. They informed me where I now lived. But when I rang the bell, no one answered. Those neighbors who noticed me told me that my wife had left to pick me up. They also told me that the sister of my wife lived on the other side of the street, directly across from our apartment.

I was in the process of leaving my sea sack on the street in front of my door, as we had always done before, when I was told that because of theft I could no longer do it. I took the sack with me, went across the street, and rang the bell of my sister-in-law, Gertrud. We greeted one another excitedly; I was expected; she only wondered why my wife and I had not met at the train station. While she led me into my unfamiliar apartment, I explained to her. The house was bomb damaged, the neighboring house completely destroyed. Otherwise ours was a nice three-room apartment, furnished with old pieces of furniture collected from all over.

We looked intensely out of the window, waiting for my wife and my son, who was now six years old. We only knew each other from pictures. Suddenly the boy appeared with his empty wagon in front of the house, but my sister-in-law had to first tell me that he was my son Günter. He had already discovered us at the window and waved to us. I opened the door for him. I had not one moment's time to think, as I had in so many lonesome nights, how our first meeting would be. He was only one year old when I left in December 1943. I opened my arms in welcome and he came to me with a laughing but pale face, and hugged me tightly.

My son led me into the apartment, but did not let go of my hand. In the kitchen he sat on my lap. He then held my ears tight in his hands and we looked at each other carefully. I could tell by many of his traits that he was my son. I asked him where his mother was, but he showed that he was very self-confident and said, "She will be coming soon, but tell me first of all why it took them so long to let you come to us. Mr. Bechthold, next door, has been with his Ilona since the easter rabbit came."

He looked at my sea sack and asked roguishly, "Do you have something for me for Christmas inside? Mama said that you would certainly bring us something like Mr. Bechthold brought his Ilona."

The doorbell rang. Günter jumped up and ran to open the door. "Oh, it is you, come in, my papa is here." He shoved a same-aged boy into the kitchen and said, "This is Dieter Ell; he is still waiting for his father, but he does not send any money."

The doorbell rang again. It was Dieter's mother, who greeted me with a forced laugh and said to her son that he must come home immediately. Then the door opened suddenly and my wife appeared in the kitchen. As I jumped toward her, Frau Ell pulled her son out of the kitchen by the nape of his neck. Now we were alone. The moment that she and I had been waiting for over four years. We threw our arms around each other. Silence. What kind of tears were they that coursed over our wet faces?

It took a while, but then Günter pulled on my pants and said, "Mama is also hungry. Do you have any chocolate?"

Oh God, I was happy that I had bought one of the famous English tea cakes. I opened my sea sack in front of her, something that I had done a thousand times in my dreams. The thick, yellow-gold cake quickly lost its wrappings and lay on the table as though heaven had thrown it through the kitchen ceiling. It was a little ragged after being carried so far, but my dear wife was soon at work on it with a knife. I had not eaten lunch, but I had no hunger.

In England I had decided what I would do when I returned home. My wife was taken aback. "You want to work at your profession, which you have not had anything to do with for over ten years?" "I have returned home completely healthy, both mentally and physically. I am excited about life, and I have the responsibility for the three of us. Hungry students learn faster than well-fed ones. Please let me step into the cold water undisturbed; I will make it."

"Good," she said after a while, "actually that is very good; there are enough idle men running around already. I was fearful you would be one as well. Many of those who have returned home, even those who have returned healthy, hang on their wives' apron strings. They are helpless or too lazy to do anything. Many have their doubts about the situation here. They have lost all belief in their own strength. They jabber about the old order. They no longer have a leader that commands them. There are no longer any marriage standards for the people who want to marry. There are no orphanage houses for the children and no money to help care for them. No money for the winter and no help for the old people. The ship is sunk. Whoever was lucky came back up to the surface."

I asked my wife how much money she absolutely needed each month to pay the rent and everything else. She did not need a pencil. She said, "Thirty-five marks and fifty pfennig a week. You must give up your smoking. There is no money for beer or other things that men often want. We will always eat at home. I have become a good cook; trust me."

That night she told me about her escape from Bruchsal. "I fled with some other people who had children, from the bomb shelter over bodies that were still burning, toward the north where there was no fire. But there the airplanes came in very low and shot at everything that moved. There were no soldiers there! It was simply murder. We were unarmed civilians—women, children, and old men. No one threatened them; there were no German airplanes around. Helmut, you were a soldier; did you ever do anything so awful? Please tell me now. I want to know, I must know, I could never live together with such a horrible person."

I was terribly shaken. Yes, we had heard about such tragedies, but we had never seen them ourselves. Now to hear such things in bed with my own wife, to be asked such questions, and to face the consequences which the answers might bring. Who could calmly light a cigarette and say, "Not us Germans!"

But that is not what she asked. She asked me personally. But I personally had not killed any human being; I had not beaten, robbed, or tortured anyone.

I wanted to become a dentist, but in order to enter dental school, I had to pay money that I did not have. Therefore I decided to take work in a laboratory as a dental technician. The employment office had plenty of positions since during the war there were hardly any dentists available for civilians.

After my probation, I negotiated a salary with my boss, explaining to him how much money we needed to live. He agreed and we lived sparingly. The articles I had brought in my sea sack were a big help during the first few weeks. I had brought with me from Delaware a nearly new army jacket that looked very much like a civilian coat. Elly sold the coat on the black market for enough food to last the three of us a week. We lived better than many other poor devils.

I wanted to immigrate to Australia after I mastered my trade. To my surprise, Elly was not opposed. Then, on June 20, 1948, the monetary reform occurred. Ten Reichsmarks were now worth only one new German mark. Every German received forty new marks, and as one radio commentator stated, "Now Germans were either all poor or all rich together." The reform did not matter to us. We had not been able to save any money. But suddenly now there were goods in the stores but people were unable to purchase them. Orders for teeth were withdrawn and three dental technicians had to be released. We older married employees escaped the first round; however, the future did not look good. The decision to immigrate burned within me and I sent my wife to begin the process of application. Because there were no Australian officials available she was sent to the Americans; after she told them our story they were not at all enthused. They said they were in the process of rebuilding Germany and therefore needed young people who had not lost the belief that they were an industrious people. They could not prevent us from immigrating, but they did tell Elly to tell me that the letter of recommendation they had from the time I was company leader at Camp Upton, New York, was impressive and that if difficulties did arise for us that I should report to them and they would help me.

I continued to work, but still carried the idea of immigrating to Australia inside me. I listened as some talked about a new war, an atomic war that would come, and that is why I wanted to go to Australia. They would not drop any atomic bombs there; that continent would simply fall into the hands of the victor without a fight.

But life went on. Elly and I enjoyed going for walks and one evening we came upon a half-destroyed pawn shop in the Kaiserstrasse. We looked into the display window and then I pointed into the left corner. "There is the foundation for our future wealth." There, unnoticed by anyone, lay the dental technician's drill and polishing machine with the flexible tubes and hand tools. It was produced for the army by the firm Bauknecht. The shop was closed, and I started to shake. I gave Elly strict orders to go there early the next morning and get the equipment no matter what the cost. On the way home I started to organize in my mind my own laboratory, which I would set up in our spacious kitchen. I did not worry about illegal work at home. Even the war had been prohibited. ...

From then on I had work in the evenings, often until late at night, which brought in extra money. By 1949 I had the total responsibility for teeth replacements for our patients. I worked hard with the hope of establishing my own practice, but circumstances ended that dream and our plans to add a daughter to our family. My wife had begun to work, and I came to the realization that there was no real purpose in working night and day.

Finally we had free time. I went fishing. We enjoyed ourselves on the weekend and if we became bored during the week we could go to a movie. We joined a book club. Then, one foggy Sunday morning in November 1950, I lay in bed reading the newspaper reports about the Korean War. Günter was at church, Elly was in the kitchen, and I had at least two hours until Sunday dinner. I slipped into my athletic suit and made my way into the basement looking for my journal entries and accounts about my own war. I found them covered with dust and some still stored in the sea sack I had brought from America. I sorted my collection. To be honest, my wife was not very enthused about my writing project. But I began to work hard, unceasingly, and sometimes as though possessed.

* * *

After he left the United States, Helmut lost contact with all of those with whom he had been a prisoner of war. He did try to visit Willi Hocker at his home in Reilingen by Mannheim. Helmut made the trip in the early 1950s on a motor bike he was able to purchase. He spoke with Hocker's sister, who informed him that her brother had been killed in France after he returned from the United States. Documents in Willi Hocker's prisoner of war file indicate that he spent his entire time in the United States at Camp Gruber, Oklahoma. On June 26, 1945, Hocker signed a request that he be employed during the remainder of his time as a prisoner of war. He did work three months, July 1945, and March-April 1946, though the nature of his work is not indicated. On September 5, 1945, Hocker fractured his right leg while playing soccer at Camp Gruber and this injury apparently kept him from work until February 1946. On November 27, 1945, Hocker withdrew fifteen dollars—nearly half of his account balance—for a donation to the Red Cross for Germany. Hocker was sent from Camp Gruber directly to Camp Shanks on April 24, 1946, one year and two days after he arrived in Oklahoma. He arrived in France on May 17, 1946. He escaped from a prisoner of war camp in France on August 19, 1946, and was crossed off the list of prisoners on November 20, 1946. The circumstances surrounding his death are clouded. Documents in his prisoner of war file did not indicate when or how he died; however, his sister told Helmut that Hocker had been killed while trying to escape.

Information from the prisoner of war files on Helmut's other comrades was not available.

Helmut continued his career as a dental technician, manufacturing prostheses until his retirement, when he and Elly moved from Karlsruhe to an apartment in Stutensee, approximately ten miles north of Karlsruhe. Their son Günter became a baker and now owns bakery shops in the city of Kassel, two hundred miles north of Karlsruhe. In July 1990, after several years of poor health and while this book was in production, Helmut was diagnosed as having cancer of the pancreas. He died on August 10, 1990.

* * *

# NOTES

### Chapter One

1. For an engaging account of the evacuation, see Walter Lord, *The Miracle of Dunkirk* (New York: Viking Press, 1982).
2. John Erickson, *The Road to Stalingrad* (London: Weidenfeld and Nicolson, 1975), 251.
3. Brian I. Fugate, *Operation Barbarossa: Strategy and Tactics on the Eastern Front, 1941* (Novato, CA: Presidio Press, 1984), 285–98.
4. See Walter Boardman Kerr, *The Secret of Stalingrad* (Garden City, NY: Doubleday, 1978) and Erickson, *Road to Stalingrad.*
5. T. Dodson Stamps and Vincent J. Esposito, eds., *A Military History of World War II* (West Point, NY: United States Military Academy, 1956) vol. 2, *Operations in European Theaters*, 398.

### Chapter Two

1. Quoted in Alan Bullock, *Hitler: A Study in Tyranny* (New York: Harper and Row, 1962), 749–50.
2. John Toland, *Adolf Hitler* (Garden City, NY: Doubleday, 1976), vol. 2, 913.
3. Eddy Florentin, *The Battle of the Falaise Gap* (New York: Hawthorn Books, 1967).

### Chapter Three

1. David Pryce-Jones, *Paris in the Third Reich: A History of the German Occupation, 1940–1944* (New York: Holt, Rinehart and Winston, 1981), 206.
2. Martin Blumenson, *Liberation* (Alexandria, VA: Time-Life Books, 1978), 159.
3. Larry Collins and Dominique Lapierre, *Is Paris Burning?* (New York: Simon and Schuster, 1965), 310–12.

### Chapter Four

1. Toland, *Adolf Hitler*, vol. 2, 953. Toland offers a fuller history of the battle in his earlier book, *Battle: The Story of the Bulge* (New York: Random House, 1959). For a more recent comprehensive history of the battle, see Charles Brown McDonald, *A Time for Trumpets: The Untold Story of the Battle of the Bulge* (New York: William Morrow and Co., 1985).

### Chapter Five

1. Arnold Krammer, *Nazi Prisoners of War in America* (New York: Stein and Day, 1979), 18.

### Chapter Six

1. Ray Allen Billington, *Land of Savagery, Land of Promise: The European Image of the American Frontier in the Nineteenth Century* (New York: W. W. Norton and Co., 1981), 54–56.
2. Richard S. Warner, "Barbed Wire and Nazilagers: PW Camps in Oklahoma," *Chronicles of Oklahoma* 64 (Spring 1986):50.
3. See Wilma Parnell, *The Killing of Corporal Kunze* (Secaucus, NJ: Lyle Stuart, 1981) and Krammer, *Nazi Prisoners of War in America*, 169–74.
4. Krammer, *Nazi Prisoners of War in America*, 13.
5. Janet E. Worrall, "Prisoners on the Home Front: Community Reactions to German and Italian POWs in Northern Colorado, 1943–1946," *Colorado Heritage* Issue 1 (1990):36, 47.
6. Allan Kent Powell, *Splinters of a Nation: German Prisoners of War in Utah* (Salt Lake City: University of Utah Press, 1989), 84–86.
7. Kenneth W. Rock, " 'Unsere Leute': The Germans from Russia in Colorado," *The Colorado Magazine* 54 (Spring 1977):155–83; the quotation is from page 156.
8. J. K. Zawodny, *Death in the Forest: The Story of the Katyn Forest Massacre* (Notre Dame, IN: University of Notre Dame Press, 1962) and Louis FitzGibbon, *Katyn* (New York: Charles Scribner's Sons, 1971).

9. Transcribed from the Twenty-eighth Annual Report of the Weld County Extension Service, 1944; quoted in Worrall, "Prisoners on the Home Front: Community Reactions to German and Italian POWs in Northern Colorado, 1943–1946, 42."

10. Hans Christian Adamson and Per Klem, *Blood on the Midnight Sun* (New York: W. W. Norton and Co., 1964).

11. Albert Speer, *Inside the Third Reich* (New York: Macmillan, 1970), 225–29.

12. See Warren F. Kimball, *Swords or Ploughshares? The Morgenthau Plan for Defeated Nazi Germany, 1943–1946* (Philadelphia: J.B. Lippincott Co., 1976) and Michael J. Hogan, *The Marshall Plan: America, Britain and the Reconstruction of Western Europe, 1947–1952* (Cambridge: Cambridge University Press, 1987).

13. Provost Marshal General's Office, Prisoner of War Division, Inspection Reports, West Point, NY, Record Group 389, Box 2675, National Archives, Washington, D.C.

14. Krammer, *Nazi Prisoners of War in America*, 219–24, and Judith M. Gansberg, *Stalag U.S.A.* (New York: Thomas Y. Crowell, 1977).

15. Krammer, *Nazi Prisoners of War in America*, 245, 255.

### Chapter Seven

1. Edward John Pluth, "The Administration and Operation of German Prisoner of War Camps in the United States during World War II" (Ph.D. diss., Ball State University, 1970), 405–13, and Krammer, *Nazi Prisoners of War in America*, 248–50.

# SELECTED BIBLIOGRAPHY

**Books About the German Prisoner of War Experience in the United States**

Bailey, Ronald H. *Prisoners of War*. Alexandria, VA: Time-Life Books, 1981.

Gaertner, Georg, with Arnold Krammer. *Hitler's Last Soldier in America*. New York: Stein and Day, 1985.

Gansberg, Judith M. *Stalag U.S.A.* New York: Thomas Y. Crowell, 1977.

Koop, Allen V. *Stark Decency: German Prisoners of War in a New England Village*. Hanover and London: University of New England Press, 1988.

Krammer, Arnold. *Nazi Prisoners of War in America*. New York: Stein and Day, 1979.

Moore, John Hammond. *The Faustball Tunnel: German POWs in America and Their Great Escape*. New York: Random House, 1978.

Pabel, Reinhold. *Enemies are Human*. Philadelphia: The John C. Winston Co., 1955.

Parnell, Wilma. *The Killing of Corporal Kunze*. Secaucus, NJ: Lyle Stuart, 1981.

Powell, Allan Kent. *Splinters of a Nation: German Prisoners of War in Utah*. Salt Lake City: University of Utah Press, 1989.

# INDEX

391